Environmental Education:
Principles and Policies

Environmental Education:
Principles and Policies

Dr Savita Mishra

KALPAZ

ISBN: 978-93-5128-189-4

Price: ₹ 1590

First Published, 2016

Published by

Kalpaz Publications
C-30, Satyawati Nagar,
Delhi – 110052
E-mail: kalpaz@hotmail.com
Ph.: 9212142040

Printed at: G. Print Process, Delhi

Cataloging in Publication Data—DK
Courtesy: D.K. Agencies (P) Ltd. <docinfo@dkagencies.com>

Mishra, Savita, author.
Environmental education : principles and policies / Savita Mishra.
pages cm
Includes bibliographical references.
ISBN 9789351281894 (hardback)

1. Environmental education—India. 2. Environmental education—Government policy—India. I. Title.

GE90.I4M57 2016DDC 333.7071054 23

Contents

Preface

The 'Environment' is an all-encompassing subject which concerns everybody, right from common man to the most elite person. The environmental problem especially the climate change is the greatest ecological change which acts as catalysts for economic and social changes of our time. Environmental education therefore assumes importance for everyone. This book has been attempted to give an insight on this very important subject to the readers which is expected to help them for preparing for their examination and also for their life.

I have been engaged in teaching this subject to college level students for last one decade. Over the years, I realised that students need a book which covers all the topics exhaustively, yet it is written in simple and lucid manner. I have tried to achieve that goal so that it serves as self instructional material to the readers.

The book in its tangible form is the result of exhaustive research on each of the topics, innovative ideas, encouragement and support from my family members, and overwhelming response from the student community to my earlier book on this subject.

—Dr Savita Mishra

1

The Environment

1.1 Introduction

We live in absolutely beautiful and breathtaking world created by God. God has created many things, all of them lovely and sights to behold and to be preserved for eternity. The lush lakes, the bottom of the ocean, the fish, the clouds, air, sky, the lovely birds, the flora, colourful flowers and many more beautiful things in nature that brings joy and vigour to all of us. Nature can set a sky aflame at sunset or magically transform a familiar landscape into a snow-white wonderland. It can paint a rainbow in the sky, paint beautiful autumn colours on trees, or paint a clump of daffodils in the grass with glow of soft sunlight. Nature is thus fascinating.

The present day civilisation has interfered with nature so much that its natural balance is being deteriorated. In a bid to make life more and more comfortable, the mankind has often destroyed forests thoughtlessly, polluted air and water recklessly, spoiled nature ruthlessly. The inevitable consequence has been an ominous deterioration of the environment. We are confronting an environmental crisis affecting the whole planet, disrupting the pace of life and destroying the environment, as well as human communities. This global crisis is very grave as the continuation of human existence itself is threatened. The overcoming of the crisis so as to provide a viable future for the mankind is therefore necessary. The humanity has the responsibility to ensure the right for life for all peoples of the earth, for future generations as well as for each and every form of life, regardless of its usefulness for humans. Once we realise this fact, the important question before all of us is- how to save environment. Obviously, education about Environment is the only answer. Recognising this fact and necessity, the Supreme Court has directed in December 2003 for compulsory Environmental Education for the students of 1st to 12th standards to bring awareness about environment among school students to enable them to become responsible citizens. A Chinese proverb rightly says, *"if you want one year of prosperity, plant corn; if you want ten years of prosperity plant trees; and if you want one hundred years of prosperity, educate people.*"

1.2 Meaning of Environment

The word 'environment' is derived from French word '*ENVIRON*' which means 'encircle'. The dictionary meaning of the word 'environment' is surrounding-that which environs or surrounds; surrounding conditions, influences, or forces, by which living forms are influenced and modified in their growth and development. *The word "environment" is most commonly used to denote "natural" environment and means the sum of all living and non- living things that surround an organism, or group of organisms.* Generally speaking, the environment is equated with nature wherein physical components of the planet earth, *viz;* land, air, water etc. which support and affect life in the biosphere is construed.

Environment of early man consisted of only physical aspects of the planet earth- land, air and water and biological communities. With the passage of time and advancement of society men extended his environment through his social, economic and political activities as has been described in the figure below:

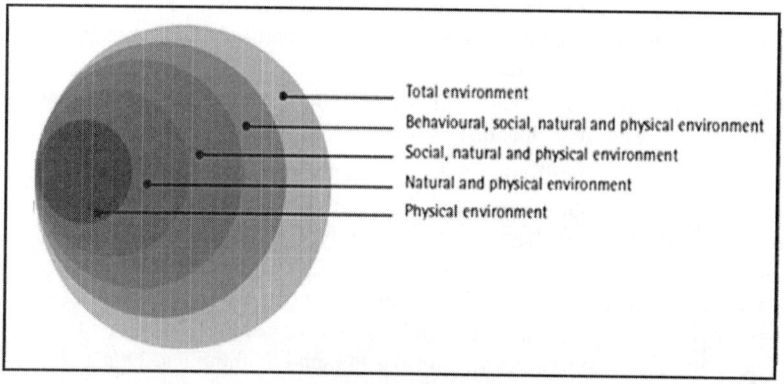

Figure 1.1: Definition of the Environment (Adapted from Smith, Corvalan and Kjelistorm, 1999).

'Environment' in present day has a larger connotation and refers to the sum total of conditions which surround man at a given point in space and time and include all elements, factors, and conditions that have some impact on growth and development of certain organism. Environment includes both biotic and abiotic factors that have influence on observed organism. Abiotic factors such as light, temperature, water, atmospheric gases combine with biotic factors (all surrounding living species) forms environment.

Thus, while the word environment is used in variety of ways, it can be described as the physical, chemical and biological surroundings of an organism at any given time. Environment encompasses everything, living and non-living, the interactions and the products of interactions. Environment can be described as all the physical, chemical and biological factors external to the human host, as well as those factors impacting related behaviours.

1.3 Definitions of Environment

Environment consists of the sum total of the stimulation that the individual receives from conception until death. This means that everything in and around an individual including various circumstances which assert their influence on the individual is covered by the term environment. In real world everything that affects an organism during its lifetime is collectively known as its environment.

The word 'Environment' has been defined by various environmentalists in different ways. Some of the definitions are as follows:

'A person's environment consists of the sum total of the stimulation which he receives from his conception until his death.'- *Boring*

'The environment is everything that affects the individual except his genes.'- *Anastasi*

'The term environment is used to describe, in the aggregate, all the external forces, influences and conditions, which affect the life, nature, behaviour and the growth, development and maturity of living organism.'

–*Douglass and Holland*

'Environment is the sum of all external conditions affecting the life, development and survival of an organism.'

–*United States Environmental protection Agency*

The term *environment* refers to an organisation's natural and human surroundings. An organisation's environment extends from within the organisation itself to the global system, and includes air, water, land, flora, fauna, as well as human beings.- *ISO 14001 (2004)*

'Environment is the sum total of the elements, factors and conditions in the surroundings which may have an impact on the development, action or survival of an organism or group of organisms. The environment is as opposed to genetics. We are the product of our genetic inheritance and our environment.'- *Medical dictionary*

The above definitions indicate that the term 'Environment' refers to the: (i) surroundings of a living organism which includes both living and non-living components and (ii) the factors responsible for growth and development of living organism. Environment includes various types of forces such as physical, social, political, economic, cultural, intellectual, moral and emotional. Environment is the aggregate of all the external forces, influences and conditions, which affect the life, nature, behaviour and the growth, development and the maturation of living organisms.

1.4 Characteristics of Environment

From the above definitions, following characteristics of environment emerge:

- Sum total of conditions which surround man at any given point of time and in space;
- It includes physical (land, air and water) and biological (plants, animals including man and his several functions, organisations and institutions) components;
- It involves physical, chemical, biological, social, economic, political and cultural processes;
- It consists of physical, intellectual, social, moral, cultural, emotional, economic and political forces which affect the life and nature of behaviour;
- It consists of all the external forces which affect the growth and development of living organism;
- Everything which affects an individual excluding his genes, and
- The sum total of the stimulation from his birth until his death.

1.5 Elements of Environment

The term environment is viewed in different ways by different people. In common parlance environment is viewed as the interacting system of physical, biological and cultural elements which are inter-related individually as well as collectively in variety of ways. Various elements of environment can be described as follows:

(i) Physical elements

As the name suggests, physical elements refers to physical part of the environment such as air, space, landforms, water bodies, climate, soils, rocks, minerals etc. These elements determine the variable character of the human habitat, its opportunities as well as limitations.

(ii) Biological elements

This refers to biospheric elements of environment such as plants, animals, micro-organisms, men, etc. These elements are inter-dependent amongst themselves and affect one another.

(iii) Cultural elements

These are economic, social and political elements and are essentially man-made features which go into making of cultural milieu.

Thus, environment consists of natural as well as socio-cultural elements and plays an important role in day-to-day life of mankind. Due to over exploitation of natural resources, population explosion, urbanisation, industrialisation and a host of other activities, serious ecological and environmental imbalances are taking place. It is common knowledge that environment degradation has adversely affected not only the human health but also the human progress and sustainability. This calls for an urgent action to improve the quality of man's environment. It is always preferable to prevent environmental damage from occurring it in the first place, rather than attempting to restore degraded environmental resources later.

1.6 Types of Environment

Environment can be described into three types duly considering the influence it makes on the personality of an individual:

(i) Physical Environment

(ii) Social and Cultural Environment, and

(iii) Psychological Environment.

(i) Physical Environment

Physical environment also encompasses biological environment. It refers to geographical climate and weather or physical conditions in which an individual lives. The human races are greatly influenced by the climate. The white, black and yellow races live in different climatic conditions. While people from cold countries are of white complexion, people from relatively warmer countries are usually black complexioned. The human working efficiency also depends on the climatic conditions. Heredity and the physique of an individual are also influenced by the physical environment and climatic conditions as the individual tries to adjust in the given physical environment.

(ii) Social and Cultural Environment

It includes the social, economic and political conditions of an individual in which he lives. The moral, cultural and emotional forces affect the life and nature of individual behaviour. There are two types of society- open and closed. While the open society is very conducive for the development of individuals, closed society does not facilitate development of individuals. So much so that even the classroom climate plays an important role towards development to find individual potentialities.

(iii) Psychological Environment

Kurt Lewin has laid emphasis on the psychological environment of an individual. The physical and social environments are common to the individual in a specific situation while every individual has his own psychological environment in which he lives. Lewin has used the term 'life space' for explaining psychological environment. Psychological environment is very important to understand the personality of an individual. Both the person and his goal form part of the psychological environment. A person cannot achieve his goal if he is unable to overcome the barriers and may lead to frustration. Alternatively, he has to change his goal for a new psychological environment. This mechanism helps the individual in his adjustment to the environment.

1.7 Structure of Environment

Environment is both physical and biological. It includes both- living and non-living components. On the basis of basic structure the environment may be divided into two basic types: (i) physical or abiotic environment; and (ii) biological or biotic environment.

(i) Physical or Abiotic Environment

On the basis of physical characteristics and state, the physical environment is sub-divided into three broad categories - solid, liquid and gas which represent the lithosphere (solid earth), the hydrosphere (water component) and the atmosphere respectively. Thus, three basic divisions of physical environment may be termed as: (i) lithospheric environment, (ii) atmospheric environment and (iii) hydrospheric environment. These may be further broken into smaller units based on different spatial scales, e.g.; mountain environment, plateau environment, plain environment, lake environment, river environment, maritime environment, glacier environment, desert environment, coastal environment, etc.

(ii) Biological or Biotic Environment

The biological component of the environment consists of flora (plants) and fauna (animals) including man as an important factor. Thus, the biotic environment may be divided into floral environment and faunal environment. All the organism work to form their social groups and organisations at several levels and thus the social environment is formed where in the organisms work to derive material from the physical environment for their sustenance and development. This process generate economic environment. Of all the organisms man is the most skilled and civilised and hence his social organisation is most systematic. The three aspects of man- physical, social and economic have different characteristics functions in the biotic environment as mentioned below:

The physical man: The 'physical man' is one of the organism populations or biological community. He requires basic elements of the physical environment, *viz*; habitat (space), air, water and food like other biological populations and releases wastes into the ecosystem.

The social man: The 'social man' establishes social institutions, forms social organisations, formulate laws, principles and policies to safeguard his existence, interest and social welfare.

The economic man: He derives and utilises resources from the physical and biotic environments with his skills and technologies. These may be termed as physical, social and economic functions of man. The economic function makes the man an environmental/geomorphic process because the transports material and energy from one component of the ecosystem to the other. So long as the exploitative functions are in harmony with the natural environment this function does not necessarily involve change in the working of the ecosystem. When these exceed the critical limit, the equilibrium of the environment/ecosystem is disturbed and several environmental and ecological problems crop up. These are detrimental not only to man himself but to whole population of human species in a given ecosystem.

The physical environment may be viewed in terms of climatic conditions providing certain types of habitat for the biological communities, *viz;* tropical environment, temperate environment, polar environment, etc which may be further subdivided into smaller but specific divisions. Physical/abiotic and biotic environments fused together for 'biome environment' like Tundra biome, Temperate biome and Tropical biome which are further sub-divided into second and third order biomes. In environmental geography the physical environment is the most outstanding feature and thus should be given more significance than the social or cultural environments. The economic function of man becomes more significant than his other functions as it is more concerned with the functioning of ecosystem. Thus, the interaction of man through his economic function is an environmental process, with natural environment. The resultant human response to the environment is the fundamental concern of environmental education.

1.8 Components of Environment

Environment is a broad concept which includes all external conditions influencing growth and development of child, animals and plants, etc. The environment has been broadly classified into physical and biological components. The physical components include land, air and water, whereas, biological components are plants, animals including man, his functions, organisations and institutions. The environmental components can be classified in the following categories:

(i) Physical component

Physical component consists of air, water and land amongst other physical components. Details are enumerated in succeeding paragraphs:

Air: Air is the most vital component without which the question of survival does not arise beyond a few minute. A human being of normal health and height respires 22,000 times a day and the air utilised in course of such respiration is about 20 times more than the quantity of food consumed by him. Natural air at mean sea level contains nitrogen (78.09 per cent), oxygen (20.94 per cent) and argon (0.93 per cent) as macro-constituents. The micro-components of air are carbon dioxide (0.0318 per cent), Krypton (0.0001 per cent) and helium (0.0052 per cent). Many other compounds, e.g., SO_4, NO_2, O_3, etc. are also present in much lower concentration than those mentioned above. Besides these, water vapour and dust particulars in varying amounts and sizes are present in air depending upon the meteorological, typographical and industrial activities of the areas under examination.

Water: Water is vital for all forms of life on this earth. In our country, the main source of water is in the form of precipitation, which is roughly of the order of 400 million hectare meter per year. Nearly 50 per cent of it percolates into the soil – about 30 per cent of it runs as surface run off and another 20 per cent evaporates into the atmosphere.

Pure and clean water is necessary for healthy environment. But whatever water bodies we have in India about 70 per cent of them are polluted. Pollution of water may be by different sources. Streams and other water systems are polluted by municipal waste and industrial effluent. The responsibility for maintaining civil amenities like water supply, drainage, slum clearance, open spaces and streets in the cities rests with our municipal bodies.

Land: Land is one of the most important components of our environment as human sustenance is primarily dependent on land. Right from our shelter to agricultural productivity, industrial growth to trade, we are dependent on land to a large extent. While it takes between 500 to 1,000 years to build landmass, it takes only one rainy season to erode it. Almost 50 per cent of our national land area *i.e.* nearly 175 million hectares suffers from one or the other type of land degradation. This is primarily because of wrong pattern of land use and has led to decline of agricultural productivity from these lands. Application of inorganic fertilisers to our crop-lands coupled with use of highly toxic insecticides and pesticides to control crop diseases has the harmful effects in agriculture. Potent agriculture land and forest cover are being destroyed for want of correct irrigation practices, brick manufacture and urban development schemes. It is thus absolutely essential to be cautious with the modern technology in agriculture and scientific land use planning and execution in our country.

(ii) Biological components

Biological components constitute plants and animals. Details are enumerated in succeeding paragraph:

Plants: Plants play very dominant role in the biosphere because they are primary producers in the biosphere and provide directly and indirectly food to all terrestrial and aquatic animal including man. The social groupings of plants species are called plant community of which plant is the fundamental basic unit. Plants directly receive and trap solar energy and prepare their own food with the help of sunlight through the process of photosynthesis. Thus, solar energy converted into the food or chemical energy is transferred to different animals and micro-organisms through different levels of food chain. Thus, plants are intermediary between biotic and abiotic components of the environment.

Animals: In the overall context of environment, animals play an important role as not only they protect the environment and help in maintaining ecological balances, they help in regulating and transforming the solar energy. Solar energy trapped by the plants is converted into food to help them grow which becomes food for the animals. On death of animals, organic substances are turned into inorganic substances such as carbon-dioxide, oxygen, nitrogen, etc. by micro-organisms. This is in turn by the plants. Thus, animals form one of the important components of the environment.

(iii) Social components

Social components consist of social system, social changes and social relations, urbanisation, etc. Social components are very important in determining the role of educational institutions. Environment and society are closely intertwined and are interdependent. Different social groups and social structures like industrial, agricultural, political, cultural, religious, aesthetic, etc; have evolved and developed during various stages of development of human civilisation. Social structure represents man's accumulated cultural experiences and resources based on natural environment. The educational process helps in the development of different structures of society and the quality of environment. Education is the creature and creator of society. The structure of the society is evolved by the process of education. The educational process utilises the natural environment and its resources. Different social structures depend on the natural resources and environment. Education is a powerful instrument for social change and social control. The social changes are essential to utilise the natural resource of the environment.

(iv) Cultural components

Cultural component of the environment encompasses political, economic, religious and moral components. Culture is a collection of concepts that are separate and distinct, but that blend together to form a single overall concept. Culture reflects itself in everything from art to politics, from architecture to family size. Importantly, culture also influences the relationships people perceive between various cultural institutions, between cultures and the physical environment, etc. Culture has arisen and evolved in a great variety of physical settings that differ in climate, natural vegetation, soils, and landforms. Culture influences natural environments and force human being to develop adaptive strategies for their survival.

(v) Psychological components

Psychological component of environment includes level of aspiration of man, life space, topology, etc. Individuals set the goals in life according to their environment. Facts, self-concepts, etc are also influenced by ones environment.

(vi) Energy components

Energy components, both solar and geothermal, play an important role in determining the environment. While solar energy is heat from the sun, geothermal energy is defined as heat from the Earth. It is a clean, renewable resource that provides energy in and around the world. It is considered a renewable energy resource because the heat emanating from the interior of the earth is essentially limitless. The heat continuously flowing from the earth's interior is estimated to be equivalent to 42 million megawatts of power. The interior of the earth is expected to remain extremely hot for billions of year to come, ensuring an essentially limitless flow of heat. Geothermal power plants capture this heat and convert it to energy in the form of electricity.

1.9 Relationship of Environment with Other Subjects

Although environment has been recently reckoned as a specific subject and accordingly curriculum have also been developed by NCERT and UGC on direction from apex court of the country, the subject has bearing with a host of other traditional subject such as geology, agriculture, chemistry, botany, zoology, humanities, etc. The Chart 1.1 describes the inert link of environment with other subjects:

Environment, as we all know, has two major components- biotic and abiotic. While biotic covers plants, animals and man and accordingly is related to botany (plants), zoology (animals), humanities, etc. In environment, we study plants, which is essentially a subject matter of botany. Similarly, when we learn about animals and their impact on environment, we know that we are covering subject matter of zoology. Studying about man and his environment

Chart 1.1

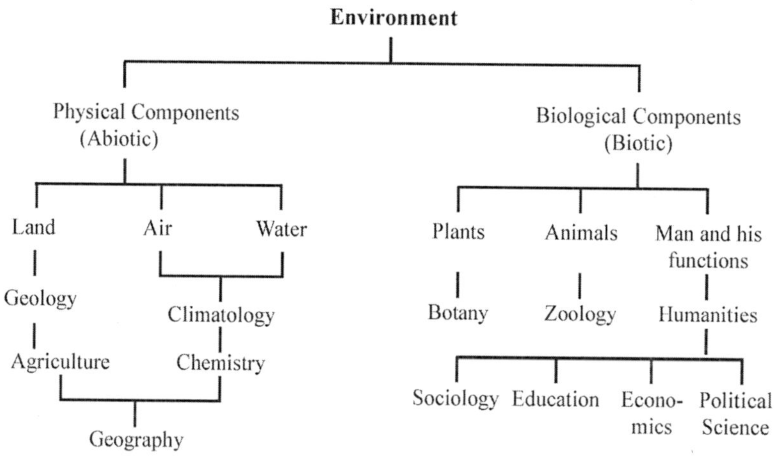

would establish link with the subjects like sociology, education, economics, political science, etc.

Abiotic components essentially deal with land, air and water amongst other physical components. While studying about air and water, we deal with chemistry and in case of land we deal with geology and agriculture. The study of environment is also linked with geography as the subject has wide coverage of environment in the form of both biotic and abiotic component.

1.10 Environmental Protection Act, 1986

Salient Features of Environment (Protection) Act, 1986

- As compared to all other previous laws on environment protection, the Environment (Protection) Act, 1986 is a more effective and bold measure to fight the problem of pollution.
- The genesis of the Environmental (Protection) Act, 1986, thus, is in Article 48A (Directive Principles of State Policy) and Article 51A (g) (Fundamental Duties) of the Indian Constitution.
- Soon after the United Nations Conference on the Human Environment held at Stockholm in 1972, the Water (Prevention and Control of Pollution) Act, 1974 came on the statute book. The Air (Prevention and Control of Pollution) Act came in 1981 and finally came the Environment (Protection) Act, 1986.
- The Environment (Protection) Act, 1986 has 26 Sections and it has been divided into four chapters relating to: (i) Preliminary, (ii) General Powers of the Central Government, (iii) Prevention, Control, and Abatement of Environmental Pollution and (iv) Miscellaneous.

- The Act consists of and deals with more stringent penal provisions. The minimum penalty for contravention or violation of any provision of the law is an imprisonment for a term which may extend to five years or fine up to one lakh rupees, or both. The Act also provides for the further penalty if the failure or contravention continues after the date of conviction. It is Rs 5000 per day. If the failure of contravention continues beyond the period of one year, then the offender is punished with imprisonment for a term which may extend to seven years.
- The Act empowers the Central Government to take all appropriate measures to prevent and control pollution and to establish effective machinery for the purpose of protecting and improving the quality of the environment and protecting controlling and abating environmental pollution.· The Central Government or any other person duly authorised is empowered to collect the samples of air, water, soil or other substances as evidence of the offences under the Environment (Protection) Act, 1986.
- The Act prescribes a special procedure for handling hazardous substances and the concerned person has to handle the hazardous substances according to the procedure of the Act.
- The Environment (Protection) Act, 1986 has relaxed the rule of "Locus Standi" and because of such relaxation even a common citizen can approach the Court provided he has given a notice of sixty days of the alleged offence and his intention to make a complaint to the Central Government or any other competent authority.
- In the commission of the offence under this Act by Government Department, the Act holds the Head of the Department as guilty of the offence unless the head of the Department proves that the offence was committed without his knowledge or that he exercised all due diligence to prevent the commission of such offence.
- This Act also empowers and authorises the Central Government to issue directions for the operation or process, prohibition, closure, or regulation of any industry. The Central Government is also authorised to stop, regulate the supply of electricity or water or any other service directly without obtaining the order of the Court in this regard.
- The Environment (Protection) Act, 1986 grants immunity to the officers of the government for any act done under the provisions of this Act or under the powers vested in them or functions assigned to them under this Act.

- The Central Government is also empowered to enter and inspect any place through any person or through any agency authorised by Central Government.
- The Act debars the Civil Courts from having any jurisdiction to entertain any suit or proceeding in respect of an action, direction, order issued by Central Government or other statutory authority under this Act.
- Under the Act, there will be supremacy of provision. In other words, the provisions of this Act and the rules or orders made under this Act shall have effect and supremacy over anything inconsistent contained in any enactment other than this Act.

2

Environmental Education

2.1 Introduction

Environmental degradation is no more a secret. We feel it on day-to-day basis in the form of unprecedented heat, scorching sun, erratic rainfall- scanty at some places and very heavy down pour at other places, very short winter, sudden and flash flood, snow melting, etc. All these call for an urgent action on the part of policy-makers, government functionaries, educators, NGOs, etc. Unless urgent action is initiated to stop this phenomenon it is not very unlikely that ecological balance would be disturbed and sustainability on the earth would been endangered. Considering this, it has increasingly been felt that education about environment, its underlying causes for deterioration and measures to reverse the trend or at least minimise the deterioration by adopting best practices is the only solution. This is how environmental education has come to the fore as syllabi for various academic courses.

The roots of environmental education can be traced back as early as the eighteenth century when Jean-Jacques Rousseau from United States stressed the importance of an education that focuses on the environment. Several decades later, Louis Agassiz, a Swiss-born naturalist, echoed Rousseau's philosophy as he encouraged students to "Study nature, not books." These two influential scholars helped lay the foundation for a concrete environmental education programme, which took place in the late nineteenth century and early twentieth century.

Environmental education emerged in the 1960s as the term for the educational dimensions of the environment movement which, at that time, was concerned about air and water quality *(pollution),* the growth in world population, continuing depletion of natural resources and environmental degradation. In the 1970s, as a result of the 1972 United Nations Conference on the Environment, the formation of the United Nations Environment Programme, and several UNESCO-UNEP intergovernmental conferences on environmental education, a set of goals and objectives for environmental education were agreed upon that have continued to form the fundamental principles for the field.

Environmental education is the education through, about and for the environment and generally refers to curriculum and programmes which aim to teach people about the natural world and particularly about ways in which ecosystems work. The term is often used to imply education within the school system, from primary to post-secondary but in effect includes all efforts to educate the people at large through various means such as lecture, workshops, seminars, print media, websites, etc. It is an organised effort to teach about how natural environments function and, particularly, how human beings can manage their behaviour and ecosystems in order to live sustainably.

Environmental education is the process of assisting people to become more sensitive to the environment, more literate about the environment and more motivated and skilled in coping with environmental problems. Environmental education aims to change people's perceptions about the value of the natural world and to teach those ways to change environmental behaviours.

2.2 Education and Environment

Human survival depends on the continued existence of natural resources. The quality of human life is intricately linked to the quality and quantity of environmental resources such as water, air, soil and so forth. Despite the efforts of thousands of environmental organisations, our environmental problems continue to worsen. Resources are being depleted and habitats are still being destroyed to make way for human progress. Other life forms that depend on these resources and surroundings also become threatened. This chain effect of resource depletion or environmental degradation ultimately affects all of us. It is every person's duty and responsibility to find ways to develop an understanding of how humans are linked to the natural order and how we can use our intellect to remedy the effects of destructive actions.

It is in this context it is perceived that education about environment alone can bring awareness and foster change in the attitude of the people. In fact, education has been used from ages as a tool for social control and also to develop a creative and regenerative influence to bring about positive changes in existing modes of thinking and living in beliefs, values, attitudes and customs. In a crisis of the kind we are witnessing vis-à-vis environmental problems, there are greater demands on education to take a more active part and make purposeful contributions by developing awareness and sensitisation towards the challenges and consequences of the environmental degradation, a proper understanding and appreciation of the phenomenon of better living and the formation and sustaining of desired values and attitudes through it.

Bernard has illustrated the relationship of environment and education. The educational process of development is organised formally in the educational institutions, where interaction takes place between the teacher and the taught. A teacher performs certain activities verbally and non-verbally to generate conducive social and emotional climate to provide new experiences to his students for desirable changes and modifications in their behaviour and thus process of development takes place in schools. The organisations' climate and health of the institutions also provide new experiences to their students. Thus, educational process of development occurs in physical, social, cultural and psychological environment as shown in figure below:

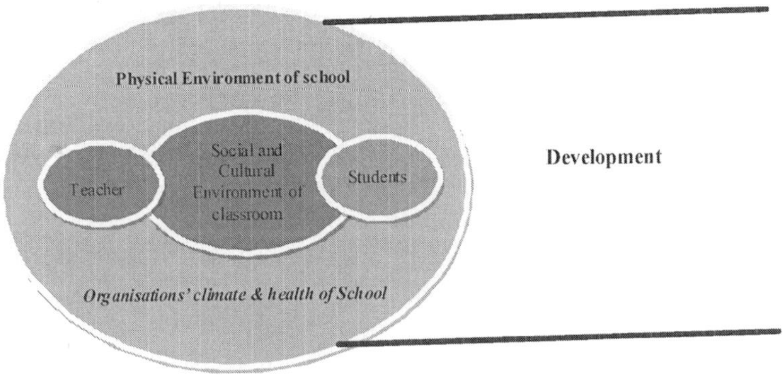

Figure 2.1: Education and Environment.

Education deals with various problems and principles, governing the relationship between students and their environment, created by school and teacher formally and informally. Similarly ecology is a new science which deals with various principles which govern the relationship between organisms and their environment.

Environmental issues are complex and our attempts to develop an insight into the problem must be a careful and systematic undertaking. The diagram below shows how the environment is really a collection of smaller systems: the biophysical, social, political and economic worlds. It does not only refer to natural resources such as air and water but consists of the total system of energy from the sun, interlinked food chains and the interactions between people and the biosphere *(i.e. our life support system)*. Humans are part of a social and technological sphere that depends on natural resources. All these smaller systems are intricately linked to each other.

Educators now prefer an approach that encourages learners to understand and transform problem environments. It is this sense that we now prefer to speak of Environmental education as education about and for the environment.

It is now seen as holistic field that draws from the tools of both the social and natural sciences. This means that planet earth should be seen as super organism consisting of interrelated and interdependent bio-physical.

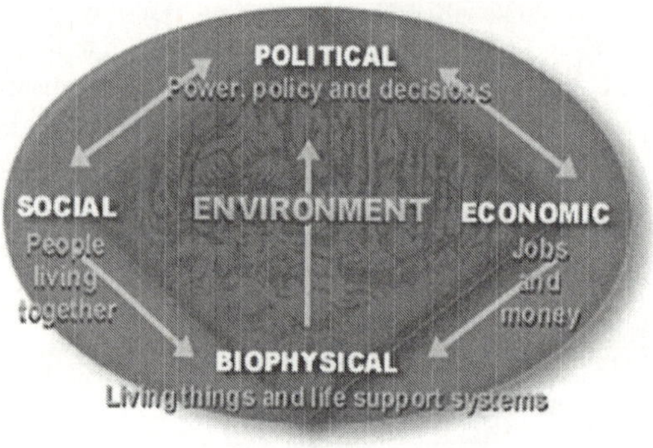

Figure 2.2: The environment as a collection of interactions and actions within various life worlds (O'Donoghue: 1995) entities that are undergoing continuous transformation.

2.3 Meaning of Environmental Education

Environmental education is an integral process, which deals with man's inter-relationship with his natural and man-made surroundings. While the natural surroundings include physical aspects of environment, man-made surroundings include social, political and economic aspects of the environment. Environmental education is a study of the factors influencing ecosystems, mental and physical health, living and working conditions, decaying cities, population pressures, etc.

Environmental education is education through environment, about environment and for environment. It is both a style and subject matter of education. In so far as the style is concerned, it means using environment as a teaching- learning aid and as an approach to education. In so far as the subject matter is concerned, it means teaching about the components and constituents of environment. In so far as the teaching for environment is concerned, it means controlling the environment, establishing proper ecological equilibrium which entails proper use and conservation of resources and also involves control of environmental pollution. It also includes proper environmental planning so that environment is not only functionally useful but is also aesthetically enjoyable. This aspect includes horticultural planning, rural planning and urban planning. The nexus of environmental education is multi-disciplinary in character. Its quintessence is a commitment on the part of one and all to prevent deterioration of air, water, land and physical and social environment including inter-relations among people. So that a nuclear war, a chemical warfare or any other cataclysm generated by man may not destroy the world.

Environmental education is a lifelong process and aim at imparting knowledge, understanding and awareness of man's total environment *(both physical and social environment)*, methods and their application for improving our near and distant surroundings, skills, the attitudes and values necessary to understand, appreciate and improve our biosphere and troposphere. It involves a child's investigation and systematic exploration of his own natural and social environment to prepare himself to solve the problems for improving his life. Environmental education enhances critical thinking, problem-solving, and effective decision-making skills, and teaches individuals to weigh various sides of an environmental issue to make informed and responsible decisions.

It is a complex process, covering not just events, but a strong underlying approach to society building as a whole. Environmental Education is meant to envision a set of organised curricular and co-curricular experiences designed to bring about the desired changes in knowledge, understanding, attitudes and skills pertaining to environment, conservation and ecological balance and sustaining it. Education must be considered as a solution for all environmental problems.

Environmental education is rooted in the belief that humans can live compatibly with nature and act equitably towards each other. Another fundamental belief is that people can make informed decisions that consider future generations. Environmental education aims for a democratic society in which effective, environmentally literate citizens participate with creativity and responsibility.

2.4 Definitions–Environmental Education

Environmental education is a process in which individuals gain awareness of their environment and acquire knowledge, skills, values, experiences, and also the determination, which will enable them to act -individually and collectively- to solve present and future environmental problems.

The term 'Environmental Education' has been defined in variety of ways. Some of the definitions are as follows:

"Environmental Education is the process of recognising values and clarifying concepts in order to develop skills and attitude necessary to understand and appreciate the interrelatedness among man, his culture and his bio-physical surroundings. It also entails practice in decision, making and self-formulation of a code of behaviour about problems and issues concerning environmental quality."- *International Union for the Conservation of Nature; 1971.*

"Environmental education is problem-centred, interdisciplinary, value-oriented, community-oriented, and concerns with man's survival as species, based on student initiated activities and involvements present and future oriented."- *Cook and Hearn; 1971.*

"Environmental education is a way to implement the goals of environmental protection. It should be carried out according to the principles of lifelong integral education."- *UNESCO seminar at Jammi; 1976.*

"Environmental education is a learning process that increases people's knowledge and awareness about the environment and associated challenges, develops the necessary skills and expertise to address the challenges, and foster attitudes, motivations, and commitments to make informed decision and take responsible action."-*UNESCO, Tbilisi Declaration; 1978.*

"Environmental education appears to be a process that equips human being with awareness, knowledge, skill, attitudes and commitment to improve environment."- *Mishra;1993.*

"Environmental education refers to the awareness of physical and cultural environment and perceives its relevance for real life situation, the problems and issues are to be identified, imbalances of environment are to be improved in view of sustainable development."- *Sharma;1996.*

Environmental education is a multi-disciplinary approach to learning that develops the knowledge, awareness, attitude, values and skills that will enable individuals and the community to contribute towards maintain and improving the quality of the environment.-*Me Ako Ki Te Tiaki Taiao.*

Thus, environmental education involves a comprehensive, life-long education, responsive to changes in a rapidly changing world. It prepares the individual and communities for life through understanding of the major problems of the interactions of the biological, physical, social, economic and cultural aspects of the individual and communities. It provides skills and attitudes required to play a productive role in improving life and values to enable people to enjoy good health and high quality of life.

2.5 Characteristics of Environmental Education

The review of the definitions of environmental education indicates the following main characteristics:

- It identifies the imbalances of environment and tries to improve it in view of sustainable development;
- It is a process of recognising the inter-relationship among man, his cultural and biological surroundings;
- It appears to be a process that equips human beings with awareness, skills, attitudes, values and commitments to improve environment;

- It refers to the knowledge and understanding of physical, biological, cultural and psychological environment and to perceive its relevance for real life situation;
- It entails proactive decision-making and self formulations of a code of behaviour about problems and issues concerning environmental quality;
- It develops skills, attitudes, feelings and values needed to play an productive role in improving life and values;
- It involves child's investigation and systematic exploration of his own natural and social environment and his life and prepares himself to solve problems for improving environment;
- It is problem-centred, interdisciplinary, value and community oriented and concerns with man's survival and development. It concerns with the present and the future;
- It provides the basis for construction and creative skills for the practice of healthy living and improvement;
- It involves both theoretical and practical aspect of environment to improve the imbalances and prevent the deterioration or pollutions; and
- It utilises educational approaches, methods and techniques of teaching to identifying the real cause of environmental problems and practice problem solving skills in formal and non-formal situations.

2.6 Environmental Awareness

We have impacted our planet more deeply in the twentieth century than ever before. Indeed, environmental problems now run rampant across the globe. The more serious issues include ozone deterioration, deforestation, global warming, suburban sprawl and other human developments that disrupt ecosystems, urban air pollution, soil erosion and species extinction. The first step in addressing our current environmental problems is to develop an environmentally-conscious society. Education is an important key towards achieving the goal of environmental awareness. In colleges and universities across the country, Environmental Science is a growing field of study, and high schools are beginning to integrate environmental studies into their curriculums as well. Classroom education has however not been able to overcome the disconnect between humans and the environment, and citizens have yet to re-establish their historical appreciation for the land. This disconnect can only be overcome through awareness about environment. World educators and environmental specialists have repeatedly pointed out that only solution to the environmental crisis is environmental awareness and understanding. For this, a deep-rooted educational system at all levels needs to be developed.

Environmental Awareness has the connotation to help social groups and individuals acquire an awareness and sensitivity to the total environment and its associated problems. The goals of environmental education were defined as creating environmental awareness; impart general knowledge for a basic understanding of environment, acquiring environmental-friendly attitudes and values and to generate new patterns of behaviour towards environment.

Although the term environmental education and environmental awareness are significantly different, these are often used interchangeably to denote same meaning and connotations. The study of physical and bio-science, geography, agriculture provides the environmental awareness. Awareness alone however does not help in developing skills and attitudes for improving environment. Therefore, it is essential to understand the concept of environmental awareness and differentiate it with educational environment.

Belgrade International workshop (1975) described the state of the art of Environmental education in all parts of the world and scope to extend and explore the Environmental awareness. It also states that environmental awareness may provide power and understanding to:

Recognise the interdependence among materials in to physical environment and plant and animal life for survival, growth and development.

- Take decisions individually and collectively and initiate actions for social, cultural and economic survival, growth and development and for conservation of nature and natural resources.
- Identify human, material, space and time resources in the environment.
- Recognise ways of making effective use of environmental resources for social, economic and cultural survival, growth and development.
- Take decisions for the effective use of resources, to recognise the special significance of conservation of natural resources and initiate or support community efforts for the purpose.

The more recently held United Nations Conference on Environment and Development in Rio de Janeiro, Brazil in 1992, popularly known as the Earth Summit, adopted an action plan for Sustainable Development, (agenda 21; Chapter 36) which is devoted to education states that "Education is critical for promoting sustainable development and improving the capacity of people to address environment and development issues."

Environmental awareness therefore refers to the understanding and competence to recognise environment and its associated problems by the individuals and the social groups. It also helps in acquiring basic understanding of environmental resources and interdependence between physical and biological components of the environment for the growth and development of all species.

Developing Environmental Awareness

The United Nation Conference of Human Environment (Stockholm, June 1971) was a major breakthrough towards recognising the deteriorating environment. As a follow up, United Nations Environmental Programme (UNEP) was formed for safeguarding the environment through international co-operation and awareness by:

- Identifying, analysing and understanding the need and problems of personal life including health, vocation, etc.
- Social life at different levels viz, family, caste, community, religion, town or village life, state and country.
- National life including civic, economic, etc.
- Appreciate, promote and use the environment to improve health, vocation and social and national life;
- Interact with government and social agencies and utilise the developmental facilities provided by these agencies in his/her individual capacity and also for organising certain community activities.
- Develop the aesthetic sense to appreciate beauty and adopt it in personal and social life.

The areas and content of environmental awareness have been enumerated in the succeeding paragraph.

Contents of Environmental Awareness

Awareness to environment is a horizon-sweeping word and encompasses in totality the social, biological and psycho-chemical factors individually or collectively that comprise the natural and man-made surroundings. Environment can be classified in to basic components such as: (i) physical component, (ii) biological component, (iii) human uses, and (iv) human values as described below:

Physical Components: Water, air, land, light, temperature, humidity etc.

Biological Components: Aquatic and terrestrial flora (plants) and fauna (animals).

Human uses: Agricultural, industrial, residential, forestry, water supply, transportation, navigation, hydropower and recreation.

Human values: Traditional life style, religious status, archaeological and economic base, community structure, etc.

Thus, while the term 'Environment' covers the whole spectrum of science and humanities, the word 'Environmental Awareness' denote inter-relations and interactions between the living system and life.

2.7 Environmental Education and Environmental Awareness-differences

Environmental education is an effective process to develop an understanding of environmental awareness. Environmental awareness is one of the most important aspects of environmental education. Thus, they are closely interwined. However, the distinction between the two can be summarised in the following manner:

- The Environmental education focuses on improving the quality of life and values through systematic productive function, whereas environmental awareness focuses on providing an understanding of physical and biological components of the environment and their interdependence. The environmental awareness provides the understanding of natural, physical and biological aspects of the environment of an organism and also helps to identify human, material, space and time resources in the environment. Environmental education, on the other hand, inculcates awareness amongst man towards identifying and investigating the methods and techniques for modifying and improving quality of life of mankind and community as a whole.
- The culture and psychological environments are crucial in environmental education because organisation, climate and health of an institution is governed by the psychological principles and social and emotional climate of classroom teaching is generated by the psychology of the subject teacher, while environmental awareness provides the knowledge and understanding of inter-dependence of physical and biological components and the ecology of the organism.
- Environmental education plans and generates the conducive environment for desirable changes in man and manipulates the environment; whereas environmental awareness involves the knowledge of both natural and manipulated environment and confines itself only to the theoretical aspect.
- The environmental education provides the opportunities and situations for performing certain tasks and activities at all levels for solving environmental problems; while environmental awareness is limited to the problems and their solutions but does not involve task and activity.
- Environmental education is an effective process for developing environmental awareness through classroom interaction between teacher and taught and through the activities like: (a) providing sanitary facilities in school, (b) keeping school, home and surrounding

clean, (c) making provisions for deposition of waste, controlling the pollution of air and water, (d) keeping the body healthy and clean through games and sports facilities in schools, etc.

Thus, although environmental education and environmental awareness most often are used interchangeably, there are differences between the two as brought out above. objective-wise difference between environmental education and environmental awareness is summarised below:

Table 2.1

Environmental Education	*Environmental Awareness*
To provide the knowledge and understanding of structure, process and solution.	
To develop feeling, attitude and values for improving environment.	To provide knowledge and understanding of structure, components, process, problems and solutions (Theoretical and suggestive).
To inculcate skills for the effective participation for solving problems.	
To prepare for evaluating the educational programmes for their work ability or effectiveness (Theoretical and practical both).	

2.8 Education Develops Environmental Awareness

Seminars, conferences and workshops on environment have become common occurrence both at national and global level. Experts and scientists of different disciplines have realised the importance of 'environmental awareness'. They also recognise the urgent need for introduction of environmental education. Under the environmental education the theoretical and practical aspects are emphasised. The awareness confines to cognitive level whereas educational environment includes cognitive, psychomotor and affective levels.

In order to help children develop knowledge, skills and values, attitudes and awareness relevant to environments, teacher is expected to impart knowledge and give information through teaching learning situations. For the purpose of profitably utilising the time and taking care of the interests of children, teacher should resort to group activities and encourage their active involvement in the classroom. The teachers must organise environment-related activities such as plantation, forest conservation, etc. Documentary film on environment conservation and its ill-effects of over exploitation, excursion programme to develop awareness about the nature and deteriorating natural resources should be organised. Students should also been courage to watch environment related T.V. programmes, read newspapers, follow radio news on environment. The ill-effects of environmental degradations should be shown to the students through teaching aids such as charts, models, etc to develop awareness about the environment.

2.9 Environmental Education and Educational Environment

There are various terms which are used for Environmental Study which is interdisciplinary in nature. Therefore, it is not possible for an expert of a discipline to provide a comprehensive and true understanding. A student can also acquire the awareness of environment, which is limited to his horizon of thinking i.e. related to educational environment not environment as a whole. Therefore, an attempt has been made to differentiate between 'Environmental education' and 'Educational Environment'.

Table 2.2

Points	*Environmental Education*	*Educational Environment*
Area	Broad based including physical, biological, social and cultural environment and organisation and climate of the schools.	It is limited to social, cultural, psychological and organisational climate of a schools' classroom.
Purpose	It provides the awareness, skills, attitudes and values a consciousness about the environments. Practical work may be taken for controlling pollution.	It develops understanding of educational processes and activities, skill and practice to following schools and classroom and to improve quality of environment.
Points	*Environmental Education*	*Educational Environment*
Discipline	It is a highly interdisciplinary edifice of knowledge of environment. Most of the disciplines are concerned with it and contribute in its own area of study.	It is also interdisciplinary, but it is mainly concerned with teachers, Principals and teacher-educators.
Organisation	It is given on national, regional, local levels. Private agencies participate in formal, non-formal and adult education and orientation courses for administration.	It is mainly at state level and a few at central level by private agencies and state organised programmes for checking environmental pollution.
Problems	Problems are pollution and degradation of environment, physical (air, water, soil), social and cultural (Population problems).	Problems are related to educational administration, examination, teaching, schools and classrooms.
Impact and Assessment	It is made in terms of quality of the environment.	It is made in terms of students' performance in the examination.
Media and Management	Media is the most important for the awareness of problems. Legal steps are also essential for preventing and controlling pollutions.	Media has evolved alternative system of Education, i.e. Distance education; open system of education, Mass Media is used in it.

2.10 Need of Environmental Education

It has been stated in the Rigveda, the oldest of all four Vedas '*The dust (dhula) of mother earth and light of father sky should remain associated with full brightness for our welfare*'. According to Rigveda, there are three forms of God- the celestial (land), the aerial (air) and terrestrial (water). The whole Brahmanda was full of peace and happiness because life and environment were so closely inter-linked that it was difficult to think man and organism as something separate from nature or environment.

In present situation man and environment are considered interrelated and there is interdependence in them. The nature or environment becomes a source of sorrow and happiness, because the dusts of earth, light and air of sky have the adverse effect on human being. Therefore, it widely recognises the need of introduction of 'environmental education.' With the recommendations of the Tiwari Committee (1980) Indian Government have accepted the need for environmental education. They recognise an urgent need for environmental education. Besides introducing the subject of 'Environmental science' at all levels of education, emphasis has been laid on the new approaches and programmes of environmental education. Thus, the idea is to bring environmental concerns in all subjects and to all facets of life.

While most people recognise an urgent need for environmental education, only some have clear ideas as to what should be done. Very few have the actual experience or knowledge about the courses that need to be taught. The chief objective of environmental education is that the individual and social groups acquire awareness and knowledge, develop attitudes, skills and abilities and participate in solving real life environmental problems. This perspective should be integrated inter-disciplinary and holistic in character. The common man in rural areas, urban population, tribal, slum dwellers, students, teachers, workers, programme implementers, planners and policy-makers all need to be educated about the environment.

International Efforts

The need of environmental education has been thoroughly discussed at several national and international seminars, workshops, conferences. After the deliberations at Fourex in 1971 and at Stockholm in 1972, an International Workshop was held on Environmental Education. In 1975, the 'Belgrade charter' was declared at Belgrade (Yogoslavia) by UNESCO which formulated the guiding principles to achieve the objectives of Stockholm conference. Later, an Inter Governmental conference was organised by UNESCO and UNEP at Tbilisi, former USSR in 1977. Tbilisi conference followed closely the footsteps of Belgrade workshop.

Efforts in India

In collaboration with the International programme on Environmental Management a national seminar was organised by the Indian Environmental society at the Indian National Science Academy, New Delhi in 1979. In it emphasis was laid on incorporating Gandhian thought and values as a part of environmental education. A number of recommendations were made in the seminar.

The First international conference on Environmental Education was held at New Delhi, in 1987. Late Mrs Indira Gandhi had observed that environmental education is to help arouse social consciousness and make community aware of the fact that the good the individual and that of community are both harmed by ecological disruptions. In 1985, the second International conference on Environmental Education was held at New Delhi. Several important points emerged from the deliberations of the international, regional, national and even local conferences on environmental education.

The Environment Education and Training Scheme of the Ministry are precisely meant for environmental awareness. Under this scheme, various programmes are conducted every year for creating environmental awareness through non-formal activities as well as formal education system. While the programmes like National Environmental Awareness Campaign (NEAC), National Green Corps (NGC), use of Electronic Media etc. fall in the non-formal sector, the Ministry's initiative of taking up a pilot project for strengthening environmental concept in the school curriculum and the linked Global Learning and Observations to Benefit the Environment (GLOBE) programme use the formal education system for conveying the message.

Formal Environmental Education

The Ministry has taken various initiatives for strengthening Environment Education (EE) in the formal education curriculum. For this purpose, the Ministry had been closely interacting with the University Grants Commission (UGC), the National Council for Education Research and Training (NCERT), the Ministry of Human Resources Development (MHRD), the All India Council for Technical Education (AICTE) and the State Education Department to ensure integration of environmental concept into the curriculum. Pilot Project on Environment Education in School System (EESS) was launched with the basic objective of strengthening Environment Education in the formal school system. During Phase I, a nationwide survey to assess the extent of its delivery in the classroom was conducted by Bhartiya Vidyapeeth Institute for Environmental Education and Research (BVIEER). As a part of this study, a national consultation on EE was organised, which suggested instead of teaching environment as a separate subject, separate space/forum should be created within the school system for integrating the various environmental concept infused/introduced in other subjects. Based on these recommendations and the outcome of the EE study carried out by the BVIEER, the EESS project was implemented in eight States namely, Andhra Pradesh, Assam, Goa, J&K, Maharashtra, Odisha, Punjab and Uttaranchal on a pilot basis under Phase II of the project. One hundred schools in each of these States were selected for pilot implementation. During the pilot implementation, the textbooks of Science, Social Studies and language of standards VI to VIII in the selected schools of the project. This exercise was also accompanied by development of other education material like teachers' handbooks/guides/manual, classroom materials, etc. Subsequently, the concerned teachers (about five in no.) from each project school were also trained for effectively teaching the environmental concept infused in the modified/greened textbooks. The modified textbooks were introduced in the project schools during the 2002-2003 and 2003-2004 academic session.

In view of the success of this initiative, the project was extended until 30th June, 2004 and seven additional States viz. Chhattisgarh, Himachal Pradesh, Karnataka, Kerala, Sikkim, Tamil Nadu, and Tripura were covered. Hundred schools from each of these States implemented the project on pilot basis as done previously for the eight States. Activities like development and printing of educational materials including textbooks, training of master trainers, training of the teachers, introduction of green textbooks in the project schools etc. were completed in the seven States.

Global Learning and Observation to Benefit Environment (GLOBE)

GLOBE is an international Science and Education programme which provides "Hand-on environmental learning" of environmental concept to the students to carry out various measurements. So that they can learn about scientific protocol and perform environmental learning activities, which have already been introduced as theory in the greened textbooks developed for EESS project. These experiments and measurement were included as a part of new curriculum to enable the students to gain a better understanding of the infused environmental contents. The Hands-on Environmental Learning Programme being an integral component of EESS project was implemented in all the EESS project schools. About 1800 teachers from about 1700 schools have been trained so far in various protocols for conducting the experiments in respect of four broad environmental parameters, namely, Hydrology, Soil, Land Cover and Atmospheric temperature/rainfall. Instruments/kits for carrying out various experiments were provided to about 800 schools.

Strengthening Environmental Education in Indian Management Schools

This initiative, which was launched by the Ministry in 2002 to integrate environmental concepts in the management education, made good progress during the year. An inventory of the courses offered in India and abroad has been prepared along with the inventory of resource material.

Environmental Appreciation Courses

In order to provide interested persons an opportunity to learn in detail about specific environmental issues, the Ministry has already got a course module developed from Indira Gandhi National Open University for Environmental Appreciation courses. It is proposed to deliver these courses through distance education mode by IGNOU. The materials for these courses have also been prepared. IGNOU has started introducing these courses at the undergraduate level on compulsory basis.

Non-Formal Environmental Education and Awareness

Environmental Education, Awareness and Training play a significant role in encouraging and enhancing people's participation in activities aimed at conservation, protection and management of the environment, essential for achieving sustainable development. Accordingly the Ministry accords priority to the promotion of non-formal environment education and creation of awareness among all sections of the society through diverse activities using traditional and modern media of communication. Some of the major activities undertaken in this regard during the year are as follows:

National Environment Awareness Campaign (NEAC)

The NEAC programme was started in year 1986 for creating environmental awareness at the National level. An action component was introduced in the awareness campaign in the year 2001-02. This programme was continued during the year with the main theme as "Solid Waste Management." The following sub-themes for action components were considered for financial assistance:

- Household waste and composting/vermin-composting
- Municipal waste
- Biomedical waste
- Plastic waste
- Waste management at higher altitude
- Electronic waste (e-waste)
- Industrial waste including fly ash

Twenty nine organisations located in different parts of the country, designated as Regional Resource Agencies (RRAs) by the Ministry, implemented NEAC programme for 2004-05 and physically monitored the activities in the areas of their jurisdiction. Seven thousand five hundred and eighty eight participating organisations were provided financial assistance for organising awareness creating activities such as padyatras, rallies, public meetings, exhibitions, folk dances, street theatres, essay/debate, painting/ poster, competitions for school children, seminars, workshops, training courses, etc. for preparation and distributions of environmental education resource material and for following these with action oriented activities. Diverse target groups ranging from students/youths/teachers to tribal, rural population, professionals, etc. were covered under the campaign. The Ministry invited applications from NGO's, VO's, Educational Institutions, and others to act as RRA's.

National Green Corps (Eco-clubs)

To impart environmental education and to encourage and mobilise participation of school children in various environmental conservation activities in the localities, the Ministry provided financial assistance to a number of schools for functioning of Eco-clubs. Each club has 30-50 members taken from the students of Class VI to X. The student members of the Eco-clubs constitute the National Green Corps (NGC). It is proposed to establish Eco clubs in at least 150 schools in each district of the country. The NGC programme addresses various issues concerning protection and improvement of environment e.g. solid waste management, pollution control, afforestation, maintenance of parks and open spaces, dissemination of information and creation of awareness. The State and Union Territory Government have been assigned the responsibility of identifying school, teacher and Nodal Agencies. The Nodal Agencies are responsible for implementing, supervising and monitoring the programme. All the States and Union Territories are implementing the programme. The Central Government provided financial assistance to the States Nodal Agencies for organising training for Master Trainers and in-charge teacher and for printing and distribution of locally relevant resource material. Besides, the Ministry also granted an annual financial assistance of Rs 1000 per Eco club. The Ministry also provided a set of resource material in the form of books, posters, booklets etc. to each Eco-club. Prominent non-governmental organisations working in the area of environmental education are associated as the Resource Agencies to assist the State Nodal Agencies in implementing the programme. It has also been decided to extend the programme to colleges.

Seminars/Symposia/Workshops/Conference

Under this programme, financial assistance is provided to educational institutions, Non-governmental organisations and other for organising seminars/symposia /conferences/workshops on environmental-related issues. Proposals are supported for financial assistance on annual basis.

Grants-in-aid to Professional Societies and Institution

The major objective of the programme is to provide assistance to professional societies and institution to augment their capability in the field of environment with an ultimate objective of involving such professional bodies in the various activities relating to protection of environment and conservation of natural resources. Organisations are provided with financial assistance under the programme.

Publication of Resource Materials

The objective of the programme is to utilise expertise available with professional societies, voluntary organisations, institutions, etc. for printing and publication of resource material for promoting environmental education and awareness. Organisations are provided with financial assistance for this purpose.

Media Action Plan

With the objective of spreading environmental awareness through various media activities, the Ministry has formulated a 'Media Action Plan'. Under the Action Plan, the Ministry has taken up several initiatives. These include: (i) launching of a 15 minute programme "Yeh Gulistan Hamara" in 12 languages on All India Radio, (ii) A National Theatre Festival on environment was organised during Feb.18 to 21, 2005 at New Delhi, (iii) Ministry has sponsored a half hour weekly Environmental Magazine Programme on television called BHOOMI, which is being telecast on Doordarshan National Channel every Sunday, (iv) To make use of the medium of documentary films for environmental awareness, a MoU has been signed with Public Service Broadcasting Trust (PSBT) for production of 13 films every year on environment and their telecast on Doordarshan and (v) To take "Vatavaran" film festival to cites other than Delhi, two screenings were organised in Chennai and Mumbai. Screening support was provided for another screening in Assam to coincide with 'Kaziranga Centenary Celebrations.'

The Ministry has sponsored 10 lakh 'meghdoot' postcards. These cards carry environmental messages relevant to rural population. Campaigns were planned for using the potential of FM channels effectively. A campaign was launched on various TV channels against the use of firecrackers during festivals. Several features were sponsored on popular magazines like 'Outlook' and 'Frontline' for highlighting the policies and programmes of the Ministry.

Other Awareness Programme

The Ministry sponsored the organisation of "Green Olympiad" (an International Environment Quiz Programme) by The Energy and Resources Institute (TERI). This was conducted in both Hindi and English this year.

More than one lakh school students from India, Russia and UAE participated in this competition. The regional winners were selected for the televised quiz programme named "TERRAQUIZ" which was telecast in 13 episodes on National channel of Doordarshan was a great success in sensitising the children about environmental issues. The Ministry sponsored organisation of "Earth Day 2004" through TERI. Nearly 500 students from various schools in Delhi participated in a series of activities associated with the event.

The National Museum of Natural History (NMNH) was set up by the Ministry to impart non-formal environmental education and conserve the example of flora, fauna and geological feature of the country. This is anchored in various awareness programmes for the student/teacher community as well as for the general public. NMNH and its Regional Museums of Natural History (RMNH) have been able to position in a network of their own to provide dedicated service to the society.

2.11 Aims of Environmental Education

"The goal of environmental education is to develop a world population that is aware of, and concerned about, the environmental and its associated problems, and which has the knowledge, skills, attitudes, motivations and commitment to work individually and collectively towards solutions of current problems and the prevention of new ones (The Belgrade Charter, UNESCO, 1976)." The world's first intergovernmental conference on environmental education adopted the Tbilisi Declaration in 1978. This declaration built on the Belgrade Charter and established three broad goals for environmental education. These goals provide the foundation for much of what has been done in the field:

- To foster clear awareness of, and concern about, economic, social, political and ecological interdependence in urban and rural areas;
- To provide every person with opportunities to acquire the knowledge, values, attitudes, commitment and skills needed to protect and improve the environment;
- To create new patterns of behaviour of individuals, groups and society as a whole towards the environment.

As the field has evolved, these principles have been researched, critiqued, revisited, and expanded. They still stand as a strong foundation for a shared view of the core concepts and skills that environmentally literate citizens need. Since 1978, bodies such as the Brundtland Commission (Brundtland, 1987), the United Nations Conference on Environment and Development in Rio (UNCED, 1992), the Thessaloniki Declaration (UNESCO, 1997) and the World Summit on Sustainable Development in Johannesburg (United Nations, 2002) have influenced the work of many educators, highlighting the importance of viewing the environment within the context of human influences.

This perspective has expanded the emphasis of environmental education, focusing more attention on social equity, economics, culture, and political structure. The environmental education aims at developing in the child awareness and understanding of the physical and social environment in its entirety. Fortunately 'environmental education' has been introduced in the curriculum from an early stage in our country. Kothari Commission (1966) recommends that "Environmental activities will lead to study of natural sciences, physical sciences, geography, history and civics; construction and creative skills will provide the basis for the practice of simple arts and crafts and practice of healthy living will serve as the foundation for environmental education."

The following are the ***main aims of Environmental Education***:

- To consider the environment in its totality (natural, artificial, technological, social, economic, political, moral, cultural, historical, aesthetic).
- To consider a continuous life process (From pre-school to all higher levels- formal as well as non-formal).
- To be interdisciplinary in approach in Environmental Education.
- To emphasise active participation in prevention and solution to environmental problems.
- To examine major environmental issues and problems from local, national, regional, and international point of view.
- To focus on current, potential environmental situation.
- To consider environmental aspects in plans for growth and development.
- To emphasise the complexity of environmental problems and need to develop critical thinking and problems-solving skills.
- To promote the value and necessity of local, national and international co-operation in the prevention and solution of environmental problems.
- To utilise diverse learning about environment and different approaches to teaching and learning about environment.
- To help learners to discover the symptoms and the real causes of environmental problems.
- To relate environmental sensitivity, knowledge, problem-solving and values clarification at every grade level.
- To enable learners to have a role in planning their learning experiences and provide an opportunity for making decisions and accepting their consequences.

- To develop the abilities of doing and understanding growth, structure approaches and problems of environmental education.

Aims of Environmental Education as per Me Ako

The aims of Environmental Education are for students to develop:

- **Aim 1: awareness and sensitivity** to the environment and related issues;
- **Aim 2: knowledge and understanding** of the environment and the impact of people on it;
- **Aim 3: attitudes and values** that reflect feelings of concern for the environment;
- **Aim 4: skills** involved in identifying, investigating, and problem solving associated with environmental issues;
- **Aim 5:** a sense of responsibility through **participation and action** as individuals, or members of groups, in addressing environmental issues.

Environmental issues related to a sustainable future are often complex. Multidisciplinary holistic teaching and learning approaches are therefore appropriate for meeting the aims of environmental education. The aims and their interactive nature are illustrated through the tree.

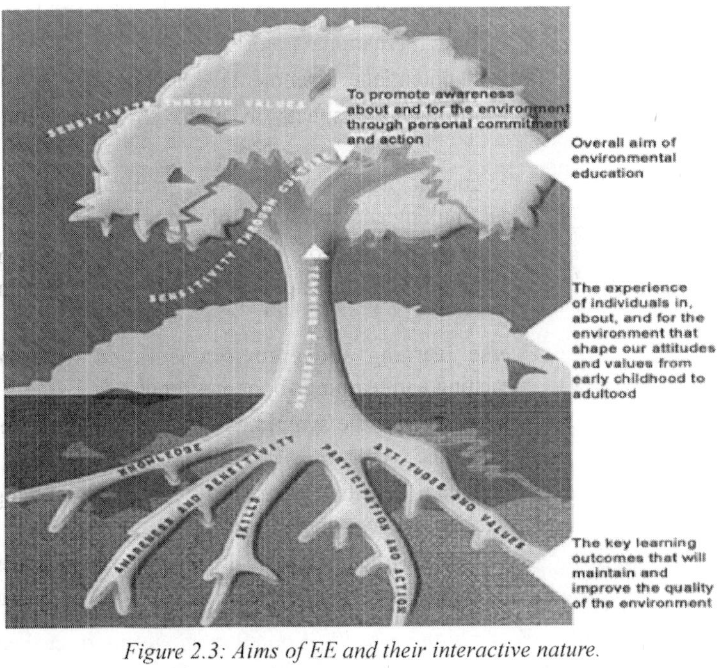

Figure 2.3: Aims of EE and their interactive nature.

2.12 Objectives of Environmental Education

The objectives of environmental education are part of the general objectives of education which have been defined variously by different thinkers, classifiers, humanists and scientists. Still most of them seem to agree with Herbert Spencer that education should prepare for complete living, which does not mean living in the material sense merely but in the widest sense. That is, an educated person should know how to lead a healthy life, how to prevent oneself from sickness, premature death and how to treat the body; what way to develop the intellect and to treat the mind; how to prepare for earning a living and to secure the necessities and comforts of life; how to rear and discipline offsprings; how to maintain proper social and political relations; how best to spend leisure time and how to use talent for the greatest advantage of the self as well as the society. For the accomplishment of most of these objectives, environmental education has been considered one of the most important mediums.

According to Bloom, the objectives of environmental education can be described in three domains cognitive, effective and psychomotor. The cognitive domain deal with intellectual skills and abilities such as remembering; problem-solving; concept formation and to a limited extent, creative thinking.

The affective domain includes the objectives that describe changes in interest, attitudes and values and the development of appreciations and adjustment. This area covers the entire continuum from ordinary attention to an object to deep down existence. It also includes contrary behaviour, that is, the aversion, antipathy or fear one shows for certain objects.

The psychomotor domain covers the manipulative or motor-skill area. This area includes neuromuscular co-ordinations found in handwriting, speech making, performing physical exercises, dancing, doing yoga, winding a screw, using a saw and in doing a lot of things which are required to be done under socially useful productive work and in vocational and technical courses.

The objectives of environmental education in all the three domains-cognitive, affective and psychomotor are given below:

Objectives in the cognitive domain

- To help acquire knowledge of the immediate environment.
- To help acquire knowledge of the environment beyond the immediate environment including distant environment.
- To help understand the biotic and abiotic environment.
- To help understand the effect of unchecked population growth or unplanned resource utilisation in the world of tomorrow.
- To examine trends in the growth of population and interpret them for the socio-economic development of the country.

- To evaluate the utilisation of physical and human resources and suggest remedial measures.
- To help diagnose the different cause of environmental pollution and to suggest remedial measures.
- To help diagnose the cause of social tensions and to suggest methods for avoiding them.

Besides the foregoing objectives, the following skills and abilities also fall in the cognitive domain:

- To help develop observational skills and notice details usually not seen by an untrained eye.
- To help develop skills required for making discriminations in form, shape, sound, touch, habits and habitats.
- To help develop ability to make meaningful suggestions.

Objectives of affective domain

We can now list the affective objectives of environmental education:

- To help acquire interest in the flora and fauna of the near and also distant environment.
- To help evince interest in the people and problem of the community and society.
- To show tolerance towards different caste, races, religions and cultures.
- To appreciate the gifts of nature.
- To love the neighbours and value mankind as a whole.
- To value equality, liberty, fraternity, truth and justice.
- To respect the national boundaries of all countries.
- To value the cleanliness and purity of our environment.

Objectives of psychomotor domain

Environmental education also fulfils some objectives of the psychomotor domain as are achieved through participation in environmental activities, excursions and camping programmes. Some of the objectives are listed below:

- To participate in afforestation programmes.
- To participate in programmes aimed at minimising air, water and noise pollution.
- To participate in programmes aimed at preventing soil erosion.
- To participate in programmes aimed at eliminating food contamination and adulteration.
- To participate in cleaning neighbourhood.

- To participate in urban and rural planning and execution programme such as, installation of gobar gas plants, solar heaters etc.

A number of objectives of environmental education have been formulated for both formal and non-formal education at all levels at the International Conference of UNESCO (1977) held at Tbilisi. These are as follows:

- To develop an awareness of environment and sensitivity (feeling and attitudes) to the total environment and its allied problems.
- To help in acquiring knowledge and variety of experiences of the environment and associated problems.
- To develop a basic understanding of structure, processes and problems of environment; interdependence of environmental components.
- To help in acquiring skills for identifying and solving environmental problems.
- To develop attitudes, a set of values and feeling of concern for the environment and encouragement or motivation for active participation in protection and improvement of environment.
- To provide an opportunity for an active participation or practice at all levels in working for the solution of environmental problems and
- To develop ability for evaluating environmental components and educational programmes in terms of ecology, economic, social, cultural, aesthetic and education factors.

The above objectives are related to all levels and both formal and non-formal system of education. In the formal system of education four different but interrelated components have been recognised which are noted below:

Table 2.3

	Objectives	*Level*
1.	Awareness of environment (Knowledge)	-Primary education
2.	Relevance for real-life situation of environment (understanding)	-Secondary education
3.	Conservation of natural resources of environment (skills)	-Higher Secondary Education.
4.	Sustainable development by solving problems of environment (Attitude and Evaluation)	-College and University Education

Thus environmental education objectives involve the doing and understanding aspects of environment.

2.13 Principles of Environmental Education

According to Tim Grant, nine principles for Environmental education are as follows:

Education should emphasise our interdependence with other peoples, other species and the planet as a whole

More than anything else, education should explore the connections between peoples, between people and other species, and between people and the planet. When we appreciate how dependent we are on having a healthy global environment, we will want to take steps to preserve biodiversity, reduce global inequalities and promote cross-cultural understanding with others.

Education should help students move from awareness to knowledge to action

Knowing about the environment doesn't necessarily lead to action. Students must have opportunities to "act" on their knowledge. It is only when we try to solve environmental problems that we can fully understand them. This can't be done solely by studying from textbooks. When students try to solve environmental problems, they discover that these issues are not black and white, and learn why these problems have not been solved already. This provides them with opportunities to develop the critical thinking skills needed to develop solutions.

Teachers, students and schools in the world's richer countries should reduce their consumption of the world's resources

It's estimated that the 20 per cent of the world's population in the richer countries consume 80 per cent of the world's resources. Does our planet have enough resources for everyone to have the same living standards as this 20 per cent? Besides asking students to consider this question, we can encourage them to think of ways their school can save energy and can use less water, paper and other resources.

Students must have opportunities to develop a personal connection with nature

It's impossible to save the environment if you don't know it. Yet, most people live in cities where it's difficult to develop an emotional bond with nature. Environmental education can help people recognise that there is more nature in cities than we realise. Many schools are replacing the concrete in their school yards with nature study areas, full of native trees and plants.

Education should be future-oriented

Traditionally, we have studied history in order to understand the present. But to solve environmental problems, we need to think about the future.

One way is to ask ourselves what kind of future we want to leave our children, may be after seven generations after us. Another method is to develop alternative views of the future. We can consider where our current path of development is taking us, and then consider environmental-friendly alternatives.

We must relearn "old wisdoms" from native peoples to re-connect to the planet

In our communities, there are grandparents and other elders who can tell us what life was like before today's consumer society. It is important for young people to realise that our consumer society is a very recent development in human history and that many people enjoyed happy, satisfying lives before this.

Teachers should incorporate media literacy into every school subject

In North America, young people encounter 2,000 advertisements each day on TV and radio, on outdoor ads and on consumer products. These advertisements help form the self-image of boys and girls, and promote materialism as a goal in itself. We need to remember that our "mental" environment can get as polluted as the natural environment.

Teachers should be facilitators

We don't need to be experts to teach about the environment. As we study environmental problems with our students, we can learn about these problems at the same time. One role is to provide opportunities for learning - we don't need to tell students what conclusions should be reached.

Teachers should be good role models for their students and "walk their talk"

As role models, teachers have an enormous influence on their students. Research shows that if students know that teachers and other adults care about the environment, it lessens their anxiety about discussing and acting on environmental issues. We thus need to practice what we preach and "walk our talk."

In conclusion, environmental education is a subject that is of a very practical nature and is also supported by sound pedagogical principles. From conception to cremation, we live in some or the other environment, and use it for meeting all our needs, comforts and luxuries. We should, therefore, understand our environment and know how to use it for our individual well being and for the welfare of the society and the future generations. Thus, environmental education is more functional than the disciplines we have been studying so far.

3

The Ecosystem

3.1 Concept

The term 'ecosystem' is made up of two words *'eco'* which means environment and *'system'* which means interacting or inter-dependent on one another and at the same time impacting on the environment. An ecosystem is a complex set of relationship among the living resources, habitats and residents of an area. It includes plants, trees, animals, fish, birds, micro-organisms, water, soil, people, etc.

An ecosystem can be defined as a dynamic entity composed of a biological community and its associated abiotic environment. Often the dynamic interactions that occur within an ecosystem are numerous and complex. Ecosystems are also always undergoing alterations to their biotic and abiotic components. Some of these alterations begin first with a change in the state of one component of the ecosystem which then cascades and sometimes amplifies into other components because of their inter-relationships. In recent years, humans have impacted the ecosystem in a number of ways to fulfil their desire for development.

As a result, number of dramatic changes has taken place to a variety of ecosystems existing on the earth - the most obvious impact of humans on ecosystems is the loss of biodiversity. The number of extinctions caused by human domination of ecosystems has been steadily increasing since the start of the Industrial Revolution. The frequency of species extinctions is correlated to the size of human population on the Earth which is directly related to resource consumption, land-use change, and environmental degradation. Other human impacts to ecosystems include species invasions to new habitats, changes to the abundance and dominance of species in communities, modification of biogeochemical cycles, and modification of hydrologic cycling, pollution and climatic change.

Ecosystems vary in size and elements that make them up, but each is a functioning unit of nature. Everything that lives in an ecosystem is dependent on the other species and elements that are also part of the ecological community. If one part of an eco-system is damaged or disappears, it has an impact on everything else. Ecosystems are hierarchical and can be viewed as nestled sets of open systems in which physical, chemical, and biological processes form interactive subsystems. Some ecosystems are microscopic, others are large, and the largest being the biosphere. Figure 3.1 below depicts a diagram of an ecosystem and its components.

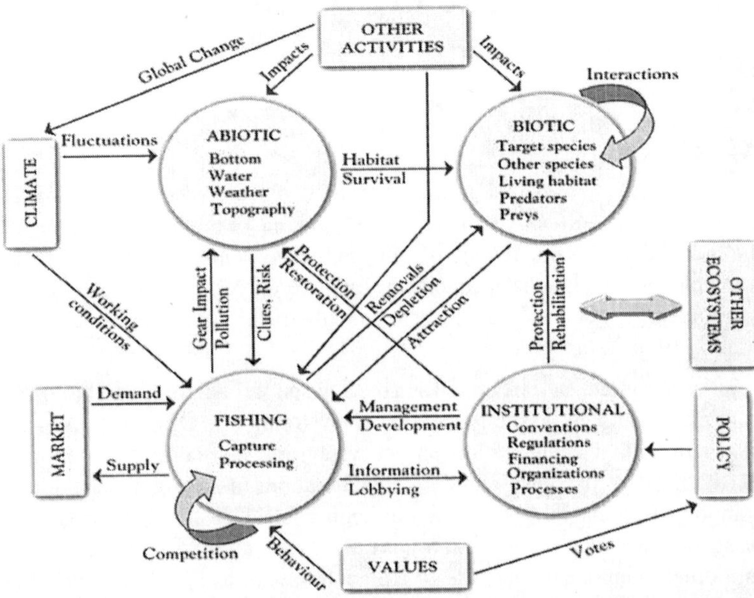

Figure 3.1: Ecosystem and components.

An ecosystem is a very complex entity with many interactive components. It can be defined as "*a system of complex interactions of populations between themselves and with their environment*" or as "*the joint functioning and interaction of these two compartments (populations and environment) in a functional unit of variable size*" (Odum, 1975; Ellenberg, 1973; Nybakken, 1982; Scialabba, 1998). Ecosystems may be considered at different geographical scales, from a grain of sand with its rich microfauna, to a whole beach, a coastal area or estuary, a semi-enclosed sea and, eventually, the whole Earth. As stated by Lackey (1999), ecosystems are defined at a wide range of scales of observation "*from a drop of morning dew to an ocean,... from a pebble to a planet.*" Since ecosystems can be as small as a single tree or as large as entire forest, there are lots and lots of different ecosystems of different size and shapes. The earth itself is an immense ecosystem. Likewise, there are ecosystems in sea, forest, river, or even in a small pond.

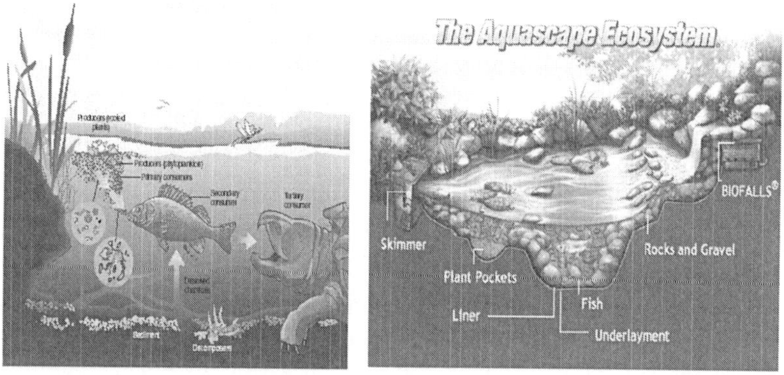

Figure 3.2: The aquatic ecosystem.

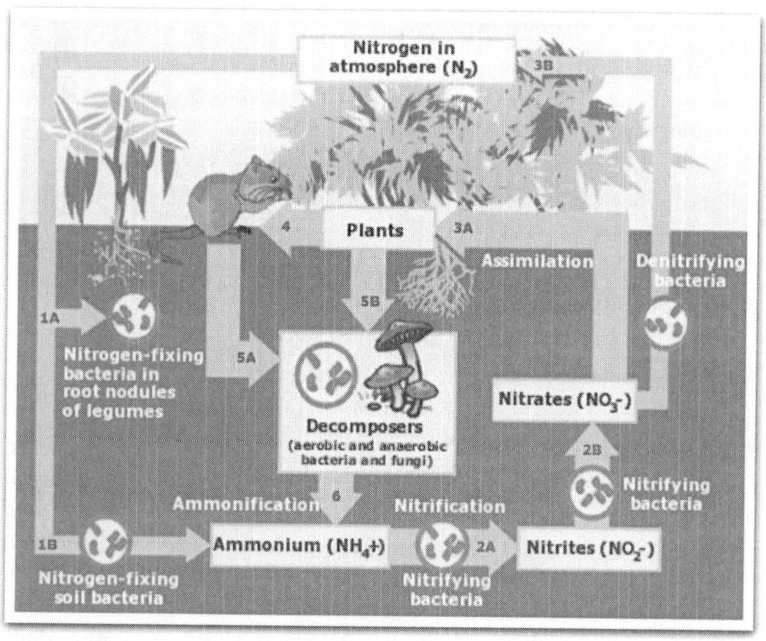

Figure 3.3: Large ecosystem comprising of nitrogen in atmosphere.

3.2 Definitions of Ecosystem

The term ecosystem was initially coined by a British ecologist, A G Tansley in 1935. According to him the system resulting from the integration of all the living and non-living factors of the environment is ecosystem. The living organisms *(biotic component)* and their non-living *(abiotic component)* environment are inseparably interrelated and constantly interact upon each other. Interaction between organisms and their physio-chemical environment is continuous phenomenon of the ecosystem. Some of the definitions of ecosystem are given below:

> Ecosystem is a dynamic system which includes organisms, biotic components and abiotic environments influencing the properties of each other and both necessary for the maintenance of life.- *Odum and Clarke*
>
> The ecosystem involves the circulation, transformation and accumulation of energy and matter through the medium of living organisms and their activities. The dynamic abiotic components of environment and the assemblage of plants and animals there, as a result of interactions between themselves keep modifying and changing each other and this leads to the development of ecosystem.- *Evans*
>
> The ecosystem as functioning, interacting system composed of one or more living organisms and their effective environment, both physical and biological.- *A G Tansley and F R Fosberg (1963)*
>
> The term ecosystem applies to any system composed of physical, chemical and biological processes within a space-time unit of any magnitude. - *R L Linderman (1942)*
>
> The total assemblage of components interacting with a group of organisms is known as ecological system or more simply an ecosystem.
> - *A N Strahler (1976)*
>
> A system of complex interactions of populations between themselves and with their environment or as the joint functioning and interaction of these two compartments (populations and environment) in a functional unit of variable size is an ecosystem.
> - Odum (1975); Ellenberg (1973); Nybakken (1982); Scialabba (1998)
>
> Ecosystems are defined at a wide range of scales of observation "from a drop of morning dew to an ocean,... from a pebble to a planet."
> - Lackey (1999)

Definition and delineation of an ecosystem can become as complicated as one want to make it. Essentially, an ecosystem can be a log in the forest and its associated micro-organisms, a small lake and its tributary, or the Gulf of Mexico. To make it simpler, each organism (including humans) is affected by and interacts with its environment. The environment is formed from a combination of interactive non-living and living elements. The non-living elements include energy, water, air, substance and chemical constituents such as nutrients. The living elements include plants, vertebrate animals, invertebrates, and micro-organisms. When we consider both forms of elements and their interactions as a single entity, we have an ecosystem at some level of organisation.

Thus, the ecosystem is the sum total of all natural organisms and substances within an area and it can be viewed as basic example of an open system in physical geography. It can be defined as fundamental functional unit occupying spatial dimension of earth spaceship characterised by total assemblage of biotic community and abiotic components and their mutual interactions within a given time unit.

3.3 Characteristics of Ecosystem

A perusal of above definitions by various environmentalists suggest following prominent characteristics of ecosystem:

- The ecosystem is a unit of organisms connected to one another and to their environment within given space and time unit;
- Any system composed of physical, chemical and biological processes within a space-time, unit of any magnitude;
- It is composed of three basic components-biotic (biome), abiotic (habitat), and energy components;
- It occupies certain well defined area on the earth- space and time unit;
- Ecosystem of any given space time unit represents the sum of all living organism and physical environment;
- It is an open system which is characterised by continuous input and output of matter and energy;
- There are complex sets of interactions between biotic and abiotic components including energy components on the one hand and among the organism on the other hand;
- Ecosystem has its own productivity which is the process of building organic matter based on the availability and amount of energy passing through ecosystem. The productivity refers to the rate of growth of organic matter in a space unit per time unit;
- It is powered by energy of various sorts but the solar energy is the most significant (radiation) and tends to be relatively stable equilibrium. It has the natural resource system;
- It is well organised and structured system. The study of ecosystem development is helpful in the environmental planning from ecological point of view.

3.4 Aspects of Ecosystem

The ecosystem has two aspects – structural and functional aspects.

(i) *Structural aspects*

Structural aspects consist of composition of biological community including species *(plants, animals and microbes)*, biomass, life cycles and distribution in space, tropic standpoint, the quantity, distribution and cycling of the non-living materials such as major and micro nutrients, trace elements and water. The range or gradient of conditions like temperature, light, rainfall, relative humidity, wind and topography form part of structural aspects.

(ii) *Functional aspects*

Functional aspects consists of the rate of biological energy flow *i.e.* production and respiration rates of the community; rate of materials/ ecological regulation which includes regulation or organisms by environment *(e.g, photoperodism)* and regulation of environment by organisms *(nitrogen fixation by organisms)*. Since, structural and functional aspects of ecosystem are inseparable, these are studied together.

3.5 Components of Ecosystem

Ecosystems are composed of a variety of abiotic (*soil, atmosphere, radiation from the Sun and water*) and biotic components (*living organisms)* that function in an interrelated fashion and are inseparable. Attempt to segregate them into Biotic and Abiotic components are usually undertaken for easy comprehension of their respective role in the ecosystem.

(i) *Biotic components*

The most important relationships between living organisms (plants, animals, bacteria and viruses) and the environment are controlled by the quantum of energy received at the Earth's surface from the Sun. It is this energy which helps to drive biotic systems. The Sun's energy allows plants to convert inorganic chemicals into organic compounds.

Ecosystems are composed of a variety of *living organisms* that can be classified as producers, consumers, or decomposers. Producers or autotrophs, are organisms that can manufacture the organic compounds they use as sources of energy and nutrients. Most producers are green plants that can manufacture their food through the process of photosynthesis. Consumers or heterotrophs get their energy and nutrients by feeding directly or indirectly on producers. We can distinguish two main types of consumers. Herbivores are consumers that eat plants for their energy and nutrients. Organisms that feed on herbivores are called carnivores. Carnivores can also consume other carnivores. Plants and animals supply organic matter to the soil system through shed tissues and death. Consumer organisms that feed on this organic matter, or detritus, are known as detritivores or decomposers. The organic matter that is consumed by the detritivores is eventually converted back into inorganic nutrients in the soil. These nutrients can then be used by plants for the production of organic compounds. Figure 3.4 below describes the major ecosystem components and their interrelationships:

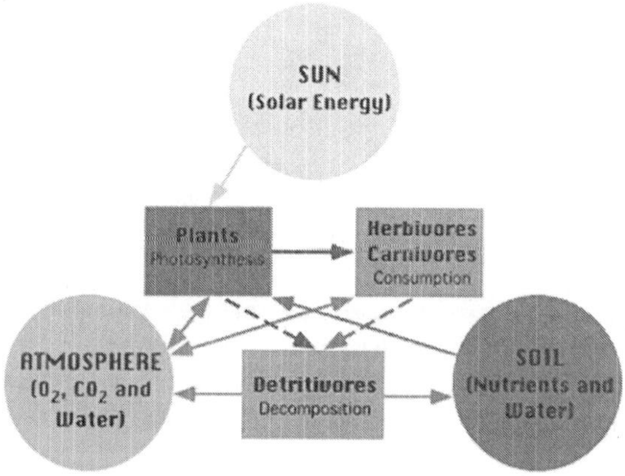

Figure 3.4: Ecosystem components and their interrelationships.

Solar energy is primarily trapped by the chloroplast machinery of green plants to build organic material. Green plants take simple inorganic materials like salt, water, carbondioxide, etc. to produce their own food. These organisms are, therefore, called as autotrophs *i.e.* self food producing. All other forms of life which do not possess chlorophyll cannot produce their own food and depend upon others and are called heterotrophy. Fungi, most of the bacteria, and animals derive their food directly or indirectly from the food produced by green plants and are examples of heterotrophy. Based on this fact of production and consumption, the green plants are called as producer components and other organisms like animals are called as consumer components. Among consumers some animals such as herbivores, like goat, cow, deer and rabbit etc. eat the green plants and are known as consumers of the first order. Other Carnivore organisms eat the herbivores e.g. frog eats a grasshopper, a carnivore fish eats herbivore fish. These are called consumers of the second order. There are in most ecosystems, some organisms that eat other carnivores like a snake eats a frog, or a bird eats all types of fish including carnivores. These are called consumers of the third order. Then there are top order carnivores like lions, vultures etc. which eat other carnivores also, but are not killed and eaten by other animals.

While the green plants are called primary producers, the heterotrophic organisms are also producer in a way as they eat plants or other organic materials as food, break them down in their digestion process and produce new type of organic materials in their body and in the process produce organic materials. Based on this concept they are also known as secondary producers. Both the primary producers and the secondary producers have their life cycles and new generation of populations develop while old ones die. Have you ever thought what happens to the dead ones? If the materials so locked in the body of the organisms are not returned to soil and atmosphere, the cycling of materials will stop and the earth will be full of dead organic matter. There is a continuous breaking up or decomposition of these organic materials taking place everywhere in all ecosystems. Some organisms with a specialised mode of nutrition and life, like fungi, bacteria, etc. constantly decompose the dead organic materials into simple inorganic substances and during the process derive their food and energy from them. These are called decomposers or reducers. In fact, decomposers are also a form of consumer who derives their food from dead parts of the primary and secondary producers. The role of decomposers is very special and important in the ecosystem as without their activity the entire cycle of minerals is liable to get blocked.

(ii) Abiotic components

The important abiotic components are *soil, atmosphere, solar radiation and water* etc. Soils are much more complex than simple sediments. They contain a mixture of weathered rock fragments, highly altered soil mineral particles, organic matter, and living organisms. Soils provide nutrients, water, a home, and a structural growing medium for organisms. The vegetation found growing on top of a soil is closely linked to this component of an ecosystem through nutrient cycling.

The ***atmosphere*** provides organisms found within ecosystems with carbondioxide for photosynthesis and oxygen for respiration. The processes of evaporation, transpiration, and precipitation cycle water between the atmosphere and the Earth's surface.

Solar radiation is used in ecosystems to heat the atmosphere and to evaporate and transpire water into the atmosphere. Sunlight is also necessary for photosynthesis. Photosynthesis provides the energy for plant growth and metabolism, and the organic food for other forms of life.

Water: Most living tissue is composed of a very high percentage of ***water***, up to and even exceeding 90 per cent. The protoplasm of a very few cells can survive if their water content drops below 10 per cent, and most are killed if it is less than 30-50 per cent. Water is the medium by which mineral nutrients enter and are translocated in plants. It is also necessary for the maintenance of leaf turgidity and is required for photosynthetic chemical reactions.

Plants and animals receive their water from the Earth's surface and soil. The original source of this water is precipitation from the atmosphere.

The abiotic components of ecosystem can be broadly grouped under two broad headings such as: (i) materials and (ii) energy. Materials are like light, heat, stored energy in chemical bonds, etc. The quantity of abiotic materials like minerals present at any given time in an ecosystem is termed as the standing state similar to standing crop which refers to the quantity of biotic components. The materials continually keep on cycling *i.e.*, entering into the living system and through death and decay returning to soil and atmosphere. This process is called mineral circulation or the bio-geochemical cycle. While the materials keep on cycling, fresh energy is continuously trapped from the sun by the green plants on the one hand and lost in space though respiration and loss of heat by all types of organisms on the other. Thus, energy flows like one way traffic.

The main abiotic factors are climatic factors such as solar radiation, temperature, wind, water, rainfall, physical factors as light, fire, pressure, geomagnetism, chemical factors as acidity, salinity and inorganic nutrients required by plants.

3.6 Food Chains

The green plants are the primary producers because they prepare their own food which is the main source of food energy for all types of organisms in the biosphere. Carbondioxide is taken by plants from the atmosphere through their leaves during day time and inorganic matter and water are taken by the roots from the soils. Plants convert water and carbondioxide into starch and sugar with the help of sun light. This process is known as photosynthesis. Thus, the green plants are primary producers. Some animals depend on plants for their foods are called herbivores. The animals take their foods from animals are known as carnivores. Some animals depend on both, plants and animals for their food are termed as Omnivores. In the ecosystem, feeding process takes place in hierarchical order. The food energy passes from one group of organisms to another group are called Trophic level.

The chain of transformation of food energy in the ecosystem from one group of organisms to other group through a series of steps or levels is called ***Food Chain***. In the biosphere the energy flows from producers to primary consumers, from primary consumers to secondary and from secondary consumers to decomposers, is known as food chain. The consumer's food chain includes the sequence energy flow – plants producers and animals consumers.

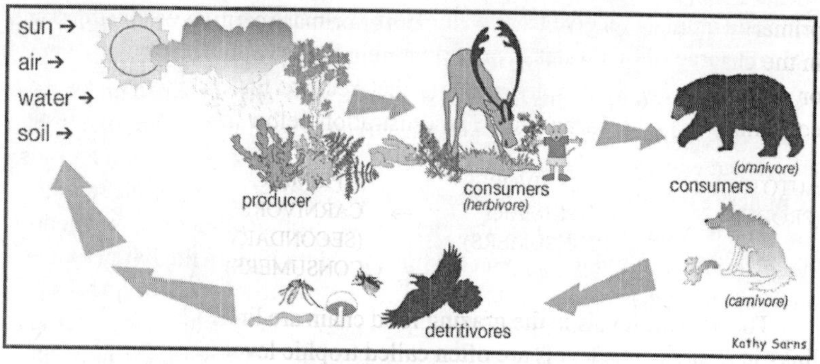

Figure 3.5: Food Chain.

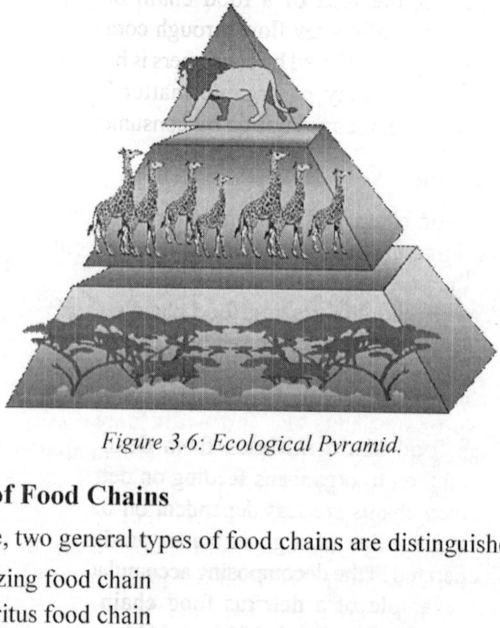

Figure 3.6: Ecological Pyramid.

3.7 Types of Food Chains

In nature, two general types of food chains are distinguished. They are:

- Grazing food chain
- Detritus food chain

Grazing food chain

The grazing food chain is a model that describes the general flow of energy in communities. This food chain starts from the living green plants and goes to grazing herbivores and on to carnivores. For most ecosystems the model begins with the photosynthetic fixation of light, carbon dioxide, and water by plants autotrophs (primary producers) that produce sugars and other organic molecules. Once produced, these compounds can be used to create the various types of plant tissues. Primary consumers or herbivores form the second link in the grazing food chain. They gain their energy by consuming primary producers. Secondary consumers or primary carnivores, the third link in the chain, gain their energy by consuming herbivores. Tertiary consumers or secondary carnivores are animals that receive their organic energy by consuming primary carnivores. The illustration below models this process.

AUTOTROPH (PRODUCER)	→	HERBIVORES (PRIMARY CONSUMERS)	→	PRIMARY CARNIVORES (SECONDARY CONSUMERS)	→	SECONDARY CARNIVORES (TERTIARY CONSUMERS)

The various levels in the grazing food chain are linked to each other like links in a chain. The levels are often called trophic levels, and they suggest a particular order for the passage of energy through the food chain. Like many very simple modules, the idea of a food chain only provides a simple abstraction of the nature of energy flow through communities. The ultimate disposition of the energy assimilated by consumers is by four routes respiration, biomass accumulation, decay of organic matter by bacteria and other decomposer organisms, and consumption by consumers.

Detritus food chain

The detritus food chain differs from the grazing food chain in several significant ways. First, the organisms making it up are in general physically smaller. Second, the functional roles of the different organisms do not fall as neatly into categories like the grazing food chain's trophic levels. Finally, detritivores live in environments (soil, sea bed, etc) that are rich in scattered food particles. As a result, decomposers are less motile than herbivores or carnivores.

The detritus food chain initiates from dead organic matter into microorganism and then to organisms feeding on detritus (detritivores) and their predators. Such chains are less dependent on direct solar energy they chiefly depend on the influx of organic matter produce in another system. This food chain operated in the decomposing accumulated litter in a temperate forest. The best example of a detritus food chain is seen in mangrove ecosystems, it is described by Head (1969) and Odum (1970). The leaves of mangrove trees fall into the warm, shallow waters. Only five per cent of the leaf material will be removed by grazing insects before leaf fall. The fallen leaf fragments are acted upon by saprotrophs such as fungi, bacteria, protozoa etc. and colonised mainly by phytoplankton and algae and later eaten and re-eaten (COPROPHAGY) by a key group of small animals. These animals include crabs, copepods, insects, larvae, grass shims, mysids, nematodes, amphipods, bivalve mollusks etc. They belong to detritus consumers and ingest animals are in turn eaten by some mini and small game fish which in turn serve as the main food for large fish and fish eating birds. A system must always be self-sufficient under natural conditions. In fact, the detritus food chain is a sub-component of another ecosystem. The grazing and detritus food chains are lined together belonging to the same ecosystem.

The transfer of food energy from one group of organism to the other group is called Trophic Level or Step. The four trophic levels of a food chain have been identified.

3.8 Steps of Food Chains

The linear food chain and energy flow have been explained in four trophic levels in the following paragraphs:

First step of food chain

The base of the food chain in the Primary Producers is known first level of trophic. The green plants produce their food through the process of photosynthesis with the help of sunlight, water, carbon dioxide and inorganic salts and consume the produced food energy to form their tissues and grow. This level is the source of food for all other organisms of the food chain.

Second step of food chain

The organisms do not produce their food themselves but depend on primary producers of first level for their food is known as second producers of trophic or second step of food chain. The organisms or animals are called primary consumers.

They basically depend on plants for their food, e.g.; sheep, cow, goats, deer and rabbits. Such animals are known as Herbivores. The food energy passed on from primary producers to primary consumers is second level of the food chain. The animals are known as herbivores.

Third step of food chain

The trophic level where energy is transferred from primary consumers to secondary animals depend on other animals, are known secondary consumers or carnivores, because they depend on primary consumers or herbivores group of second level, e.g. lions, leopard, beers. etc. Carnivores are land animals, soil animals and aquatic animals.

Fourth step of food chain

The animals which take food either directly or indirectly from primary producers or primary and secondary consumers are known as 'omnivores'. Man is the most important member of fourth level, because man takes food and fuel from green plants, primary and secondary consumers. Decomposers also take their energy from all these levels.

A simple food chain is formed with the help of four steps. It is the sequence of energy transfer from lower levels to higher levels. This chain may be summarized as follows:—

I. Primary producers——Primary consumers——Secondary consumers ——Higher secondary consumers.

II. Plants——Herbivores animals——Carnivores animals——Omnivores animals.

III. Grass (Producers)......sheep, cows, goats (primary consumers)—tigers, lions (secondary consumers).

IV. Vegetation——Vegetarian food——Non-vegetarian food——all the earlier food.

3.9 Food Webs or Complicated Food Chains

Food chains in natural conditions never operate as isolated sequences, but are interconnected with each other forming a sort of inter lacking pattern, which is referred to as food web. The linear arrangement of food chains hardly occurs and they are interconnected under natural conditions thus, there are found alternatives in nature. In a grazing food chain of a grass land, in the absence of rabbit, grass may also be eaten by mouse. The mouse may in turn be eaten directly by hawk or by snake first which is then eaten by hawk. For example, there are five linear food chains in the food web of a grass land.

I. Grass—— Grasshopper——Hawk.

II. Grass—— Grasshopper—— Lizard —— Hawk.

III. Grass—— Rabbit —— Hawk (Vultures / Fox / Man).

IV. Grass—— Mouse—— Hawk.

V. Grass—— Mouse —— Snake —— Hawk.

All these five chains are interlinked with each other at different points forming a food web. The Food Webs are important in maintaining the stability of an ecosystem in nature. For example, decrease in the population of rabbit would naturally cause an increase in the population of alternative herbivore, the mouse. This may decrease the population of the consumer that prefers to eat rabbit.

Five possible food chains interlocked together making the food web. Another example of complicated food web is a polar (arctic) ecosystem where there are several inter-connected food chains, e.g. (i) Man eats Caribou which feeds on grasses; (ii) Man feeds on whales which eat Crustacea which feed on diatoms; (iii) wolf eats caribou and hares which feed on grasses; (iv) Fox eats lemmings and hares which feed on grasses and (v) Polar beer feeds on fish which feeds on Crustacea which feed on diatoms and so on.

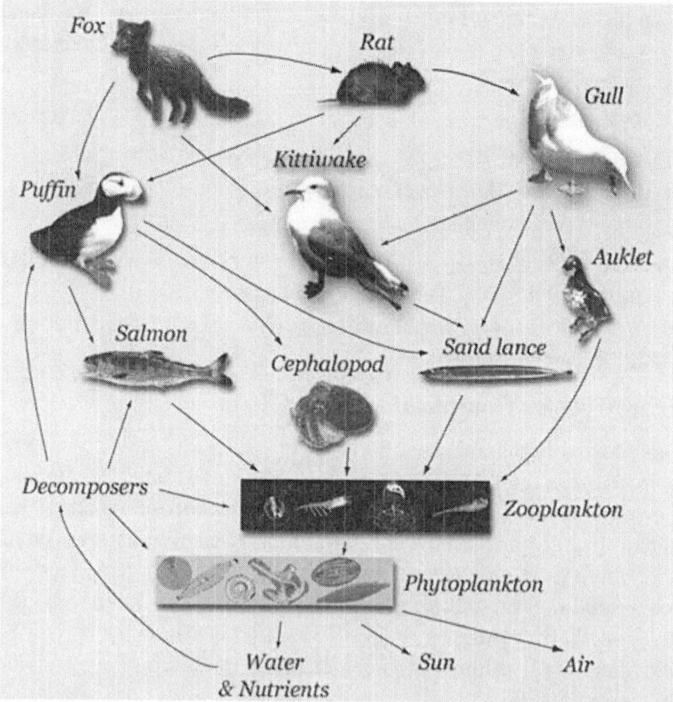

Figure 3.7: Diagrammatic sketch showing a food web in a grassland ecosystem.

A balanced ecosystem is essential for the survival of all living organisms of the system. Thus, food chains and food webs form a natural check to balance the ecosystem. The complexity of any food web depends upon bio-diversity of the system. The biodiversity is based on length of the chain and alternatives in the length of the food chain.

Food chains and food webs require sunlight or solar energy as a basic input which enters into the ecosystem. The plants are the primary producers which require sunlight, water and minerals for preparing their own foods. Thus, the food chain involves solar energy flow and biogeochemical cycle to maintain ecological balance. The brief description of solar energy flow and biogeochemical cycles has been given in the following paragraphs:

3.10 Solar Energy Flow

The plants prepare their food in sunlight with photosynthesis. It requires one per cent solar radiation which is received on earth. This solar energy passes through the hierarchy of levels of a food chain and food web. The solar energy is a basic input and becomes output through respiration from each level of food chain. The process of formation of organic tissue which indicates the transformation of solar energy into food energy is known as biosynthesis. The process of decomposition of organic matter which refers to the release of nutrients and food energy in the form of heat, is called biodegradation. The transfer of organic molecules in the ecosystem is unidirectional or non-cycle which cannot be recessed.

The solar energy is received by green plants and it is used in photosynthesis to prepare food at level first. The solar energy is transformed into organic tissues. It is the source of energy directly to the vegetarian animals of second level which are the primary consumers. The plant energy is transferred to plant-eating animals are known as herbivores. The organic tissues are formed among herbivores by eating plants.

The stored energy in the bodies of herbivores now becomes the source of energy for carnivore animals at the third level of food chain. Some part of chemical energy is lost through respiration from herbivores at second level of food chain. The animals consume energy for their movement for getting food from green plants. The carnivores eat herbivores at third level of food chain, thus, some part of potential energy is transferred to carnivores at this level through intake of food from herbivores. Some part of energy is released by herbivores as wastes and their dead bodies decompose in soil.

The stored energy in the bodies of carnivores now becomes the store house of energy for omnivores which eat both plants and animals; man is most important example of omnivores at the fourth level of food chain. The animals of the fourth level take energy from both primary producers (plants) and herbivores (animals), i.e.; first and second levels of food chain. Some part of energy is released by respiration of omnivores; their dead bodies are decomposed in soil by the decomposers. Dead bodies are decomposed in soil by the decomposers. The omnivores take their food directly from plants and herbivores and also from carnivores.

Ways of energy flow

There are three ways of flow of energy under food chain and food web in a natural ecosystem – first way, First path- The chemical energy flows in a hierarchical order, i.e. I level – II level – III level – IV level; Second path- The Chemical energy flows in a bypass manner, i.e. I level – IV level.

The second way of flow of energy is that animals of all levels release energy by respiration as heat which is lost in the atmosphere as output which cannot be released.

The third way of transfer of chemical energy from dead bodies of animals and waste of plants are decomposed in soil by the decomposers at all levels of food chain. The chemical energy which is transferred by decomposers can be recessed by plants. Thus, there is cycle of flow of chemical energy.

3.11 Biogeochemical Cycles in Food Chain

The biogeochemical cycles include the intake of inorganic elements by plants through their roots in solution from the soil where these inorganic elements are stored. The nutrients are taken up by plants through the process of osmosis and prepare their own food. The chemical energy is transferred to the higher levels along the food chains and food webs through flow of energy. The nutrients are used and assimilated in developing plants tissues and their bodies. When these are transferred and assimilated among different animals of different levels of food chains or food webs are known as organic matter.

There are three cycles through which organic elements flow in a food chain or food web.

- The waste materials released by plants and animals such as leaves, dung, etc, are decomposed by decomposers, changed into inorganic elements which are again used by plants through the process of osmosis. It is first cycle of inorganic matter to organic matter and organic matter into inorganic matter in a food chain.
- The dead bodies of animals and plants are decomposed by the bacteria into soil as inorganic matter. The organic materials are converted into inorganic materials in soil. It is the second cycle of biogeochemical energy.
- The process of deforestation and burning of vegetation by lightening or accidental forest fire releases, the organic material to the atmosphere these again fall down on the ground surface, and become soluble inorganic form of element of soil which can be re-used by plants.

Carbon cycle in food chains and food webs

The carbon-dioxide of the atmosphere is used in the biological cycles in food chain through the process of photosynthesis of green plants. The carbon, oxygen and hydrogen are combined by green plants with the help of sunlight and thus, organic compounds are formed by the processes of osmosis and photosynthesis of green plants.

Thus, the carbon-dioxide assimilated by green plants is stored in the form of body tissues. The green plants produce the carbohydrates as chemical energy which is consumed by herbivorous animals of the second level of food chain and by omnivorous animals at the fourth level. The animals release carbon-dioxide during respiration. The fallen leaf, animals waste and dead bodies are decomposed by bacteria or decomposers, thus carbon and carbon-dioxide are returned to the atmosphere. The decomposers release carbon in gaseous form through respiration and dead organic tissues.

Oxygen cycle in food chain

Oxygen is very essential for the living organisms because they cannot survive without oxygen and plays a significant role in the biosphere. It is very active gas because it combines with majority of the elements in the biosphere. It is produced through the process of photosynthesis by the green plants of different ecosystems and enters into the atmosphere. The atmospheric oxygen is used by the plants and animals during the process of respiration. The process of respiration among green plants takes place during night-time. Thus, the oxygen cycle includes the input of oxygen to the atmosphere by the photosynthesis of green plants and output of oxygen to the atmosphere through respiration of plants and animals in the food chain and food web.

Water cycle in food chain

The water, oxygen, hydrogen and carbon are the most essential elements for the survival of living organisms plants and animals. These elements constitute 90 per cent of the organic matter in the biosphere. Hydrogen in the form of water and oxygen together constitute 80.5 per cent of the total weight of all the living organisms. The water is the combination of hydrogen and oxygen which enters into biosphere and goes out of the biosphere in the form of moisture mainly in liquid form. The food involves the major part of water. The hydrogen cycle also represents the water cycle in the food chain and food webs. The water cycle is regulated by the solar energy.

Phosphorous cycle in food chain

The phosphorous is the most important second level substance in the biosphere which is not essential for the growth and development of organisms. It has very limited gaseous phase and has the main phase in the biogeochemical cycle.

The plants take up phosphorous in the form of inorganic phosphate from the soil through their roots by the process of root osmosis. The inorganic phosphates are converted into organic forms in the plants which are circulated in the food chain through different levels.

Plants ——— Herbivores ——— Carnivores ——— Omnivores

↓

Dead Organisms

↓

Decomposition in Soil

Figure 3.8: Various Cycles in the Food Chain.

Thus, the phosphate is returned back to the soil when dead organisms and their wastes are decomposed by soil organisms. The organic compounds of phosphate are returned to the soil when these are again converted into mineral forms. This cycle is completed after a long time. The Phosphorous Cycle is slow and gradual.

3.12 Factors Affecting Food Chains and Food Webs

The biosphere usually contains several kinds of food chains, food webs and ecosystems. Many of these are interconnected by one more species which in more than one food chain to form food web. These involve energy flow, bio-chemical cycles, hydrogen, carbon and oxygen cycles. There is interdependency between biotic, abiotic and solar energy which maintains the ecological balance in nature. There are several factors which are affecting the food chains and may be broadly classified into two categories-(a) Human Activity and (b) Natural Disasters and Hazards. Another way to classify these factors may be the food chains, i.e. Disturbance of food chain and quality of food. Both types of the factors are interrelated and interdependent which ultimately affect the quality of food. The descriptions of these factors have been given below:

Factors disturbing the food chain

The food chains are disturbed by human activities; natural disasters and hazards.

Human Activities: Man is trying to exploit the natural resources through industrial development, transportation and automobiles, deforestation, agriculture development, use of chemical fertilisers and pesticides, indiscriminating hunting animals, development of tourism, power plants, explosion of population, urbanisation etc. These human activities have polluted heavily the environment, i.e. air, water, soil have disturbed ecological balance and natural food chains.

The deforestation and indiscriminating hunting of animals is harmful. It is found that the removal of even one type of organism from the food chain will upset the whole ecological balance in nature.

Natural disaster and hazards: The natural accidents also disturb ecological balance of nature. The floods, forest fire, earthquakes, storms, volcanic eruptions, etc. disturb natural functioning used to maintain the ecological balance of nature.

Factors affecting the quality of food

Human activities and natural hazards not only disturb the ecological balance but also deteriorate the quality of food even for primary producers.

These may be of two types–(a) Human activities and (b) Natural disaster and hazards.

Human Activities: Man is trying to utilise natural resources as far as

Pyramids of numbers: They show the relationship between producers, herbivores and carnivores at successive trophic levels in terms of their numbers. In a grassland ecosystem, the producers which are mainly grasses are always maximum in number. This number then shows a decrease towards the apex, as the primary consumers (herbivores) like rabbits, mice etc, are less in number than the grasses. The secondary consumers such as snakes and lizards are lesser in number than rabbits and mice. Finally, the top (tertiary) consumers like hawks (or) other birds are least in number thus, the pyramid becomes upright. In a pond ecosystem the pyramid is upright.

- The producers, which are mainly the phytoplankton as algae, bacteria etc. are the maximum in number.
- The herbivores which includes small fish, rotifers, cladocerans, copepods etc. are lesser in number than the producers.
- Secondary consumers (carnivore) such as small fish eating each other, water beetle etc. are less in number than the primary consumers.
- Finally, the tertiary consumers i.e., bigger fish are least in number.

However, in a forest ecosystem, the pyramid of number is different in shape.

- The producers, which are mainly large-sized trees are less in number and form the base of the pyramid.
- Primary consumers (herbivores) includes fruit-eating birds, elephants, deer, etc. and they are more in number than producers.
- There is a gradual decrease in the number of successive carnivores, thus, making the pyramid again upright.

The pyramids are always inverted in a parasitic food chain. A single plant may support the growth of many herbivores and each herbivore in turn provides nutrition to several parasites, which support many hyper parasites. Thus, from the producer towards consumers, there is a reverse position i.e., the number of organisms gradually shows an increase making the pyramid inverted in shape.

The pyramids of numbers do not give actual picture of the food chain as they are not very functional. They do not reflect the relative effects of the geometric, food chain and size factors of the organisms. They generally vary with different communities with different food chains in the same environment. Sometimes, it becomes very difficult to represent the whole community on the same numerical scale (as in forests).

Pyramids of biomass: They are more fundamental and show the quantitative relationships of the standing crops.

- In grassland and forest, generally there is a gradual decrease in biomass of organisms at successive levels from the producers to the top carnivores. Thus, these pyramids are upright.

- However, in a pond ecosystem, the producers are small organisms and hence their biomass is least. This value gradually shows an increase towards the apex of the pyramid, thus making the pyramid inverted in shape.

Pyramids of energy: The energy pyramids reflect the best picture of overall nature of the ecosystem. In this pyramid, the number and weight of organisms at any trophical level depends on the rate at which food is being produced but not on the amount of fixed energy at any level in a given time. Its shape is always upright since in most cases there will be always a gradual decrease in the energy content at successive trophic levels from producers to various consumers.

3.14 Energy Flow in an Ecosystem

Due to unidirectional flow of energy the behaviour of energy in ecosystem is termed as energy flow. From energetic point of view energy flow explains–

- The efficiency of the producers in absorption and conversion of solar energy,
- The use of this converted chemical form of energy by the consumers,
- The total input of energy in form of food and its efficiency of assimilation,
- The loss through respiration, heat, excretion, etc. and
- The gross net production.

Models of energy flow

Single channel energy models: From energetic point of view, the principle of food chains and the working of the two laws of thermodynamics can be discussed by single channel energy model. Out of the total incoming Solar radiation (118,872 g cal/cm^2/yr), 118,761 g cal/cm^2/yr remain unutilised. Thus, gross production (net production + respiration) by autotrophs is 111.0 g cal/cm^2/yr with an efficiency of energy capture of 0.10 per cent. 21 per cent of this energy or 23 g cal / cm^2 / yr is consumed in metabolic reactions of autotrophs for their growth, development, maintenance and reproduction.

Herbivores consume 15 g cal/cm^2/yr which amount to 17 per cent of net autotroph production. Decomposition (3 g cal/cm^2/yr) accounts for about 3.4 per cent of net production. The remainder of the plant material, 70 g cal/cm^2/yr or 79.5 per cent of net production is not utilised at all but becomes part of accumulating sediments.

Of the total energy incorporated at the herbivores level, i.e., 15 g cal/cm^2/yr, 30 per cent or 4.5 g cal/cm^2/yr is used in metabolic reactions. Thus, there is a considerable energy loss via respiration by herbivores (30 per cent) than by autotrophs (21 per cent). Again there is considerable energy available for the carnivores, namely, 10.5 g cal/cm^2/yr or 70 per cent which is not entirely used. In fact, only 3.0 g cal/cm^2/yr or 28.6 per cent net production passes to the carnivore. At the carnivore level, about 60 per cent of the energy intake is consumed in metabolic activity and the remainder becomes part of the not utilised sediments. Only an insignificant amount is subjected to decomposition yearly. The respiratory loss of energy is 30 per cent in herbivores and 21 per cent in autotroph.

From the single channel model of energy flow, two things become clear. Firstly, there is one-way street along which energy moves (unidirectional flow of energy). The energy that is captured by the autotrophs does not revert back to solar input as it moves progressive through the various trophic levels, it is no longer available to the previous level. Models source, the sun, were cut off. Secondly, there occurs a progressive decrease in energy dispirited as heat in metabolic activities. The energy inflows balance outflows as required by the first law of thermodynamics and energy transfer is accompanied by dispersion of energy into unavailable heat (i.e., respiration) as required by second law. Further, there is a successive reduction in energy flow at successive trophic levels. Thus shorter the food flow at successive trophic levels. Thus, shorter the food chain, greater would be the available of food energy.

Y-shaped energy flow model: Odum (1983) gave a generalised model of Y-shaped or two-channel energy flow model applicable to both terrestrial and aquatic ecosystems.

Importance of Y-shaped model: In Y-shaped model the two food chains are not isolated from each other. Y-shaped model is more realistic and practical working model than the single-channel energy model.

- It confirms to the basic stratified structure of ecosystems.
- It separates the grazing and detritus food chains (direct consumption of living plants and utilisation of dead organic matter respectively) in both time and space.
- The micro consumers (absorptive bacteria, fungi) and the macro consumers (phototrophic animals) differ gravely in size-metabolism relations.

Odums universal model: Universal model is applicable to any living component, whether a plant, animal, micro-organism, or individual, population or a trophic group. Such a model may depict food chain as already shown in single and Y- shaped energy flow systems, or the bioenergetics of an entire ecosystems.

Use of universal model of energy flow

- It can represent a species population in which case the appropriate energy inputs and links with other species.

- The model can represent a discrete energy level in which case the biomass and energy channels represent all or parts of many populations supported by the same energy source. Foxes, for example, usually obtain part of their food by eating plants (fruit, etc.) and part by eating herbivores rabbit, field mice, etc.

Limitations of the models

These models depict the basic pattern of energy flow in ecosystem. In practice, under natural conditions, the organisms are interrelated in a way that several food chains become interlocked. This results into a complex food web. The complexity of food web depends on the length of the food chains. Thus, in nature there operate multi-channel energy flows. In these the channels belong to either of the two basic food chains grazing or detritus food chain. Interlocking pattern of such several chains in food web of an ecosystem may lead to a multi-channel flow of energy. Thus, in practice one might face difficulties in measuring the energetic of ecosystem under field conditions.

4

Ecology

4.1 Introduction

Ecology is a branch of science which deals with the study of inter-relationship between biotic and abiotic components of nature as well as relationship among the individuals of the biotic components. The term 'oecology' or 'oekology' was first coined and used by the German biologist, Ernst Haeckel in 1869, derived from two greek words, 'Oikos' meaning 'house' or 'dwelling as habitat' and 'Logos' meaning 'the study of' to denote the relationship between the organisms and their environment.

4.2 Definitions

The term Ecology has been defined in variety of ways. Some of the definitions are as follows:

> Ecology is the science of interrelation between living organisms and their environment including both the physical and biological environments and emphasizing inter-species as well as intra-species relations.
> – *Alles et al. (1949)*

> Ecology is a science which investigates organisms in relation to their environment.- *Woodbury (1954)*

> Ecology is the study of inter-relations of plants and animals with their environment which includes the influences of other plants and animals as well as those of the physical features.– *Clarke (1954)*

> Ecology is a science which concerns itself with the inter-relationships of living organisms, plants, animals and their environment.
> – *Macfadyen (1957)*

> Ecology is the science of living beings as members of the whole of nature.
> – *Friederichs (1958)*

Ecology is the science of organisms in relation to their total environment and the inter-relations of organisms inter-specifically and between themselves. – *Fraser Darling (1963)*

Ecology is the body of knowledge concerning the economy of the nature, the investigation of the total relation of animal to its inorganic and organic environment, including above all its friendly and animical relations with those animals and plants with which it comes directly or indirectly into contact. – *Ernest Haeckel (1866)*

Ecology is the study of the way in which individual organisms, populations of some species and communities respond to those changes.
– *Taylor (1967)*

Ecology is the study of the structure and function of ecosystems or the study of structure and function of nature. – *Odum (1969)*

Ecology is the study of relations between organisms and the totality of the biological and physical factors affecting them or influenced by them. –*Pinalea (1973)*

Ecology is the scientific study of the relationship of living organisms with each other and with their environments. – *Southwide (1976)*

Ecology is the scientific study of the interactions that determine the distribution and abundance of organisms. – *Charles Krebs (1985)*

Thus, modern ecologists have broadened the definitions of ecology considering all the fundamental aspects in the subject. Ecology plays a significant role in our day-to-day life. It is concerned with agriculture, horticulture, conservation of soil, wildlife, forest, water resources, etc. The study of ecological principles provides background knowledge for understanding the problems of forests, soil, surface water etc.

4.3. Characteristics of Ecology

The review of the definitions of Ecology indicates the following main characteristics:

- It is the scientific study for analysing the relations between organisms and environment.
- It is the study of Inter-relationships and interdependence between organisms and environment.
- It includes the structure and function together for full understanding of this vast nature.
- It is also a philosophy in which the world of life is interpreted in terms of natural processes.
- It is the scientific approach for controlling and regulating the welfare of living organisms.

- It is the science of all the relations of all organisms to all their environments.
- It is the study of organisms in relation to their environment.
- It is the science of ecosystems. The ecosystem is an important ecological unit.
- It is the science of inter-relation between organisms and their environments and also emphasises inter-organisms as well as intra-organisms relations.

4.4 Basic Fundamental Principles of Ecology

There are basic fundamental principles which govern the various aspects of organisms and components of environment. The following are the fundamental principles of ecology:

- All living organisms and physical environment arc mutually reactive. The organisms interact among themselves and affect each other and physical environment.
- Environmental principles of holistic nature of natural environment which largely affect the biological communities in a biospheric ecosystem.
- Sustained life on earth is a characteristic of ecosystem, not of individual organisms or population.
- The physical and biological processes follow the principle of uniformitarianism which states the same physical and biological processes, as the environment is influenced by human activity.
- Natural hazards affect adversely the biological communities in general and in particular. When biological processes are associated with physical events, yet severe hazards are created.
- Ecosystem is a fundamental unit of ecological study because it comprises both biotic and abiotic components.

The ecosystem productivity depends on two factors: (a) The availability of the amount of solar radiation to the primary producers and (b) The efficiency of plants to convert solar energy into chemical energy.

- Ecosystem functions through the input of energy mainly solar radiation which is trapped by green plants and is used to prepare food through the process photo-synthesis. The solar radiation is the main driving force of the ecosystem. In any system of constant mass, energy is neither created nor destroyed but it can be transformed from one type to another type.
- Man being an active agent of environmental change, modifies the ecosystem through the exploitation of natural resources.

- Ecosystem instability results when an ecosystem becomes unable to adjust with environmental changes.

4.5. Objectives of Ecology

The importance of ecology lies in the comprehensive understanding of its objectives. The following are the main objectives of ecological studies:

- To study the relationships between living organism and environment.
- To provide the true understanding of the structure and functions of the vast nature.
- To analyse the interdependence between organisms and environmental components.
- To interpret the world life in terms of natural processes.
- To evolve scientific approaches for controlling and regulating the welfare of living organisms.
- To explore the evolutionary development of the interrelations between living organism and environment.
- To evolve mathematical models to relate interaction of environmental components and predict their effects by employing system analysis approach.
- To provide the comprehensive awareness of all the relations between all the living organisms and their all environments.
- To study the conservation and management of natural resources and environmental pollution. It is the main focus of applied ecology.
- To observe the biological productivity of physical environment or nature and how the products may best serve the mankind or improve the quality of man.

4.6 Classification of Ecology

Broadly speaking, the important sub-divisions of ecology are animal ecology and plant ecology. It is also classified as autecology and synecology. Autecology deals with the ecological study of one species of organism. Synecology deals with the ecological studies of communities or entire eco-systems. However, we can classify ecology into following branches:

- **Habitat Ecology:** It deals with ecological study of different habitats on planet earth and their effects on the organisms living there.
- **Community Ecology:** It deals with the study of the local distribution of animals in various habitats. Also, it is related with the recognition and composition of community units and succession.
- **Population Ecology:** This is also known as demecology. It deals with the study of the pattern of growth, structure and regulation of

population organism. The population ecology also deals with interactions between populations of different species in a community.

- **Evolutionary Ecology:** It is concerned with the problems of niche segregation and speciation.
- **Taxonomic Ecology:** It is related with the ecology of different taxonomic groups of living organisms.
- **Human Ecology:** It is mainly related to population ecology. It studies the inter-relationship between man and man along-with the environment. Effects of human beings on the biosphere and the implications of these effects for mankind is the subject matter of human ecology.
- **Applied Ecology:** It is an important sub-division of ecology. It deals with the practical aspect of ecology. Mainly the application of ecological concept to human needs is the field of this study. We find wild-life management, forestry, conservation, insect control, animal husbandry, aquaculture, agriculture, horticulture, land use, population ecology etc. as the application of ecology in practical life.
- **Eco-system Dynamics:** It deals with the ecological study of the

- **Geographic Ecology:** It focuses light on the study of geographical distribution of animals and plants.
- **Space Ecology:** It is concerned with the development of partially or wholly regenerating eco-systems for supporting the life of man during long space flights.
- **Pedology:** It deals with the study of soil, especially their acidity, human contents, mineral contents, soil types, etc. and their influence on their organism.
- **Radiation Ecology:** It studies the gross effect of radiation and radio-active substances over the environment and living organisms.
- **Ethology:** It studies the animal behaviour under natural conditions.
- **Sociology:** It is the study of ecology and ethology of mankind.
- **System Ecology:** It deals with the analysis and understanding of the function and structure of eco-system through the use of applied mathematics, advanced statistical techniques, mathematical models etc.

4.7 Ecological Succession

The term ecological succession refers to the changes in the biotic communities over a period of time at a particular place. The changes are due to climatic or physiographic conditions. When there happens a change in environment, due to biological activities the modified form of environment may be not be suitable for the existing community. Such a process induces the formation of a new and developed community in place of old ones one after another over the same area. The process continues and successive communities develop one after another over the same area until a relatively stable community is established. This relatively stable community is known as climax community which has potentiality to tolerate the changing environment, thus, the sequential changes of communities with the modification of environment over a period of time in the same area are known as ecological succession.

4.8 Causes of Ecological Succession

A number of causes induce together the process of succession. Some important causes may be outlined as below:

- **Climatic causes:** The climatic causes include temperature, rainfall, light intensity, light intensity, gaseous composition, wind etc.
- **Biotic causes:** In a community, there is competition amongst different members for their existence. In such a process, some of the members are not found suitable and thus are gradually replaced by new ones.

- **Ecesis Causes:** The soil condition is also changing by the process of invasion, migration, competition and reaction of the population.
- **Stabilising causes:** Succession is taking place in order to attain the climax stage.

4.9 Characteristics of Ecological Succession

Ecological succession has the following characteristics:

- It results from modification of the physical environment of the community.
- It is an orderly process of community development.
- It involves changes in species structure and it increases diversity of species.

4.10 Types of Ecological Succession

Some basic types of successions may be outlined as below:

- **Primary Succession:** This type of succession begins in a sterile area or barren land or in an inorganic environment. When a bare or nude area is colonised by organisms for the first time and subsequently the communities are changed in a successive form, the process is known as primary succession.
- **Secondary Succession:** The community development on area previously occupied by another well-developed living community amidst the interruption due to adverse conditions like natural calamities, biotic intervention etc. are designated as secondary succession. The natural calamities include forest fire, diseases, flood, grazing etc.
- **Autotrophic Succession:** When the population of autotrophs (plants) dominates the population of heterotrophs, the succession caused is known as autotrophic succession.
- **Heterotrophic Succession:** It is characterised by early dominance of heterotrophs like bacteria, fungi and some animals in an organic environment. Since the environment is dominated by heterotrophs, the succession is called heterotrophic succession.
- **Autogenic Succession:** Due to the continuous interaction of community with environment, there happens a modification of the later such a modification of environment causes the replacement of an old community by a new one, which is known as autogenic succession.
- **Allogenic succession:** When the replacement of a community is caused by any other external condition and not by the existing organisms, the cause of succession is known as allogenic succession.

- **Habitat succession:** Successions are also named differently basing upon the type of habitat from which the phasic replacement starts.
- **Hydrosere:** The succession starting from aquatic habitat is known as 'Hydrach' and the series of changes occurring in the vegetation of hydrach are called 'Hydrosere'.
- **Mesarch:** The succession starting from a habitat where adequate moisture conditions are present.
- **Halosere:** The succession occurring at saline water or soil is known as halo sere.
- **Xerosere:** The succession taking place in xeric habitat like sand or rocks where moisture is present at minimal amount is known as xerosere. Xeroseres can further be subdivided into:
- **Psammosere:** Where the succession starts on sandy habitat.
- **Lithosere:** Where the succession starts on the surface of rocks.
- **Oxylosere:** The succession starting on acidic soils is known as oxylosere.

4.11 General process of Ecological Succession

The entire process of primary autotrophic succession is completed through a series of sequential steps followed by one after another. The different sequential steps may be outlined as blow:

- **Nudation:** It is a process of developing a bare area without any form of life for the arrival of new species. The causes of nudation may be:
    - **Topographic:** The existing community may disappear due to soil erosion (by gravity, water or wind), land slide, volcanic activity etc.
    - **Climatic:** The existing community may be destroyed due to storm, fire, frost and drought.
    - **Biotic:** The community may also be destroyed by anthropogenic activities like destruction of forest, destruction of grassland etc. Besides, diseases induced by bacteria and virus can also destroy the population.
- **Invasion:** The successful establishment of a species in a bare area is called as invasion. The process of establishment is completed in three successive steps:
    - **Migration (dispersal):** The seeds, spores or other progagules of the species are brought to the bare area by the agents like air, water etc.

- **Ecesis (Establishment):** The process of successful establishment (germination and growth) of the species in the new area as a result of adjustment with the prevailing conditions is known as ecesis.
- **Aggregation:** After ecesis, the individuals of species increase their number by reproduction and thus, are aggregated in a particular area.

- **Competition and co-action:** As the species aggregate at a limited space, there happens competition (inter as well as intra specific) mainly for space and nutrition. Secondly, the life process of one individual is affected by the surrounding species in various ways which is known as co-action. The species which are found unable to compete with others in the existing environment get discarded.
- **Reaction:** The species present in an environment constantly interact with it there by causing its modification. The mechanism of the modification of the environment though the influence of living organisms on it, is known as reaction. Reaction induces changes in soil composition, water content, light condition, temperature etc. Due to drastic modifications of the environment, it may not be suitable for the existing community. Hence, the existing community may be replaced by another community. The whole sequence of communities that substitute one another in the given area is known as sere and the various communities constituting the sere are known as seral communities or seral stages.
- **Stabilisation (Climax):** At last, a final or terminal community is established which is stabilised for a longer period of time and which can maintain equilibrium with the environment of that area. This community is known as climax community and the stage is as climax stage.

4.12 Ecology and Education

The concept of 'ecology' has been widely used in physical and biosciences but it has very broad areas of its application in social sciences as well as behavioural sciences. It is considered both art and science. Education is the process of development or all round development. Behaviour Psychologists have claimed that environment is all in all in the development of a child and heredity has nothing to do in the process of development. Behaviourists have given much more importance to environment. This school of psychology is also termed as environmental psychology. Educational processes create environments for the students to gain experiences which result in learning. Both types of environment, natural and the man-designed, are essential in education. Thusm education is the study of interaction between child and his environment. The ecology includes the structure and function together for with understanding of the environment. Similarly, education also designed the structure for the functions of students which helps in their development. Education is a scientific approach for controlling and regulating the behaviours for the desirable change among the students. The teaching is an art and learning is the science. The teaching is the doing or action part whereas learning is the understanding aspect in the educational process. Ecology has also both doing and understanding aspects. Education is also philosophy which helps in formulating aims and objectives for the human welfare whereas ecology interpret world of life in terms of natural processes. Education includes several systems. A school is a unit of the system which has its own organisational climate which is same as ecosystem of ecology. Every institution has its own inputs and output or productivity, it functions like ecosystem. Education and ecology have their broad areas of doing and understanding.

5

Natural Resources

5.1 Introduction

The sum total of all the physical, chemical, biological and social factors surrounding a man may be termed as environment. Each element in the surroundings forms a resource on which the human beings depend, in order to develop economically and socially a better life system. Thus, a resource may be defined as any part of the environment such as land, water, air, mineral, forest, wildlife, fish, population etc. which the human beings utilise to promote their welfare. In other words, all means of satisfying human needs, at a given time and place are called resources.

The functioning of ecosystem or of technological civilisation involves a continuous flow and consumption of energy, sun being the source of it as regards ecosystem and fuels as regards technological civilisation. In the light of this fact, a resource may be defined as one of the various forms of primary energy present in the nature. The five basic ecological variables like energy, matter, space, time and diversity combined are referred as natural resources. Some resources are essential for the survival of all the living organisms like air, soil, water, plants and animals while others are specially valued by man to satisfy his material needs and desires such as minerals and fossil fuels. Thus, land, water, air, minerals, forests, wildlife as well as human beings are resources.

5.2 Definitions

The sum of all physical, chemical, biological and social factors which compose the surroundings of man is referred to as environment and each element of these surrounding constitutes a resource on which man draws in order to develop a better life. Thus, any part of our natural environment such as land, water, air, minerals, forest, rangeland, wildlife, fish or even human population that man can utilise to promote his welfare may be regarded as a natural resource. Those components of the natural environment which can be drawn upon for the survival, development and prosperity of human beings are called as natural resources.

A resource is a form of energy and/or matter which is essential for the functioning of organisms, populations and ecosystems.- *Ramade (1984)*

5.3 Classification of Natural Resources

Natural resources can be classified variously into different groups:

5.3.1 On the basis of availability and abundance

All the natural resources can be put under two broad categories on the basis of availability and abundance: (a) Inexhaustible and (b) Exhaustible

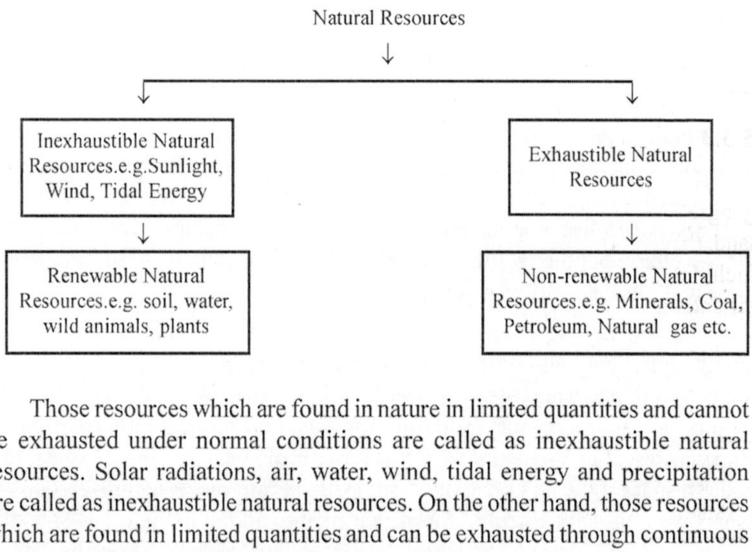

Those resources which are found in nature in limited quantities and cannot be exhausted under normal conditions are called as inexhaustible natural resources. Solar radiations, air, water, wind, tidal energy and precipitation are called as inexhaustible natural resources. On the other hand, those resources which are found in limited quantities and can be exhausted through continuous or excessive use are called as exhaustible natural resources.

The exhaustible natural resources are further classified into two broad categories: (i) Renewable and (ii) Non-Renewable natural resources.

Those natural resources which are exhausted through continuous-use but are renewed by nature after some times, are called as renewable natural resources –soil, water, wild animals and forests are renewable natural resources. There are some exhaustible natural resources that cannot be renewed or recycled in nature. Those are called as Non-renewable natural resources. Minerals, coal, petroleum and natural gas cannot be renewed in nature hence they are called as non-renewable natural resources. Though these natural resources can be renewed in nature but their renewal can take very long time. That's why these are considered as non-renewable resources.

5.3.2 On the basis of chemical nature

Natural resources can be put under three categories on the basis of chemical nature:

(a) Inorganic (b) Organic and (c) Mixed Natural Resources.

Air, water and ores are some of the inorganic natural resources whereas plants, animals, microorganisms and fossil fuels are organic natural resources. Some examples of mixed natural resources are different types of rocks and soils.

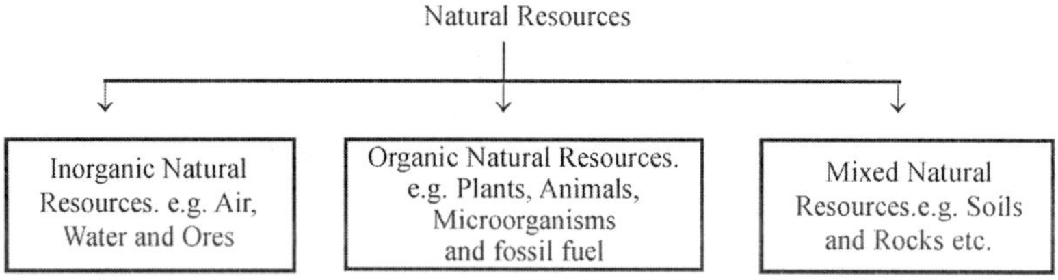

5.3.3 On the basis of geographical distribution

Natural resources can be put under three categories on the basis of geographical distribution: (a) National natural Resources like minerals and land, (b) Multinational Natural Resources like some rivers, lakes, wild animals including migratory birds, (c) International Natural Resources like sunlight, air and earth.

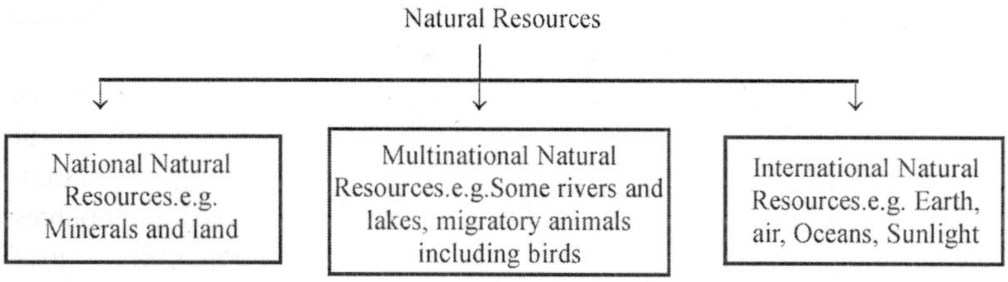

5.3.4 On the basis of origin

Natural resources can also be classified on the basis of origin:

(a) Biotic Natural Resources and (b) Abiotic Natural Resources

(a) *Biotic Resources:* When a resource is living organism or originated from living organism, it is known as biotic resource i.e., it is obtained from the biosphere. Some examples of such type of resources are coal, mineral oil, forest etc.

(b) *Abiotic Resources*: When a resource is neither derived from living organism nor living organism, it is termed as abiotic resource i.e., such resources are composed of nonliving inorganic matter. Some examples of such type of resources are air, land, water, minerals etc.

Natural Resources

Biotic Natural Resources.e.g. Coal, Mineral oil, Forest	Abiotic Natural Resources.e.g. Air, land, water, minerals

5.4. Land Resources or Soil Resources

The life supporting natural resource formed by mixing of weathered rock materials and decomposed biomass consisting of organic matter is called as soil. It is the upper most part of the earth's surface which is used for the production of crops and other biological materials needed for food, fodder, medicine and associated material. The stones, sand and gravels are used in the construction work. Some micro-organisms present in the soil maintain the soil fertility through nitrogen fixation and others are responsible for return of essential elements back to soil by the decomposition of dead organic matter. The processes like nitrogen fixation, antibiosis, soil formation, decomposition of organic matter etc. take place within the soil. The surface soil also acts as a feeding zone of plants. The soil is constituted as a result of long-term processes of complex interaction leading to the production of a mineral matrix in close contact with organic matter both living and dead, after a long time, the parent mineral matter takes the modified shape which forms soil. The interactions among climatic, topographic and biological factors pave the process of transformation and modification of mineral matter into soil.

5.4.1 Components of Soil

Soil has mainly the components like: (i) Mineral matter, (ii) Soil organic matter (Humus), (iii) Soil water, (iv) Soil air, and (v) Soil organisms.

(i) **Mineral Matter:** This is the mixture of particles of different minerals formed during the time of weathering of rock by physical, biological and chemical processes.

(ii) **Soil Organic Matter:** This is the decomposed form of various plants, animals and micro-organisms living in and above the soil. This is the accumulated form of partially decayed and partially synthesised organic substances called as HUMUS. Humus helps in increasing water holding capacity of soil and improves its aeration. Since it remains rich in nutrients, it enhances growth of plants.

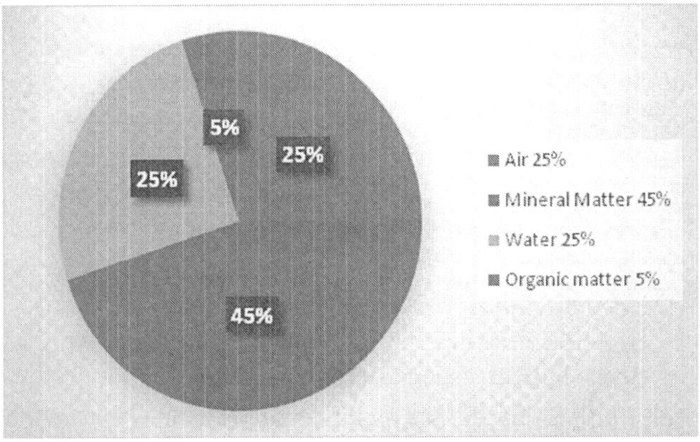

Figure 5.1: Composition of Soil.

It is usually black in colour. Hence, it absorbs solar heat and keeps the soil warm.

(iii) Soil Water: Soil contains water. This water is, in fact, a solution of many organic and inorganic compounds.

(iv) Soil-Air: There is air in the spaces found between soil particles, that air is called as soil-air. It contains oxygen and carbondioxide along with some other gases but the concentration of carbondioxide remains higher than other gases.

(v) Soil Organisms: Various types of bacteria, algae, fungi, protozoa, rotifers, nematodes, molluscs and arthropods are found in the soil. These are called as soil organisms.

5.4.2 Formation of Soil

The soil development may be classified into two major phases: (i) Weathering of parent rock and (ii) Maturation and profile development.

(i) Weathering of Parent Rock: The weathering is the process by which large rocks are broken down to small pieces and converted to a fine powder. This is a long-term process occurring mostly under the influence the climatic condition of the area and hence called weathering. The weathering may be due to physical processes and/ or chemical process and/or biological processes. The physical weathering takes place by the movement of rocks with running water and by the action of gravitational forces as landslide in mountainous regions. In deserts, large fluctuation in day temperature also causes breaking down of the rocks. The chemical weathering includes oxidation, hydrolysis and carbonation of minerals in the rock by weak acids like carbonic acid (H_2CO_3). The biological weathering includes the action of various organisms particularly lichens and mosses which secret various organic acids and produce humic acids after death and decay.

(ii) **Maturation:** The maturation process determines the structure of the soil profile and the type of the soil. It is largely influenced by climatic condition of the area. There are four major maturation processes:

(a) *Melanisation*: In the region of low humidity, the humus derived from the dead organic matter gets mixed in the upper layer of the soil which becomes dark coloured.

(b) *Podzolisation*: In the regions of high humidity high rainfall and low temperature, the minerals in the humus get leached from the upper horizon and get precipitated in middle of B-horizon forming a hard pan. This leaves an ash coloured surface layer of the soil from which the soil derives its name Podzol.

(c) *Gleisation*: In very cold climates, the underground water lying above the rock layer continuously reacts with the partly weathered mineral matter. The hydrolysis and reduction of the minerals results in the formation of a hard gley horizon.

(d) *Laterisation*: In very hot and humid climate, the rapid decay of organic matter and release of bases from organic combination results in the solubalisation of silica and formation of oxides of Fe, Al, Mn, etc. This results in a red coloured soil, rich in iron and deficient in bases and organic matters.

5.4.3 Soil Erosion

The loss of nutrient rich top soil or disturbances to the soil structure by some natural processes or anthropogenic activities is known as soil erosion. According to Odum (1966) soil erosion is a part of the soil pollution. According to Rama Rao (1962), the soil erosion is creeping death of the soil. When the rate of removal of soil exceeds the rate of soil formation, the soil erosion occurs. The soil erosions are of two types:

(i) Natural or geological or background soil erosion

(ii) Accelerated soil erosion.

The natural soil erosion takes place by normal or natural conditions without any interference of man. But the accelerated soil erosion is due to active interference of man and animals in disturbing the equilibrium in between the rate of soil formation and rate of soil loss. The magnitude of soil erosion is governed by the factors like corosivity of the eroding agent, erodibility of the soil, scope, steepness and length, land use practices and conservation strategies employed. These factors are summarised in the universal soil loss equation as follows:

$$E = R\,K\,L\,S\,C\,P$$

where **E** is annual soil loss, **R** is rainfall corosivity index, **K** is soil erodibility index, **L** is slope length, **S** is slope sleepiness, **C** is cropping factor and **P** is conservation practices. The process of soil erosions is caused by the following agents:

(a) *Water Erosion*: Water is a powerful agent causing soil erosion either in the form of rain drops or in the form of surface flow. When the soil is lost like a thin covering from a large surface area, the process is known as sheet erosion. When the sheet erosion takes place with full momentum, leading to cutting of soil surface as thin channels, it is known as rill erosion. Several rills from the steep slope converge forming wider channel known as gully erosion.

(b) *Wind Erosion*: In dry (arid) regions, the soil is mainly sandy and the vegetation is grossly inadequate. In such places, wind causes loss of soil.

(c) *Land slide or Slip Erosion*: When the rocks at cliffs face heavy rains, their weights undergo sharp rise due to gravitational forces. Such rocks with high weights slip over lower rocks causing land slide and there by slip erosion.

(d) *Stream bank erosion*: During flood, the rivers splash their water against banks and cut through them taking away soil from the bank.

(e) *Deforestation and overgrasing*: Loss of natural vegetation due to deforestation and overgrasing leads to dry and dust soil which can be taken away easily by wind and water.

(f) *Mining Erosion*: A lot of soil is also eroded due to mining and industrial activities.

- Since soil is very precious for the existence of living organisms, it is the need of the hour to prevent the loss of soil by adopting suitable mechanisms. The process of soil loss can be checked by the following means.
- Protection of soil from the severity of rain drops through afforestation.
- Preventing water from concentrating and passing through the slopes.
- Slowing down the momentum of water flow adopting various scientific techniques.
- Growing vegetation covers to minimise wind velocity.

- Growing soil binders like grasses to prevent direct contact in between soil and eroding agents.

5.5 Air Resources

The complex mechanical mixture of several gases surrounding the earth is called as air. The concentric layers of air with varying density and temperature forming the vast envelop of the earth constitute the atmosphere. The atmosphere is held to the earth by the force of gravity. The air is composed of two major gases: Nitrogen (78 per cent) and oxygen (21 per cent). Besides these, it also contains gases like carbon dioxide, ammonia, ozone and noble gases like helium and argon. These constitute the remaining one per cent volume of the air.

We know that atmosphere is divided into five different zones known as Troposphere, Stratosphere, Mesosphere, Ionosphere and Exosphere. The troposphere is the first zone of atmosphere found adjacent to the earth. It lies up to an attitude of 10 to 12 km. from the earth surface. Besides containing other gases, dust and smoke this layer contains oxygen also, which is most essential for life. Ozone is usually not found in the troposphere but, if found; it acts as a pollutant causing various ill effects in organisms. Atmospheric disturbances and human activities add Ozone in the troposphere where it causes damage to crop plants. Stratosphere is the zone of atmosphere which extends between 10 km. to 60 km. from the earth surface. This zone contains Ozone (O_3) gas which is found in the form of a dense layer called as Ozone belt or the Ozonosphere. The Ozone layer in the stratosphere is called as the protective umbrella of the earth as it protects the earth from harmful radiations (like ultraviolet radiations).

The Mesosphere is the third layer of atmosphere which usually extends up to an attitude of 80 km. In this, the temperature decreases with increasing height and falls up to -100°C at the height of 80 km.

The Ionosphere is characterised by its electrically charged nature which can reflect radio waves back to the earth's surface. It extends from 80 km. to 400 km. and helps in wireless communications. The temperature increases with the increasing height in this zone. The Exosphere is the upper most Zone of atmosphere which extends up to the attitude of about 400 km. Some of the important functions of air are given below:

- It is an essential part of life support system as it supplies oxygen, carbon dioxide and nitrogen to the biosphere. Oxygen is essential for respiration which is the universal characteristic feature of all life forms. Carbon dioxide is essential for the process of photosynthesis, the ultimate source of food supply in the biosphere. Nitrogen is very essential as it is the principal constituent of protein, the body-building substance.

- Air, regulates humidity and temperature in the biosphere and it is also responsible for causing rains and other weather phenomena.
- Air serves as a medium for flying organisms like insects and birds and also helps us in flying aero-planes.
- It serves as important medium for communication because sound cannot travel without air.
- Most of our artificial satellites are stationed in the thermosphere at different altitudes.
- Air in motion (wind) is utilised as a source of energy in running wind mills and in sailing of boats.

5.6 Water Resources

Water is the most important element of the biosphere which is essential for the existence of all forms of life. Water is a renewable resource and its availability depends upon the climate, geographical and physical conditions, affordable technological solutions and the efficiency with which water is conserved and used. In a civilised society, the human activities and economic development are dependent upon water.

Out of the total water resources, 97 per cent remains in oceans as salty water, 2 per cent remains as ice and rest 0.6 to 1.0 per cent remains as fresh water either on surface or as ground water. That is the available fresh water resources are very limited. The fresh water is used by living organisms for their different activities. Of the three major uses of water that is domestic, agricultural and industrial, agriculture is the greatest consumer of water (65 per cent of total consumption). Industries consume 25 per cent and five per cent is used for domestic purpose. In India, 96 per cent is consumed by agriculture, three per cent by industries and one per cent by domestic use.

5.6.1 Source of fresh water

The fresh water required for the human beings is obtained from two natural sources:

(a) Ground water

The water present under the surface of the earth is known as ground water. The average magnitude of the total round water content is about 210 billion m^3 including recharge through infiltration, seepage and evapotranspiration. The storing of ground water occurs by the passage of water molecules through the intermolecular spaces between the soil, rock, sand and gravel particles. The downward flow of water stops when it reaches the rock without porosity. These water molecules get collected at different zones giving ground water. Similarly a part of the river water or streams can pass through the voids (inter particle spaces) giving ground water.

Due to good quality and non-polluted nature of ground water, it can be used for drinking and other uses of human beings. It can be withdrawn for human consumption by the following ways: Wells (dug well or bore well), Spring intake chamber and Infiltration galleries.

(b) Surface water

The water present over the surface of the earth in rivers, ponds, streams, etc. is known as surface water. The freshwater bodies may be lotic (i.e. running water as spring, steam, river, etc.). The river water system serves about 80 per cent of the total population of the country. The surface water contains a lot of pollutants, micro-organisms, and manual nutrients for the feeding of bacteria and virus. The surface water gets polluted by the run of water from agricultural fields containing pesticides and fertilisers, soil particles, waste chemicals from industries and sewage from cities and rural areas. However, the surface water can be purified and reused.

5.6.2 Uses of water

The fresh water can be used for different purposes as given below:

- Domestic use for drinking, cooking, cleaning and sanitation etc.
- Irrigation for agriculture.
- Industrial use for cooling, processing, cleaning etc.
- For fisheries and aqua-culture.
- For waste disposal.
- For power generation.
- For recreation.

5.6.3 Factors responsible for increasing water demand

Following factors for responsible for increasing water demand are as follows:

- Expansion of irrigation.
- Increasing demand by industry.
- Rising demand due to growing population.
- Increasing water use due to changing life style.

(a) Expansion of irrigation

India is an agricultural country hence plenty of water is needed for irrigation. About 80 per cent of the total water is used in irrigation. The remaining percentage (20 per cent) of water is used for domestic, industrial and other purposes. There has been a rapid increase in the irrigated area in India since independence. Thus, the demand for irrigation in India has been increasing continuously. The reasons for the increasing demand for irrigation are:

- Regional and seasonal variation in the distribution of rainfall.
- Uncertainly of rainy season.
- Growing demand of water for commercial crops.
- Changing cropping pattern.

More efficient and environmentally sound irrigation technologies can greatly reduce water demands and waste on fields by delivering water more precisely to crops. For example, low pressure sprinklers (allows 80 per cent of water to reach crops) and micro irrigation (delivers small amounts of water precisely to crops).

(b) Industrial use of water

Most industries require water at various stages of production of goods and products. Water is used in industries in both consumptive and non-consumptive ways. Be it agro based industries (cotton, textile, jute, sugar and paper) or mineral based industries (iron, steel, chemical and cement). Water is needed in large amounts during the production process or as heat exchanger for cooling various machine parts which get heated up during the production process. In power plants water is used as a power source as well as a cooling agent. The ore and oil refining industries use water in various chemical processes.

(c) Rising demand for growing population

Population of India has been increasing continuously and it has increased three times since independence. Due to this increase in population, the demand for water has increased. We need water for drinking, for flushing or draining sewage or human waste, domestic use, irrigation, industries etc.

- Rising demand for water due to growing population is a single most important factor leading to water scarcity in our country and elsewhere.
- It is becoming impossible for the state to supply clean drinking water to its people.
- Most other human activities like washing, cleaning, cooking, flushing of waste etc. require water.
- More the number of people, more is the demand for water to carry out day-to-day work.

(d) Changing life style

Industrial development led to economic development. Purchasing capacity of individuals has increased. Thus, the life style of people changed and the standard of living has gone up. Large number of attractive appliances, gadgets and fittings for kitchen and bathroom are available in the market and people are generally tempted to use them, for example, taps and showers are designed in such a way that large amounts of water come out when they are turned on. Washing machines and dish washers use large amounts of water but are convenient and suit the present day life style.

Lot of water is used for recreational purposes like water parks are becoming extremely favourite place for people to enjoy holidays. Most of the sports or games here require huge quantity of water. Although much of the water used in various water games are actually recycled and reused. Water in the reservoirs is used for recreational purposes- boating, swimming and angling etc. Golf is becoming a very favourite sport and many golf courses are coming up at various places. Golf courses use excessive amount of water for its maintenance. Private and public gardens too require water for their maintenance. Private and public swimming pools require water supply and sanitation.

5.6.4. Causes for the depletion of water resources

The depletion of water resources is attributed to the following causes:

- ***High demand for water***: Coupled with population explosion, the rapid industrialisation and technological development require large quantity of water for their maintenance.
- ***Poor storage facility and careless attitude towards conservation***: Due to poor storage facility and careless attitude, a lot of rain water is carried off to the seas and oceans.
- ***Poor ground water resources***: The ground water resources are declining due to overgrazing and deforestation which cause soil erosion and make the soil unable to permit water infiltration.
- ***Over exploitation of ground water***: In order to meet the demand of increased population, the ground water is withdrawn by suitable mechanism and it is over exploited.
- ***Bad water management***: Due to bad water management and ignorance, a lot of water is lost.
- ***Evaporational loss***: The water stored in large reservoirs undergo evaporation and due to such process, a lot of water is lost.
- ***Loss by seepage***: During the passage of water in long canals a part is lost due to seepage.
- ***Dumping of pollutants***: The usability of the available water decreases with dumping of different pollutants in water bodies.
- ***Siltation of bodies of water***: The degradation of vegetational cover in the hills and catchment areas, there is siltation of water bodies.

5.6.5. Conservation of water

We can do conservation of water by using various methods such as reforestation, re-use, recycle, increase water use efficiency, water harvesting and ground water recharge.

Reforestation

There is a continuous interchange of moisture between earth and atmosphere, constituting the hydrological cycle. The movement of water through the hydrological cycle has a major influence on rainfall distribution and temperature modification. Plants play an important role in hydrological cycle through the process of transpiration. In tropical forest, 75 per cent of the annual precipitation is returned to the atmosphere by the plants. Thus forests play a very important role in maintaining water balance of the soil and atmosphere. Forests play a protective function and conserve soil and water. Reforestation is the process of planting of trees on the deforested area or of increased tree cover from regrowth and planting of trees. Reforestation increase soil fertility by preventing soil erosion, prevents run-off of eroded soil into aquatic systems and prevents flooding. Thus, reforestation plays a major role in conservation of water.

Recycling of water

The waste water from industrial or domestic sources can be used after proper treatment for irrigation, recharging ground water and even for industrial and municipal use. Agricultural lands close to cities can be irrigated with municipal waste water. Household level recycled 'grey water' (untreated household water which does not come in contact with toilet waste) can be used for various purposes. Grey water from shower, bath, wash basins, laundry troughs and washing machines can be put to various uses to reduce pure water requirement. Pure water after used in bath and shower can be used for watering plants.

Reuse of wastewater

Wastewater is containing lots of nutrients. These nutrients may help the growth of plants when such water is used in irrigation. Reuse of wastewater occurs most effectively with on-site or small treatment system. The reuse option in the local context at the community level must be seriously considered.

Water harvesting

Water harvesting is collecting rainwater that falls on a house or on and around any building and then putting it to use later on or simply replenishing the ground water by allowing the water to reach underground. Time has come when we should work on our ancient methods of water management including capturing of water from swollen streams and rivers during monsoon season and storing it in various forms of water bodies.

5.6.6 Recharging of groundwater

The available groundwater is about 13-20 times as much as water available on surface. The groundwater consists of water contained in the soil or aquifers (underground natural water reservoir).

- Flood water may be injected into aquifers through series of deep pits or ditches.
- Small reservoirs and percolation tanks can be dug to hold runoff water recharging ground water.
- Storm water, used water (municipal and domestic), domestic drains can be fed into pits, trenches, depressions to be filtered and percolated through the soil for recharging ground water.
- Desiltation of canals and tanks should be done regularly.
- Pre-monsoon tillage of fields helps to conserve soil moisture.

5.6.7 Management of water resources

The total amount of water available for use by humans is limited. In view of the variability of rainfall in our country, this precious resource needs to be effectively managed and conserved. Due to the unwise use of water resources by our enormously large population and poor distribution and maintenance practices, the existing system has resulted in serious shortages. Effective management and conservation of water has to incorporate the following two strategies:

- Reduction in loss and wastage of water.
- Harvesting, collection and improved storage of water.

Reduction in loss and wastage of water

Reduction in loss and wastage of water can be best achieved by launching awareness campaigns to involve all sections of the society for the conservation of water. Such awareness is possible through different media such as newspapers, radio and T.V. other ways would be to organise short plays, street plays or lectures.

- Any agency either government or otherwise responsible for water meters and charging for water use should make it a point to install efficient meters and decide to charge a rate which will force the public to reduce use of municipal water.
- Tap, shower flow restrictors and low volume toilet flushes can help in reducing water use.

- Any leak in water pipes and faucets should be detected and repaired immediately.
- Lawns and gardens should be watered in the early morning or late in the evening so that water evaporation losses are minimised.
- Rain water is the major source of water for irrigation of agricultural fields in the country and for recharging the ground water. Rain fall is restricted to three months in a year therefore rain water should be stored and use of ground water well planned as ground water is a renewable water source and gets replenished by natural process of recharge. Loss of water through seepage and evaporation, water wasted on weeds, cost of bringing water from ponds to place of use should be minimised.

Harvesting, collection and improved storage of water

(a) Recharging of ground water

- Flood waters may be injected into aquifers (underground water reservoirs) through series of deep pits or ditches.
- Small reservoirs and percolation tanks can be dug to hold runoff water recharging ground water.
- Rain water harvesting carried out by building power for recharging ground water.
- Storm water, used water, domestic drains can be fed into pits, trenches, depressions to be filtered and percolated through the soil for recharging ground water.
- Desiltation of canals and tanks should be done regularly.
- Pre-monsoon tillage of fields helps to conserve soil moisture.

(b) Removal of pollutants to transform polluted water into usable form

- Proper treatment of domestic and municipal waste water which is rich in organic matter and pathogens material also helps to conserve water. Treatment ensures the removal of pollutants, germs and toxic elements.
- Growing algae or floating masses of water hyacinth also helps in cleaning the water polluted by absorbing phosphates, nitrates and other nutrients. These aquatic plants can be harvested for producing biogas.

5.7 Marine Resources

About 71 per cent of earth surface is covered by water. Out of the total water content, about 97 per cent lies in seas and oceans. Since the beginning of civilisation, the ocean space has been used by mankind as a source of food and an area for commerce, colonisation and welfare.

There are three major productive regions in ocean e.g. estuaries, near-shore and continental shelf water. The estuaries are the store house of fishes and other marine products consumed by human beings. The continental shelf is the major region of petroleum reserves. Some important uses of marinc system (ocean) are outlined below.

- **Potential food reserve:** The Ocean acts as a potential food reserve. The protein requirement of world population is met by marine fishes.
- **Diverse biological form:** The Ocean has varieties of species like Phytoplanktons, dineflagellates, zooplanktons, fishes of a number of types, crabs and several bentic flora and fauna.
- **Source of Fuel:** The Fuel sources like oils and natural gases are plenty available from the off shore areas. As per statistics, about 30 per cent of world's exploitable hydrocarbon is found below ocean water.
- **Lot of Minerals:** A number of elements are present in sea water in their compound forms e.g. Chlorine (55 per cent), Sodium (30.6 per cent), sulphur (7.7 per cent) along with trances of bromine, carbon, strontium, boron, silicon, nitrogen, lithium, rubidium, phosphorous, zinc, tin, aluminium, molybdenum, copper etc. Nowadays, only NaCl, Mg and Br_2 are being extracted from sea or oceah using economic procedure.
- **Source of Energy:** A lot of energy can be generated from the tides and waves adopting suitable technique.
- **Vast area for commerce:** The Ocean area can be used by the human being as a place of commerce in between different countries.
- **Diffuser of pollutants:** The Ocean water acts, as a diffuser of pollutants (water pollutants and radioactive pollutant).
- **As a laboratory:** The Ocean acts as a laboratory for the testing of different traditional and nuclear weapons.
- **Universal supplier of Oxygen:** The living organisms present in ocean, release a lot of oxygen by photosynthesis which is used by the living organisms on the surface in the process of respiration.
- **Major component of hydrologic cycle:** The Ocean acts as a major component of hydrologic cycle which maintains climatic condition and ecological balance.
- **Novel drug sources:** The biological species present in ocean or sea can be used for the preparation of a number of novel drugs.

Rapid population explosion and higher tendency of human beings to become more and more civilised, exert tremendous pressure on marine resources and the ocean is facing serious threats to maintain its standard. The different stresses on marine resources may be outlined as follows:

(a) To provide food to increased population, there is extensive fishing using motor boats, launches, trollers and ships. These devices are not only catching fishes but also destroying a number of living organisms in marine system.

(b) Effluents released from different industries are discharged into marine system causing its pollution.

(c) The municipal wastes are introduced in marine system causing its pollution.

(d) The chemical pollutants and radioactive pollutants are also introduced into marine system.

(e) The testing of traditional and nuclear weapons on the surface of ocean causes potential hazards in aquatic environment.

Since the marine resources are very important for our food, energy, transportation, natural security etc. There should be proper marine resource management so that the stress can be released to some extent.

5.8 Forest Resources

A forest is a natural ecosystem having multi-species and multi-aged trees as dominant community. Forests cover about one-third of the earth's land surface of which about 50 per cent is occupied by tropical forest. It constitutes the largest, complex and most important resources and remains almost in a fixed and self-regulated condition over a long time. It supplies the civilised society fuel, timber, paper pulp, raw material for synthetic fibre etc. It regulates the earth's temperature regime, hydrologic cycle, control of flood and soil erosion and helps the balance of the carbon dioxide and oxygen in atmosphere. The natural forests maintain soil fertility by returning the nutrients to the soil. In addition, these act as suitable habitat for varieties of wild life which are essential for maintaining ecological balance. Some other benefits of forests are checking of air pollution, attracting rainfall, preventing soil erosion, contributing substantially to the socio-economic development of the society or country etc.

As per the national forest policy, there should be 33 per cent of land under forest. But the present statistics suggests that there is only 12 per cent of land in the form of forests.

5.8.1 Importance of Forests

Functions of a forest may broadly be classified into following three categories:

- ***Protective functions***: These include the protective role of forests against soil erosion, droughts, floods, intense radiation etc.
- ***Productive functions***: Forests are the source of wood and many other products like germs, resins, fibres, medicines, Katha, honey, bidiwrappers, pulp, paper etc.
- ***Accessory functions***: These include the role of forests in recreation, aesthetics, and as habitat of diverge wildlife etc.

Thus, it can be said that forests are important in two ways- ecologically and economically.

Ecological Significance

Environmentally, the forests are very important. They help in balancing oxygen and carbon dioxide level in atmosphere, regulate earth's temperature regime and hydrologic cycle. Forests increase local precipitation and water holding capacity of soil, thus, preventing drought situation. Vegetation cover provided by forest impedes the velocity of runoff on soil surface checks soil erosion, silting and landslides, thus reducing the danger of flood. The litter derived from fallen leaves maintains fertility of soil by returning the nutrients. Forests also act as refuge of wild animals and provided protection to them against strong, cold or hot and dry winds, solar radiation, rain and enemies.

Economic Significance

Wood which has various applications in domestic and industrial processes, is the chief product of forest. Wood when used as fuel, has certain advantages over coal as its sulphur and ash contents are very low but, at the same time excessive use of fuel wood results pressure on forests which have many functions to serve. Wood may also be converted into solid, liquid and gaseous fuels. Timber is an important material in building construction and day-to-day uses. Forest provides raw material for various wood-based industries, viz., pulp and paper, composite wood, rayon and other man-made fibres, sport goods, furniture, boat building matches etc. Miscellaneous products, like bamboos, resins, gums, some oils, fibres, medicines, Katha, lac, shellac etc. are also obtained from forests.

5.8.2 Depletion of Forests

Increased urbanisation, industrialisation and mining have entailed indiscriminate felling of trees resulting denudation of forests. Nobody will, however, ever learn that who set the first assault on which tree in the history, but this practice of logging down trees for human use has been going on for centuries unabated. Colonists used logs for fire wood and making huts. They also made handles for their tools, furniture and fence posts, etc. from it. For them forest had only a present and a past but no future; thus, they resorted to ruthless and accelerated exploitation of available forest a story that shill continues with more serious black-lashes earth has ever witnessed. India alone is losing more than 1.5 million hectare of forest cover each year and according to Tiwari (1982), 22 million hectare of forests have been destroyed during the last three decades due to over exploitation and misuse and conversion to agricultural fields. The depleted forest wealth would simply deprive the man of economic and environmental values offered by forest.

5.8.3 Management of Forests

In forestry, the yield is chiefly obtained from the accumulated growth of the past, so this industry has to depend upon the annual growth. Forests are managed to obtain a sustained yield which is obviously possible through sustained growth. Following considerations are important in this direction.

- A forest should have in correct proportion of the trees of different ages and classes so that continuous removal of exploitable produce would not affect the future yield.
- Each tree crop should put on normal growth increments.
- No obstacle should exist to the continuous harvest of exploitable stems.
- Unrestrained felling should be prevented.

For all such planning and decision making, sound ecological knowledge is desirable that includes knowledge about climatic conditions, of biotic community, successional trend, life cycle of important tree species, methods of arresting growth of undesirable trees and promoting growth of high yield tree species, and biotic inter-relationship (such as weeds, competitions, pets, parasites and diseases, etc.) of various tactics employed in forest management, some deserving special considerations are as follows: (i) restrained felling, (ii) block and selective cutting, (iii) reforestation, (iv) control of disasters and (v) recycling of forest products.

5.9 Wildlife

Webster's Dictionary defines wildlife as living things that are neither human nor domesticated, specially mammals, birds and fishes hunted by man. In American usage, term 'wildlife' is used to designate the games and excludes fish, thus they have fish and wildlife services at the federal level. In India too, the common understanding of the people regarding wildlife is of wild animals and shikar, more particularly mammals, birds and reptiles. However, a report entitled wildlife conservation in India (1970) of the Indian Board for Wildlife states wildlife as the entire native uncultivated flora and fauna of the country.

The Wildlife (Protection) Act, 1972, also defines wildlife as any animal, bees, butterflies, crustacean, fish and moth, and aquatic as well as land vegetation which form part of any habitat. Thus, a comprehensive definition of wildlife may be given as any or all non-cultivated and non-domesticated life including both, plants and animals.

5.9.1 Importance of wildlife

The wildlife resources provide aesthetic recreational and economic benefits and at the same time are important ecologically. Nature's millions of forms of life on this earth perform some or the other definite biological function which keeps the delicate balance of our exosphere. In nature flora and fauna go hand-in-hand and one cannot exist without the other. Bird and insects are necessary for the cross-pollination of flowers and these with other animals also serve for dispersal and propagation of vegetation. Not only this, the health of vegetation also depends on natural browsing and grazing. Needless to mention that animals directly or indirectly depend on green plants for their food. Besides food, plant, also provide shelter to a variety of animal as species equally important are the relations among animal populations. If too many herbivores are killed, the predators, deprived of their natural food, will leave forest, become vermin, and prey upon domestic livestock or even man. On the other hand if too many carnivores are killed the herbivores because of release of predation pressure will become too numerous and acquire the status of pest for agricultural crops. Thus, most important is the balance of nature of which wildlife is an integral and important part.

5.9.2 Depletion of Wildlife

India is endowed with rich biological heritage and her various scriptures and epics are full of vivid and beautiful account on wildlife. Over 372 mammalian and 1,200 avian species contribute to the riches of the wealth. Unfortunately, today the Indian wildlife is threatened because of man's unprecedented intervention with nature. Nearly 1,500 plant species have been declared threatened as against 173 species of mammals, 101 species of birds, 15 species of reptiles respectively. Great Indian bustard, (*choriotis nigriceps*) confined to the semi-arid regions of Rajasthan and Gujarat, and the White-windged wood duck (*Cairina scutalata*) Inhabiting the Brahamaputra Swamps and the flood plains of Assam are both on the brink of extinction.

We often comes across the headlines in newspapers like 'Last of the blue whales', 'Save the golden langur', 'tragedy strikes sea turtles', 'Major downfall in rhino population', 'great Indian bustard' on the road of extinction and so on which narrate the sad story of abuse and depletion of our wildlife heritage. According to an estimate in last 2,000 years the world has lost, by way of extinction about 160 species of mammals and 88 species of birds.

5.9.3 Wildlife management

The conservation is the practice embracing preservation, maintenance, sustainable utilisation, restoration, and enhancement of the natural environment. Wildlife conservation in this sense is the management of nature's living resources if we consider wildlife as consisting both of wild flora and fauna. Since one cannot manage living resources while being indifferent to the non-living environment, the concept of wildlife management becomes the concept of management of natural ecosystems. It also overlaps "forestry" in so far as it is based on multiple land use concept and implies management of wild plants as well as wild animals. However, under present dispensation wildlife management implies management of wild animals as distinct from forestry, and it implies maintenance of habitats suitable to the different species.

During past decades the wildlife management implied the understanding, increasing, and controlling of some species. Sanctuaries and National parks were mostly meant to protect a particular species or a group of species and to limited extent for tourism and recreation. Today, however, the emphasis is shifting from the management of species to the management of ecosystem. The objective of wildlife management, as outlined in the world conservation strategy, are thus as given below.

- **To maintain essential ecological processes and life support systems in natural ecosystems, on which human survival and development depends:** These essential ecological processes and life support systems can be defined to include maintenance of both the biotic and abiotic components of the ecosystems.
- **To preserve genetic diversity:** The range and variety of genetic material found in the world's wild plants and animals on which depend the breeding programmes, necessary for the protection and improvement of cultivated plants and domesticated animals, as well as much scientific advance, technical innovation, and the security of the many industries that use living resources.
- **To ensure the sustainable utilisation of species and ecosystems:** This will include the proper utilisation of wild animals for game, forest and grazing, and to achieve proper integration for economy both of rural communities as well as trade and industry.

Fortunately, people have been alerted now and the strong measures being taken in favour of restoring, maintaining, and increasing wildlife population, gives hope that our rich legacy of wildlife will not only be saved for future but developed further ways and means employed in wildlife conservation include: (i) protection of breeding stock by enacting game laws and developing wildlife refuges; (ii) artificial stocking including introduction of exotics; (iii) control of predators; (iv) habitat improvement and (v) game farming.

5.10 Minerals Resources

India has extensive and rich deposits of industrially important minerals. Minerals like water and land are invaluable treasure of the earth. Minerals play a significant role in industrialisation and economic development of a country. Like oil and petroleum, minerals are non-renewable resources, hence they must be used carefully and judiciously so that they are conserved for future. Along with population explosion, industrialisation and technological growth have led to an increase demand in per head consumption of minerals. According to geologists, the known reserves of minerals may not last long and most of them will be exhausted within 100 to 200 years. So now the scientists are in search of new sources of minerals in the sea bed which may reduce the futuristic fears of exhaustion of resources. The mineral resources are of two types:

Terrestrial mineral resources

The mineral resources present in the land surface are known as terrestrial minerals. The chief mineral resources are mineral oils (fossil fuels), natural gases, ores of different metals, coal etc. As per available report, the original stock of petroleum and coal were about 1,250 billion barrels and 6000 billion ton respectively and by 1960, nearly 100 billion barrels of petroleum and 100 billion tons of coal had been exploited. The different types of minerals are:

(a) Mineral or ore containing structural metals (e.g. Fe, Al etc.)

(b) Mineral or ore containing noble metals (e.g. Pt, Au, Ag etc.)

(c) Minerals or ore containing scarce metals (e.g. Cu, Pb, Zn, Mn, Ni, Hg etc.)

As per geological survey of India, the different types of minerals present in India are bauxite, coal, lignite, dolomite, gypsum, haematite, lime stone, ores of Cu, Au, Pb, Zn, Mn, Ni etc.

Marine mineral resources

The mineral resources present in sea water, on the sea bed and below the sea bed are referred as marine mineral resources. The mineral resources contain elements like Na, Mg, Cl_2, Br_2, Sr, B, Si, Ar, N_2, Li, Rb, Zn, Fe, Ni, V, Ba, Mo etc. The deep sea basin of Indian Ocean is found to contain three types of mineral resources. These are:

- Terrigeneous minerals which have plenty of limnite (ore of titranium, monazite (ore of thorium) and calcareous sands,
- Biogeneous deposits consist of shell pieces and skeletal debris present at the ocean floor;

- Chemogeneous deposits consist of manganese nodules (Mn=19 per cent, Fe=12 per cent) and other deposits containing elements like Ni, Co, Cu etc.

5.10.1 Minerals and their characteristics

Minerals are the nonliving substances obtained from the earth through the process of mining. Formation of minerals took place predominantly in weak zones like mountains, folded and faulted regions, lakes, troughs, and continental shelves through geological processes going on since billions of years. They hold some peculiar characteristics, as discussed below, which distinguish them from other natural resources.

- **Exhaustibility:** Minerals are non-renewable or depleting assets and once mined out the deposit get depleted and lost forever without any chance of replenishment. Refuse or waste, however, can be consumed afterwards through improved beneficiation technology. If the rate of mineral consumption is increasing fast, the knowledge about more reserves and potential substitutability of many minerals is also being improved.
- **Localised occurrence:** Minerals are mainly localised in their occurrence and the total area occupied by them is far limited. Most of the mineral deposits are very sporadic in distribution, for instance, Kolar gold fields of India occupy an area of 8 km. by 1.6 km. formations containing coal and petroleum are, in general, bigger as compared to metalliferous deposits. The coal-bearing formation of India, for example occupy about four per cent of the country's total area.
- **Unpredictable occurrence:** The quantity and quality of a mineral in any region is not easy to predict. Uncertainties prevail with respect to their occurrence, extent of depth, cost of mining (often linked with depth) and the grade.
- **Risk involvement:** The process of mining involves large number of problems for miners. Abnormal temperature and pressure variations, rock burst, fire and gas hazard, lack of ventilation and drainage, collapse of roof and side walls are the peculiar problems encountered only in mining industry.
- **Dependence on other factors**: Mineral production is largely affected by factors like the changing needs of consumer industries, availability of stock, fluctuation in prices, and reuse of metallic scrap in production process. A technologically poor country possessing richer grades of ores may have to face keen competition in international market with technologically richer countries may,

however, possessing poorer grades of ores, since in later case, the cost of production is considerably low due to improved mining methods.

- **International character:** Minerals know no political boundaries. Virtually, no country within its own boundaries has adequate production and reserves of all the minerals needed for its industrial development. Thc unequal distribution of minerals makes the international trade in its inevitable. Some countries are bestowed with monopolistic rights in respect of certain mineral deposits which result in what is known as geopolitics.

5.10.2 Impact of mineral activities on environment

The mining activities have significant impact on environment. Some major impacts may be outlined as follows:

- To develop mining, there is cutting trees causing deforestation which subsequently induces soil erosion.
- Mining activities release a lot of particulates into environment which become sites for accumulations of toxic substances and cause severe damage to living system.
- The release of various effluents after the operations like concentration, beneficiation and refining can cause pollution of water bodies.
- The poisonous gases released during mining causes air pollution.

5.10.3 Conservation of mineral resources

The conservation of mineral resources means efforts to utilise mineral in best possible ways depending upon the industrial needs and changing technological requirements, so that the life of the deposits is increased. On the basis of whether the minerals are completely utilised or not, these are divided into two categories: (i) Expendable and (ii) Non-expendable. The minerals which are completely lost on their consumption, are known as expendable minerals, e.g. coal, fossil fuel, natural gases etc. The minerals which can be used again and again through recycling except those quantities that are lost due to corrosion and abrasion are known as non-expendable minerals e.g. metals. Some important efforts to conserve minerals resources are as follows:

- Selection and adoption of suitable methodology of mining which will have negligible effect on environment.
- Economic and optimum use of minerals.
- Recovering all associated elements as co-products or by-products.
- Use and reuse of scraps after suitable treatments.

- Replacing rare and costly minerals with those which are abundant and cheaper.
- Encourage a search for substitutes and promote resource conservation.
- Encourage exploration of new deposits, stimulate development of better mining technology and make it profitable to mine lower-grade ores.

5.11 Energy Resources

Human beings and all other living organisms require energy for their activity and physiological functions. The energy acts as an important parameter for any developmental process. There exists a direct correlation between degree of economic growth, the size of per capita income and per capita energy consumption. Since energy is an essential input in economic growth, the betterment of life requires higher amount of energy which is used in household activities, transport, agriculture and industrial processes. The world's primary energy sources are fossil fuels which include oil, coal, natural gases and nuclear materials.

Basing upon the energy sources, the energies are of two types: (i) Non-commercial energy (ii) Commercial energy. The sources of non-commercial energy are fire, wood, agricultural wastes, cow dung etc. The sources of commercial energy are coal, lignite, oil, electricity and atomic energy. Basing on whether the energy sources are renewable or not, these may be divided into two groups: (A) Conventional energy sources and (B) Non- conventional energy sources.

(A) Conventional Energy Sources

The energy sources which cannot be compensated, once these are used (after their exploitation) are termed as conventional energy sources. Some important conventional energy sources are discussed below:

Coal

Coal is a major conventional energy sources. It was formed from the remains of the trees and ferns grew in swamps around 500 million years ago. The bacterial and chemical decomposition of such plant debris (which remained buried under water or clay) produced an intermediate product known as peat which is mainly cellulose $(C_6H_{10}O_5)_n$. Due to progressive decomposition by heat and pressure, the cellulose lost moisture, H_2 and O_2 and got converted into coal as per the given equation.

$$\text{Plants} \xrightarrow[\text{and chemical action}]{\text{Becterial}} \text{Peat} \xrightarrow[\textit{pressure}]{\Delta} \text{Lignite} \xrightarrow[\textit{pressure}]{\Delta\Delta} \text{Bitu min ous coal} \xrightarrow[\textit{pressure}]{\Delta\Delta\Delta} \text{Anthracite coal}$$

The average formula of coal is $(C_3H_4)_n$. Out of the 6000 billion tons coal stocks under earth crust, 200 tons have been exploited the present society. The coal reserves are found in the states like Jharkhand, Orissa, West Bengal, M.P. and A.P. some important coal fields are Talcher, Raniganj, Jharia, Bokaro, Panch Konkam, Signoulli, Chanda etc.

Petroleum and natural gases

Petroleum is a complex mixture of hydrocarbons, mostly alkanes and cycloalkanes. It occurs below the earth crust entrapped under rocky strata. In its crude form, the viscous black liquid is known as petroleum and a gas in contact with petroleum layer which flows naturally from oil wells is termed as natural gases. The composition of natural gas is a mixture of mainly methane (95 per cent), small amounts of ethane, propane and butane (3.6 per cent) and traces of CO_2 (0.48 per cent) and N_2 (1.92 per cent). A liquid mixture of propane and butane can be obtained from natural gas or refinery gases at room temperature under a pressure of 3-5 atmospheres. This is stored and distributed in 40-100 litre capacity steel cylinders.

The crude petroleum after being refined and purified, are available as petrol, diesel, kerosene, lubricating oil, plastic etc. for commercial and domestic use. In India, the oil deposits, are found at Ganga-Brahmaputra valley, Bombay high, Plains of Gujarat, Thar desert of Rajasthan and area around Andaman Nicobar islands. On the world basis, petroleum deposits are found at Saudi Arab, Iraq, Iran, Kuwait, USA, Mexico, Russia etc. As per the current survey, it is found that world petroleum deposits are diminishing at a very faster rate. If preventive steps are not taken, the existing petroleum will be available maximum upto 40 years.

Fuel woods

The rural peoples require fuel wood or fire wood for their day-to-day cooking which are obtained from natural forests and plantations. Due to rapid deforestation, the availability of fire wood or fuel wood becomes difficult. This problem can be avoided by massive afforestation (plantation) on degraded forest land, culturable waste land, barren land, grazing land etc.

Hydropower

Energy obtainable from water flow or water falling from a higher potential to lower potential, is known as hydro-power. It is a conventional and renewable form of energy which can be transmitted to long distance through cables and wires. In India, hydroelectric power is generated by a number of multipurpose river valley projects e.g. Hydro-power project– Hirakud, Bhakra Nangal Project, Narmada valley project, Nagarjun Sagar project, Sardar Sarovar Project etc.

Nuclear energy

A small amount of radioactive substance (U^{235}) can produce a lot of energy through the process of nuclear fission. For example, one ton of uranium can provide energy which is much higher than three million tons of coal or 12 million barrels of oil. In order to obtain nuclear energy, nuclear reactors are required. There are around 300 nuclear reactors all over the world. India has only four nuclear power stations (reactors). The nuclear energy can be used in production of electrical energy, as a fuel for marine vessel and space crafts and for the generation of heat in chemical processing plants. In India, uranium deposits are found at different parts of Rajasthan and Singhbhum of Jharkhand. Thorium is recovered from monazite sand found in the state of Kerala. Due to the higher energy releasing tendency of these radioactive substances, these can be used in nuclear reactors to release energy crisis. But the radioactive substances are exhaustible and can be used to develop nuclear weapons of mass destruction. In addition, dumping or radioactive wastes cause serious environmental hazards.

(B) Non-conventional energy sources

The conventional energy sources discussed above are exhaustible and in some cases, installation of plants to get energy is highly expensive. In order to meet the energy demand of increased population, the scientists developed alternate non-conventional sources of energy which should be renewable and provide a pollution free environment. Some non-conventional, renewable and inexpensive energy sources are described below:

Solar energy

Solar energy, a primary energy source, is non-polluting and inexhaustible. There are three methods to harness solar energy.

- Converting solar energy directly into electrical energy in solar power stations using photo cells or photovoltaic cells or silicon solar cell.
- Using photosynthetic and biological process for energy trapping. In the process of photosynthesis, green plants absorb solar energy and convert it into chemical energy, stored in the form of carbohydrate.
- Converting solar energy into thermal energy by suitable devices which may be subsequently converted into mechanical, chemical or electrical energy.
- Since solar energy is non-ending and its conversion to some other energy form is nonpolluting, attention should be paid for the maximum utilisation of solar energy.

Wind energy

Wind is air in motion. The movement of air takes place due to the convection current set out in the atmosphere which is again due to heating of earth's surface by solar radiation, rotation of earth etc. The movement of air occurs both horizontally and vertically. The average annual wind density is 3 kW/m^2/day along coastal lines of Gujarat, Western Ghat central parts of India which may show a seasonal variation. Since wind has a tremendous amount of energy, its energy can be converted into mechanical or electrical energy using suitable devices. Nowadays, wind energy is converted into electrical energy which is subsequently used for pumping water, grinding of corns etc. As per available data nearly 20,000 MW of electricity can be generated from wind. In Puri, wind farms are set up which can generate 550 kW of electricity.

Tidal energy

The energy associated with the tides of the ocean can be converted into electrical energy. France constructed the first tidal power plant in 1966. India could take up ocean thermal energy conversion (OTEC) and by the process, it will be capable of generating 50,000 MW of electricity, to meet the power requirements of remote oceanic islands and coastal towns. The Netherlands is famous for windmills. The largest wind farm has been set at Kanyakumari which generates 380 MW of electricity.

Geothermal energy

The geothermal energy may be defined as the heat energy obtainable from hot rocks present inside the earth crust. At the deeper region of earth crust, the solid rock gets melted into magma, due to very high temperature. The magma layer is pushed up due to some geological changes and get concentrated below the earth crust. The places of hot magma concentration at fairly less depth are known as hot spots. These hot spots are known as sources of geothermal energy. Nowadays, efforts are being made to use this energy for generating power and creating refrigeration etc. There are a quite few number of methods of harnessing geothermal energy. Different sites of geothermal energy generation are Puga (Ladakh), Tattapani (Suranguja, M.P.) Cambay Basin (Alkananda valley, Uttaranchal).

Bio-mass based energy

The organic matters originated from living organisms like wood, cattle dung, sewage, agricultural wastes etc. are called as bio-mass. There substances can be burnt to produce heat energy which can be used in the generation of electricity. Thus, the energy produced from the bio-mass is known as bio-mass energy. There are three forms of bio-mass.

(a) **Bio-mass in traditional form:** Energy is released by direct burning of bio-mass (e.g. wood, agricultural residue etc.)

(b) **Bio-mass in non-traditional form:** The biomass may be converted into some other form of fuel which can release energy. For example, carbohydrate can be converted into methanol or ethanol which may be used as a liquid fuel.

(c) **Biomass for domestic use:** When organic matters like cow dung, agricultural wastes, human excreta etc. subjected to bacterial decomposition in presence of water in absence of air, a mixture of CH_4, CO_2, H_2, H_2S etc. is produced. These gases together are known as biogas. The residue left after the removal of biogas is a good source of manure and biogas is used as a good source of non-polluting fuel.

Biogas

Biogas is an important source of energy to meet energy requirements of rural area. As per given data, around 22,420 million m^3 of gas can be produced from the large amount of cow dungs obtained in rural areas in a year. The gas is generated by the action of bacteria on cow dung in absence of air (Oxygen).There are two types of biogas plants namely, Fixed done type and floating gas holder type. These plants are commonly known as gobar gas plants because the usual raw material is cow dung. The methodology involves in the process is to prepare a slurry of cow dung with water. Sometimes form waters can also be added to the slurry. The slurry is subjected to bacterial decomposition at 35°C. There are about 33,000 biogas plants in India. All India dung production is about 11.30 kg per cattle and 11.60 kg per buffalo with about 67.10 m^3 of gas per ton of wet dung.

Petro plants

In order to release the pressure on mineral oils (a non- renewable resource), the scientists have discovered some potential plant species from which liquid hydrocarbons can be extracted. The liquid hydrocarbons present in such plants can be converted into petroleum. Such plants are known as petro plants which belong to families Apocynaceae, Ascalepiadaceae, Euphrobiaceae, Convolvulaceae and Spontaceae. Still research is on to increase the biomass of the petro plants and effective method of converting their hydrocarbons in petroleum.

Dendrothermal energy (Energy plantation)

Due to rapid deforestation and overgrazing, a number of denuded wastelands are formed. On these wastelands, fast growing trees and shrubs may be planted which will provide fuel wood, charcoal, fodder etc. Through gasification, these plants can produce a lot of energy.

Baggasse-based plants

Baggasse is generated as a waste product in sugar mills. This can be utilised to produce electrical energy. As per available data, the sugar mills in India can generate about 2000 MW surplus electricity during crushing season.

Energy from urban waste

Sewage and solid municipal wastes can also generate energy on their suitable treatments.

5.11.1 Conservation of Energy

The need for conservation of energy becomes essential in view of the following simple facts:

- Most of the activities of present day are nothing but the large and growing population requiring massive energy inputs, thus, per capita and total demands for energy are fast increasing.
- We are not endowed with much these are not to last for long at the present rate of consumption. At the same time much talked about possible alternate source of energy are, in fact, still in tentative state of development, so far their practical applicability is concerned.
- There are economic constraints for many countries even if they want to develop conventional sources of energy, what to talk about sources like nuclear energy.
- Unplanned exploitation and use of energy result in widespread environmental damage, the cost of which is to be borne by humanity.

Conservation of energy means not simply the curtailment of energy consumption but to curtail unnecessary or wasteful consumption of energy and make thrifty use of energy producing resources to ensure their steady supply for generations.

6

Environmental Pollution

6.1 Introduction

We have already learnt that the ecosystems on earth play very important role in maintaining the balance of nature for survival of both living and non-living substances. All organisms are inter-dependent upon each other and also on their abiotic component of environment. They interact with each other and with the environment to maintain the balance in nature. At times, this ecological balance is disturbed due to introduction of contaminants into environment leading to instability, disorder, harm or discomfort to the ecosystem which is commonly known as pollution.

The term pollution has been derived from Latin word "pollutioneum" which means to defile or make dirty. When the contaminants pollute or degrade the natural balance in the environment causing harmful effect is known as pollution. Pollution therefore can be defined as any undesirable changes in the physical, chemical or biological properties of the environmental components causing harmful effects on all organisms and non-living substances.

Although pollution was present in the environment since the centuries preceding the Middle Ages, it became a popular issue after World War II, due to radioactive fallout from atomic warfare and testing followed by the great smog of 1952 in London killing at least 4,000 people.

The environmental pollution as we know it today is primarily due to industrial revolution. The emergence of great factories and consumption of immense quantities of coal and other fossil fuels gave rise to unprecedented air pollution. Industries began manufacturing and using synthetic materials such as plastics, polychlorinated biphenyls (PCBs), and inorganic pesticides like dichloro diphenyl trichloroethane (DDT) etc which are not only toxic but are non-biodegradable. The large volume of industrial chemical discharges added to the growing load of untreated human waste. International catastrophes such as the wreck of the Amoco Cadiz oil tanker off the coast of Brittany in 1978 and the Bhopal disaster in 1984 have demonstrated the universality of such events and the urgency to address them.

Figure 6.1: Amoco Cadiz oil tanker off Figure.

6.2: Bhopal disaster in 1984 the coast of Brittany in 1978.

The borderless nature of atmosphere and oceans inevitably resulted in the implication of pollution on a planetary level. Growing evidence of local and global pollution and an increasingly informed public over time have given rise to environmentalism and the environmental movement, which generally seek to limit human impact on the environment.

6.2 Meaning and Definitions of Pollution

Environmental pollution and degradation are used interchangeably by most people as both the terms are broadly concerned with the lowering of quality of environment. The terms however differ. Environmental degradation, on the one hand, means deterioration in the environmental quality at global, regional and local levels by both natural process and human activities. The environmental pollution, on the other hand, has two aspects i.e., lowering the quality of environment and deterioration of the quality of environment. While lowering of quality of environment at local level caused by human activities for exploitation of resources is commonly known as environmental pollution; deterioration of environmental quality refers to the magnitude or intensity of the area covered.

The environmental pollution has now become a global concern. Fortunately, increased awareness about pollution has emerged of late. A comprehensive study of pollution involving definition, its types, sources, effect and monitoring and abatement of pollution has therefore become desirable for environmental geographers, environmental scientist and future strategists for formulation and implementation of proper resource utilisation and comprehensive environmental management programme.

A few definitions of pollution are given below

Environmental pollution may be defined as the unfavourable alterations of our surroundings wholly or largely as a by product of man's action through direct or indirect effects of change in energy pattern, radiation levels, chemical and physical constitution and abundance of the organism. – *US President's Science Advisory Committee (1966) in Report of the Restoring the Quality of Our Environment*

Pollution is an undesirable change in physical, chemical and biological characteristics of air, water and soil that may harmfully affect the life or create a potential health hazard for living organism. – *Odum (1971)*

Pollution is the release of harmful substances or energy into the environment by man in quantities that damage health and resources. – *Edward (1972)*

Pollution includes all those activities conscious or unconscious of human beings and their domestic cattle and the result thereof, which detract in any way in the long-term or short-term form enjoyment of his environment and his ability to derive full benefit there from. – *D M Dixon (1972)*

Residuals or wastes are generated in all stages of production and consumption of goods or services. Residuals become pollutants or an environmental problem of some kind and in some degree when they have harmful effects in the atmosphere, the oceans or the terrestrial environed. Harmful effects that are harmful to man, or to animals, plants or inanimate objects or conditions that are important to man. Their importance to man may be biological, economic, religious, moral aesthetic or intellectual. – *N Lee and C Wood (1972)*

Pollution is the accumulation of substances in the environment or at rates of flow which exceed the capacity of ecosystem to either neutralise or disperse them to harmful levels. – *Dasmann (1975)*

Pollution is viewed as the release of substances and energy as waste products of human activities which result in changes, usually harmful, within the natural environment.
– *Natural Environmental Research Council (NERC), 1976*

Pollution is defined as the presence at large of substances or energy patterns which have been involuntarily produced, have outlived their purpose, have escaped by accident, or have unforeseen effects, in quantities which harm his (man's) health or do offend him.
– *Lord Kenett (1978-79)*

Pollution is defined as the addition of extraneous materials (inorganic, organic, biological or radiological) to water, air or land which adversely affects the natural quality of environment. – *Kudesia (1994)*

Pollution, therefore, can be defined as "an undesirable change in the physical, chemical and biological characteristics of air, water and soil that may harmfully affect the life or create a potential health hazard of any living organism." Pollution is thus direct or indirect change in any component of the biosphere that is harmful to living organisms and man affecting adversely the industrial progress, cultural and natural resources or general environment.

6.2.1 Criteria of pollution

A perusal of the definitions of pollution suggest following criteria for environmental pollution:

- Unfavourable alterations of our surroundings;
- Undesirable change in characteristics of air, water and soil;
- A by-product of man's action;
- Harmfully affect the life;
- Create a potential health hazard;
- Accumulation of harmful substances / extraneous materials;
- Residuals generated during production-consumption process; and
- Residuals become pollutants and create environmental problem.

6.3 Pollutants

In our day-to-day life, we are grossly engaged in production and consumption of variety of goods and services. In the process, residuals or wastes are generated in all stages of production and consumptions. These residues become pollutants when they harmfully affect the atmosphere, the oceans or the terrestrial. It is in the form of waste from factories, air by gases, thermal power plants etc. A pollutant is thus a waste material that pollutes air, water or soil. Three factors determine the severity of a pollutant: its chemical nature, the concentration and the persistence. In other words, substance which causes lowering the quality of environment or pollution is called *pollutant.*

According to Smith (1977), "Every human society, be it rural, industrial and most technologically advance society disposes of certain kinds of by-products and waste products which are injected into the biosphere in great quantities and they affect the normal functioning of ecosystems and have an adverse effect on plants, animals and man are called pollutants."

The Massachusetts Institute of Technology (MIT 1970) has identified more than a million kinds of products produced by man which are both waste and useful products that eventually turn to be wastes after their uses. MIT has also specified a series of key pollutants which create environmental problem such as: carbon dioxide, particulate matter, sulphur dioxide, oxides of nitrogen, toxic heavy metals (lead, mercury, arsenic, cadmium, nickel, manganese, copper, zinc), oil, chlorinated hydrocarbons (especially DDT and

Poly-chlorinated biphenyl; PCB), other hydrocarbons, radioactive, heat and nutrients.

6.4 Environmental Pollutants

The main source of pollutants which pollutes our environment include

- deposited matter such as dust, smoke, tar, grit, etc;
- gaseous such as nitrogen, carbon monoxide, sulphur oxides;
- solid waste; radioactive waste; noise; complex organic substances such as ether, acetic acid, benzene, etc; metals; fluorides; photochemical oxidants; and
- agrochemical such as fungicides and fertilisers; etc.

The major forms of pollution are listed below along with the particular pollutants relevant to each of them:

Table 6.1

Pollution	***Pollutants***
Air pollution	Air pollutants include carbon monoxide, sulfur dioxide, chlorofluorocarbons (CFCs) and nitrogen oxides produced by industry and motor vehicles. Photochemical ozone and smog are created as nitrogen oxides and hydrocarbons react to sunlight. Particulate matter, or fine dust is characterised by their micrometre size PM to PM.
Noise pollution	Encompasses roadway noise, aircraft noise, industrial noise as well as high-intensity sonar.
Light pollution	Includes light trespass, over-illumination and astronomical interference.
Soil contamination	Occurs when chemicals are released by spill or underground leakage. Among the most significant soil contaminants are hydrocarbons, heavy metals, MTBE, herbicides, pesticides and chlorinated hydrocarbons.
Radioactive contamination	Resulting from twentieth century activities in atomic physics, such as nuclear power generation and nuclear weapons research, manufacture and deployment.
Thermal pollution	A temperature change in natural water bodies caused by human influence, such as use of water as coolant in a power plant.
Visual pollution	Refers to the presence of overhead power lines, motorway billboards, scarred landforms (as from strip mining), open storage of trash or municipal solid waste.
Water pollution	Release of waste products and contaminants into surface runoff into river drainage systems, leaching into groundwater, liquid spills, wastewater discharges, eutrophication and littering.

6.4.1 Types of pollutants

A pollutant is defined as any form of energy or matter that caused degradation and pollution in the existing natural balance of ecosystem. On the basis of source of genesis pollutants are divided into two categories i.e. Natural pollutants and Man-made pollutants.

A natural pollutant is a pollutant created by substances of natural origin such as volcanic dust, sea salt particles, photo chemically formed ozone, and products of forest fibers, rayon, pollen, and mold spores etc. Natural pollutants are thus the direct result of decaying organic matter, wind born smoke and particulates from such natural events as plain and forest fires (ignited by heat or lightning), volcanic ash, sand and dust which can spread over a large area of the countryside.

Man-made pollutants are the result of human activities and include smoke from factories and vehicles, photo chemical ozone, smog, chlorofluorocarbons, nitrogen oxides, sulfur dioxides, carbon monoxides, etc.

Pollutants can also be divided into bio-degradable and non-biodegradable based on degradability. **Biodegradable pollutants** are materials like sewage that quickly decompose by natural processes. Such pollutants cause problems only when they are added to the environment faster than the rate of their decomposition. The **non-biodegradable** pollutants on the other hand are those pollutants which do not decompose in the soil or decompose very slowly. Once these pollutants are added in the environment it becomes difficult to remove them.

Pollutants are further divided on the basis of visibility in two types viz: (i) Visible pollutants; and (ii) Invisible pollutants. **Visible pollutants** include smoke, gaseous, dusts coming out of chimneys, waste water or sewage water coming out from factories and urban areas, heaps of garbage, animal and human wastes etc. whereas **invisible pollutants** include several types of bacteria, toxic chemicals mixed with water and soils etc.

Pollutants may be classified on the basis of their nature and state such as **Solid particulate pollutants** e.g. aerosols, industrial wastes such as lead, mercury, tailings, asbestos etc. **Gaseous pollutants** e.g. Chlorofluorocarbon gases, Carbon dioxide, Sulphur dioxide, Nitrogen oxide etc. and (iii) Liquid pollutants e.g leaked oil slicks in sea water, dissolved solids ammonia, urea, nitrate, chloride, fluoride, carbonates insecticide and pesticides – all in dissolved form oil, and grease etc.

Pollutants are also divided into: (i) Physical pollutants; (ii) Cultural pollutants and (iii) Biological pollutants. **Physical pollutants** include all natural as well as man-made pollutants in gaseous, solid and liquid state as referred to above. **Cultural pollutants** include over-population or say explosive population, poverty, crime, richness, cultural backwardness etc. whereas **biological pollutants** include eutrophication, lowest swarms etc.

Pollutants may also be divided on the basis of areas polluted by specific polluted by specific pollutant and ground of pollutants such as: (i) **Air pollutants** e.g Sulphur oxide, nitrogen oxide, carbon di-oxide, carbon monoxide, hydrocarbon, ammonia, lead aldehydes, asbestos, aerosols etc, (ii) **Water pollutants** e.g. dissolved and suspended solids, chlorine ion, Sodium ion, potassium ion, magnesium ion, insecticide and pesticide residues, toxic metals such as lead, mercury and cadmium, radioactive wastes etc. and (iii) **Land pollutants** e.g. human and animal wastes/excreta, garbage, pesticides, insecticides and chemical fertilisers, machines and tools radioactive substances etc.

Besides, the United States National Academy of Sciences National Research Council (USNAS-NRC) has identified eight broad types of pollutants which enter water courses. These pollutants include heat from power plants, sediments from land erosion and radioactive substances. These pollutants are: (i) Domestic Sewage and other oxygen demanding wastes, (ii) Infectious agents, (iii) Plants nutrients, (iv) Organic Chemical which are highly toxic at very low concentrations such as insecticides, Pesticides, detergents, and petrochemicals, (v) Minerals and chemicals (including chemical residues salts, acids, silts and sludge), (vi) Sediments from land erosion, (vii) Radioactive substances and (viii) Heat from power and industrial plants.

6.5 Sources of Pollution

The pollutants, as described earlier, are produced by both natural and anthropogenic processes and therefore the sources of pollution on this basis are divided in two categories: (i) Natural source of pollution and (ii) Anthropogenic source of pollution as described below.

Natural source: Natural sources of pollution are caused by nature. It is due to undesirable substances brought to the surface owing to natural phenomena due to fracture and faults caused by seismic events, flood water in low lying areas. It includes pollutants such as volcanic ashes and dusts from volcanic eruptions leading to reduction of air temperature.

Anthropogenic source: Anthropogenic source of pollution is varied and many. It is the main reason for environmental pollution as natural pollutants are taken care of to a large extent by nature with the in-built mechanism in the nature to absorb any changes brought in by the nature. Anthropogenic sources of pollution include: (i) industrial, (ii) urban, (iii) agricultural and (iv) population etc. Most of the pollutants come from industrial and urban sectors.

The **Industrial source** contributes a host of pollutants such as gaseous pollutants and solid pollutants. The gaseous pollutants include nitrogen oxides, sulphur dioxide, carbon monoxides, hydrocarbons as methane and numerous toxic gases, etc. The solid pollutants include dissolved and suspended solid waste water having numerous chemical ingredients, heat etc.

The **Urban sources** of pollution contribute sewage water, solid waste, gaseous exhaust, liquid effluents, pollutants emitted by chimneys of factories located within the urban centres etc.

Agricultural source of pollution includes the pollutants related to chemical fertilisers, pesticides and insecticides. Human population is the most important source of pollution because all forms of anthropogenic pollution are the creation of human activities. On an average, the increase in the population of a nation has been positively correlated with pollution. The ever increasing population in the developing countries is posing as much the problem of pollution as in the developed countries through industrial growth and urban expansion. Poverty and underdevelopment are yet another source of pollution.

6.6 Types of Pollution

Various types of pollutions classified on the basis of nature, medium, area, etc. are given in the chart below:

Chart 6.1

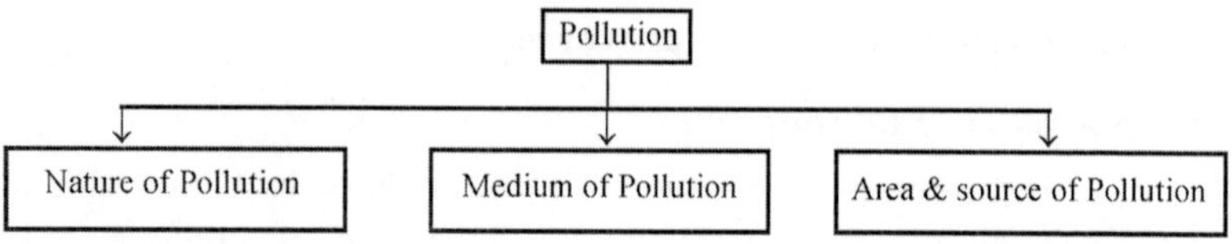

Nature of Pollution

Pollution is divided into two categories viz. physical pollution and social pollution. **Physical pollution** means lowering of the quality of physical components of the environment such as land, air and water. Physical pollution is further divided into: (a) land pollution, (b) water pollution and (c) air pollution.

Social pollution means degradation of human communities due to a variety of factors and through a number of processes. Social pollution is further divided into: (a) Economic pollution based on economic poverty and underdevelopment, (b) Religious pollution (communal riots and violence), (c) Political Pollution (wars), (d) Ethnic pollution (ethnic riots such as in Sindh, Pakistan, Northern peninsula of Sri Lanka, Punjab and Kashmir in India etc.).

Medium of pollution

Pollution is divided on the basis of medium through which pollutants are transported and diffused into three categories e.g. (a) Land Pollution, (b) Water pollution and (c) air Pollution. This has been dealt in detail in subsequent chapters.

Area and Source of Pollution

Pollution is divided on the basis of area affected by pollution and sources of major pollutants into: (i) Urban Pollution, (ii) Rural Pollution, (iii) Industrial Pollution and (iv) Agricultural Pollution.

Nature of pollutants

The pollutants are broadly classified into two categories:

Non-degradable Pollutants: These are the materials and poisonous substances like aluminium, mercuric salts, etc which do not degrade or degrade very slowly in nature. They are not cycled in ecosystem naturally.

Bio-degradable pollutants: These are the domestic wastes that can be rapidly decomposed under natural conditions. They may create problems when they accumulate.

Cost pollution

The following are the main basis for evaluation of cost pollution:

- Damage to crop production.
- Loss of resources by unnecessary wasteful exploitation.
- Medical care of health due to diseases.
- Soiling of building and textiles.
- Corrosion of metals as iron, steel, copper, brass, zinc, lead etc.
- Pollution control involving money funds manpower etc. for disposal of pollutants and for control devices developed.

Location of pollution

Pollution is divided into two major types on the basis of locational aspect e.g. (i) Point pollution and (ii) Non-point pollution.

Point pollution: Point pollution is always visible and hence can be easily identified. Discharge of effluent from a drain or pipe into a river channel is termed Point source pollution or simply point pollution. In fact, point pollution means coming out of pollutants from a specific location such as outfall of sewer drains in a river or a crack, outfall of drains in industrial waste water, chimneys of factories, etc.

Non-point pollution: Non-point pollution means pollution of the area from unspecified location. It includes washing of fertilisers and pesticides from agricultural land into streams. Thus, non point pollution is seldom visible. For example, chemical fertilisers and pesticides and insecticides used in the agricultural fields are washed out during rains and thus are brought to the streams. Non-point pollution mostly occurs from agricultural practices. The chemical used in the form of plant nutrients as fertilisers and in the form of pesticides and insecticides in the agricultural farms are brought to the tanks and ponds, lakes and streams in dissolved and solid forms. The main medium or agent of non-point pollution is surface runoff resulting from atmospheric rainfall. The rainwater transport pollutants in two directions viz (i) lateral movement of pollutants through surface runoff and (ii) downwards movement of pollutants through infiltrating and percolating water.

Thus, non-point pollution involves both surface water and ground waters. In fact, non-point pollution is a slow poisoning of our physical environment mainly surface and subsurface waters and soils. The polluted water in turn adversely affects biological communities in general and human community in particular. Soil pollution results in phenomenal decrease in fertility and productivity which causes drastic reduction in agricultural production. Substantial shortage of food supply due to reduced agricultural productivity may cause economic pollution through poverty, sustainability and deaths.

Non-point pollution is further divided into two types viz (i) Rural non-point pollution and (ii) Urban non-point pollution.

Rural non-point pollution: The major source of non-point pollution in rural areas is agricultural activity. Since rural non point pollution is basically related to agricultural activities, it is also called as agricultural pollution. Nature and amount of chemical fertilisers, pesticides and insecticides applied to the farms, types of soils, amount and intensity of annual rainfall, other climatic conditions, methods of ploughing and farm management techniques, nature and slope of ground surface, nature of crop, etc. are the factors which determine the nature and magnitude of non-point pollution in rural areas.

Urban non-point pollution: Though the sources of urban non-point pollution are varied and uncertain yet these are divided into three categories viz (a) pollutants coming from residential areas, the amount of which depends on the density of houses, (b) pollutants coming from small scale industries, and (c) pollutants coming from large scale industries.

6.7 Pollution: Role of Education

Education plays an important role in the programme of management for the control of pollution. The education must be broad based and it should reach everyone including the scientists, the engineers, administrators, policy and decision-makers as well as general public through popular and common media such as newspaper, radio, television and documentary films. It is the responsibility of all of us and primarily of the government to bring awareness amongst general public to combat and control the pollution. The educationist and scientists must educate and apprise the decision-makers through the following steps:

- To provide and arouse awareness about the different types of pollution among general public.
- To train the administrators and policy-makers to handle the situation created by pollution by providing detailed maps of the problem area.
- To assess the impact of plans, projects, dams, reservoirs, factories deforestation in view of their adverse impact on human life.
- To educate the people for moral and religious values and discourage overstressing for economic values to maintain the quality of environment.
- To educate masses to protect their psychological and cultural environment (internal environment) from pollution.

Hence, systematic, environmental education is essential for maintaining harmony between man and his environment. Education is a way of thinking, doing and feeling pertaining to natural as well as social sciences and behavioural science. It suggests a way out to integrate moral values and cultural education to environmental education. It is the need of the day that educationists must have full understanding of physical, biological, social, cultural and psychological environment - its components and their operations. In other words the ecological studies are of great importance in our education in present day situation.

7

Air Pollution

7.1 Introduction

The pollution of atmosphere is not a new phenomenon. It can be traced to the pre-historic period when the cave man discovered fire. With the passage of time and gradual increase in population coupled with switch from wood-burning to coal-burning fires created clouds of smoke over cities as early as the eleventh century. This was followed by the Industrial Revolution across countries which witnessed use of coal as common affairs even in private residences. Air pollution was first recognised in 1273 in England. Similarly, air pollution came to focus in the United States on 26th October 1948 when a thick, malodorous fog enveloped the small industrial town of Donora, Pennsylvania killing at least twenty people and affecting 7,000 with respiratory problems. To combat the air pollution, the Clean Air Act, 1963 was enacted by the US Government which was later strengthened in 1970. In our country, air pollution was first recognised in 1974.

Fig. 7.1: Fading Taj Mahal

Fig. 7.2: Leak of Chlorine gas in Mumbai

Government took immediate action and regulations on Air pollution was first introduced in1974 by setting up of Central and State Pollution Control

Boards to enforce the Water (prevention and control of pollution) Act, 1974. Additionally, the Boards were asked to control Air (prevention & control) Act, 1981; Environment Protection Act, 1986; etc. The World Health Organisation estimates that about two million people die prematurely every year as a result of air pollution while many more suffer from breathing ailments, heart disease, lung infections and even cancer. Fine particles or microscopic dust from coal or wood fires and unfiltered diesel engines are rated as one of the most lethal forms of air pollution caused by industry, transport, household heating, cooking and ageing coal or oil-fired power stations. Air pollution is thus the presence of any chemical, physical (e.g. particulate matter), or biological agent that modifies the natural characteristics of the atmosphere.

The primary reasons for air pollution can be attributed to emissions from vehicles, thermal power plants, industries and refineries. India's environmental problems are exacerbated by its heavy reliance on coal for power generation which has led to a nine-fold jump in carbon emissions over the past forty years. Exhaust from vehicles has increased eight-fold over levels of twenty years ago and are responsible for 70 per cent of the country's air pollution in the recent time. Industrial pollution has risen four times over the same period. The effects of air pollution are obvious and abundantly visible. Rice crop yields in southern India are falling as brown clouds block out more and more sunlight; the brilliant white of the famous Taj Mahal is slowly fading to a sickly yellow; birds and species are affected as disclosed by the studies conducted by the Zoological Survey of India as there were drastic fall in butterfly in the western Himalayas. A latest example of industrial pollution is the leak of chlorine gas on July 14, 2010 from industrial are meant for storage and delivery of cargo and containers in Mumbai leading to hospitalisation of nearly 76 people. With pollution level rising across the country, the worst hits are the metropolitan cities like Kolkata, Delhi, Mumbai and Chennai. To tackle the problem, the Government of India revised the National Ambient Air Quality Standards on 18th November 2009 equivalent to the European level which exceeds even the standard prevalent in the US.

7.2 Meaning and Definitions of Air Pollution

The present-day atmosphere is quite different from the natural atmosphere that existed before the Industrial Revolution in terms of chemical composition. The chemical composition of air today makes it impure owing to presence of undesirable foreign substances in air. This is known as air pollutants and the state of air is known as air pollution.

Defining "air pollution" is not simple. One could claim that air pollution started when humans began burning fuels. In other words, all man-made (anthropogenic) emissions into the air can be called air pollution, because they alter the chemical composition of the natural atmosphere. The increase in the global concentrations of greenhouse gases CO_2, CH_4 and N_2O can be called air pollution. It is true that air is never pure because some gases such as sulfur dioxide, carbon monoxide, hydrogen sulfide emissions from volcanoes, swamps, dusts, salt spray, pollens from plants etc. are continuously added to the air by these natural processes. The air becomes polluted when its natural composition is disturbed either by natural or man-made sources or activities or by a combination of both. The contamination of air with dust, smoke and harmful gases are called air pollution.

Some specific definitions of air pollution are given below:

"Air Pollution means the presence in the outdoor atmosphere of one or more contaminants, such as dust, fumes, gas, mist, odour, smoke or vapour, in quantities, with characteristics, and of durations such as to be injurious to human, plant or animal life or to which unreasonably interfere with the comfortable enjoyment of life and property."
– *Engineers Joint Council (U SA) H. Perkins (1974)*

"Air Pollution is the presence in ambient atmosphere of substances, generally resulting from the activity of man, in sufficient concentration, present for a sufficient time and under circumstances which interfere significantly with the comfort, health or welfare of persons or with the full use or enjoyment of property."
— *Indian Standards Institution IS – 4167 (1966).*

"Air pollution is the excessive concentration of foreign matter in the air which adversely affects the wellbeing of the individual or cause damage to property." – *American Medical Association.*

Air pollution is defined as limited to situation in which the outdoor ambient atmosphere contains materials in concentration, which are harmful to man and his surrounding environment."- *World Health Organisation (WHO)*

Air Pollution thus can be defined as the disequilibrium condition of the air caused due to introduction of foreign elements from natural as well as anthropogenic sources to the air so that the air becomes injurious to biological communities in general and human community in particular.

7.3 Nature of Air Pollution

Man-made pollutants are injected and concentrated in certain localities of their sources mainly in highly industrialised and urbanised pockets of the world. In other words, the pollutants coming out of natural sources are generally absorbed by the natural environment and no pollutional problem arises. Man-made pollutants however pollute the air as the pollutants get concentrated in certain parts of the atmosphere. The nature, dimension and magnitude of air pollution depend on a variety of factors such as duration of stay of pollutants in the atmosphere, sources of pollutants, nature of pollutants, quantity of pollutants, etc. The duration of pollutants in the atmosphere (residence time of pollutants in the atmosphere) also vary considerably, depending upon the nature of the pollutant itself, upon the way emission had taken place, on meteorological factors and on sink mechanism (absorption of pollutants such as nature of vegetation, water bodies etc.).

7.4 Sources of Air Pollution

Major sources of air pollution are natural sources and man-made sources. The natural sources include volcanic eruption (dust, ashes, smoke, carbon dioxide and other gases), extra-terrestrial bodies (cosmic dusts, dusts produced due to collision of Asteroids, meteors, comets etc. with the earth), green plants (vapour through evaporation, pollen of plant flowers, carbon dioxide from bacteria), fungi (fungal spores, viruses), land surface (salt spray from seas and oceans, dusts and soil particles from ground surface), deflation of sands and dusts, forest or wild fires of natural vegetation etc. Man-made sources include industries (smoke from chimney, industrial waste, heat), urban centres (solid waste and particulate matter, incineration of municipal and domestic garbage), automobiles (smoke, dust), aircrafts (smoke from engines), agriculture (chemical run off), power plants (gases, chemical emission), mines (muck, dust), domestic waste (kitchen waste, gases, solid waste), railways (smoke from coal and diesel engines), nuclear (radioactive substances, nuclear fuel, nuclear explosion), etc.

7.5 Air Pollutants

From the different sources of air pollution, a variety of pollutants are released into atmosphere. The principal air pollutants emitted from different sources are as follows:

Carbon compounds: These are mainly carbon dioxide (CO_2) and carbon monoxide (CO) the former released by complete combustion of fossil fuels and the later by automobile exhaust.

Sulfur compounds: These include SO_2, SO_3, H_2S and Sulfuric acid (H_2SO_4), mostly released by fossil fuel (coal, etc.) based power generating plants (thermal plants) and industrial units as refineries.

***Nitrogen oxides*:** These include chiefly nitrogen monoxide, nitrogen oxide, nitric acid mostly released by automobiles, power plants and industries.

Ozone (O_3): Its level may rise in atmosphere due to human activities.

Fluorocarbons: These come from industries, insecticides spray etc.

Hydrocarbons: These are chiefly benzene, benzpyrence etc. which are mostly discharged by automobiles and industries.

Metals: These include chiefly lead, nickel, arsenic, beryllium, tin, vanadium, titanium, cadmium, etc., present in air as solid particles or liquid droplets or gases. They are produced mostly by metallurgical processes, automobiles, seas prey etc.

7.6 Types of Air Pollutants

Air pollutants can also be broadly classified into two general groups–primary air pollutants and secondary air pollutants.

Primary air pollutants

The natural air is in the pure state in the troposphere. When it moves towards earth's surface, the air collects the products of both natural events (dust, storms and volcanic eruptions) and human activities (emissions from cars and smoke stacks). These pollute the air and the potential pollutants are called primary air pollutants. These pollutants are emitted directly from identifiable sources. Examples of Primary air Pollutants are: (i) Finer particles (less than 100 μ in diameter), (ii) Coarse particles (greater than 100 μ in diameter), (iii) Sulfur compounds, (iv) Oxides of nitrogen, (v) Carbon monoxide, (vi) Halogen compounds, (vii) Organic compounds and (viii) Radioactive compounds. These pollutants are emitted by man-made sources like transportation, fuel combustion, industrial operations, solid waste disposal and various other activities. Finer aerosols include particles of metal, carbon, tar, resin, pollen, bacteria etc.

Secondary air pollutants

Secondary air pollutants are produced in the air by the interaction between two or more primary pollutants, or by reaction with normal atmospheric constituents, with or without photo activation. Examples of Secondary air Pollutants are: (i) Ozone, (ii) Formaldehyde, (iii) PAN (peroxy acetyl nitrate), (iv) Photo chemical smog, (v) Formation of acid mists (H_2SO_4) due to reaction of sulfur dioxide and dissolved oxygen, when water droplets are present in the atmosphere.

7.7 Classification of Air Pollution

Air pollution is classified on the basis of: (i) types of pollutants, (ii) types of sources of pollutants and (iii) stationary and mobile sources.

On the basis of types of pollutants

Pollution is divided into two categories on the basis of types of pollutants: (i) Gaseous air pollution, and (ii) Particulate air pollution. Gaseous air pollution is due to the presence of different types of gaseous air pollutants which are given below:

- Carbon dioxide (CO_2), Carbon monoxide (CO) from combustion of fossil fuels; transportation, industrial processes and garbage disposal;

- Hydrocarbons (carbon and hydrogen containing compounds in oxygenated hydrocarbons) from incomplete combustion of fuels;
- Fluorocarbons from aerosol cans, and refrigeration systems;
- Sulfur compounds such as SO_2 (Sulfur dioxide), SO_3 (sulfur trioxide), H_2S (Hydrogen sulphide) and H_2SO_4 (sulphuric acid) from the burning of sulphur containing fossil fuels;
- Nitrogen oxides and other nitrogenous compounds such as N_2O (nitrous oxide), NO (nitric oxide), NO_2 (nitrogen dioxide) and NO_3 (nitrogen trioxide) from high flying aircrafts, combustion of fuels and chemical fertilisers;
- Aldehydes from thermal decomposition of fats, oils or glycerol and Chlorine from bleaching cotton cloths and flour and many other chemical processes.

Particulate air pollution is due to the presence of different types of particulate air pollutants such as aerosols, smokes, dust, etc. The details are given below:

- Aerosols are those fine particles which are around 1 to 10 microns in size, these are added to the atmosphere by industry, power generation, automobiles, space heating, agricultural activities;
- Smokes, soot and fumes are smaller than aerosols in size and are added to the atmosphere through the incineration of municipal and domestic wastes (garbage), power plants and almost all types of manufacturing processes;
- Dusts include those solid particles which are larger than aerosols in size. These are added to the atmosphere from all types of combustions and agriculture; and
- The particulate air pollutants are also divided into living and non-living type. Living particulate air pollutants include bacteria, pollen grain, fungal and other spores, all of which belong to the category of natural air pollutants. Non-living particulate air pollutants types include all of the pollutants whether gaseous or particulate from man- made sources.

On the basis of types of sources of pollutants

These are further sub-divided into six categories such as: (i) Automobiles, (ii) Industrial, (iii) Thermal, (iv) Urban, (v) Rural and (vi) Nuclear pollution.

Automobiles Air Pollution

In our country, pollution from vehicles account for 65 percent. Vehicles powered by gasoline (passenger cars, motorcycles, scooters and auto rickshaws) usually exhaust gases roughly 65 per cent, evaporation from the fuel tank and carburetor account for roughly 15 per cent and blow by or crank case emission (gases that escape around the piston rings) for about 20 per cent. Carbon monoxide, nitrogen oxides and lead compounds are emitted almost exclusively in the exhausts gases. Similarly, large buses and trucks powered mostly by four stroke diesel engines exhausts only about a tenth of the amount of carbon monoxide exhausted by a gasoline engine, although hits hydrocarbon emissions may be more than those of the gasoline engine. Blow by negligible in the diesel, since the cylinders contain only air on the compression stroke. Evaporative emissions are also low because the diesel engine uses a closed injection fuel system and is less volatile than gasoline. The major problems of diesel engines are smoke and odour.

Industrial Air Pollution

Even though there are many different sources which contribute to air pollution, industries contribute a major share. There are a number of industries which are responsible for air pollution, but it is not possible to mention all of them. A few examples are given below:

Table 7.1: Air pollution problems from some of the Industries and other sources

Source	*Following specific pollutants besides smoke, sulphur dioxide, Oxides of nitrogen and fly-ash may also be found*
Fertiliser, industry and aluminum manufacturing plant	Hydrogen fluoride, ammonia, fluorides, fertiliser dust and sulphuric acid mist
Lead casting and melting heavy	Tin, lead etc. fumes and oxides solvents and thinners, Acid fumes
Tanneries, Leather industry	Mercaptans and sulphides
Cement industry	Cement and lime dust
Carbon black manufacture	Polynuclear hydrogen sulphides
Paints and pigments	Nitrobenzene and aniline, thinners, solvents and base material
Coal tar industry	Polynuclear hydrocarbons and aerosols after
Paper and paper products	Hydrogen sulphide and mercaptans
Refinery and petrochemical industry	Hydrogen suphide, hydrocarbons, odours of mercaptans
Metallurgical industry	Metallic fumes, dust
Electrolytic manufacture of chlorine	Chlorine
Coal burning (power plants)	Soot
Vehicle emission	
(a) Petrol	Hydrocarbons, HCHO
(b) Diesel	Hydrocarbons, HCHO

Thermal Air Pollution

There are a number of thermal power stations and super thermal power stations in the country, primarily setup by National Thermal Power Corporation (NTPC), a Government of India Corporation. The plants consume several million tons of coal which emit pollutants such as fly ash, sulfur oxide and other gases and hydrocarbons. The gascous pollutants from the thermal power plants are aldehydes, carbon monoxide, hydrocarbons, oxides of sulphur, particulate matter and ash. The different sources of air pollution release a variety of pollutants into the atmosphere, such as carbon compounds, sulfur oxides and compounds, nitrogen oxides, ozone gas, fluorocarbons, hydrocarbons, metals, photo chemical products, particulate matter and toxicants other than heavy metals increasing urban air pollution in major cities, especially in developing countries. Over 90 per cent of air pollution in cities in these countries is attributed to vehicle emissions brought about by high number of older vehicles coupled with poor vehicle maintenance, inadequate infrastructure and low fuel quality.

It is estimated that more than one billion people are exposed to outdoor air pollution annually and is linked to up to one million premature deaths and one million pre-native deaths each year. Urban air pollution is estimated to cost approximately two per cent of GDP in developed countries and five per cent in developing countries. While most developed countries have put in measures to reduce vehicle emissions, in terms of fuel quality and vehicle emission reduction technologies, these measures are yet to be adopted in most cities in developing countries. United Nations Environment Programme (UNEP) through the Partnership for Clean Fuels and Vehicles has been coordinating programmes that aim at reducing vehicular emissions in developing countries to improve urban air quality. UNEP and United States Environmental Protection Agency (USEPA) have also been supporting the establishment of air quality monitoring capacity in two cities in Africa.

Rural Pollution

Pollution is an ever increasing problem in modern society. The ever increasing pollutants released from cities and industrial areas in urban locations affect rural areas. This is primarily owing to reactions which alter the chemical composition in rural areas. This is known as rural pollution. Much of this pollution is anthropogenic (man-made) in origin. Sulphur dioxide (SO_2), hydrocarbons (VOC), carbon monoxide (CO) and oxides of nitrogen (NOX) are largely anthropogenic. While the primary pollutants are higher in cities; secondary pollutants, like ozone, are higher in rural areas. Acid rain affects both urban and rural areas. Acid rain and ozone can damage crops and materials. Much of the pollution is anthropogenic in origin which can greatly affect rural areas.

Nuclear pollution

Nuclear pollution is the result of release of radio nuclides in the environment. A radio nuclide is an atom with an unstable nucleus which has excessive energy. While breaking down through radioactive decay item its gamma rays. According to the UN Atlas of the Oceans, the main sources of radio nuclides released into the marine environment include nuclear weapon testing, fallout from accidents such as the Chernobyl accident in 1986, foundering of nuclear submarines, dumping of nuclear waste into the deep ocean, and discharges from nuclear power plants and nuclear reprocessing plants. Other sources are oil extraction, phosphate rock processing and radioactive transport at sea. Ocean currents can transport radio nuclides over large distances. Radioactive waste can be in gas, liquid or solid form and may remain radioactive from a few hours to hundreds of thousands of years.

Radioactive contamination can enter the human body through ingestion, inhalation, absorption, or injection. Long-term exposure to radiation, at doses less than that which produces serious radiation sickness, may harm the DNA causing cancer or birth defects. Higher levels of exposure may lead to radiation sickness with symptoms depending on the exposure levels ranging from decreased blood cells to nearly immediate death. Marine organisms may also be affected and the reproductive stages and growing tissues are the most sensitive in marine fish. Mammals appear to be the most sensitive of all fauna followed by birds and then insects. The effects of man-made radio nuclides discharged into the sea still loom large in the minds of the general public.

According to UNEP/GPE 2006 the most significant authorised releases of radio nuclides to the sea are from nuclear fuel-cycle installations, particularly spent fuel reprocessing plants located at Sellafield (UK), La Hague and Marcoule (now closed) (France), Trombay (India), and Toki-Mura (Japan). So long as they are well operated and regulated their routine emissions present relatively minor risks to human health on a regional or global scale. A serious potential risk both for people and the environment of the region is the transport of radioactive material by ship especially in the Caribbean Sea and Panama Canal.

Air pollution due to stationary and mobile sources

Air pollutants may be classified by sources as stationary or mobile. Stationary sources are those sources which come from one place such as smoke from industry. The stationary source can either come from a particular point which in other words are large stationary sources or from a particular area, in other words small stationary sources. Mobile sources are those sources which are not concentrated to one place but keeps on moving such as emission from vehicles. This can come from two sources i.e. line and area. While the line sources are definite, the area sources are largely indefinite. The detail explanation is given below in the table:

Table 7.2

Point sources	*Area sources*	*Line sources*	*Area sources*
Industrial processing	Residential heating coal gas oil	Highway vehicles	Motor vehicles Light-duty Medium duty Heavy duty
Power plants	Institutional oil gas and commercial heating coal, oil, gas	Railroad locomotives	Railway yard locomotives
Fuel combustion (industrial) combustion (industrial) coal, oil, gas	On site incineration	Channel vessels	Port vessels
Solid waste disposal	Open burning		Aircraft (airports)
Municipal incinerators	Evaporative losses		Miscellaneous
Miscellaneous	Miscellaneous		

7.8 Methods of Identification, Detection and Measurement of Air Pollution

There are three methods of identifying air pollution i.e. Sensory recognition, physical measurements of pollution and effects on plants, animals, and building.

Sensory recognition

Usually the first awareness of an air pollution problem is through some effects on the individual. These are strong or unusual odours, reduction invisibility, eye irritation, acid taste in the mouth, feel of grit under foot. These are highly subjective phenomena and vary from individual to individual.

Physical measurements of pollution

While sensory perception may provide the first indication of the presence of most of the contaminants in the air, it is often not possible to detect or trace quantities of many airborne toxic substances or the presence of radioactive matter through the senses. Their identification required physical measurements by standard methods of sampling and analysis.

Effects on plants, animals and buildings

Effects of air pollution can be observed on the growth of plants and health of animals. Similarly, its deleterious effect on building can also be observed. Thus, plants, animals, and buildings act to some extent as indicators of certain atmospheric impurities.

Measurement

Air pollution is usually measured by sampling of air by thermal and by electrostatic, sonkin impactor and electro static and dust collectors. The particulate pollution is examined by the instrument which is called deposit gauge or by owen's dust counter. The thickness of the smoke measured by Liegean spheres and by Ringelmann chart. The rough estimate of sulphur dioxide in air by laboratory chemical analysis of the dust collected in a deposit gauge or by bobber method. Fluorides are estimated by colour reaction.

There is separate department at Bhava Atomic Energy Centre at Bombay which is known as 'Air Monitoring Department' to measure and estimate atomic experiments conducted by any country of the world. The dust collected in a deposit gauge on International Aeroplanes which travel over the world. The dust is analysed for several purposes as to how far the atomic particle are harmful for man and what will be the remedy for the adverse effect on man.

7.9 Adverse Effects of Air Pollution

The effects of air pollution on the environment (both components– abiotic and biotic) may be grouped in six broad categories viz. (i) effects on weather and climate, (ii) effects on Human Health, (iii) Effects on Animals, (iv) Effects on plants, (v) Economic effects of Air pollution and (vi) Effects on Art Treasures.

Effects of Air pollution on weather and climate

Different types of air pollution caused by gaseous and particulate pollutants modify weather and climate at local, regional and global levels. A few of the climatological effects of air pollution are given below:

> Depletion of ozone is caused by chlorofluorocarbons (CFCs). CFCs are emitted from air conditioners, refrigerators, foam, plastic, hair driers, perfume, fire extinguishers and many cosmetic goods. Nitrogen oxides released by large fleets of supersonic jets. The overall effect of ozone depletion is increase in the ultra-violet solar radiation that reaches the earth's surface and lead to rise in air temperature. Substantial increase in the surface temperature of the earth causes global warming of the environment which in turn causes climatic changes at regional and global levels. Increased temperature also causes melting of glaciers and ice caps such as those of Antarctica and Greenland, which in turn causes rise in sea level and consequent submergence of coastal lands of low lying countries.

Effects of Air Pollution on Human Health

Air pollution is one of the greatest environmental evils. The air we breathe has not only life supporting properties but also life damaging properties.

Under ideal conditions the air we inhale has a qualitative balance that maintains the well-being of man. But when the balance among the air components is disturbed or in other words, if it is polluted, it may affect human health.

An average man breathes 22,000 times a day and takes in 16 kg of air each day. It far exceeds the consumption of food and water. It has been estimated, that a man can live for weeks without food and five days without water, but only for five minutes without air. All the impurities in thc inhaled air do not necessary cause harm. Depending upon the chemical nature of the pollutants, some may be harmful depending in their concentrations. The duration of exposure of the body to polluted air is also an important factor. Therefore, the prime factors affecting human health are nature of the pollutants, concentration of the pollutants, duration of exposure, state of health of the receptor, etc. Generally speaking susceptibility to the effects of air pollution is great among infants, the elderly, and the infirm. Those with chronic diseases of the lungs or heart are also at great risk. Likely health effects on human includes eye irritation, nose and throat irritation, irritation of the respiratory tract, increase in mortality and morbidity rate, chronic pulmonary diseases like bronchitis and asthma, etc.

Effects of Air Pollution on Animals

The air pollution effects equally to animals. Medical research laboratories here reported the result of experimental exposure of small animals to various air pollutants such as mice, rabbits, rats, guinea pigs, etc.

Air pollution effects on Farm Animals

The farm animals also get poisoned owing to polluted atmospheres, in two step process - accumulation of the air-borne contaminant in the vegetation and forage; and subsequent poisoning of the animals when they eat the contaminated vegetation. In case of human beings working in polluted atmospheres in factories, the concern is for the harmful substances that are directly inhaled, whereas in the case of the farm animals, the danger obviously is not in inhaling the polluted air, but rather than ingestion of forage which has been contaminated with pollutants like fluorine from the air. The three pollutants responsible for most livestock damage are fluorine, arsenic and lead. These pollutants originate from industrial sources or from dusting and spraying.

Effects of Air pollution on plants

Air pollution adversely affects plants. At first, it was only sulphur dioxide that was considered a dangerous pollutant. Now, with the advent of various pesticides and new industrial processes, the range of harmful pollutants has multiplied tremendously. Sometimes, vegetation over 150 km away from the source of the pollutant has been found to be affected. The increased ultra-violet solar radiations have been adversely affecting plant and animal communities in a variety of ways. Photosynthesis, water use efficiency and yields of plants are substantially reduced. Soil-moisture is significantly reduced resulting in marked decrease in food production.

Table 7.3: Air Pollutants Affecting Plants

Sulphur dioxide	*Fluoride compounds (hydrogen fluoride) (like hydrogen fluoride)*
Ozone	Chlorine
Hydrogen chloride	Nitrogen oxides (NO, NO_2, etc.)
Ammonia	Hydrogen sulphide
Hydrogen cyanide	Mercury
Ethylene	PAN (Peroxy acetyl nitrate)
Herbicides (sprays of weed killers)	Smog

The above pollutants interfere with plant growth and phenomenon of photosynthesis. Smog, dust, etc., reduce the amount of light reaching the leaf and also by clogging the Stomata may reduce carbon dioxide intake to some extent and thus interfere with photosynthesis.

Table 7.4: Forms of Damage to Leaves

Necrosis	Necrosis is the killing or collapse of tissue.
Chlorosis	Chlorosis is the loss or reduction of the Green plant pigment, chlorophyll. The loss of chlorophyll usually results in a pale green or yellow pattern. Chlorosis generally indicates a deficiency of some nutrient required by the plant. In many respects, it is analogous to anaemia in animals.
Abscission	Leaf abscission is dropping of leaves.
Epinasty	Leaf epinasty is a downward curvature of the leaf due to higher rate of growth on the upper surface.

The effects of various pollutants like sulphur dioxide, ozone, fluorides, etc., on plants is shown in Table.

Table 7.5: Effects of pollutants on plants

Pollutant	*Dose*	*Effect*
Sulphur dioxide	Mild	Interveinal chlorotic bleaching of leaves
	Severe	Necrosis in interveinal areas and skeletonised leaves

(Contd...)

Ozone	Mild	Flecks on upper surfaces, premature aging and suppressed growth.
	Severe	Collapse of leaf necrosis and bleaching
Fluorides	Mild	Cumulative Necrosis at leaf tip
Nitrogen-dioxide	Mild	Suppressed growth, leaf bleaching
Ethylene	Mild	Epinasty, leaf abscission
PAN	Mild	Bronzing of lower leaf surface, suppressed growth leaf surface (upper surface normal), suppressed growth, young leaves more susceptible

Table 7.6: Air Pollution Damage to various materials

Materials	*Principal air pollutants*	*Effects*
Metals	SO_2, acid gases	Corrosion, spoilage of surface, loss of metal, tarnishing
Building materials	SO_2, acid gases	Discolouration, bleaching
Paint	SO_2, H_2S	Discolouration particulates
Textiles	SO_2, acid gases	Deterioration, reduced tensile textile Dyes NO_2 ozone strength and dading
Rubber	Oxidants, Ozone	Cracking, weakening
Leather	SO_2, acid gases	Disintegration, powdered surface
Paper	SO_2, acid gases	Embrittlement
Ceramics	Acid gases	Change in surface appearance

Effects of Air Pollution on Art Treasures

Air pollutants have caused great damage to art objects throughout the industrialised world. Some excellent monuments of antiquity have been silently eaten away by pollutants. This can be clearly seen in many works of art sculptures and carvings on historic buildings, cathedrals, temples, etc. A few examples of such works of art which have been affected by air pollution have been described below:

Taj Mahal: The Taj Mahal is one of the Seven Wonders of the World, a miraculous piece of sculpture, is facing grave danger from pollution created by existing foundries, power house, railway yards and other industrial units. According to some environmentalists, the problem has been aggravated because of the commissioning of the Mathura Oil Refinery, about 40 km away of the priceless monument.

Belur temple: The renowned temple of Sri Channakeshava at Belur (Hassan district, Karnataka State) is threatened with a similar hazard.

Some factories located close to the temple emit soot laden fumes which get deposited on the sculptures in the temple and discolour the surface both inside and outside.

7.10 Control and Prevention of Air Pollution

Control and prevention is very important. Unless, we take urgent measures, air pollution will continue to rise and affect more and more people and properties of various nations. A concerted effort at all levels is required to check the air pollution.

Control measures are indicated below:

- To create awareness among all walks of people in society and government bodies and officials towards the causes and effects of air pollution.
- To conduct extensive survey and regular monitoring of the existing level of air pollution and to predict, on the basis of existing information, the possible level of air pollution and adverse effects emanating from it in near future.
- To acquaint the general public with the adverse effects of air pollution on their health and wealth.
- To make efforts to disperse and dilute the pollutants in the upper air to reduce their concentration at ground level.
- To reduce the total pollution load of the atmosphere.
- To eradicate extremely hazardous forms of air pollution which cause irreparable loss to human society.
- To make efforts to search alternative less harmful products such as solar powered cars (as done recently in the U.S.A).
- To improve the existing devices of air pollution control and to make efforts to invent new effective devices to control air pollution.

The Automobiles air pollution control measures may involve the following steps:

- To check pollutants emission from vehicular exhaust,
- To control evaporation from fuel tank and carburetor,
- To use the filters, and
- To control through law- Motor Vehicles Act 1988 and other Acts.

The Industrial air pollution control measures may involve the following steps

Air pollution by industry and power plants waste can be checked by devising measures for removal of the particulate matter and gaseous pollutants from the wastes. The three types of equipment or devices used are: (a) Cyclone collectors, (b) Electrostatic precipitators and (c) Control through law–Act of industry.

The Gaseous Pollutants control measures involve the following steps

The following four methods can be used to control air pollution from gaseous pollutants : (a) Wet systems: The alkali liquid reacts with sulphur dioxide to produce a precipitate; (b) dry systems: water is in contact with sulphur dioxide produces sulphuric acid; (c) Wet dry systems: This method is very effective in dry cleaning plants, printing shops, paint factories, food processing plants, etc. and (d) control through Law, Acts for Industries are to be enforced to prevent gaseous pollution.

It may be pointed out that comprehensive control measures of air pollution and air quality management strategy must be based on holistic perspective of air pollution involving different aspects of pollutions, its impact on human society and over all environment. Such as time and place of air pollution, its impacts on human health, natural resources, ecosystem equilibrium ecological balance, human needs, essential commodities like food, medicine, clothes, houses, transport, domestic products and above all costs of control measures. The immediate concern of human community is to reduce the emissions of chlorofluorocarbons, halogen, hydrocarbons, oxides of sulphur and nitrogen, carbon monoxide and greenhouse gases and particulate matter and smokes.

7.11 The Air (Prevention and Control of Pollution) Act, 1981

An Act to provide for the prevention, control and abatement of air pollution, for the establishment, with a view to carrying out the aforesaid purposes, of Boards, for conferring on and assigning to such Boards powers and functions relating thereto and for matters connected therewith whereas decisions were taken at the United Nations Conference on the Human Environment held in Stockholm in June, 1972, in which India participated, to take appropriate steps for the preservation of the natural resources of the earth which, among other things, include the preservation of the quality of air and control of air pollution; and whereas it is considered necessary to implement the decisions aforesaid in so far as they relate to the preservation of the quality of air and control of air pollution. It was enacted by Parliament in the Thirty-second Year of the Republic of India. It was amended in 1987. The features of the act have been mentioned below:

- The Act deals with the particular type of pollution and presents an integrated approach to tackle the problem of pollution. This Act is an important legislative measure which has been enacted to implement the decision taken in the United Nations Conference on Human Environment held in June 1972 at Stockholm.

- Air (Prevention and Control of Pollution) Act 1981 is an appropriate step for the preservation of the natural environment on the Earth which includes the preservation of the quality of air and control of air pollution. In other words, this is an Act to provide for the prevention, control and abatement of air pollution.
- The Air (Prevention and Control of Pollution) Act 1981 has 54 Sections and is divided into seven chapters relating to: (i) Preliminary, (ii) Central and State Boards for the Prevention and Control of Air Pollution, (iii) Powers and Functions of Boards, (iv) Prevention and Control of Air Pollution, (v) Funds, Accounts and Audit, (vi) Penalties and Procedures, and (vii) Miscellaneous.
- The Act provides that the State Government, in consultation with the State Board, is empowered to declare any area or areas within the jurisdiction of the concerned State an "Air Pollution Control Area."· The Act provides that the Central and State Boards established under the Water (Prevention and Control of Pollution) Act, 1974 will also exercise and perform powers and functions respectively under the Air (Prevention and Control of Pollution) Act, 1981. In other words, the Air Act, 1981 provides that the Central or State Board for prevention, control and abatement of water pollution shall exercise the powers and perform the functions of the Central or State Board for the prevention, control and abatement of air pollution.
- The Act provides that the State Government in consultation with the State board has a power to give instructions to the registration authority under the Motor Vehicle Act, 1939 (Act 4 of 1939) for ensuring standard for emission from automobiles driven with the help of petrol or diesel.
- The Act provides for the imposition of restriction on the use of certain industrial plant in any pollution control area without the previous permission and consent of the State Board.
- The Act provides that the Board has the power to make an application to the Court for restraining persons from causing air pollution.

The Act provides that whoever:

- operates or establishes any industrial plant in an pollution control area without the consent of the State Board, or
- allows emission of an air pollutant in excess on the standard laid down by the State Board, or

violates any direction issued by the Board, in the above situation, is punished with imprisonment for a term which shall not be less than one year and six months but which may extend to six years and with fine. If this fails or contravention continues, the guilty person is punished with the additional fine which may extend to five thousand rupees for every day during which such failure or contravention continues even after the conviction for the first such failure or contravention.

7.12 Role of Education in Air Pollution

Education is considered as cure of all ills in the society, therefore, proper emphasis on pollution control and prevention in educational system will be very effective considering the fact that pollution is essentially a social and human problem. Hence, human attitude change can alter the entire situation.

Education is a powerful instrument to control social problems: Air pollution is a serious social problem of recent time. Everyone is concerned by this. The Government of India brought out Air and Noise Pollution Prevention Act to control air pollution and noise pollution as they are inter-related. The Act provides legal framework for the local government to initiate appropriate steps for controlling air pollution. Education can also play a significant role in the prevention and controlling of air pollution. This is more so as education enriches individual with requisite knowledge on environment and air pollution and at the same time bring awareness about environmental problem which may be encountered by air pollution. Proper education brings consciousness about the problem and feelings and also inculcates appropriate attitudes to curb the menace through behavioural change. The behavioural change can be brought about by developing advertisement materials on print and electronic media depicting charts and mottos on air pollutions and remedial measures.

8

Water Pollution

8.1 Introduction

The total volume of water on Earth is around 1.37 billion km. The volume of freshwater resources is around 35 million km, or about 2.5 per cent of the total volume. Of these freshwater resources, around 24 million km or 68.9 per cent is in the form of ice and permanent snow cover in mountainous regions of the Antarctic and Arctic regions. Around 30.8 per cent of the world's freshwater is stored underground in the form of groundwater. Freshwater lakes and rivers contain an estimated 1.05 million km or around 0.3 per cent of the world's freshwater. The total usable freshwater supply for ecosystems and humans is about 200 000 km of water which is less than one per cent of all freshwater resources.

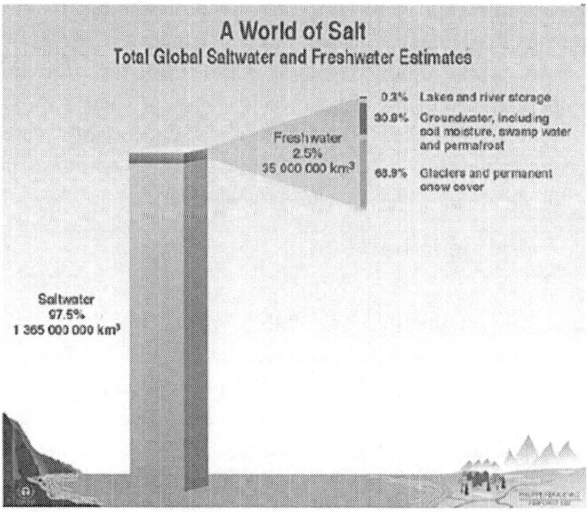

Source: Igcr A. Shilomenov, State Hydrological Institute (SHI, St. Petersburg) and United Nations Educational, Scientific and Cultural Organisation (UNESCO, Paris), 1999.

Fig. 8.1: A World of Salt

Water is essential to life. Clean, safe, and adequate freshwater is not only vital to the survival of all living organisms but also for the smooth functioning of ecosystems, communities and economies. This is because of this fact all human settlements initially began near a water source. Unfortunately, the importance of clean water was not understood until the second half of the nineteenth century and as a result of indiscriminate dumping of wastes and other harmful substances into water bodies led to pollution of rivers and lakes. As human populations grew, industrial and agricultural activities expanded and climatic conditions changed over a period of time, quality of the world's water is increasingly threatened. This worsening of water quality, primarily owing to pollution, is threatening the major alterations of the hydrologic cycle.

Water pollution is a major global problem. It is one of the leading worldwide causes of deaths and diseases and accounts for more than 14,000 deaths daily. An estimated 700 million Indians have no access to a proper toilet, and 1,000 Indian children die of diarrheal sickness every day. Some 90 per cent of China's cities suffer from some degree of water pollution, and nearly 500 million people lack access to safe drinking water. In addition to the acute problems of water pollution in developing countries, industrialised countries continue to struggle with pollution problems as well. In the most recent national report on water quality in the United States, 45 per cent of assessed stream miles, 47 per cent of assessed lake acres, and 32 per cent of assessed bay and estuarine square miles were classified as polluted.

Water pollution is a concern for everyone as the poor water quality threatens the health of people and ecosystems, reduces the availability of safe water for drinking and other uses, and limits economic productivity and development opportunities. Its effects are devastating. There is thus an urgent need for the global community both the public and private sector to join together to take on the challenge of containing the water pollution, protecting and improving the quality of water in our rivers, lakes, aquifers, and taps.

8.2 Water Pollution in India

Water has defined life in the Indian subcontinent for thousands of years. On an average, the combination of rainfall, surface and groundwater resources are ideally sufficient for providing adequate water to the Indian population. In many cases, these sources have however been rendered unsafe for human consumption as well as for other activities such as irrigation and industrial needs owing to pollution. The most polluting source for rivers is the untreated city sewage and industrial waste discharge. Realising the severity and importance of the problem, the Government of India passed the Water Pollution Act, 1974 requiring each state to set up water pollution control authorities. Accordingly, State Pollution Control Boards have been set up in all the states

Fig. 8.2: Polluted River

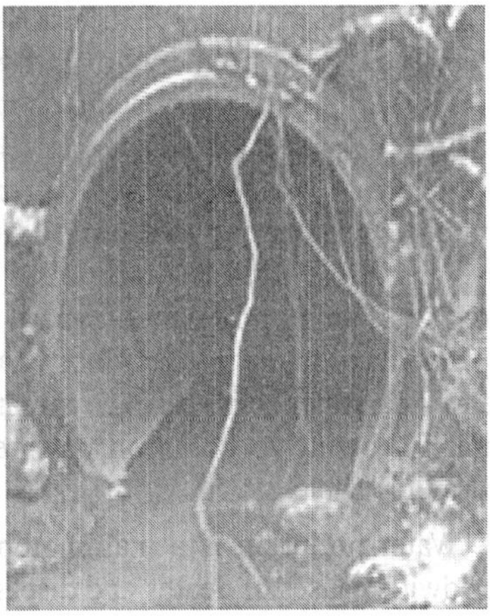

Fig. 8.3: Untreated Seusage

and at Central level, Central Pollution Control Board have been set up to give policy perspective and directions to State Pollution Boards.

In 1995, the Central Pollution Control Board identified severely polluted stretches on 18 rivers in India, majority of these stretches were located in and around large urban areas. The Study Report of Ministry of Water Resources, Government of India during the year 2000 recorded Water pollution as one of the serious problems in India as almost 70 per cent of its surface water resources and a growing percentage of its groundwater reserves are contaminated by biological, toxic, organic and inorganic pollutants.

8.3 Meaning and Definition of Water Pollution

Water is said to be polluted when the water bodies (e.g. lakes, rivers, oceans and groundwater) are contaminated. Water is typically referred to as contaminated (polluted) when it is impaired by anthropogenic contaminants and does not support a human use, such as drinking water, and/or undergoes a marked shift in its ability to support its constituent biotic communities, such as fish. Water Pollution is thus the presence of harmful and objectionable material in water in sufficient concentrations to make it unfit for use.

Water pollution occurs when pollutants are discharged directly or indirectly into water bodies without adequate treatment to remove harmful compounds. Water pollution affects plants and organisms living in these bodies of water. In almost all cases, the effect is damaging not only to individual species and populations, but also to the natural biological communities. Natural phenomena such as volcanoes, algae blooms, storms, and earthquakes also cause major changes in water quality and the ecological status of water.

Some specific definitions of air pollution are given below

"Foreign materials either from natural and other sources are contaminated with water supplies and may be harmful to life, because of their toxicity, reduction of normal oxygen level of water, aesthetically unsuitable effects and spread of epidemics.-*World Health Organisation (1966)*

Water pollution is defined as a natural or induced change in the quality of water which renders it unsuitable or dangerous as regards food, human and animal health, and agriculture, fishing or leisure pursuit.
– P Viver (1958)

Water pollution may be defined as 'alteration in physical chemical and biological characteristics of water which may cause harmful effects on human and aquatic life.-*Report, 1965 Restoring the quality of our Environment, President's Science Advisory Committee, Washington, USA*

The term water pollution refers to deterioration in chemical, physical and biological properties of water brought about by human activities and/or by natural (e.g. hydrological processes which induce decomposed and vegetable materials and weathering products of rocks etc.-*C. S. Southwick, 1967 Ecology and the Quality of our Environment, New York.*

'Water pollution refers to deterioration of physical (such as colour, odour, turbidity, taste, temperature etc.) chemical (such as acidity, alkalinity, salinity etc.) and biological (presence of bacteria, Caliform MPN, algae etc.) characteristics of water from various storages (such as river water, lake water, pond water, ground water) though natural (e.g. fallout of volcanic dust, landslide near the water bodies, sediments supplied by soil erosion and weathering processes) and anthropogenic (e.g. industrial, urban agriculture domestic, radioactive, mining sources etc.) process to such an extent that it becomes harmful to human beings, plants and animal communities.'- *Singh (1991)*

Thus, water pollution refers to:

- Deterioration in physical, chemical and biological quality of water.
- Deterioration of water quality takes place owing to natural and anthropogenic reasons.
- Causes the harmful effects on man, animals and vegetation and also quality of environment due to toxicity, reduction of normal oxygen level, etc.
- Deterioration in quality of environment.

8.4 Sources of Water Pollution

The sources of water pollution can either be natural or man induced. The ***natural sources*** include dissolved chemical in water that percolates through the soil erosion, volcanic eruption, landslides, coastal and cliff erosion, floods, decomposition of plants and animals. Similarly, ***human (man-induced)***

sources include agriculture, mining, construction, industry, business, urbanisation, cultural sources such as religious fair and pilgrimage, etc. Kumbha mela at Allahabad is an example of cultural source of water pollution.

Sources of water pollution can also be classified as Point Sources and Non-Point Sources based on the place from where pollution emerges in the water.

Point source water pollution refers to contaminants that enter a waterway from a single, identifiable source, such as a pipe or ditch. Examples of sources in this category include discharges from a sewage treatment plant, a factory, or a city storm drain; storm water runoff from combined storm and sanitary sewer lines in urban areas; industrial plants and animal feedlots where large numbers (sometimes 10,000 or more) of animals are scientifically fed in tightly restricted quarters before slaughter, etc. The U.S. Clean Water Act (CWA) defines point source for regulatory enforcement purposes. The CWA definition of point source was amended in 1987 to include municipal storm sewer systems, as well as industrial storm water, such as from construction sites.

The main sources of point pollution of river waters are industries and urban centres wherein pollutants are discharged into the rivers through urban sewage drains and industrial effluents at specific points (outfall points) at the river banks.

Non-point source pollution refers to diffused contamination that does not originate from a single discrete source. This pollution is often the cumulative effect of small amounts of contaminants gathered from a large area. A common example is the leaching out of nitrogen compounds from fertilised agricultural lands. Nutrient run-off in storm water from "sheet flow" over an agricultural field or a forest are also categorised as Non-point sources of pollution. Besides, runoff of sediment from natural and human caused forest fires, construction, logging and farming; runoff of chemical fertilisers, pesticides and saline irrigation water from croplands; urban storm water runoff; drainage of acids, minerals and sediments from active and abandoned mines and spills of oil and other hazardous materials also fall under non-point sources of pollution.

Fig. 8.4: Polluted River Banks

Non-point pollution of river water involves discharge of pollutants mainly from agricultural fields through surface runoff. Rainfall generates surface runoff which removes chemical substances from land applied to the agricultural fields in the form chemical fertilisers, pesticides, insecticides and herbicides and transports them to nearby rivulets, streams and rivers. Huge amount of sediments caused by accelerated rate of soil erosion effected by human activities (such as deforestation) reaching the rivers is major source of non-point pollution of river water because these sediments increase the sediments land of the rivers and thus increase turbidity of the water.

The Principal sources of water pollution are:

- industrial discharge of chemical wastes and byproducts;
- discharge of poorly-treated or untreated sewage;
- surface runoff containing pesticides;
- slash and burn farming practice, which is often an element within shifting cultivation agricultural systems;
- surface runoff containing spilled petroleum products;
- surface runoff from construction sites, farms, or paved and other impervious surfaces e.g. silt;
- discharge of contaminated and/or heated water used for industrial processes;
- acid rain caused by industrial discharge of sulfur dioxide (by burning high-sulfur fossil fuels); and
- excess nutrients added by runoff containing detergents or fertilisers underground storage tank leakage, leading to soil contamination, thence aquifer contamination.

8.5 Nature of Water Pollution

The nature and intensity of water pollution is linked with many factors like waste water disposal and treatment system, hydrological conditions of dilution bodies and self-purification capacity of streams, characteristics of effluents discharging from an area, socio-economic conditions of the communities generating the wastes and in cases, types of soil and vegetation. Even rainwater is never pure because when it falls as rainfall, atmospheric carbon dioxide is mixed with it. Dissolution of atmospheric CO_2 in rainwater enhances the acidity of rainwater while rainwater passes through several pathways such as lateral movement as surface runoff and downward movement as ground water several contamination mix with the water. Further, a host of pollutants are discharged from various e.g. industrial, urban and agricultural into different water storages such as river water lake water, pond water and ground water. All these pollutants pollute the water to various levels depending upon the nature and amount of pollutants. It is significant to point out that unlike air, water has dissolving capacity and therefore water, while moving through various pathways, further dissolves several chemical substances and thus, is further polluted by numerous organic and inorganic methods.

The water pollution is assessed on the basis of: (i) Physical, (ii) Chemical and (iii) Biological parameters. Generally, Biological Oxygen Demand (BOD) Chemical Oxygen Demand (COD), Dissolved oxygen (DO) and pH value are important indicators of water quality.

Physical Parameters are used to ascertain the quality of water including temperature, colour turbidity, conductivity, density, suspended, dissolved and total solids.

Chemical Parameters include nature and amount of soluble salts, hardness of water, acidity and alkalinity of water dissolved oxygen (DO), biological oxygen demand (BOD), chemical oxygen demand (COD), concentration of hydrogen (pH), amount of ammonia, nitrate and nitrites, amount of heavy metals, mercury lead chromium, chlorides, pesticides, insecticides, detergents etc.

Biological Parameters include bacteria, Coli form, MPN, algae, virus etc.

8.6 Water Pollutants

The substances which degrade the quality of water are called water pollutants. The eight major types of water pollutants are: (i) Oxygen-demanding wastes (domestic sewage, animal manure, and some industrial wastes); (ii) disease-causing agents (bacterial, parasites and viruses); (iii) inorganic chemicals and minerals (acids, salts and toxic metals); (iv) organic chemicals (pesticides, plastics, detergents, industrial wastes and oil); (v) plant nutrients (Nitrates and phosphates); (vi) sediments (soil, silt and other solids from land erosion); (vii) radioactive substances; and (viii) heat (from industrial and power plant cooling water).

The United Nations Environment Programme (UNEP) identified following contaminants which cause surface and ground water pollution.

Contaminants of water

- **Nutrients** from agricultural runoff and from industrial and domestic waste water;
- **Erosion and sedimentation** due to human activities;
- **Acidification** from power plants emitting large quantities of nitrogen and sulfur dioxides, or downstream of mines releasing contaminated groundwater;
- **Pathogenic organisms** from human or animal feces and introduced pathogenic microorganisms;

- **Trace metals/non-metals** like arsenic, copper, zinc, fluoride, chromium and selenium from human activities like mining, industry, and agriculture;
- **Human-produced chemicals** and other toxins from diverse organic chemicals produced by humans, including pesticide use and industrial processes;
- **Introduced species** and other biological disruptions etc.

8.7 Classification of Water Pollutants

Water pollutants may be classified on the basis of sources of pollutants and physical and chemical properties of the pollutants as discussed in the following pages.

On the basis of sources of pollutants

On the basis of sources of pollutants, water pollutants are divided into four types such as: (i) industrial pollutants, (ii) Agricultural pollutants, (iii) Urban pollutants and (iv) Natural pollutants.

Industrial pollutants are industrial waste water which includes several chemical pollutants such as chlorides, sulphides, carbonates, ammonical nitrogen, nitrites, nitrates, heavy metals such as mercury, lead, zinc, arsenic, barron etc; organic chemical compounds synthesised for industrial purposes, radioactive wastes etc.

Agricultural pollutants include chemical fertilisers, pesticides, insecticides and herbicides and several other synthetic chemical compounds weeds and plant remains.

Urban pollutants are various types of ions such as sulphates ion, nitrate ion (representing air pollutants emitted from automobiles and other forms of fossils fuel combustion) chlorine ion and sodium ion (coming from deriving salts used to melt ice spread over roads and streets) calcium ions and bicarbonate ions (from lime and chemical fertilisers used in the lawn and the gardens within the city) sulphate, nitrate and potassium ions and a host of chemical ions contained in urban sewage water, household sewage stored in septic tanks, phosphates and nitrated ions from body wastes of human and animals etc.

Natural pollutants include volcanic dusts sediments to weathering and erosion, debris caused by landslides decayed and decomposed organic matter (both plants and animals).

On the basis of physical and chemical properties of the pollutants

On the basis of physical and chemical properties of the pollutants water pollutants are divided into two types such as: (i) physical pollutants and (ii) chemical pollutants.

Physical pollutants are colour, turbidity sediments, volcanic dust, oil and grease dissolved and suspended solids, total solids, etc.

Chemical pollutants are chlorides, sulphides, carbonates, ammonical nitrogen, nitrites, nitrates, pesticides, insecticides, herbicides, several other synthetic chemical compounds etc.

On the basis of degradability

Water pollutants are also classified into: (i) Degaradable and (ii) Non-degradable. Degradable pollutants are those pollutants which are biodegradable such as domestic sewage, garbage, leaf litters and other oxygen-demanding wastes plant nutrients, human and animal excreta, some synthetic organic chemicals etc. These pollutants break down and decompose by biological means such as decomposery micro-organism or are simply degradable pollutants. These pollutants are also called organic pollutants.

Non-degradable pollutants are those pollutants which cannot be degraded by biological means. Such pollutants are also called as inorganic pollutants. Examples of Non-biodegradable pollutants are some metals (such as mercury, lead and arsenic), some salts of metals, sediment, some synthetic organic compounds (such as plastics), some bacteria and viruses etc. These pollutants must be controlled either by removing them through waste treatment or by preventing them from entering the environment.

8.8 Classification of Water Pollution

Water pollution may be classified into two categories based on: (i) water sources and its storage (surface water pollution, lake/ pond water pollution, ground water pollution, sea water pollution and river water pollution); and (ii) sources of water pollution (sewage water pollution, domestic waste pollution, industrial waste water pollution, solid waste water pollution, thermal water pollution and water pollution by agricultural discharges). These are discussed in detail below.

On the basis of sources and storage of water

Water pollution is classified on the basis of water sources and the places where water is stored. It includes surface water pollution, lake/ pond water pollution, ground water pollution, sea water pollution and river water pollution. The details are enumerated below:

Surface water pollution

Surface water is polluted through the mixing of different quantities of dissolved inorganic matter in the form of ions (positively charges ions = anions) and (negatively charged ions = anions). It may be pointed out that the major source of surface water is precipitation which contributes water to surface storage through rainfall and melt-water. Fresh rainwater, considered as pure water in general public is seldom pure as it contains numerous ions from different sources viz ions of sulphate (SO_4), Chlorine (Cl^-) sodium (Na^+), Magnesium (Mg++) calcium (Ca++) and potassium in those areas which are free from industrial and urban influences. These ions reach the atmosphere to join rainwater from land soil, bedrock and ocean water. In addition to the aforesaid ions which are added to the rainwater from natural sources some new pollutants are also added to the rainwater when it comes in contact with the land surface e.g. fresh input of chlorine ion; and sodium ion from deicing salts, calcium and bicarbonate ions from the use of lime and fertilisers. Besides these pollutants, there are other contaminants which pollute surface waters whether moving (river) or stagnant (lakes ponds and inland seas) such as (i) pesticides, which are used to remove unwanted weeds from crops and to prevent plant diseases, (ii) toxic metals such as lead mercury, cadmium, zinc, asbestos and (iii) radioactive wastes from the processing and use of nuclear fuel etc. These pollutants react with chemical substances and introduce several types of chemical and physical changes in surface waters and in the process contaminate and pollute waters. This adversely affects plants and animals including man. For example, combustion of fossils fuels (coal and petroleum) in the power plants factories and automobiles releases sulphur dioxide (SO_2) which after reacting with films forms down sulphric acids (H_2SO_4). These sulphuric acids come down on the earth's surface with precipitation as acid rains. Acid rains increase the acidity of surface water and reduce pH of soil water and also surface waters.

Pond water pollution

Ponds are polluted through natural and anthropogenic sources. Siltation of ponds due to dumping of enormous quantities of sediments derived through accelerated rate for soil erosion caused by rapid rate of deforestation in hilly source areas of the streams is the major form of anthropogenic source of pond/lake pollution. Numerous ponds/lakes in the Kumaun region of Uttaranchal (India) have disappeared or are near extinction due to increased rate of weathering and erosion consequent upon reckless felling of trees. Some of them are Sukha Tal (dry lake), Saria Tal (rotten lake). It denotes the level of pollution of lakes in Kumaun region. Most of the artificially created reservoir/lakes behind major dams or big rivers are facing the acute problem of siltation and resultant reduction in their water accommodating capacity.

Washing and dumping of tailing or waste sludge from factories into stagnant water of lakes and tanks pollutes them more than they pollute the rivers because the river water is mobile while the lake water, in most cases, is stagnant. If the concentration of a single matter becomes very high, it may become a killing factor and the water so contaminated may turn into killer water. For example, increase in the concentration of asbestos in the lake water causes lung cancer in human beings and the killer disease is called asbestosis.

Inorganic nutrients from the agricultural fields are also brought to the lakes by surface runoff, rivulets, streams and rivers. Besides, nitrates, phosphates and organic matters are contributed by sewage treatment plants. Similarly, toxic chemical from factories enter the lake water. The abundance of nutrients causes uncontrolled growth of plants and animals while increased concentration of toxic chemicals causes death of aquatic organism resulting into considerable decrease in lake populations.

Ground water pollution

Groundwater is polluted through a variety of sources viz leaching and downward movement of pollutants from agricultural field (such as nitrates, phosphorous, potash and several insecticides and pesticides), from industrial dumping areas, from urban and rural garbage's, from earthen septic tanks and from polluted ponds and tanks. The main controlling factors of groundwater pollution are lithological characteristics of sub-soils and subsurface materials, depth of water table of groundwater, nature of aquifer, amount and nature of annual rainfall, general outlook of society nature and rate of infiltration of rainwater and stagnant pond and tank water and above all the nature and amount of pollutants.

The loose and friable sandy soils high water table and moderate to high annual rainfall accelerate the rate of infiltration of rainwater and rapid downward movement of pollutants with percolating water and consequently high rate of pollution of groundwater is the ultimate result. Generally, industrial wastes including waste water are dumped, where steams are not available in the nearby areas, into ponds or dug-out tanks. The dissolved chemical pollutants are moved downward with percolating water (the process is known as leaching) to meet the ground water resource and thus groundwater is polluted which is readily reflected in the polluted water of dug-wells. Similarly, pollutants are leached downward form the municipal dump sites of city garbage. Leaching of polluting ions form the earthen soak pits and septic tanks and rotten and damaged underground sewer pipe lines downward very often pollute groundwater up to a depth of 400 m. The pollutants which move downward with percolating water are called leachates. The leached pollutants are seldom stationary in the groundwater rather they move in the aquifers with the movement of groundwater as guided by groundwater contour.

Sea water pollution

Sea water is polluted mostly near the coast through the disposal of urban and industrial waste into the coast water. Concentration of a single matter in the literal water causes serious environmental problem. For example, concentration of mercury-rich sludges from *minamate* city into the bay caused severe mercury poisoning. The resultant disease known as *minamata* took several lives in the city of Japan in early 1950s. Dumping of industrial wastes, urban effluents and toxic chemical into the coastal water leaves adverse effects on marine organisms. Many of the corals are reported to have been killed off the Andaman and Nicobar Coast because of toxic industrial effluents. Fishes are mostly adversely affected due to sea water pollution.

Leakage of immense quantities of crude oils from oil tankers and offshore oil wells is a major source of sea water pollution. On an average about 284 million gallons of mineral oil are leaked every year from the oil tankers. Leaked crude oil rapidly spreads on water surface as oil licks and makes the water poisonous with the result numerous sea organisms including invaluable fishes die. Thus, oil leakage causes ecological disaster in the coastal ecosystem.

River water pollution

The major sources of river water pollution are industries urban centres, agricultural and other human activities. Discharges of urban sewage water, industrial effluent carrying industrial solid wastes, non-degradable and long lasting pollutants from leather tanneries, sugar factories, beet sugar refining, meat-packing distilleries etc. into nearby rivers pollute the water of streams rivers and nalas.

On the basis of sources of water pollution

Sewage water pollution

Sewage is the waterborne waste derived from home (domestic waste) and animal or food processing plants. It includes human excreta, paper, clots, soap, detergents etc. These are a major proposition of the pollutants entering our water. There is uncontrolled dumping of wastes of rural areas, towns and cities into ponds, lakes, streams or rivers. The primary source of sewage pollution is the discharge of untreated sewage in water bodies sometimes due to improper sewage. This is very common in major cities of the country.

Sewage constitutes of 99.9 per cent solid and 0.1 per cent liquid. 70 per cent of these are organic constitutes and the remaining 30 per cent are inorganic. 65 per cent of organic portion are proteins. While carbohydrates and fats are represented by 25 per cent and 10 per cent respectively, many viruses and bacteria are also present in sewage which causes disease in human beings. Well treated sewage may still contain pathogenic bacteria and virus, unless properly chlorinated before its discharge into any water course. Sewage on drying after treatment is known as sullage. Sewage further diluted by kitchen and other domestic wastes are known as sludge. Sewage may be strong, average and weak. Assessment of its strength is determined on the basis of chlorine content, the ratio of BOD and permanganate value and on the basis of a combination of chemical parameters as shown below:

Table 8.1

Chemical	Weak sewage	Storage sewage
Chlorine	60 ppm	150 ppm
BOD/Pv	60 per magnate value	170 per magnate value

The following methods are used to check the water pollution through sewage waste:

- To stimulate water must be treated before its discharge into lake or river. This would limit its nutrients input;
- To stimulate bacterial multiplication in order to reduce the amount of nutrients solubilised in water. This would help disruption of algal food web;
- To check recycle of nutrients into the water through harvest and removal of algal blooms upon their death and decomposition;
- To remove dissolved nutrients from water by physical or chemical methods. For instance, phosphorous can be removed by precipitation nitrogen by biological nitrification and denitrification or by air stripping of NH_3 from an alkalised waste water, or by ion exchange electro dialysis or reverse osmosis.

Domestic waste water pollution

The existence of human beings itself is a source of water pollution. In primitive ages, the purifying capacity of nature was much greater than the rate of water pollution caused by human beings. But as time passed, men began to settle near water sources for the convenience of living, than they developed various industries which provided them with the foundation of civilised life. The increasing concentration of the population has also invited the concentration of pollution sources. As a result, the rate of environmental pollution exceeded the rate of natural purification. Untreated domestic wastes pollute the water where they accumulate in water bodies. It includes human sewage and waste from other facilities such as waste water, kitchen wastes, unutilised food, vegetables, etc.

The following methods are to be used to check the water pollution from domestic wastes:

- The domestic wastes must be treated before its discharge into water bodies;
- There should not be accumulation of domestic wastes in water bodies;

- Dissolved nutrients from water should be removed by physical or chemical methods;
- Phosphates major ingredient of most detergents favour the luxuriant growth of algae which form water blooms and decrease O_2 level in water for the disruption of algal food web bacterial multiplication should be stimulated in order to reduce the amount of nutrients solubilised in water.

Industrial waste water pollution

A wide variety of both inorganic and organic pollutants are present in effluents form breweries, tanneries, mining operations, etc. The pollutants include oils greases, plastics, plasticisers, metallic wastes, suspended solids, phenols, toxins, acids, salts, dyes, cyanides, DDT, etc. many of them are not readily susceptible to degradation and thus cause serious pollution problems. Sulphuric acid water from coal mines is a serious pollutant that increases the hardness of water and cause disastrous effect on living organism and corrodes concrete etc. Nitrates, copper, chromium, calcium, mercury, lead, etc. are the heavy metal effluents discharged from industries.

The following methods are to be used to check the water pollution from Industrial wastes:

- Physical, biological and chemical treatment of liquid wastes before disposal in water bodies;
- Treatment and recycling of process water to reduce fresh water requirement as well as pollution;
- Equalisation and proportioning of liquid wastes;
- Incorporation of process changes to keep the pollutant concentration at a lower level; and
- Recovery of useful chemicals.

Solid water pollution

Solid waste substances are those materials which become useless and hence waste after short period of their use such as newspapers, different types of cans, bottles, broken glass wares, plastic containers, polythene bags, ashes and domestic garbage. These discarded solid substances after their uses are variously called as refuse garbage, rubbish solid waste etc. These solid wastes acquire proper and ample space for their dumping and disposal. The environmental pollution caused by these solid wastes is rapidly increasing in tune with rapid rate of industrial growth and urbanisation. The problem of disposal of ever-increasing quantities of solid substances has become a headache for not only industrialised and developed countries but also for most of the developing countries. The dump sites in the western world are generally stakes underground pits and sea water. These wastes pollute the water and create ecological problem causing death of marine organisms including fishes and corals.

The following steps are given to check the water pollution by solid waste:

- The collection and clearance of municipal wastes from various collection sites in the cities is the first step in the management of solid waste water pollution;
- The second step of the management of solid waste water pollution is the proper and scientific method of disposal of solid wastes;
- Garbage disposal involves sorting of waste substances dumping of non-combustible substances into suitable dump sites and incineration of combustible substances;
- The solid wastes are separated into the following categories of substances: (i) compostable organic matter, (ii) Non-combustible solid wastes, (iii) Highly combustible waste (e.g papers card boards, plastics rubber etc.), (iv) Combustible wastes (e.g. wood scrap cartons, floor sweepings etc.) and (v) Animal and vegetable wastes and reusable wastes.

Thermal water pollution

The two chief pollutants are heat and radioactive substances. These are the wastes chiefly from power plants– thermal and nuclear, which are large qualities of water. Some other industries also give our waste after use. Nuclear power plants are the source of radionuclide.

The quantity of water is highest in the thermal power plants in the country. This waste water is returned after use at very high temperature to the streams a river, lake. This affects the aquatic life in these water bodies. This is also called thermal pollution since heat acts as a pollutant. Similarly, nuclear power plants besides causing fall out problems also release waste heat.

This also contributes to thermal pollution. Some plants and animals are killed outright by the very hot water. Through waste water from nuclear power plant is not as hot, but still has adverse effects on aquatic life. These are: (i) early hatching of fish egg, (ii) failure of trout eggs to hatch, (iii) failure of salmon to spawn, (iv) increase in BoD, (v) change in diurnal and seasonal behavior and metabolic responses of organisms and (vi) significant shift in algal forms and other organisms towards more heat-tolerant forms. This leads to decrease in species diversity, affect changes in macrophytes and migration of some aquatic forms. The problem of thermal pollution can be alleviated to some extent by using artificial cooling lakes and ponds, cooling towers and improvements in efficiencies of electric generation plants.

Agriculture discharge water pollution

Agriculture has been a victim of water pollution in many instances but sometimes, it is also responsible for polluting water. Water pollution caused by agricultural practices is mainly the outcome of uses of fertilisers and agricultural chemicals such as insecticides, pesticides and herbicides. Fertilisers applied to crops are sometimes not fully consumed. A part of it is absorbed by soil which influences the underground river and sea waters.

Fertilisers as the sources of water pollution are non-point sources in contrast to point sources such as sewage and industrial waste waters. The non- point sources are not only hard to eliminate, but also hard to measure their quantity. Organic fertilisers such as compost, farmyard manure, human waste and fish meal produce nitrogen and phosphorus when they are decomposed, and also become the sources of pollution.

Agricultural chemicals comprise a variety of chemicals such as insecticides, sterilisers, pesticides, herbicides and weed killers and have played important roles in the operation of modern agriculture, but they have also caused serious environment pollution. They are harmful and disturb the natural ecosystem. These chemical affects the quality of the food stuffs. The chemical make water unfit for drinking and also causes diseases.

Pesticides are the chemicals used for killing the plant and animal pests. There is a wide scope of chemicals used as biocides but these are most harmful to man by entering into our food chain. Pesticides create various types of disease related to kidney, blood, urine and brain tissues.

8.9 Assessment and Monitoring of Water Quality

Water quality monitoring is one of the first steps required for the rational development and management of water resources. Water quality assessment and monitoring is a complex subject, and the scope of it is both deep and wide. It has a direct relation with chemistry, biology, statistics and also economics. Its scope is also related to the types of water uses and functions which are manifold and the nature of the sources of water such as surface water (rivers and lakes), sea water, groundwater.

One of the important provisions of the Water Act, 1974 is to maintain and restore the 'wholesomeness' of our aquatic resources. To define the level of 'wholesomeness' to be maintained or restored a system of water use classification was developed. If a water body or its part is used for multipurpose, then the use which demands highest quality of water is designated as 'designated best use' and accordingly water body or its part is designated. Now through regular water quality monitoring, existing water quality is assessed and compared with the desired quality as identified under designated best use class and gaps are identified. Based on the identified gaps the water body or its part is identified as polluted.

In India, Central Pollution Control Board has developed and identified a concept of five designated best use. This classification helps the water quality managers and planners to set water quality targets and design suitable restoration programmes for various water bodies.

Table 8.2: Water quality criteria in India

Designated Best Use	*Class of water*	*Criteria*
Drinking Water Source without conventional treatment but after disinfection	A	Total Coliforms Organism[1] MPN/100 ml shall be 50 or less pH[2] between 6.5 and 8.5 Dissolved Oxygen (DO)[3] 6 mg/l or more Biochemical Oxygen Demand (BOD)[4] -5 days 20°C 2 mg/l or less
Outdoor bathing (Organised)	B	Total Coliforms Organism MPN/100 ml shall be 500 or less pH between 6.5 and 8.5 Dissolved Oxygen 5 mg/l or more Biochemical Oxygen Demand - 5 days 20°C 3 mg/l or less
Drinking water source after conventional treatment and disinfection	C	Total Coliforms Organism MPN/100 ml shall be 5000 or less pH between 6 to 9 Dissolved Oxygen 4 mg/l or more Biochemical Oxygen Demand - 5 days 20°C 3mg/l or less
Propagation of Wild-life and Fisheries	D	pH between 6.5 to 8.5 Dissolved Oxygen 4mg/l or more Free Ammonia (as N) 1.2 mg/l or less
Irrigation, Industrial Cooling, Controlled Waste disposal	E	pH between 6.0 to 8.5 Electrical Conductivity at 25°C micro mhos/cm Max.2250 Sodium absorption Ratio Max. 26 Boron Max. 2 mg/l
	Below E	Not Meeting A, B, C, D & E Criteria

References

1. Coliforms organisms like fecal bacteria are an indicator of water quality.
2. It is a measure of the acidity or basicity of a solution. Since pH can be affected by chemicals in the water, pH is an important indicator of water that is changing chemically.
3. DO is a relative measure of the amount of oxygen that is dissolved or carried in the water body. Adequate dissolved oxygen is needed and necessary for good water quality.
4. BOD is a chemical procedure for determining the uptake rate of dissolved oxygen by the biological organisms in a body of water and is widely used as an indication of the quality of water.

From the user's point of view, the term "water quality" is defined as "those physical, chemical or biological characteristics of water by which the user evaluates the acceptability of water." For example, drinking water should be pure, wholesome, and potable. Similarly, for irrigation dissolved solids and toxicants are important, for outdoor bathing pathogens are important and water quality is controlled accordingly. Textiles, paper, brewing, and dozens of other industries using water, have their specific water quality needs.

Table 8.3

Water quality monitoring involves 8 steps as explained below:

Step-1 Setting Water Quality Monitoring Objectives

|

Step-2 Assessment of Resources Availability

- Laboratory facilities and competence
- Transport
- Manpower –adequate number and competence

|

Step-3 Reconnaissance Survey

- Map of the area
- Background information
- Human activities
- Potential polluting sources
- Water abstractions and uses
- Hydrological information
- Water regulation

|

Step-4 Network Design

- Selection of sampling locations
- Optimum number of locations
- Parameters to be measured
- Frequency of sampling
- Component to be samples – water, sediment or biota

|

Step-5 Sampling

- Representative sampling
- Field testing
- Sample preservation and transport

|

Step-6 Laboratory Work
- Laboratory procedures
- Physical, chemical analysis
- Microbiological and biological analysis

↓

Step-7 Data Management
- Storage
- Statistical analysis
- Presentation
- Interpretation
- Reporting

↓

Step-8 Quality Assurance
- Production of reliable data
- Quality control
- Internal AQC
- External AQC

Besides, the various policy documents, Acts also stipulates about water quality assessment, monitoring and protection of water for its best designated use as detailed in the paragraphs 1 to III below:

1: 'Protection of Environment' Provisions in India's Constitution

The Forty Second Amendment to the Constitution in 1976 underscored the importance of 'green thinking'. Article 48A enjoins the state to protect and improve the environment and safeguard the forests and wildlife in the country. Further, Article 51A (g) states that the "fundamental duty of every citizen is to protect and improve the natural environment including forests, lakes, rivers and wildlife and to have compassion for living creatures."

II: Policy Documents on Natural Resource Conservation Policy Statement for Abatement of Pollution (1992)

The Policy suggested developing relevant legislation and regulation, fiscal incentives, voluntary agreements and educational programmes and information campaigns. It emphasises the need for integration by incorporating environmental considerations into decision-making at all levels by adopting frameworks namely, pollution prevention at source, application of best practicable solution, ensure polluter pays for control of pollution, focus on heavily polluted areas and river stretches and involve public in decision-making.

The National Conservation Strategy and Policy Statement on Environment and Development, 1992 aimed at "integrating environmental concerns with developmental imperatives.... [to] meet the challenges....by redirecting the thrust of our developmental process so that the basic needs of our people could be fulfilled by making judicious and sustainable use of natural resources." The priorities mentioned in this policy document include the sustainable use of land and water resources, prevention and control of pollution and preservation of biodiversity.

The National Water Policy, 2002 contains provisions for developing, conserving, sustainable utilising and managing this important water resources and need to be governed by national perspectives. Concern due to water logging, ingress of soil salinity and over-exploitation of groundwater will be addressed on the basis of common policies and strategies. The policy includes improvements in existing strategies, innovation of new techniques to eliminate the pollution of surface and groundwater resources to improve water quality. It has emphasised on water resource planning, development of institutional mechanism, water allocation, groundwater development and participatory approach to water resource management. Regular water quality monitoring programme for both surface and groundwater will be undertaken with particular emphasis on pollution control at source.

III: Indian Laws and Regulation on Water Quality Management

The conservation of water resources expressed in the Constitution is embodied in the following regulations:

The Water (Prevention & Control of Pollution) Act, 1974 as amended deals comprehensively with water issues. It empowers the government to constitute Pollution Control Boards to maintain the wholesomeness of national water bodies. It enables Central and State Pollution Control Boards to prescribe standards and has provisions for monitoring and compliance and penal provisions against the violators of the Act. It provides the permit system i.e. **"Consent"** procedure to prevent and control of water pollution. The Act empowers State Boards to issue directions to the defaulters.

Water Cess Act, 1977 was adopted to strengthen the Pollution Control Boards financially, to promote water conservation. This Act empowers the Central Government to impose a Cess on water abstracted from natural resources by industries and local authorities.

Environment (Protection) Act, 1986 has a broad coverage in which 'Environment' includes water, air and land and there exists an interrelationship among water, air, land, human beings and other creatures. It empowers to take measures in protecting and improving the quality of the environment through preventing, controlling and abating environmental pollution. The government is authorised to set national standards for ambient environmental quality and controlling discharges to regulate industrial locations, to prescribe procedure for hazardous substance management and to collect and disseminate information regarding environmental pollution. The Act provides for severe penalties for those who fail to comply with or contravenes any provision of the Act.

The Manufacture, Storage, Import of Hazardous Chemicals Rules, 1989 and its amendments under EPA, 1986 has identified the responsibilities of various stakeholders for management of chemicals and containment of spillage.

The Hazardous Wastes (Management and Handling) Rules, 1989 and its subsequent Amendment 2000 were created to provide 'cradle-to grave' or comprehensive guidance to the generators, transporters and operators of disposal facilities among others, and monitoring norms for State governments.

The Municipal Wastes (Management and Handling) Rules, 1999 fix responsibilities to every municipality responsible for the collection, segregation, storage, transportation and disposal of municipal wastes.

The Bio-medical waste (Management and Handling) Rules, 1998 are likewise directed at institutions that generate and bio-medical wastes in any form.

8.10 Adverse Effects of Water Pollution

The effects of pollution in the water are myriad. In rivers, oceans and seas, the water pollution can be lethal, killing the fish and plant life. This in turn can kill the birds and other animals that eat this contaminated food supply. The effects of water pollution have also been considered the leading cause of human deaths worldwide. Almost every type of contamination found in water has a detrimental effect on humans. Blood diseases, heart disease and nervous system disorders are commonly linked to the effects of water pollution. Many of the toxins found in polluted water are carcinogenic, which means they can cause cancer. Some substances can even effect generations to come by changing the body's chromosomal makeup. Less severe effects of water pollution can include diarrhea, skin lesions, and vomiting.

Water contamination weakens or destroys natural ecosystems that support human health, food production and biodiversity as discussed below:

Impact of water pollution

On human health

Unsafe or inadequate water, sanitation, and hygiene cause approximately 3.1 per cent of all deaths – over 1.7 million deaths annually. Women, children, and the economically disadvantaged are the most affected by water quality impacts. Over 90 per cent of those who die as a result of water-related diseases are children under the age of five.

On food production

Most polluted freshwater ends up in the oceans, damaging coastal areas and fisheries. Livelihoods such as agriculture, fishing, and animal husbandry all rely on water quality as well as quantity.

On biodiversity

Studies have estimated that the value of ecosystem service is double the gross national product of the global economy, and the role of freshwater ecosystems in purifying water and assimilating wastes has been valued at US $ 400 billion. Freshwater ecosystems are among most degraded on the planet, and have and have suffered proportionately greater species and habitat losses than terrestrial or marine ecosystems.

8.11 Control and Prevention of Water Pollution

Water pollution causes irreparable damage to both plants and animals including man. The most sufferers are human beings and micro-organisms. Polluted water is the major cause for the spread of epidemics and several dangerous diseases such as cholera, tuberculosis, jaundice, dysentery, typhoid, paratyphoid, diarrhea, etc. For example, the consumption of water contaminated by fibers as asbestos causes lung cancer and stomach diseases called as asbestosis, water polluted with mercury causes minamata disease etc. Water pollution mainly caused by toxic chemicals cause death of aquatic organism including both plants and animals.

The use of polluted water of rivers, lakes and ponds and even polluted groundwater for irrigating agricultural fields severally damages crops and decreases agricultural production. Heavily polluted water also pollutes soils, decrease their fertility and kills soil micro-organisms such as useful bacteria. The use of water, polluted by high concentration of sand load for irrigational purposes increases the sand ratio of soils and thus reduces soil fertility and raises water requirement of the soils. The use of water contaminated with salts increases alkalinity in the soils. Rise in the concentration of inorganic and organic nutrients in lake and river waters causes eutrophication which leads to rapid rate of increase in the populations of plants and animals in the aquatic ecosystem beyond controllable limit. On the other hand phenomenal increase in the concentration of toxic chemicals and harmful metals in different water bodies cause elimination of plants in general and animals in particular due to their sudden death. Contamination of sea water due to oil slicks resulting from leakage of crude oils from huge oil tankers and due to discharge of industrial and urban wasters causes ecological disaster in the littoral ecosystems because of mass death of sea organisms including fishes.

There are three fundamental solutions to water quality problems: (i) prevent pollution; (ii) treat polluted water; and (iii) restore ecosystems.

Solutions to water quality problems

Pollution prevention

It is the reduction or elimination of contaminants at the source before they have a chance to pollute water resources – and it is almost always the cheapest, easiest, and most effective way to protect water quality. Pollution prevention strategies reduce or eliminate the use of hazardous substances, pollutants, and contaminants; modify equipment and technologies so they generate less waste. Pollution prevention will also require better design of human settlements to improve water infiltration and reduce non-point source pollution. As the world takes on the challenge of improving water quality, pollution prevention should be prioritised in international and local efforts. Pollution prevention can be undertaken by source water protection of rivers/lakes/ground water and by means of programmes for reducing/eliminating use of harmful solvents in the industrial processes, reducing the use of toxic chemicals in processes, reducing the overall water use in industrial processes and closing the water cycle within industries and eliminating waste water discharge. Programmes can also be introduced for tackling agricultural non-point source pollution of rivers by measures like promoting the use of organic manure, crop rotation, mulching, composting, cover cropping, banning use of synthetic pesticides and fertilisers, integrated pest management, use of drip irrigation, contour farming and terracing.

Treat polluted water

Many water sources and watersheds are already of poor quality and require remediation and treatment. Both high-tech, energy-intensive technologies and low-tech, low energy, ecologically focused approaches exist to treat contaminated water. More effort to expand the deployment of these approaches is needed; they need to be scaled up rapidly to deal with the tremendous amount of untreated wastes entering into waterways every day; and water and wastewater utilities need financial, administrative, and technical assistance to implement these approaches.

Restore Ecosystems

Healthy ecosystems provide important water quality functions by filtering and cleaning contaminated water. By protecting and restoring natural ecosystems, broad improvements in water quality and economic well-being can occur. In turn, ecosystem protection and restoration must be considered a basic element of sustainable water quality efforts.

Control of water pollution requires several remedial measures involving individuals, community, governments at national and international levels. The individuals must be educated enough to understand the nature of water pollution and its adverse effects on human health and wealth. There must be mass awareness and right perception at community level about various aspects of water pollution.

Control of water pollution requires several remedial measures and Central Water Control Acts suggested: (i) maintaining stability of the ecosystem; (ii) reutilisation and recycling of waste; (iii) removal of water pollutants; and (iv) management of water pollution as measures to control water pollution as detailed below.

Maintaining Stability of the Ecosystem : It is the most scientific method to control and prevent water pollution. The basic principles are the reduction in waste input, thus water pollution is controlled at source. Several methods biological as well as physical can be used to restore species diversity and to maintain ecological balance in the water bodies.

Reutilisation and Recycling of waste: The various types of wastes include industrial effluents and thermal pollutants which may be reutilised. The urban waste is reused to generate cheaper fuel gas and electricity. The efforts are being made in the development of suitable technology for waste water so that it can be utilised in agriculture and prepare some useful products.

Removal of water pollutants: There are various types of pollutants present in water bodies which can be removed by suitable methods, e.g, absorption, electrodialysis, on exchange, reverses osmosis etc. This process is used for purveying water from sewage. The solar power can also be used for cleaning up polluted water cheaply. Such type of experiments is being conducted in our country and also in western countries.

Management of water pollution: There is lot of industrial liquid waste, very poor urban sewage, sewage treatment facilities which have caused heavy water pollution. There is an urgent need to maintain the quality of water at surface level as well as ground water. The Central Government has constituted 'Water Control Acts'.

The water quality can be managed by both short-term and long-term measures. Short-term devices include pollution control at urban settlement, proper sewage system, sewage regulation, control at industrial source, planning of industrial estates and protection of drinking water. Long-term devices include preparation of water use map, evaluation of pollution in river basin, preparation of water quality map and water quality assessment.

8.12 The Water (Prevention and Control of Pollution) Act, 1974

An Act to provide for the prevention and control of water pollution and the maintaining or restoring of wholesomeness of water, for the establishment, with a view to carrying out the purposes aforesaid, of Boards for the prevention and control of water pollution, for conferring on and assigning to such Boards powers and functions relating thereto and for matters connected therewith. The salient features of this Act are:

- Water (Prevention and Control of Pollution) Act, 1974 is an appropriate step for the management of water pollution; the maintenance or restoration of wholesomeness of water; the establishment, with a view to carrying out the purposes aforementioned, of Boards for the prevention and control of water pollution; conferring on and assigning to such Boards powers and functions relating thereto and for matters connected therewith.
- The Act deals with a particular type of pollution and presents an integrated approach to tackle the problem. It is an important legislative measure which has been enacted to implement the decision taken in the United Nation's Conference on Human Environment held in June 1972 at Stockholm.
- The Water (Prevention and Control of Pollution) Act, 1974 has 64 Sections and has been divided into eight chapters relating to: (i) Preliminary, (ii) Central and State Boards for the Prevention and Control of Water Pollution, (iii) Joint Boards, (iv) Powers and Functions of Boards, (v) Prevention and Control of Water Pollution, (vi) Funds, Accounts and Audit, (vii) Penalties and Procedures, and (viii) Miscellaneous.
- The Act provides for the creation of the Central Pollution Control Board and State Pollution Control Boards. It authorises the establishment of the Joint Boards. The main function of the Central Board, under Section 16(1) of the Act, is to promote cleanliness of streams and wells in the States. Section 16(2) provides certain functions in the nature of advice, planning, co-ordination, publications, education and programmes for preventing, controlling and abating water pollution.
- The State Boards (under Section 17) of the Act are expected not only to plan comprehensive programmes for the prevention and control of water pollution in the State but also to inspect sewage or trade effluents, works and plants for their treatment, to lay down standards for such effluents, their treatment and for the quality of receiving waters, and to make orders for waste disposal and the like.
- The Act provides that the State Government in consultation with the State Board is empowered to declare any area or areas within the jurisdiction of the concerned State as "Water Pollution Prevention and Control Area."

- The Act provides for the appeal by any person aggrieved by an order made by the State Board under Section 25 (Restrictions on new outlets and new discharges), Section 26 (Provision regarding existing discharge of sewage or trade effluent), Section 27 (Refusal or withdrawal of consent by the State Board) may within thirty days from the date on which the order is communicated to him, refer an appeal to such an authority or appellate authority as the State Government may think fit to constitute.
- The Act provides that the State Government may at any time, either of its own motion or on an application made to it in this behalf, call for the records of any case where an order has been made by the State Board under Section 25 (Restrictions on new outlets and new discharges), Section 26 (Provision regarding existing discharge of sewage or trade effluent), or Section 27 (Refusal or withdrawal of consent by the State Board) for the purpose of satisfying itself as to the legality or propriety of any such order and may pass such order in relation thereto as it may think fit after giving reasonable opportunity of being heard in the matter to the appealing person.
- The Act provides that where the consent of the Board is subject to the condition of execution of work and the person to whom such conditional consent is given fails to execute the works, the State Board can get those works executed at his cost.

8.13 Oil Pollution

Oil pollution refers to layers of oil on water bodies. Oil spills are most glaring of all oceanic pollution. Every marine transport vessel posses a potential danger of oil spill.

8.13.1 Causes of oil spill

The most common cause of oil spill is leakage during marine transport. It includes both small scale and large scale leakages. Oil spill could occur during off shore-oil production. There is a continuous oil slick concentrated along the supply lines used by oil tankers. Motors boats may release oil into the seas. On an average a ton of oil is discharged into the seas for every 1000 tons of oil transported by sea.

8.13.2 Impact of oil spill on marine life

Within hours of oil spill the fishes, shellfish, plankton die due to suffocation and metabolic disorders. Within a day of oil spill birds and sea mammals die. Death of these organisms severely damages marine ecosystems. Oil spills also either poison or suffocate algal blooms. This in turn makes water body deficient in oxygen. Water deficient in oxygen in turn, is responsible for the deaths of enormous number of fish/marine life.

8.13.3 Impact of oil spills on terrestrial life

Bays, estuaries, shores, reefs, beaches particularly near large coastal cities or at the mouth of river are relatively more susceptible to the hazards of oil spills. A number of coastal activities, especially recreational such as bathing, angling, diving, rafting are affected. As a result tourism and hotel business in the coastal areas suffers seriously.

9

Land Pollution

9.1 Introduction

The rapid growing population and economic development is leading to a number of environmental issues in India as elsewhere in the world. Ever increasing desire for fast paced economic progress has witnessed uncontrolled growth of urbanisation, unprecedented pace of industrialisation, massive intensification and expansion of agriculture and the destruction of forests. These activities put a lot of pressure on land which ultimately results in land degradation or land pollution besides the resource (water, mineral, forest, sand, rocks, etc.) depletion, public health, loss of biodiversity, loss of resilience in ecosystems, livelihood security for the poor, environmental degradation, etc.

It is estimated that the country's population will increase to about 1.26 billion by the year 2016. The projected population indicates that India will be the first most populous country in the world and China will be ranking second in the year 2050. India with 2.4 per cent of world's total area would be supporting 18 per cent of the world's population. This will further increase

Fig. 9.1: Degraded Land.

the pressure on its natural resources and this would be manifested by water shortages, soil exhaustion and erosion, deforestation, air and water pollution and above all land pollution.

9.2 Land Pollution: Meaning and Concept

Land pollution is the degradation of earth's land surfaces often caused by human activities and their misuse of land resources. Urbanisation and industrialisation are primarily responsible for land pollution. While the industrial revolution set a series of events into motion which destroyed natural habitats and polluted the environment, causing diseases in both humans and other species of animals; the urbanisation leads to concentration of population in small areas with better opportunities for livelihood and economic progress causing excessive pressure on land. The indiscriminate disposal of urban and industrial wastes, exploitation of minerals and improper use of soil by inadequate agricultural practice contributes to land pollution.

In a general sense, land **pollution (or soil pollution)** is the presence of toxic chemicals (pollutants or contaminants) in soil in high enough concentrations to be of risk to human health and/or ecosystem. Additionally, even when the levels of contaminants in soil are not of risk, soil pollution may occur simply due to the fact that the levels of the contaminants in soil exceed the levels that are naturally present in soil (in the case of contaminants which occur naturally in soil).

The ***soil pollution*** is ***defined*** as the presence of materials in the soil which are harmful to the living beings when they cross their threshold concentration levels. The factors or substances which affect the soil are not static. It can be positive or negative. In the negative soil pollution there occur an overuse of soil and erosion. The erosion occurs by water and air. The water erosion occurs by the high speed rivers which remove the top layer of soil. It occurs near the hills.

Land pollution is characterised by the contamination of Earth's surface. One of the major causes of land pollution is human activities. Land pollution not only affects the landscape but also the air and groundwater sources, thereby compounding its effects.

Thus, the soil pollution can be defined as:

- The contamination of soil with excess of chemicals, fertilisers, and insecticides.
- The decrease in the quality of soils either due to human activities or natural sources or by both.

9.3 The Problem of Land Pollution in India

The problem of land pollution in India have arisen owing to two major characteristics of the country- its population and its rapidly developing economy. India is the second most populous country in the world with more than one billion people. This makes it four times larger than the US and almost three quarters the size of China. India's population is also its greatest challenge, both politically and economically. The amount of farmland necessary to feed such a huge appetite and the amount of space to house such a huge number of people puts a great deal of strain on the agricultural sector. Many modern agricultural practices increase the yield of crops but increase the land pollution in India. This large population is also an environmental challenge for the world. Land pollution in India takes two main forms- soil erosion and deforestation.

Soil erosion: The near draught condition in some parts of the country increases, the difficulty of protecting agriculturally rich terrain. Rainfall in these areas is small, scattered and tends to aid in erosion. Moisture is one of the central problems leading to land pollution in India. The uneven ground, thin top soils, and strong winds add to these problems. The rainy season wash away much of the healthy agricultural layer.

Deforestation: India is one of the countries which had rich flora and fauna. However, in a bid to modernise and also to achieve fast paced development, forests have been cut at unprecedented rate. This fast depletion led to deforestation and added to land pollution. The forest which helps in protecting the soil gave way to land pollution owing to deforestation.

9.4 Nature of Soil Pollution

Soil sustains innumerable microbes and a large number of plants and animals along with plenty of mineral resources for purposeful exploitation. Soil has different meaning to different people. Chemists consider the soil like an object endowed significantly with high buffering capacity while to a Geologist; the soil is a means for ascertaining the age of the earth from a large number of isotopes present in it. The soil to a limnologist is a dependable source of nutrition for the biota. To a farmer, the soil in the form of land is a source of living whereas to a sanitary engineer, it is nothing more than dumping ground for all kinds of wastes. Above all, the soil is a living record from where originated all major ecological events of the past.

India is losing nearly 6,000 million tons of top soil per year in Ganga basin alone, caused mainly due to ruthless deforestation, leading to soil erosion. Soil erosion is caused by wind, water, overgrasing, forest fires and growing same crops repeatedly. Erosion makes the soil waterless and causes the death of wild animals. It increases the possibility of floods. Statistics prepared by the Ministry of Agriculture, Government of India indicate that out of 304 million hectare (mh) of land, nearly 175 mh is becoming less and less productive year after year. Such increasing trend of desertification is really devastating and needs our urgent attention towards better land management.

9.5 Sources of Land Pollution

The major sources of soil pollution are accelerated rate of soil erosion, soil eruption, deforestation, excessive use of chemical fertilisers, pesticides, insecticide and herbicides, polluted waste water from industries, urban areas, forest fires, a few micro-organisms, dumping of urban and industrial wastes, water-logging and related capillary process, leaching processes drought, etc. It can be categorised to following sources:

Physical Sources: The physical source of soil pollution is related to soil erosion and consequent soil degradation caused by natural and anthropogenic factors. The natural factors of soil erosion include quantity and intensity of rainfall, temperature and wind, topographic factors, lithologicial factors, vegetation and soil characteristics. These factors are further accelerated by human activities such as land use changes (e.g. deforestation).

Biological Sources: The biological sources or agents of soil pollution include those micro organisms and unwanted plants which degrade the quality and therefore fertility of the soils. The soil pollutant biological agents are grouped into four major categories, such as: (i) Pathogenic microorganisms excreted by human beings; (ii) Pathogenic microorganisms excreted by domestic animals; (iii) Pathogenic microorganisms already present in the soils; and (iv) Enteric bacteria and protozoa. These micro organisms enter the soils from various sources and degrade them and to human bodies through food chains.

Fig. 9.2: Deforestation.

Air borne sources: Air borne sources of pollutants are released into the atmosphere by 'human volcanoes' (Chimneys of factories), automobiles, thermal power plants and domestic sources. In fact, gaseous and solid particulate pollutants emitted by factory chimneys and other sources are transported to the areas far away from the source of the emission of pollutants by prevailing wind. The fallouts of these pollutants are deposited in the soils which are polluted due to toxic substances. Sulphur emitted from the factories causes acid rains which lower the pH of the soils. Acid rains increase the acidity of the soils. Highly acidic soils are injurious to plant growth.

Huge quantities of particulate matters emitted from cement factories, lime kilns, coal mining, loading and unloading of coal, thermal of plants, flakes and chips of mica mines, magnetite dust etc. reach the soils and thus pollute them by altering their chemical and physical prosperities. Similarly, high concentration of lead pollutes the soils to large extent.

Chemical Fertilisers and Biocides Sources: Excessive use of chemical fertilisers to boost agricultural production causes alteration in the physical and chemical properties of soils, though chemical fertilisers act as inorganic plant nutrients. The most dangerous pollutants are different kinds of biocides which destroy micro-organisms including useful bacteria and thus lower down the quality of soils significantly. In fact, rapid growth of population and commercialisation of agriculture have been responsible for the phenomenal increase in the production and consumption of chemical fertilisers and bodies.

The use of biocides has also gained momentum in India with the Green Revolution since 1960s. According to an estimate about 1000,000 tons of biocides are used in India annually. According to the report of World Health Organisation (WHO) about 500,000 persons become the causalities of biocides in one way or the other every year. The annual production of various biocides in India has increased from 2,350 tons in 1955 to 1,49,795 in 1983 thus registering more than 63 times increase in their production. This rate of increase continues even today. Generally, biocides (pesticides, insecticides, herbicides etc.) are used to get rid of unwanted plants and to kill harmful insects and destroy pests to boost agricultural production such as organic Phosphate Compounds, Chlorinated Hydrocarbons, Arsenic Containing Pesticides, etc. Organic phosphate compounds such as Malathions are used to kill insects by damaging their nerve systems. Frequent use of these chemicals result in the accumulation of acetyl chlorine in the soils and ultimately these chemicals are transported to plant tissues. The mammals depending on these plants are thus adversely affected.

Chlorinated Hydrocarbons such as D.D.T., dieldrin and aldrin are generally used to kill insects and micro-organisms. Chlorinated hydrocarbon compounds were developed as potent pesticides after World War II. D.D.T. proved to be boon to human society in the beginning because its use helped in killing a host of disease carrier insects such as mosquitoes and millions of people could be saved of typhoid, malaria etc. It however, affects negatively on human and animal health.

Thus, pollution sources include a variety of pollutants emanating from plastic factories, chemical plants, oil refineries, nuclear waste disposal activity, large animal farms, coal-fired power plants, metals production factories and other heavy industry. Some of the examples of main soil pollutant, their potential sources and common effects are given below:

Table 9.1

Main Soil Pollutant	*Potential Specific Sources*	*Some Common Symptoms/ Effects of Poisoning with the Polluted Soil*
Lead (Pb)	Lead, paint, Mining, Foundry, activities; Vehicle exhaust; Construction activities; Agriculture activities (pesticide with lead such as lead arsenate that was banned but has been historically used).	Affect the nervous system and memory, growth and development, as well as cognitive development (lower IQs); Learning difficulties; Autism in genetically predisposed people; Growth reduction and weight loss; Impair pituitary-thyroid endocrine system; and Favour osteoporosis at old age.
Mercury (Hg)	Mining; incineration of coal, alkali and metal processing; Medical and other waste; Volcanoes and geologic deposits (natural sources); accumulation in plants and vegetables grown on polluted soils.	Itching, burning, pain; Damage to brain, kidney and lungs; Pink disease (acrodynia) – skin discoloration (pink cheeks, fingertips, toes), while red cheeks and nose in affected children; Desquamation (peeling off in layers of dead skin); High blood pressure and hyper salivation, tachycardia, Loss of hair, teeth, nails, photofobia, kidney dysfunction, memory impairment, insomnia - in children.
Arsenic (As)	Mining Coal-fired power plants; Lumber facilities (used as CCA – chromate copper arsenate in pressure treated wood); Electronic Industry; Foundry activities; Agriculture (Pesticides including some of those currently used).Natural accumulation under specific conditions.	If ingested –the most specific effects relates to **skin pattern changes** and **cancer** (including liver, kidney, bladder, prostate and lung cancer); even lower doses affect the digestive system such as: nausea, vomiting, stomach irritation, diarrhea, damage of blood vessels; If inhaled – skin changes; irritation of throat and lungs, circulatory problems, nervous system disorders.
Other metals (Mn, Cd, Cu, Zn, Ni, etc.)	Mining; Foundry activities and Construction activities.	Depends on metals.
PAHs (polyaromatic)	Coal burning.	Harm to skin, body fluids.

(Contd...)

Hydrocarbons	Vehicle emissions- Accumulation in plants and vegetables grown on polluted soils; Cigarette smoke- Wildfires, Agricultural burning Wood burning, Asphalt roads (construction activities); Industrial plants (e.g., coal tar, bitumen, coal-gasification); accumulation in plants and vegetables grown on polluted soils; construction activities.	Auto immune system; eye irritation, nausea, vomiting, diarrhea, cataracts, kidney and liver damage; cancer (skin, lung, bladder, gastrointestinal); difficulty in reproduction in animals (not yet confirmed in humans).
Herbicides/ Insecticides	Agricultural activities; and Gardening.	Large range of effects from skin rashes to death

9.6 Causes of Soil Pollution

The soil is polluted by both natural events (volcanic eruptions, tsunamis, etc.) and man-made (improper waste dumping, construction activities, deforestation and soil erosion, agricultural activities and mining activities). When the large amounts of sulfuric acid poured out into the atmosphere during volcanic eruptions, acid rain and soil acidification might take place where the acid rain falls on the soil. Similarly, when tsunamis hit the coastal land, the flush of saline water onto soil can lead to soil salination. When natural disasters hit, many of these man-made infrastructure (buildings, roads, sewage systems) break down and litter the streets with debris and even sewage overflow. Man-made objects such as television sets, plastic pails or even rubber toys may pour out of homes and float around in flooded roads. Chemicals from industries may leak out onto the surrounding land or water bodies when the buildings containing these hazardous materials are devastated in the disasters. It is usually not the natural events per se but these man-made pollutants that are the cause of land pollution. Thus, the land pollution is often linked directly or indirectly to man's activities.

The man, made causes of land pollution include increase in urbanisation, increase in agricultural land, domestic waste, agricultural activities, industrial activities, etc. which are discussed in detailed below:

- **Increase in urbanisation:** Increased urbanisation warrants more and more construction of houses, conversion of agricultural land to dwelling units, water requirement, more and more vehicles to facilitate transportation, etc. More constructions mean increased demand for raw materials like timber leading to deforestation. There is more demand for water. Reservoirs are built leading to the loss of land. All these put pressure on land leading to land pollution.
- **Agricultural activities and malpractices:** As the human population grew there was a greater demand for food. This caused more land

Fig. 9.3: Urbanisation.

allocated to agriculture. Forests were cut down for this purpose and led to land pollution.

Similarly, agriculture malpractices are another cause of land pollution. As the demand for food increases with the growing human population, the pressures for farmers to increase their yields also rise. Soil nutrients are necessary for plant growth and development, so farmers generally use fertilisers to correct soil deficiencies and pesticides to kill unwanted insects, fungi, bacteria or viruses. However, when farmers adopt maladaptive agricultural practices like the overuse of synthetic fertilisers and pesticides, problems arise. Fertilisers and pesticides can contaminate the soil with impurities and toxins (e.g. dioxin) causing land pollution. Agricultural wastes including the waste matters produced by crop, animal manure and residues of the farm land is also one of the major causes of land pollution.

Domestic waste: Every single day, tons and tons of domestic waste is dumped ranging from huge pieces of rubbish such as unused refrigerator to fish bones. If all these wastes are not disposed of properly, the damage they can do to the environment and humankind can be devastating. While waste collected from homes, offices and industries may be recycled or burnt in incinerators, a large amount of rubbish is neither burnt nor recycled but is left in certain areas marked as dumping grounds. We throw away more things

Fig. 9.4: Land Pollution due to Garbage.

today and there is an increase in the quantity of solid waste. This has given rise to problems as new dumping grounds have to be found.

- **Industrial activities and waste:** Industrial activity is a contributing factor to land pollution. For example, in open cast mining, huge holes are dug in the ground and these form dangerously deep mining pools. Heaps of mining wastes are left behind and these wastes often contain several poisonous substances that will contaminate the soil. **Industrial waste** is another major contributor of land pollution. Dumping of toxic materials such as chemicals and paints make the areas surrounding the industries, look very filthy.
- **Waste dumping at landfills and other sites:** The dumping of waste at landfills is often cited as a major cause of land pollution. Landfills are well-known for their pollution. One of the common causes of land pollution in the landfills is the contamination of landfill soil with toxic and even hazardous substances. These substances may be part of the waste itself (e.g. engine oil), are leeched from the waste (e.g. heavy metals from discarded batteries) or are produced by the waste (e.g. dioxins from plasterboards) after some time in the landfill. These toxic substances greatly reduce the quality of the soil in the landfill and the ability of soil to support life. The contaminants could include household waste (that in itself includes a large range of materials from organic to inorganic and toxic), sewage waste (in some cases, the waste may even be inadequately treated or untreated) from treatment plants, chemicals and waste materials from industries or factories, radioactive waste (treated or untreated) from nuclear plants, and oily sludge waste from oil refineries, etc.
- **Construction Activities:** With an exploding human population and urbanisation, more and more construction activities is taking place to create infrastructures like homes, offices, roads, buildings and factories. However, construction activities are another significant cause of land pollution. New construction projects often require deforestation either to free up land for the new building or road, or to extract raw materials for the building project. In addition, construction projects are also responsible for the creation of large amounts of construction waste, which in turn contribute to the cause of land pollution in the landfills. One of the main problems with construction waste is the large waste articles like concrete and metal debris. Some construction wastes like oils and paints are hazardous waste, and could also leach harmful chemicals into the ground which is a cause of land pollution.

- **Deforestation and Soil Erosion:** Deforestation is another major cause of land pollution. Deforestation often arise from the need to extract more raw materials (e.g. wood) from the forests for industries, or the need to clear more land for human activities, such as agriculture, urban development or building of industries. Deforestation often results in soil erosion – a cause of land pollution. Without the roots of plants and trees to hold the soil particles, the particles become more prone to being dislodged by wind and water. The eroded soil loses its nutrients and organic matter, as well as its ability to hold water. As such, soil erosion can render fertile land infertile which is no longer suited for agriculture, or even turn originally fertile land into barren deserts.
- **Mining Activities:** With increasing demand for goods by the growing population, the demand for raw materials has also increased. Some of these raw materials like metals (e.g. copper), coal and precious stones are extracted from the earth via mining. However, mining activities have large impact on the environment. In particular, it is a big cause of land pollution. With mining activities, especially surface mining projects, the destruction of existing vegetation becomes inevitable. The land area, void of vegetation, then becomes very susceptible to soil erosion, which is a cause of land pollution. The mining and mining-related activities (e.g. road construction) also destabilises the land structures in the area, exacerbating the frequency at which soil erosion occurs, especially when little or no preventive and control measures are employed. Mining produces large amount of waste rocks (rocks not containing the desired substance such as coal or copper) that need proper disposal, for otherwise they would bring about environmental problems.
- **Non-biodegradable wastes:** The disposal of non-biodegradable wastes, including containers, bottles and cans made of plastic, used cars and electronic goods, leads to the pollution of land.
- **Improper treatment of sewage:** Improper treatment of sewage leads to the accumulation of solids, such as biomass sludge. These solid wastes overflow through the sewage, making the entire area look dirty.
- **Burning of solid fuels:** Burning of solid fuels leads to the formation of ashes, which is yet another cause of land pollution.

The natural causes of land pollution includes following:

- **Natural accumulation of compounds in soil:** This is due to imbalances between atmosphere deposition and leeching away with precipitation water (e.g. concentration and accumulation of perchlorate in soils in arid environments).

- **Natural production in soil under certain environmental conditions:** The natural formation of perchlorate in soil in the presence of a chlorine sources, metallic object and using the energy generated by a thunderstorm.
- **Leaks from sewer lines into sub-surface**: The adding of chlorine which could generate trihalomethanes such as chloroform.

9.7 Effects of Land Pollution

Land pollution may affect all of us as well as plants and animals. While anyone is susceptible to soil pollution, soil pollution effects may vary based on age, general health status and other factors. Children are usually more susceptible. This is because kids are more sensitive to various pollutants and they may come in close contact with soil by regularly playing in the ground.

The harmful effects of land pollution can be summarised below:

- ***Environmental impacts:*** The environmental impacts of land pollution depend upon nature of the pollutant. Herbicides and fungicides degrade relatively quickly in the environment. However, non-selective pesticides can potentially harm any organism that comes in contact with it, regardless of whether it was the initial target. These poisonous agents can cause cancer and birth defects, as well as short-term skin irritations.
- ***Slow plant growth and reduce crop yield:*** Industrial pollution can slow plant growth and reduce crop yield. Some toxins persist in the environment without breaking down readily. This lack of action allows these pollutants to accumulate and become more toxic in higher concentrations.
- ***Cost of clean up:*** Adding to the effects and significance of land pollution is the cost of clean up. Decontamination of polluted soils requires extensive measures that can be costly. The effects of land pollution become not only environmental, but also economic.
- ***Exterminates wildlife***: The land pollution also affects wildlife and may risk their existence.
- ***Acid rain***: The extreme land pollution may lead to acid rain and can kill trees and other plants, vegetation that provides food and shelter is destroyed. It can seriously disrupt the balance of nature.
- ***Ill effects of pesticides***: The pesticides can damage crops, kill vegetation, poison birds, animals, and fish. Most pesticides kill or damage life forms. For example, pesticides used in an effort to

control or destroy undesirable vegetation and insects often destroy birds and small animals. Some life forms develop immunity to pesticides used to destroy them.

- ***Unhealthy environment:*** Tons and tons of domestic wastes are dumped every day. Since people do not follow proper methods for the disposal of such wastes, it leaves the places look dirty and makes them unhealthy.
- ***Health problem:*** Land pollution indirectly affects the human health problem such as respiratory, skin problems, birth defects, etc. Breathing in polluted dust or particle can result in a number of health problems related to the respiratory system. Improper disposal of household wastes leads to allergic reactions on the skin and cause skin problems. Land pollution has been found as one of the leading causes for birth defects. Pregnant women living in unhealthy and dirty environment can incur breathing problems and a number of diseases, which may affect the health of the baby as well.
- ***Effect on wildlife***: Land pollution has serious effect on wildlife. Flora, which provides food and shelter to wildlife, are destroyed.

9.8 Control of Land Pollution

It is not only desirable but is also necessary to control land pollution because the very existence of human beings and animals depends upon soils. It is very necessary not only to maintain but also to enhance the quality of soil because the food supply for billions of world population, fodder for animals and a host of raw materials come from soil. To check the land pollution, we need to ascertain the causes and initiate action to control and regulate theses activities as detailed below:

- ***Minimise urbanisation***: It is a natural phenomena for the present generation to migrate towards urban locations in search of better employment avenues, enhanced facilities and comfort. We need to change our outlook and with the help of policy shift by the government to create necessary infrastructure and employment opportunities in rural areas to arrest migration to urban areas. In fact, Mahatma Gandhi National Rural Employment Generation Scheme, guarantee 100 days of employment to each households and Integrated Development of Small and Medium Towns scheme etc have been implemented by Government of India with a view to arrest migration to urban areas. Many more such programmes need to be initiated by the government.
- ***Organic farming***: With ever increasing population and shrinking of agricultural land, it is necessary to use soil nutrients for better yield.

However, in a bid to do so, farmers use fertilisers and pesticides in excess of requirements, which needs to be controlled. The government may promote organic farming to check soil pollution.

- ***Proper disposal of domestic and industrial waste***: Solid waste generation is assuming larger proportion with each passing day and its disposal is posing a challenge. We need to check the generation and try to minimise by reuse and recycling, proper disposal at land fill sites, etc. The non-biodegradable wastes, including containers, bottles and cans made of plastic, used cars and electronic goods, etc may be burn through incinerators and turned into ashes. Three Rs – Reduce, Reuse and Recycle needs to be practiced by each household.
- ***Afforestation***: Deforestation is another major cause of land pollution. The government has already put a ban on deforestation for any developmental purposes unless it is urgent and indispensable. Even in that scenario, equal or double the area of deforestation is required to be planted to compensate the deforestation. It is commonly known as Compensatory Afforestation under Forest Conservation Act, 1986. A stringent monitoring of implementation of the provisions of this act by all concerned is the call of the hour.
- ***Mining Activities:*** Mining activities is to be undertaken to the minimum. The necessary and required amount of preventive and control measures must be employed in the mining areas. These measures include proper disposal of waste rocks, muck, appropriate amount of afforestation, etc.
- ***Arrest soil erosion:*** It is necessary to check soil erosion to control land pollution as soil erosion is one of the important factors for land pollution. It can be checked by using controlling measures such as planting trees, bushes and grass; arrest soil flow with the help of dams and retaining walls; contour ploughing, deep ploughing, step farming; and mixing of organic matter; etc.
- ***Proper treatment of sewage***: Proper treatment of sewage through sewerage network is necessary to ensure its proper treatment and disposal.
- ***Stringent monitoring of by law enforcement authorities:*** A need to stringent monitoring by law enforcement authorities such as Forest, Urban Development, Industry, etc are necessary to ensure proper adherence to the laws and rules relating to land pollution. The public representatives' right from panchayat level to Member of Parliament must engage the attention of general public towards inculcating the habits of strict adherence to proper precautionary measures to check land pollution.

9.9 Radiation Pollution: Sources and Hazards

Radiation pollution is the increase in over the natural background radiation. There are many sources of radiation pollution such as nuclear wastes from nuclear power plants, mining and processing of nuclear materials. The worse case of nuclear pollution was the Cherndoyl disaster in Russia in 1986 but the effects still longer today.

9.9.1 Radiation

Radiation is a form of energy travelling through space. The radiation emanating from the decay of radioactive nuclides is a major source of radiation pollution. Radiations can be categorised into two groups namely, the non-ionising radiation and the ionising radiation.

- **Non-ionising radiations** are constituted by the electromagnetic waves at the longer wave length of the spectrum ranging from near infrared rays to radio waves. These waves have energies enough to excite the atoms and molecules of the medium through which they pass causing them to vibrate faster but not strong enough to ionize them. In a microwave oven the radiation causes water molecule in the cooking medium to vibrate faster and thus raising its temperature.
- **Ionising radiations** cause ionisation of atoms and molecules of the medium through which they pass. Electromagnetic radiations such as short wavelength ultraviolent radiations (UV), X-rays and gamma rays and energetic particles produced in nuclear processes, electrically charged particles like alpha and beta particles produced in radioactive decay and neutrons produced in nuclear fusion, are highly damaging to living organisms. Electrically charged particles produced in the nuclear processes can have sufficient energy to knock electrons out of the atoms or molecules of the medium, thereby producing ions. The ions produced in water molecules, for example, can induce reactions that can break bonds in proteins and other important molecules. An example of this would be when a gamma ray passes through a cell, the water molecules near the DNA might be ionised and the ions might react with the DNA causing it to break. They can also cause chemical changes by breaking the chemical bonds, which can damage living tissues. The ionising radiations cause damage to biological systems and are, therefore, pollutants.

9.9.2 Radiation damage

The biological damage resulting from ionising radiations is generally termed as radiation damage. Large amounts of radiation can kill cells that can dramatically affect the exposed organism as well as possibly its offspring. Affected cells can mutate and result in cancer. A large enough dose of radiation can kill the organism.

Radiation damage can be divided into two types: (a) somatic damage (also called radiation sickness) and (b) genetic damage. Somatic damage refers to damage to cells that are not associated with reproduction. Effects of somatic radiation damage include reddening of the skin, loss of hair, ulceration, fibrosis of the lungs, the formation of holes in tissue, a reduction of white blood cells, and the induction of cataract in the eyes. This damage can also result in cancer and death. Genetic damage refers to damage to cells associated with reproduction. This damage can subsequently cause genetic damage from gene mutation resulting in abnormalities. Genetic damages are passed on to next generation.

9.9.3 Radiation dose

The biological damage caused by the radiation is determined by the intensity of radiation and duration of the exposure. It depends on the amount of energy deposited by the radiation in the biological system. In studying the effects of radiation exposure in humans, it is important to realise that the biological damage caused by a particle depends not only on the total energy deposited but also on the rate of energy loss per unit distance traversed by the particle (or "linear energy transfer"). For example, alpha particles do much more damage per unit energy deposited than do electrons.

9.9.4 Radiation effects and radiation doses

A traditional unit of human-equivalent dose is the *rem*, which stands for radiation equivalent in man. At low doses, such as what we receive every day from background radiation (< 1*m rem*), the cells repair the damage rapidly. At higher doses (upto100 *rem*), the cells might not be able to repair the damage, and the cells may either be changed permanently or die. Cells changed permanently may go on to produce abnormal cells when they divide and may become cancerous.

At even higher doses, the cells cannot be replaced fast enough and tissues fail to function. An example of this would be "radiation sickness." This is a condition that results after high dose is given to the whole body (>100 *rem*).

Nuclear explosions and accidents in nuclear reactors are a serious source of radiation hazard. The effects of atomic explosions in Nagasaki and Hiroshima are still not forgotten. They nuclear reactor accident at Chernobyl in 1986 led to deaths of many reactor personnel and a very large release of radionuclide to the environment causing a long-term radiation damage to the people living in the neighbouring regions.

9.9.5 Accidents at nuclear power plants

Nuclear fission in the reactor core products lot of heat which if not controlled can lead to a meltdown of fuel rods in the reactor core. If a meltdown happens by accident, it will release large quantities of highly dangerous radioactive materials in the environment with disastrous consequences to the humans, animals and plants. To prevent this type of accidents and reactor blow up, the reactors are designed to have a number of safety features.

Inspite of these safety measures two disasters in the nuclear power plants are noteworthy- namely at "Three Mile Island" in Middletown (USA) in 1979, at Chernobyl (USSR) in 1986. In both these cases a series of mishaps and errors resulted in over heating of the reactor core and lot of radiation was released into the environment. The leakage from Three Mile Island reactor was apparently low and no one was injured immediately. However, in case of Chernobyl the leakage was very heavy causing death of some workers and radiation spread over large areas scattered all over Europe. People of the city had to be evacuated to safer places and the plant had to be closed down. These two disasters are a reminder that nuclear power reactors require a constant up gradation of safety measures. Accidents with nuclear submarines also points to the same.

10

Noise Pollution

10.1 Introduction

In simple terms, noise is unwanted sound. The word 'Noise' is derived from the Latin word "nausea" implying unwanted sound or sound that is loud and unpleasant. The noise originates from human activities especially that of increased urbanisation. Most of the outdoor noise primarily arises from construction and transport related activities. It is the urban population which is affected most by noise pollution, however small towns and villages are also not spared especially those situated along side roads and industries. Interestingly, despite its omnipresence in the small or big form, it still remains relatively unnoticed form of pollution even in the developed countries. This is because of the fact that unlike other forms of pollution, noise pollution contaminants are not physical particles. These are rather waves that interfere with naturally-occurring waves of a similar type in the same environment.

In India, the problem of noise pollution is widespread. Several studies report that noise level in metropolitan cities exceeds specified standard limits. It is responsible for rising incidence of deafness among the inhabitants.

Fig. 10.1: Noise Pollution due to aircraft.

Even at the "calm" places, it does not fall below 60 dB. The noise pollution is defined as the unwanted sound released into the environment. It disturbs the human being and cause an adverse effect on the mental and psychological wellbeing. The prominent adverse effect includes annoyance and aggression, hypertension, high stress levels, tinnitus, hearing loss, sleep disturbances, and other harmful effects. Chronic exposure to noise may cause noise-induced hearing loss.

10.2 Sound and Noise

Sound and noise is almost one and the same thing except for the fact that sound is soothing and essential means of communication since generations, noise is unpleasant and disturbing. The difference between sound and noise is very subjective and differs from one person to another. Sound may be defined as pressure in air, water or any medium that a human ear can detect. It becomes discordant and unpleasing to the ear when produced in irregular succession and causes disturbances. This is when sound becomes noise. In fact, noise is that higher level of sound which becomes unpleasant, and causes discomfort and fatigue to human bodies by damaging hearing ability, brain and balancing mechanism.

Sound which pleases the listener's ear is music and that which causes pain and annoyance is noise. Although a soft rhythmic sound in the form of music and dance stimulates brain activities removes boredom and fatigue, but its excessiveness may prove detrimental to living things and may be termed as noise.

Noise is an unwanted sound without agreeable musical quality. Thus, otherwise sound and noise can be taken to mean the same thing but in considering our acoustic environment, we must differentiate between these two terms. In acoustics, noise is defined as any undesired sound. Usually, noise is a mixture of many tones combined in a musical manner. It is only when the effects of a sound are undesirable it may be termed as noise.

Table 10.1: The differences between sound and noise can be summarised below

Sound	*Noise*
Sound pleases the listener's ear.	Noise causes annoyance and pain.
It is rhythmic and soft.	It is excessive and causes fatigue.
Sound is desirable.	Noise is undesirable.
Sound may be defined as pressure in air, water or any medium that a human ear can detect.	Usually, noise is a mixture of many tones and not detectable.

(Contd...)

It is in regular succession and is musical.	It is in irregular succession, discordant and unpleasing to the ear.
Sound is ecologically essential for environment.	Noise is undesirable for ecological environment.
Sound is meaningful.	Noise is higher level of sound which is not meaningful.

10.3 Meaning and Definition of Noise Pollution

Noise is unwanted or undesired sound. Unbearable high pitched sound is called noise pollution. The sweetest music, if it disturbs a person who is trying to concentrate or to sleep, is a noise to him, just as the sound of a pneumatic reverting hammer is noise to nearly everyone. In other words, any sound may become noise if circumstances cause it to be disturbing.

Encyclopaedia American defines noises as "Noise by definition is unwanted sound, what is pleasant to some ears may extremely unpleasant to others, depending on a number of psychological factors." Thus, noise as pollutant produces contaminated environment which becomes a nuisance and affects the health of a person, his activities and mental activities. Hence, "Noise Pollution is unwanted sound 'dumped' into the atmosphere not – withstanding the adverse effects, it may have on living and non-living things."

Noise pollution may be defined as the state of discomfort and restlessness caused to humans by unwanted high intensity sound known as noise. Noise is thus the main pollutant of noise pollution which may be both natural and artificial. Natural noise pollution results from natural sources such as cloud thunder, high intensity rainfall, hailstorms, waterfalls etc. It may be widespread, sporadic, frequent or rare.

On the other hand, artificial noise pollution is caused by high intensity sound created by human activities. There for artificial or simply called noise pollution is increasing in high dimension and intensity with increasing urbanisation and industrialisation. It is apparent that the main source of noise pollution is sound which may be caused naturally or artificially. Unlike other pollutants, sound/noise is not an element, compound or substance instantaneous effects on nearby organisms. Unlike other pollutants, it cannot be carried far away and spread from its source area.

10.4 Nature of Noise Pollution

Noise pollution is often misinterpreted by most of the people as sound pollution. As a matter of fact, sound is a pure tone and harmonically related, having fixed frequencies and amplitudes. It occurs at regular intervals and produces meaningful communication and pleasure in hearing. Musical lectures given by teachers, leaders and the preaching by saints are the examples of sound. On the other hand, 'unwanted sound' is termed as noise. It is a complex mixture of a number of pure tones of various frequencies and amplitudes. These sound waves fluctuate and repeat themselves in a highly haphazard manner.

Noise pollution has become a part of industrial life in modern times. Urban people are at constant exposure to such pollution contributed by disorderly maintained vehicles. Rural populations are increasingly being exposed to noise pollution by 'Loudspeakers', an amplifier of music, especially during social functions. The people working in non-industrial establishments are also vulnerable to noise pollution, significantly contributed by ill-maintained type-writers and electronic instruments.

10.5 Measurement of Noise Pollution

Depending upon the types of experiments to be done, the instruments needed for the measurement of noise pollution are many and varied. For examples, sound level meter, noise dosimeter and frequency analyser are the instruments, commonly used for measuring the total intensity of noise, the actual noise that the worker receives during working hours and the frequency bands respectively. Brief description of each of the instruments is given below:

Sound Level Meter: A sound level consists of a microphone, amplifier, rectifier and a display meter. The sound pressure level in db is directly read out from this instrument.

Noise Dosimeter: This instrument measures directly the different noise levels, existing close to or away from the machines. The total levels of noise that workers receive during their working period are indicated whereas, the total intensity of sound produced in the campus shown by the sound level meter.

Frequency Analyser: It measures the frequency-cum-noise level distribution. It helps to device control measures to reduce the potentially effective part of the noise level.

10.6 Sources of Noise Pollution

The sources of noise pollution can be broadly categorised under following two categories:

(i) **On the basis of general sources**

- **Natural sources:** It include cloud thunder high velocity wind such as hurricanes, gales, thunderstorms, high intensity rainfall, hailstorm, waterfalls, surf currents, etc.
- **Biological sources:** Biological sources are sounds of varying intensities of wild tame animals such as roars of lions in circus cages. Street dogs are perpetual sources of noise pollution in the neighbourhood of villages and fringes in urban areas.

Man also creates different types of sounds and noise such as during laughing, crying, singing, weeping, quarreling etc.

- **Artificial sources:** They are noise created by man through his activities and creations such as musical instruments, automobiles, aircraft's, factories etc.

(ii) On the basis of area of specific sources

- **Rural sources of Noise Pollution:** Rural source generates least noise pollution because of general absence of ingredients of industrial and urban areas. There are certain occasions when the level of pollution becomes higher than normal permissible level (25 – 35 db) e.g. during festivals (Holi, Diwali, Moharram etc.), religious rituals (marriages) mourning elections, quarrels, fairs etc. Street dogs are perpetual sources of high level of noise pollution. Very often barking dogs disturb the sleep of villagers during night. Diesel engines used for pumping sets and flour mills cause high level noise pollution.
- **Urban sources of Noise Pollution:** Urban source of noise pollution includes noise produced from: (i) automobiles (motorcycles and scooters, tempo, cars, lorries and buses, trucks, trains) and aircrafts, (ii) rockets, (iii) defense experiments, rifles shooting, motor firing, other firing explosions, (iv) hawkers, (v) vegetable and fruit markets, (vi) children playing, (vii) electioneering, (viii) religious propaganda, (ix) cultural programmes, (x) musical rights, (xi) festivals, (xii) worships (prayers in temples and mosques), non-stop recitation of Rama Charita Manas, Geeta, Upanishads etc. (xiii) advertisements, (xiv) mourning at the time of death, etc.

Loud speakers are the most significant noise pollutants as these are used at large scale during all types of festivals and religious fairs of all communities, national festivals like Independence Day and Republic Day, electioneering, advertisement, political and religious propaganda, worships, bhajan and kirtan, speechs etc.

- **Industrial sources of Noise Pollution:** It includes noise produced from factories and all other sources of noise pollution in urban areas such as noise created from automobiles, loud speakers, defence establishment, markets, religious and cultural gatherings etc. Industrial sources of noise pollution also include noise caused by mining operations such as operations of bulldozers, trucks, and machines, blasting of rocks by dynamites, operation of drillers etc.

10.7 Classification of Noise Pollution

Noise pollution may be classified in a number of ways on different criteria such as:

- On the basis of sources of noise;
- On the basis of aerial source of noise; and
- On the basis of periodicity and intensity of noise.

On the basis of sources of noise

On this basis, noise pollution may be divided into:

- Natural noise pollution caused by noise created from natural sources as referred to above,
- Biological noise pollution caused by noise produced by different animals including man (such as tamed elephants, lions in circus cages and in zoological gardens, dogs, jackals, donkeys, birds etc.) and
- Man-made noise pollution.

On the basis of aerial source of noise

On this basis, noise pollution may be divided into four types viz.

- rural noise pollution,
- urban noise pollution,
- industrial noise pollution, and
- mining noise pollution.

On the basis of periodicity and intensity of noise

On this basis, noise pollution may be divided into:

- Pollution caused by intermittent or non-uniform noise,
- Pollution caused by continuous or uniform noise, and
- Pollution caused by instantaneous or impulsive sounds such as explosions, gunshots, thunder etc.

The noise pollutions caused by intermittent and continuous noise are most injurious to human being because they are quite annoying, disturbing and fatiguing as they cause much discomfort to human health and mind. These pollutions are generally caused by the noise created from entertainment establishments (cinema halls, dance halls, etc.), public addresses by politicians, religious addresses, hospitals, schools, common vegetable fruit and fish markets, vacuum cleaner, television and radio sets, sewing machines, stereo music players, grinder, mixer, fans etc. Sonic booms created by supersonic jet aircrafts, high intensity sound waves caused by the explosion of high power bombs, blasting of rocks by high power dynamites, etc also cause discomfort and health hazard. It creates such powerful sound waves that even window glass panes are ratted. In fact, sonic boom is the noise which is caused by the objects travelling faster the speed of sound and is produced instantaneously.

10.8 Acceptable Noise Standard

Sound is essential for life. Organisms are at constant exposure to some or other forms of energy, without which the brains may not function. At the same time adage, "Too much of everything is bad", is also applicable in this case. The 'Unwanted Sound', what is called as noise, is not at all ecologically desirable at any level. However, the permissible noise levels in db is dependent upon the time of exposure, 80 db of noise level for eight hours a day, 90 db of noise for four homes per day, 95 db of noise for two homes per day, 100 db or noise for one hour/ day, 105 db of noise for hour per day, 110 db of noise for hour (15minute) /day and 115 db of noise for hour per day have been permitted by almost all the countries of the world. Exposures to continuous or intermittent noise level higher than 115 db should not be permitted. However, 90 db of noise level for eight hours /day of exposure has been granted in case of mining occupations for worker in India. The maximum desirable limit for noise levels in residential areas and recreational activity centers around the habitations has been fixed as 40 db in night, 45 db evening and 50 db during daytime.

The noise is measured in the units of decibels and is denoted by the db. The industrial limit of sound in the industries must be 75 db according to the world health organisation. Ambient noise standards has been prescribed in The Environment (Protection) Act, 1986 (amended in 2006) as detailed below:

The unit of the expression of the Noise Pollution intensity is decibel (db), i.e., the logarithmic ratio of noise intensity (10) to reference level (I). The minimum intensity of sound audible by man is termed as reference level (I), approximately equal to the sound pressure of 0.0002 microbars (dynes per cm^2) or an energy of about 10 – 16 watts). According, 10, 20 and 100 db represent 101, 102 and 1010 times the threshold intensity of sound required for human hearing is zero db, the ratting of leaves produces 10 db. Sound level of 30 db is generated during broad casting is 20 db. Sound level of 30 db is generated is bedroom at night pillow talk, 40 db in a library and 60 db in normal conventional speeches. The play of the radio at average volume induces a sound level of 70 db, light traffic produces noise at 74 db and 80 db of noise is produced by a typical factory. Running train generates a noise of 90 db, orchestra of 100 db, rock band of 10 db while an aircraft take off produces noise of 120 db. The threshold of pain is of 140 db.

Table 10.2

Ambient noise standards *Category of Area/ Zone*	*Limits in db* during* *Day*	*Night*
Industrial area	75	70
Commercial area	65	55
Residential area	55	45
Silence zone	50	40

** The limit in db denotes the time-weighted average of the level of sound in decibels on the scale which is relatable to human hearing.*

10.9 Effects of Noise Pollution

There is no doubt that the noise affects human health adversely. The noise may result in loss of hearing, stress, high-blood pressure, loss of sleep, distraction affecting productivity, and a general reduction in the quality of life. The effects of noise are difficult to quantify because tolerance levels among different populace and types of noise vary considerably. The adverse effects of noise have not even spare the birds. Those living near busy roads could not hear each other and thus unable to contact for propagation. The noise interferes with communication, disturbs the sleep and reduces the efficiency of individuals under its umbrella. Generally, growing age bears the brunt of excessive noise pollution.

The effects on human beings can be summarised on the following categories:

- Physiological Effects.
- Psychological Effects.
- Behavioural Effects.
- Person logical Effects.
- Effects of noise pollution on animals
- Effects of noise pollution on non-living thing
- **Physiological Effects:** This form of environmental degradation has implications for health as air or water pollution. It can change man's physiological state by speeding up pulse and respiratory rates. It can impair hearing either permanently or temporarily; millions of industrial workers are threatened with hearing damage. Medical evidence suggests that noises can cause heart attacks in individuals with existing cardiac injury, and that continued exposure to loud noise could cause chronic effects as hypertension of ulcers, and of course deafness. Audio grams of pop musicians show typical hearing loss in both the ears. For the connoisseur of this music, it takes 20 to 50 hours of quiet to make the loss of hearing caused by a four–hour–

rock concert. The adverse effects of noise pollution on the human beings are manifested through physiological indications such as loss of hearing, occupational deafness and noise induced diseases. Some empirical research conducted on pregnant female mice reveals that aircraft taking of which bring in 120 to 160 decibels caused miscarriages in them. If the findings on mice are made applicable to human beings, high noise is equally capable of creating similar disturbances in human beings also. Several birds have been observed to have stopped laying eggs. Apart from this animals change their places. It has been observed that less and less number of migratory birds moves to a particular place if the noise level at that place increases. Prolonged chronic noise can also produce stomach ulcers as it may reduce the flow of gastric juice and change its acidity. It may lead to abortions and other congenital defects in unborn children.

- **Psychological Effects**: Many behavioural changes are recorded as a result of exposure to high noise in human beings as well as animals. Certain symptoms can be observed out rightly. The undesired sound may cause annoyance. Intolerable agony may result when the source of the sound in not known. Interruptions in speech communications may impair performance, lead to errors and lower output and efficiency. Noise can cause tension in muscles, nervous irritability and strain. No doubt the noise reaction varies to large extent in different individuals.
- **Behavioural Effects:** By lowering down the auditory sensitivity of person, noise result in poor attention and concentration. It has been observed that performance of school children is poor in 'comprehension' tasks where schools are situated in busy areas of a city and are subjected to noise pollution. Noise causes irritation which results in learning disabilities. Sudden noise distracts a person and can create nervousness in him. Housewives working in kitchen with all kinds of electric gadgets have been seen to get headache due to noise and vibrations of these gadgets. Perhaps, this may be for meditation away from residential localities and free from noise.

It has been found that in the Toda of the Nilgiris that the hearing capacity of a 50-year old man is as good as that of a 20 - years old. A study by an organisation in Ahmedabad found an increased incidence of birth defects; still births and unusually low weight among children born to mothers living near airports affected indicating that foetal development is adversely affected if the mother is subjected to continuous noise stress during pregnancy.

- **Person logical Effects:** If the injurious effects of noise lend to persist for long, they cause stable maladaptive reactions in the individual disturbing his total personality make up. The lowered performance level among children may develop a feeling in adequacy, lack of confidence, poor perception of one's own self which may jeopardise their optimal person logical development as a growing child. Once the feeling of ineptness, worthlessness and inadequacy are developed by a child in the growing age, its disastrous effects are not going to be removed easily without learning their marks behind.

People suffering from insomnia, fatigue, hypertension, blood pressure and deafness were all showing symptoms of living in noise polluted areas. A bus or truck without silencer may emit noise upto 110 decibels. Today noise is also being used as a third degree measure for interrogation. In the early twenty first Century a German Noble Laureate, Robert Pock has predicted that a time is likely to come when man will die due to sheer noise.

10.10 Control of Noise Pollution

As we know that noise pollution has become omnipresent in the small or big form. However, it still remains relatively unnoticed form of pollution, more so in our country. In India, the problem of noise pollution is widespread. This calls for control measures to check the noise pollution to save environment and also the living beings from it sill effects. The following control measures are suggested:

- **Reduce noise at source:** The first approach has been to reduce noise at source. Design and fabrication of silencing devices and their use in aircraft engines, trucks, cars, motorcycles, industrial machines and home appliances would be an effective measure. Protection to workers can be provided through wearing devices such as ear plugs and earmuffs.
- **Change in design and operation:** Making a change in design and operation of machines, vibration control, sound proof cabins and sound-absorbing materials can reduce it.
- **Noise limits for vehicular traffic:** It can get reduced by prescribing noise limits for vehicular traffic, ban on honking of horns in certain areas and planning main traffic arteries, industrial establishments, amusement areas, residential colonies, creation of silent zones near schools and hospitals and resigning of building to make them noise proof. Other measures can involve reduction of traffic density in residential areas giving preferences to mass public transport system.

- **Control of Indoor Noise:** Where outdoor noise levels have been high, the following methods can be applied for reducing their effect.
  - Locate in the building as far as possible from noise source. The noise level drops about 6 db each time the distance is doubled.
  - Trees and shrubs may be planted in front of building to provide some absorption for the sound.
  - Locate non-critical areas such as corridors kitchens, bathrooms, elevators and service spaces in the noisy side and critical areas each as bedrooms and living spaces on the quiet side.
  - Back to back bathrooms or toilets should be avoided unless they are effectively sound isolated. Bathrooms, kitchen and laundry rooms should not be adjacent to the floor.
  - Bathroom walls, floor and ceiling should be sound insulated using construction of high sound insulation glasses.
  - Noisy toilets, is bettered by quiet siphon jet type flush toilets should be installed to reduce the noise from the source. Commode seats with double siphon system are now available and may be adopted wherever possible.
- **Road Noise:** Vegetation buffer zones must be created in different parts of the city. Efforts should be made for roadside plantations.

11

Environmental Education: Teaching Approaches

11.1 Introduction

We have studied in previous chapters that environmental education is the education through, about and for the environment and generally refers to curriculum and programmes which aim to teach people about the natural world and particularly about ways in which ecosystems work. The term is often used to imply education within the school system, from primary to post-secondary. In effect it includes all efforts to educate the people at large through various means such as lecture, workshops, seminars, print media, websites, etc. It is an organised effort to teach about how natural environments function and, particularly, how human beings can manage their behaviour and ecosystems in order to live sustainably. It is, therefore, important that a proper and effective teaching approach is developed and practiced for imparting environmental education to our future citizen through schooling system. The role of teachers both in-service and prospective thus assumes importance.

Environmental education is relatively a new field of study under the discipline of education which is concerned with the advancements and development of good practices for sustainable development. The environmental problems are interdisciplinary in nature and therefore should be resolved by employing interdisciplinary approaches. Considering its importance, environmental education has been included in the syllabi of teacher education programme at various levels.

11.2 Need for Environmental Education

Teacher education has always been recognised as one of the most crucial means of social and national development. The National Policy on Education, 1986 emphasised for continuous professional improvement and career enhancement of teachers. The programme of Action of the Policy highlighted the role of distance education in teacher education programmes. Thus, it is evident that there should be two types of teacher education programmes for preparing teachers i.e., Teachers training for conventional teaching; and teachers training for distance teaching. Teachers in present times are looked upon as facilitators and managers of learning experiences, organisers of situations and guides for all round development of students. The National Policy of Education, 1986 has rightly placed major thrust on child - centred approach in teaching learning process. It asserts that a human being is a positive asset and precious national resource which needs to be developed and nurtured with tenderness and care, coupled with dynamism.

Belgrade charter section [1976] has emphasised the need for environmental education and redefined, environmental ecology, objectives of environmental and environmental education. A meeting of Regional Asian nations held in 1976 at Bangkok passed 15 resolutions, broadly falling under four areas, such as Programmes for environmental education, Training for personal environmental, Non-formal environmental education and Preparation of material for environmental education.

Tbilisi Conference, USSR (1977) of UNESCO had recommended medium term plans. While these first two First Medium Term Plan (1977-82) and (1984-89), organised under these plans several conferences and seminars on environmental science at various levels, Third Medium Term Plan (1990-95) emphasised on Environmental Education. This included development of environmental curriculum of in-service and pre-service teachers training programmes. The Universities and colleges of China are providing in-service teachers training in Environmental Education. The following are the main objectives of the Teachers Training Programmes:

- Training to graduates and post-graduate students for environmental education.
- Preparing instructional material for teaching environmental education.
- Training to In-service teachers for teaching environmental education.
- Integrating environmental sciences and development.

Environmental education occupies the important place for pre-service and in-service school Teachers Training. Teacher education programmes have to prepare teachers by providing the awareness, skills, attitudes and values of environmental education. It is essential to develop environmental resource efficiency among teachers. The teachers' education institutions have to share this responsibility in the present context.

11.3 NCERT's Emphasis on Environmental education

NCERT is providing training for pre-service and in-service teachers. Environmental education is interdisciplinary in nature, therefore, it is essential to have some changes in teacher education programmes. The teacher has to provide the awareness about the problems of environment, which the students have to encounter and eventually bear the consequences. Five principles for developing teacher education programmes are noted below:

- Course contents have to be designed in such a way to accord priority on improving the quality of the overall environment.
- The basic scientific and social aspects of environment are to be taught to the pre-service teachers.
- The environmental awareness, assumptions and course-content should be taught.
- The environmental content should be included in school curriculum.
- The awareness of technical impact on society and environmental problems should be inculcated.

For the above following points need consideration

- Environmental education should be considered as an independent field of study.
- The course content should be content-cum-methodology to provide theoretical knowledge for all the essential features points of environment. Provision for observation, exhibition, experimentation, discussion and similar other methods for teaching different points of environment would have to be developed.
- Activity-based approach should be employed to provide the awareness to the students. The competency should be developed among teachers through training programmes.
- The lesson plans are to be developed on the content of environment during teaching practice.
- An interdisciplinary approach should be followed for explaining the concepts of environment related to social studies, sciences, humanities, physical sciences, etc.

11.4 Objectives of Environmental Education

International conferences of Environmental Education (give name of place/country and year) outlined following objectives:

- To develop an awareness of environment and sensitivity to the environment and its problems.

- To help in acquiring knowledge and various type of experiences of the environmental problems.
- To develop the basic understanding of structure, processes, problems and interdependence of environmental components.
- To help in acquiring skills for identifying and solving environmental problems.
- To develop attitudes, a set of values and feelings of concern for the environment and to encourage for active participation.
- To develop ability for evaluating environmental components and educational programmes in terms of ecological, economic, social, cultural, aesthetic and educational factors.

The above content of "Environmental Education" is directly or indirectly related to 'Environment'. It concerns with physical, social, biological, psychological and educational environment as a whole. The core content is the understanding of ecology and ecosystem and inter-dependency of biotic and abiotic factors. The content of 'Environmental Education' is inter-disciplinary in nature. Therefore, various methods of teaching and research such as experimental and non-experimental methods, philosophical and historical methods are employed. Some legal laws have also been formulated to protect the quality of the environment.

11.4.1 Objectives of Environmental Education as Primary to University level

At primary level, the emphasis is on imparting awareness about environment to the children relating to their life situation. At secondary stage, the relevance for real life situation of environment are emphasised for providing the basic understanding. The conservation of natural resources of environment is explained and skills are developed at Senior Secondary stage. The attitudes, feelings and values are to be developed for sustainable development by solving problems of the environment. The ability for evaluating environmental components and programmes are developed at the university level.

Thus, the effort in curriculum development for environmental education is in graded form from the primary to the university level, so as to realise objectives of environmental education in full.

11.4.2 Objectives of Environmental Education at B.Ed. and M.Ed. Courses

N.C.T.E. has formulated objectives of teacher education programmes at B.Ed. and M.Ed. levels and prepared course content. The course content has been classified into three parts: (i) Theory, (ii) community work and

(iii) practical work. The environmental education form part of community work along with its practical work. Following are the objectives of environmental education which are to be realised through out teacher – education programmes.

- To develop knowledge and understanding of environment and its problems.
- To help in acquiring skills for identifying and solving environment and its problems.
- To develop set of values, attitudes and feelings concerned for the environment and to encourage for active participation in protection of environment.
- To develop an ability for evaluating and managing environmental components in terms of social, economic and cultural factors.

These objectives can be realised by introducing the course content of environmental education since the primary stage as an integral part of education. The teachers training course should include environmental education at all levels.

Table 11.1

Levels of Teacher Education	*Objectives*
Primary Teachers	Awareness of environment
Secondary and Higher Secondary Teachers	Understanding and skills for real life situation of natural resources
College and University Teachers	Ability of solving environmental problems

11.5. Contents of Environmental Education

Environmental education consists of curricular courses that are formal and co-curricular activities that is non-formal. So far as the first part is concerned our whole syllabi is full of topic relating to environment. An integrated multidisciplinary and holistic perspective is to be adopted. Hence, co-curricular activities must be linked with formal teaching relating to real life situation. In order to cope with this a teacher should pay the following roles:

- While teaching his own subject matters he would correlate the topics of environmental issue.
- He can help individuals in awareness of and positivity to the total environment and its allied problem.
- A teacher may create awareness regarding renewal and non-renewal resources of environment.

- The teacher can help his pupils to basic understanding of the total environment, its associated problems and humanity's critically responsible presence and role in it.
- The teacher should organise seminars, workshops on environmental issue like soil erosion or population explosion etc.
- The teacher should arrange lecture on topics of environmental concern.
- A teacher should discuss environmental issue with simple teaching activities through which pupils understand the significance of environmental resource.
- A teacher should help his pupils to evaluate environmental measures and educational programmes in terms of ecological social and aesthetic factors.

11.6 Approaches of Environmental Education

There are two approaches of environmental education:

A. Multidisciplinary Approach

B. Interdisciplinary Approach

11.6.1 Environmental Education- A Multidisciplinary Approach

This approach is also known as infusion model. In this model a distinct environmental education unit course model is created by selecting presenting and dwelling upon relevant components of various disciplines. In this approach various concepts of environmental education are taken into different discipline such as physics, chemistry, biology, geography etc. It is called infusion model because in this approach different subjects are used for infusion and environmental education will be taught as a part of various subjects. In this model environmental education is not treated as a separate discipline or subject. It is incorporated in different subjects where possibilities are there. This model is known as infusion model which intended to draw out units from different disciplines and to put them in to one namely, environmental education. It is multidisciplinary in nature. This is taught at different levels of education i.e. from primary to university levels.

First part: Concept of Environmental Education: Meaning and concept of environment, concept of environmental education, structure of environmental education etc. as an independent field of study.

Second part: Ecology and Environmental Pollution: Concept of ecology and ecosystem, quality of environmental pollution and degradation, human ecology and environmentalism, food chains and food webs, flow of energy and biogeochemical cycles.

Third part: Educational and psychological environmental: Concept of educational environment, growth and development, mental health, population explosion and environmental problems.

Fourth part: Environmental Management: Concept and meaning of environmental management, teacher education, adult education, role of mass media, problems and remedies, impact of environmental education, evaluation of environmental education.

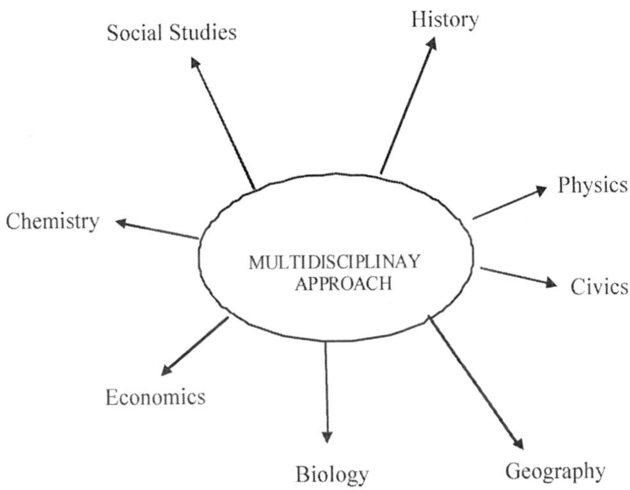

Figure 11.1: Multidisciplinary Model.

11.6.2 Implementation of Multidisciplinary Approach

Environmental education as a separate subject may be taught at higher levels. Environmental education involves both theoretical and practical aspect of environment to improve the quality and prevent deterioration due to this maturity level, age factor in taking up environmental issues in integrated way. At this stage detail study of the subject is required. So it can be used as a separate discipline in primary, middle and higher secondary stage.

Implementation of multidisciplinary approach in the primary level

- Environmental topics can be handled by a single teacher with some basic elementary training.
- Children will have the basic understanding about the environment.
- No additional subject will be introduced and therefore there will not any over loading in the primary school curriculum.
- At primary stage children are very small in age, so it becomes necessary to teach them the basic concept of environmental education.

11.6.3 Components of Multidisciplinary Approach

The contents of environmental education have four components:

- **Awareness:** It includes conscious about physical, biological, social, cultural aspects of environment. The environment is linked with the life support system which in itself has six components such as air, land, water, flora, fauna, and sunlight. These components have dynamic relationship. Man is the most important organism and has great responsibility.
- **Real life situation:** It links environment to life, these conditions are location specific thus problem and priorities of each area are different.
- **Conservation:** It means utilisation of natural resources not only by the present generation. It does not include the process of exploitation.
- **Sustainable development:** It aims at utilisation of resources for development. Therefore, resources should be used in a wise manner. All resources are finite and there is also limit to growth of living system.

11.6.4 Course Contents of Environmental Education

The course contents of environmental education have been classified stage-wise. These classifications of contents have been made in the following five stages:

(i) Primary Education stage
(ii) Lower Secondary Education Stage
(iii) Higher Secondary Education Stage
(iv) College Education Stage and
(v) University Education Stage

A brief outline of content has been provided in the following paragraphs:

(i) ***Primary Education Stage***: Here the emphasis should be mostly (75 per cent) on building up awareness, followed by real life situations (20 per cent) and conservation (five per cent). Thus, attempt should be to only sensitise the child about environment. The contents to be used are surroundings from home to school to outdoor situations. Teaching strategy includes audio-visual and field visits.

(ii) ***Lower Secondary Education Stage***: From the lower Secondary stage onwards, the quantum of awareness must decrease and there should be increased knowledge of real-life situations, conservation and sustainable development. At lower secondary level, objective must

be real life experience, awareness and problem identification. The contents to be used are those used at Primary School level supplemented with general science. Teaching, practical and field visits are to be done.

(iii) ***Higher Secondary Education Stage***: Here the emphasis must be on conservation, assimilation of knowledge, problem identification and action skills. The content used may be science-based and action oriented work. There should be proper teaching, practical and field work.

(iv) ***College Education Stage***: At this level, the picture would be almost reverse of the primary level, as maximum emphasis would be here on knowledge regarding sustainable development based on experience with, conservation followed, in a descending order by conservation, real-life situations and awareness. The content must be college/university based on science and technology. Teaching, practical and action-oriented field work is to be done.

In the school education NCERT has been playing vital role in designing, syllabi, text books, help books, guide books, charts, kit, teaching materials and aids both for students and teachers.

(v) ***University Education Stage***: Environmental education at this level is being looked after by the University Grants Commission. There is a High Powered Committee to suggest areas of Environment Education at postgraduate level. There are about 10 universities providing courses in environmental areas. Besides these, there are also research institutes and professional institutions as Indian Institute of Technology, Engineering Colleges, Schools for Planning and Architecture, which offer courses in environmental engineering. The university education has three major components: teaching, research and extension. At post-graduate level, four major areas are recognised:

Environmental Engineering: It includes the subjects like architecture, civil engineering, town and country planning, including human settlement, slum improvement, landscape architecture, industrial design, regional science and urban ecosystem studies.

Conservation and Management: It includes fields like land use, forestry, agriculture, energy, waste management, wildlife management, national parks, biosphere reserves, biological diversity, water management, mining management, non-polluting renewable energy development etc.

Environmental Health: This deals with public health and hygiene, sanitary and chemical engineering, occupational health, toxicology, nutrition and drug use etc.

Social Ecology: It includes subjects like human ecology, sociology, social planning, cost- benefit, community organisation and services, Psychology and counseling, environmental ethics and related areas of humanities.

11.6.5. Environmental Education-An Interdisciplinary Approach

Environmental Education is a powerful instrument to maintain ecological balance that equips human beings with awareness, knowledge, skills, attitudes and commitment to improve the quality of environment. Environmental education has its own independent course content while it is interdisciplinary in nature. The interdisciplinary model of curriculum construction for environmental education is also known as infused model. It occupies the status of a separate discipline and examples from different subjects find their due weightage in the content of environmental education. The contents of environmental education are directly and indirectly related to environment. It concerns with physical, social, biological, psychological and educational environment as whole. The core is the understanding of ecology and ecosystem and interdependency of biotic and abiotic factors. Various factors have to be studies which are polluting the environment.

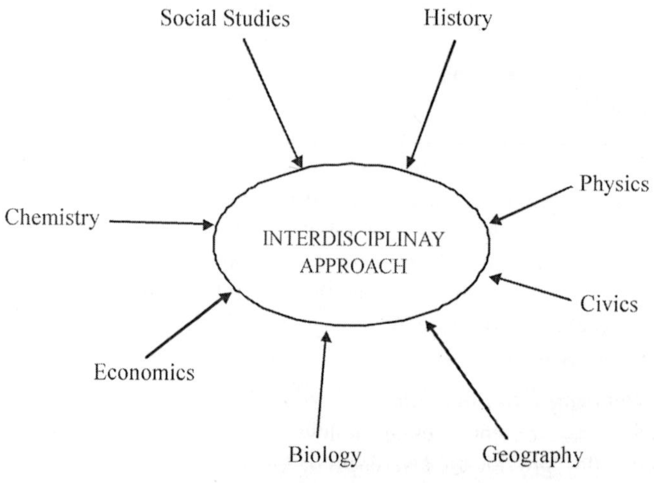

Figure 11.2: Interdisciplinary Model.

Environmental education is a leading subject from primary to university level. The inter-related components are to be taught for different levels. Thus, the curriculum for environmental education is to be developed in the graded form from the primary to the university level, so as to realise the objectives of environmental education. National and International Conferences and seminars have attempted to develop the content of environmental education which is at emerging stage as the environmental education itself is an emerging field of study. Following is an outline of the course content which is to be taught at different levels of teachers training programme.

Table 11.2

Section	*Course brief*	*Details*
1st	Concept of Environmental Education	Concept of environment and its components, Concept of Education, Meaning of Environmental Education and relationship with other subjects and Environmental Education as a Discipline.
2nd	Ecology and Environmental Pollution	Concept of Ecology and Ecosystem, Quality of Environment – Pollution and Degradation, Environmental Pollution – Air, Water, land and noise, Human Ecology and Environmentalism, Interdependency in Environment – food chains and food web. Flow of energy and biochemical cycles.
3rd	Educational and Psychological Environment	Concept of Educational Environment; Organisations, climate and health; Growth and Development; Psychological Environment and Mental Health; and Population Explosion and Environmental problems.
4th	Environmental Management	Meaning of environmental management; Teacher – Education and Environmental Education; Role of Media in Environmental Education; Social Forestry and Environmental Education; Problems and Remedies of Environmental Education; and Evaluation of Environmental Education.

The core content of Environmental Education is highly interdisciplinary in nature but the difference lies in the level of objectives. The purpose of other subject is to provide the awareness of environment and environmental studies, but environmental education has to develop cognitive, affective and psychomotor abilities and efficiencies. In Indian situation, infused model is appropriate for primary level and infusion model for secondary level. At primary level teaching of daily living skills and identification of different aspects of nature is important. But in secondary stage habit formation towards a particular aspect is important. So the children should learn about environment through different subjects. Environment education as a separate subject may be taught at higher level. Environment education involves both theoretical and practical aspect of environment to improve the quality, imbalance and prevent the deterioration.

11.7 Goals for Pre-service Teacher Training on Environmental Education

UNESCO-UNEP International Environment Education Programme stipulates that the ultimate aim of Environment Education is to aid citizens in becoming environmentally knowledgeable and, above all, skilled and dedicated for working, individually and collectively, towards achieving and/or maintaining a dynamic equilibrium between quality of life and quality of the environment. Goal-wise details are given below:

Goal level - I

The Ecological Foundations Level

Upon completion of a middle level teacher education programme specialisation designed to develop an effective environmental educator, the in service middle level teacher should be expected to be able to:

- Communicate and apply in an educational setting, major ecological concepts including those which focus on individuals and species populations; communities and ecosystems; biogeochemical cycles; energy production; storage; transfer and degradation; interdependence; niche; adaptation; succession; homeostasis; and human as an ecological variable.
- Apply knowledge of ecological concepts to the analysis of environmental problems and issues, and be able to identify important ecological principles involved.
- Apply knowledge of ecological concepts in predicting the probable ecological consequences of alternative solutions to environmental problems.
- Understand principles of ecology in order to identify select and utilise appropriate sources of information in a continuing effort to investigate, evaluate and develop solutions for environmental problems.

Goal level - II

The Conceptual Awareness Level

- Understand and communicate how human cultural activities (e.g., religious, economic, political, social, and others) influence the environment from an ecological perspective.
- Understand and communicate how people's behaviours, individually and collectively, impact upon the environment from an ecological perspective.

- Identify a wide variety of local, regional, national, international, and global environmental issues, as well as the ecological and cultural implications of these issues.
- Identify and communicate the viable alternative solutions available for remediating crucial environmental issues, as well as the ecological and cultural implications of these various solutions.
- Understand and communicate the need for environmental issues investigation and evaluation as prerequisites for sound decision-making.
- Understand the roles played by differing human beliefs and values in environmental issues, as well as the need for personal values clarification as an important part of environmental decision-making.
- Understand and communicate the need for responsible citizenship action in the solution of environmental issues.

Goal level - III

The Investigation and Evaluation Level

- Apply the knowledge and skills needed to identify and investigate environmental issues (using both primary and secondary sources of information), and to synthesise the data gathered.
- Demonstrate the ability to analyse environmental issues, and the associated value perspectives for their ecological and cultural implications.
- Demonstrate the ability to identify alternative solutions for important environmental issues, and the value perspectives associated with those issues.
- Demonstrate the ability to evaluate alternative solutions and associated value perspectives for their ecological and cultural implications.
- Demonstrate the ability to identify and clarify personal value positions related to important environmental issues and to their associated solutions.
- Demonstrate the ability to evaluate, clarify, and modify personal value positions in light of new (additional) information.

Goal level - IV

The Environmental Action Skill Level

- Demonstrate the ability to design action plans using citizenship action strategies associated with each of the following categories of strategies: consumer action, physical action (eco-management), persuasion, political action, and legal action.

- Demonstrate the ability to evaluate specific (selected) action strategies in light of their ecological and cultural implications.
- Demonstrate the ability to implement action plans and apply action skills for the purpose of resolving or helping to resolve one or more environmental issues.

Goal level - V

The Instructional Application Level

- Demonstrate the ability to both select and develop curricular/ instructional materials which address each of the four EE goal levels, and which are appropriate for use in middle level settings.
- Demonstrate the ability to organise and implement instruction at each of the four EE goal levels using those teaching strategies which have proven effective, and which are appropriate for use in middle level settings.
- Demonstrate the ability to design and carry out appropriate assessments of student learning at each of the four EE goal levels in middle level settings.
- Demonstrate the ability and a willingness to modify one's selection of instructional materials and/or strategies based upon the results of classroom evaluations and assessments.

11.8 Areas of Research

The university education has recognised three major components: teaching, research and extension work. At post-graduate level four major study areas are identified:

- *Environmental Engineering*: It includes civil engineering, planning, human settlement, industrial design, urban ecosystem studies.
- *Environmental health*: It concerns with public health and hygiene, sanitary, chemical engineering, occupational health, institutional health, nutrition etc.
- *Conservation and management*: It includes land use, agriculture, energy flow, waste management, wildlife management, national parts, water management, non-polluting renewal energy development.
- *Social Ecology*: It includes human sociology, human ecology, population explosion, urbanisation and services guidance and counselling and environmental ethics.

11.9 Environmental Education

As we know that the Environmental education is the lifelong process for the welfare of mankind and the development of the society. Therefore, it is designed for any age group, participating in social, economic, cultural development of the community. They form groups or clubs and arrange exhibitions, public lectures, meetings, environmental campaigns. The following constitute main content of non-formal education:

Adult Education: Adult may influence other members for better ways of life. In local language, information packs, posters, slides, audio, audio-visuals etc. may be generated.

Rural youth and non-student youth: They may organise into groups. The programmes of education can be taken up by involving their community leaders, women and youth. They are an important content of our forest wealth, for tribal and forest dwellers.

Children Activities: This can be ensured through essay competitions of different age groups. Department of Environment with the help of United School organisation of India organised such activities. On the spot painting, modelling and poster design contests are conducted for children by the National Museum of Natural History (NMNH) short-term courses are also given by NMNH in EE every year.

Eco-development Camps: They help in sound rural development involving youth. A set of guidelines has been prepared by Department of Environment (1984). The main objectives are: to create awareness in student and non-student youth about basic ecological principles; to identify root course of ecological/environmental problems and to develop a spirit of national integration and emotional integration.

Non-governmental Organisations (NGOs): There are over 200 NGOs, of which most are involved in EE and awareness, others in nature conservation, pollution control, afforestation and social forestry, floristic and faunal studies, rural development, wildlife conservation and waste utilisation and eco-development.

Public Representatives: India has Environmental Forums for MPs and MLAs to discuss environmental problems facing the country. They may build up sound public opinion and stimulation public interest.

Training Senior Executives/Administrators: Regular courses should be arranged for various institutes imparting such training. These are general environmental management, industry-specific environmental management. It should be included in M.B.A. Course.

Foundation courses: The courses for the probationers selected for the IAS, IFS, IPS, and cadets and three wings of Armed Forces need to be supplemented with foundation courses on environment relevant to their area of work.

Research and Development Programmes: Such programmes are supported by Department of Environment in Man and Biosphere and basic and applied environmental problems.

Centres of Excellence: Department of Environment has established two centres of Excellence in the country. They generate knowledge and methodology and training in areas of Tropical Ecology (Bangalore) and Environmental Education (Ahmedabad).

Development of Trained Manpower: There must be training programmes for the trainers, professionals, technical personnel, and legal experts.

Development of Educational Material and Teaching aids: Audio, Audit-visual materials, materials, for media (TV, Radio, Films newspapers etc.), mobile exhibitions etc. must be designed by competent manpower. One such centre is centre for Environment Education, Ahmedabad.

World Environment day: All governments in the States, UTs, academic institutions, universities, colleges, schools and voluntary organisations organise suitable activities on this day (June 5) and Department of Environment Supports this financially.

National Environment Awareness Campaign/National environment month: Commencing from 1986, Department of Environment conducts NEAC and NEM, from November 19th to December 18th every year is observed as NEM. Each year there is an environmental theme.

11.10 Environmental Education and Non-governmental Organisation (NGOs)

The emergence of NGOs represents an organised response by the civil society, especially in those areas in which the state has either failed to reach or done so inadequately. The importance of public awareness and NGOs involvement in environmental protection is acknowledged worldwide. It was also highlighted in Rio-Conference in 1992.

- NGOs have been taking a number of steps to promote discussion and debate about environmental issues, outside the broad spheres of popular media and the educational system. Advocacy and awareness is especially crucial in promoting concepts such as sustainable development, natural resource conservation and the restoration of ecosystems. NGOs can sensitise policy-makers about the local needs and priorities. They can often intimate the policy-makers about interests of both the poor and the rich about the ecosystem as a whole. In providing training facilities, both at community and government levels, NGOs can play a significant role. They can also contribute significantly by undertaking research and publication on environment and development related issues. It is necessary to support and encourage genuine, small, local level NGOs in different parts of the country which can provide much needed institutional support specific to the local needs. NGOs can make the following contributions:

- All NGOs should include environmental education in their package of activities.
- NGOs should catalyse public involvement in environmental programmes.
- NGOs have a vital role to play in creating environmental awareness at all levels.
- NGOs should begin a decade of consumer and environmental education and involve youth organisations in their work.
- NGOs should harmonise their activities with government bodies.
- NGOs can and should undertake environment-based adult education.
- A newsletter of NGOs efforts in the environmental field should be published.
- The Department of Environment should provide a nodal point for NGO activities and act as a clearing house for information on NGO work in environmental education, action and programmes.

11.11 Methods of Teaching Environmental Education

A teaching method comprises the principles and methods used for instruction. Commonly used teaching methods may include class participation, demonstration, recitation, memorisation or combination of these. The choice of teaching method to be used depends largely on the information or skill that is being taught, and it may also be influenced by the aptitude and enthusiasm of the students. In order to make children learn effectively, the teacher has to adopt the right method of teaching. In the field of environmental education, teaching methods play an important role along with its content. These teaching methods are determined by the teacher keeping in mind the capability of students and the curriculum. Thus, with the help of these methods the teacher imparts understanding of the subject matter along with the knowledge of the curriculum.

The teaching methods tell the teacher how he should teach his students. This is true that "in the absence of correct direction, a person cannot reach his destination in the same way in the absence of proper method the student cannot be given correct knowledge."

Guiding principles for selection of a Teaching Method

The teacher should keep in mind these guiding principles while selecting teaching methods:

- The appropriate method should be selected to achieve the objectives of teaching environmental education.
- The teacher should have proper knowledge of teaching methods.
- Teaching method selected by teacher should be based on an understanding of the students in the classroom.
- Before selecting teaching method, the teacher should take care of age, class and capability of the students.
- We should select teaching methods based on the realisation that the word education is a "drawing out" and not a "putting in."
- Teacher should select teaching method which leads the pupils to a sense of achievement through interest and purpose.
- Teacher should select teaching method which stimulates the pupils to think and cooperate actively.
- Teaching method should be selected on the experimental nature of the method.
- Teaching method should be selected for catering the needs of individual differences.
- Before selecting teaching method, a teacher should check the availability of apparatus and materials in the school required in that particular method.

Various methods of teaching environmental education

The methods used for teaching of environmental education are given below:

1. Project method
2. Discussion method
3. Problem-solving method
4. Excursion or Field trips

A short discussion of these methods of teaching is given here:

1. Project Method

The project is defined in Oxford's Advanced Learner's Dictionary as a plan of action. It usually involves a task or problem, calling for constructive thought or action or both on the part of the student. Project method of teaching has evolved from the philosophy of pragmatists. It is experience-centred strategy related to life-situation. This teaching strategy focus on-to socialise a child and to achieve cognitive, affective and psychomotor objectives. This method was given by Dewey- the American philosopher, psychologist and practical teacher. The project method is a direct outcome of this philosophy. This method of teaching gives more importance and recognition to the group activity.

Definitions of Project

"A project is a unit of activity in which pupils are made responsible for planning and purposing." -*Parker*

"A project is a problematic act carried to completion in its natural setting." -*Stevenson*

"A project is a whole-hearted purposeful activity proceeding in a social environment." -*Kilpatrick*

"A project is a bit of real life that has been imparted into school." -*Ballard*

By analysing these definitions, we see that a project has some purpose and there is planning to achieve that purpose which is achieved in social, real and natural situations created in the school.

Thus, it can be said that a project is a special kind of experience which is outcome of a desire of the students. Therefore, teaching by this method is based upon the use of desire of the students. Project method can be best explained through the phrase 'Learning by Living'. This phrase clearly explains the fact that human beings are social animals who cannot learn gain any kind of information by living in isolation. They always learn better in a group or society in which they are being placed. If any human beings intend to live harmoniously in society then he should be provided with well-balanced opportunities in schools and educational institutions to solve out similar kind of problems which he usually face in his real or actual life.

Human life is full of projects, and all of us make different kinds of attempts to carry out these projects successfully. This method is designed on the idea that gap between social life and home life of the students should be bridged down. Such kind of atmosphere should be created in the schools in which students feel themselves in a small society. Under this method, around a central theme, connected facts are being developed, which can be in the form of scientific principles or facts.

Under this method, a suitable project is being picked up by the students, which they are required to complete in a cooperative and natural way. Generally, such projects are inspired by needs and problems which students encounter in their day to day life. Students try to solve these problems through advice and guidance of the teacher.

Students are required to perform various kinds of activities while planning and executing the project in reality. As a result of felt needs of the students, what they learn through this method comes in a natural way. Thus, it can be said that teaching conducted through this method is a kind of incidental learning where teaching is undertaken as a result of mere coincidence in a very informal way.

This teaching method is based on the following principles:

- **Principle of utility:** Choose those projects which are closer to the social life.
- **Principle of readiness:** Involve the learners in finding the solution of the problem with their active participation.
- **Learning by Doing:** Learner performs certain tasks and experiences new things. This adds to his knowledge and results in learning.
- **Principle of socialisation:** It develops the feeling of cooperation and group work.
- **Inter-disciplinary approach:** To involve the knowledge of different subjects in solving the social problems.
- **Learning by Living:** Students learn how to live together by performing tasks together in group.
- **Principle of Freedom:** Students are given full freedom for selecting and completing their project.
- **Principle of Activity:** Learner performs so many activities for completing any project.
- **Principle of Purpose:** Every project has some purpose and students complete the project to fulfill the purpose.
- **Principle of Reality:** Every project is a replica of real object. It gives the complete idea of real object.
- **Principle of experience:** Learner gains various experiences by doing project.
- **Principle of correlation:** Students learn to correlate various things while doing any project.
- **Principle of Interest:** It develops interest among students towards teaching-learning process. Students can utilise their leisure time in a proper manner.

Types of project method of teaching

Kilpatrick has classified the project method in four types.

- **Constructive:** When learners have to construct some things related to social life. e.g. charts, models, maps, parcels etc.

- **Artistic:** These projects are generally allotted in the aesthetic fields of life e.g. in music, drawing, painting, art and culture.
- **Problem-solving:** These projects are given to solve the problems related to any life-situation or related to any subject. e.g. Problems related to food and nutrition, improvement in health etc. These general problems if solved will make a child efficient for social-life.
- **Group-work:** A team of students is assigned a work to be performed. e.g. to develop a botanical garden in the school.

Steps involved in the project method

This method involves the following steps of project method:

(i) Providing a situation

(ii) Choosing and purposing

(iii) Planning of the project

(iv) Executing the project

(v) Judging the project

(vi) Recording the project

(i) Providing a situation

A project should arise put of a need felt by pupils and it should never be forced on them. It should be purposeful and significant. It should look important and must be interesting. For this the teacher should always be on the look out to find situation that arise and discuss them with students to discover their interest. Situations may be provided by different methods. Some such methods may be included by talking to students on the topics of common interest.

(ii) Choosing and purposing

The children should be tempted to choose a project. While choosing the project the teacher should bear in mind that it should be of real need to pupils. The purpose of the project should be clearly defined and well understood by the pupils. A project which is very ambitious may prove to be a flop and a total waste of teacher and student time. The points to be taken in consideration are: (a) the student's interest, (b) degree of complexity of project, (c) time allotted to furnish the project and (d) availability of material resources.

(iii) Planning of the project

Planning in a project is very important for the success of a project depends upon good planning. The teacher should be actively involved in this stage in order to guide the students to choose the most practical plan of action: (a) the students should themselves do the planning with the teacher as a guide,

(b) discussion may be held among the student, (c) After a discussion, the best of plans is agreed on and (d) the planning is recorded in their projects book.

(iv) Executing the project

The teacher assigns work to the various group members according to their interests and abilities. Each member of the group should be actively involved in the execution of the project. In this step: (a) the work assigned by the teacher to each group in further sub-divided by the students among themselves thus distributing the various activities and duties, (b) the students collect information, visit various places, keep accounts and perform a variety of activities.

(v) Judging the project

The evaluation of the project should be done both by the pupils and the teacher. The pupils should estimate the qualities of what they have done before the teacher gives his evaluation. The evaluation of the project has to be done in the light of plans, difficulties in the execution and achieved results. Let the students have self-criticism and look through their own failings and findings. This step is very useful because as a result of the project, the pupils can know the values of the information; interest, skills and attitudes have been modified by the project.

(vi) Recording the project

The students keep a complete record of work including the choice of the project, the planning methodology, the discussions held and duties assigned. Also, references and books consulted and readings taken, difficulties faced, guidance sought and so on.

Format of a Project Report

The following format can be adopted:

- **Title:** A brief title should do, if accuracy requires more than a few key words, a subtitle may be considered.
- **Abstract:** This is a brief summary of the entire project highlighting the objectives, methods used and conclusions arrived at.
- **Introduction:** A description of the topic being studied, along with relevant background information is given here. A clear statement of the purpose, scope and the method of the study should be included.
- **Materials and Methods:** A description of the equipment/chemicals, methods and procedures used and experiments performed is given.
- **Observations:** The recorded observations and data are noted under this section.

- **Results:** The findings from the study are given in detail in this section. Students can be taught to interpret their findings, comparing their results with other workers in the same field.
- **Appendix:** Students can insert any supplementary information in this section.
- **Bibliography:** A list of references is given to help other students to follow up if they so wish.

Criteria of a Good Project

- A project should be purposeful and complete in itself. It should be useful and practically applicable to the daily life of the students with clear, well-defined objectives.
- The learning activity is life-like, purposeful and natural.
- The learners plan and direct their own activity.
- The project should be timely.
- The project should be challenging.
- The project should be feasible.
- The level of complexity of the project is of prime importance for its success or failure.
- The project should be aimed at problem-solving.
- The learning experiences gained during the progress of the project should be useful.
- There should be full freedom for the students to work of their own accord.

Role of the Teacher

The teacher should assume the following role in accomplishment of project goals:

- He is a guide, friend and philosopher.
- He helps the student in solving their problems just like an elder brother.
- He encourages his students to work collectively, amicably in the group.
- He also helps his students to avoid mistakes.
- He makes it a point that each member of the group contributes something to the completion of the project and in this process helps the shy and weaker students to work along-with their classmates.
- If the students face failure during execution of some steps of the project the teacher should only explain to his students the reasons of

their failure and should suggest them some better methods that may be used by them next time for the success of the project.

- During the execution step teacher also learns something.
- Teacher should always remain alert and active during execution, step and see that the project goes to completion successfully.
- During execution of the project teacher should maintain a democratic atmosphere.
- Teacher must be well read and well informed so that he can help the students to the successful completion of the project.

Advantages of Project Method

The advantages of project method of teaching environmental education are as follows:

- It helps in developing social norms and social values among the learners.
- It provides invaluable opportunities for correlation of various elements of the subject matter and for transfer of training or learning.
- It helps in growing knowledge very effectively as a result of their close cooperation on social participation in the spirit of democracy.
- As students get proper freedom to execute the project in accordance with their interest and abilities, because of which they get their psychological needs satisfied to considerable extent.
- This method is not only subject centred, but due importance is being provided to the students also. Students are permitted to choose projects on their own, as a result of which they make use of their abilities to maximum possible extent.
- Through this method, students are provided with various opportunities by which they can satisfy their interests and desires.
- Habit of critical thinking gets developed among the students through this method. Not only get this, an urge to make use of scientific methods to solve various problems also developed among the students through this method.
- With this method, students get the ample chances in which they can develop coordination among their body and mind. Through this method, teacher can lead a well-balanced development of the students.
- As students gain knowledge directly through their own efforts, thus, they acquire permanent kind of information, which is retained by them since a long period of time.

- Mostly the projects are undertaken in classroom as classroom assignments, because of which load of home work from the students get reduced to considerable extent.
- This is based on 'learning by doing'.
- This is a psychological method.
- The students develop qualities of patience, contentment and satisfaction.
- The students have to perform mental and physical work thus they develop the quality of dignity of labour.
- A project affords opportunity to develop to keenness and accuracy of observation and produces a spirit of enquiry.

Limitations of Project Method

This method has certain limitations, which are as follows:

- The project cannot be planned for all subjects and whole subject matter cannot be taught by this strategy.
- It is not economical from the point of view of time and cost.
- It is very difficult for a teacher to plan or to execute the projects to the learners and supervise them.
- Such method can only be proving successful if the teacher is highly knowledgeable, alert and exceptionally gifted.
- Systematic and adequate learning is not provided by this method, as it is a method of incidental learning. Thus, through this process, it is not possible to treat. The curricular areas in systematic and orderly manner.
- Generally, it is found that teachers do not possess much information regarding the manner in which this method should be used as a result of which they hesitate from using this method, as a result of which, its utility remains more or less limited to negligible extent.
- This method leaves a gap in pupil's knowledge.
- Sometimes the projects may be too ambitious and beyond pupils capacity to accomplish.
- The education given by projects is likely to emphasise relationships in breadth than in depth.
- Text-books and material written on these lines are not available.

Suggestions of Project Method

This method has following suggestions:

- This method should not be used an independent teaching strategy but as a supplementary teaching technique.

- Teacher should try to utilise the inexperience and waste projects to prepare models etc.
- To avoid the problem of supervision, teacher may appoint a leader to each group of students.
- Teacher should fix a time limit for each project.
- Project should have definite objectives.
- All students should be given responsibilities according to their capabilities.
- All figures should have graphical representation.
- The students should be given the freedom to interact among themselves.
- The charge of disorganised and irregular study can be removed by making a provision in the time-table for formal class teaching of subjects.
- The problem of expenditure can be easily solved by undertaking some such projects in which we can earn something or in other words the project should be made economically self-sufficient.

2. Discussion Method

According to Lee, "Discussion is a group education work. In this the students discuss a problem together." This method is found quite suitable for those topics in environmental education which cannot be easily explained by demonstration or other such techniques. In this method a topic is taken and the teacher encourages the students to discuss it. The teacher develops the lesson with the help of the answers and reactions of the students. In this method there is ample space for interaction among the teacher and the students. For the success of this method, it is important that the students be given freedom of expression. All students should be encouraged to express their views but there should be control over the situation by the teacher. The teacher also suggests them various reference books, text books and other books. It helps the students to prepare on the topic for discussion.

Types of Discussion

There may be four types of discussion or interactions.

- Teacher – Learner Interaction (TLI)
- Learner – Learner Interaction (LLI)
- Teacher – Material Interaction (TMI)
- Learner – Material Interaction (LMI)

When teacher is discussing, TLI may be initiated. When students are discussing in small groups, like tutorials, LLI may be initiated. When teacher is discussing with demonstration, he is using some teaching aids (material), he can use TMI along with TLI for more effective teaching. When students are doing some experiments in small groups, LMI will be of better use along with LLI and TLI.

Suggestions for Improvement of Discussion Method

The teacher should keep in view the following points while using this method:

- The topics for discussion should be chosen very carefully. It should be of common interest of students – neither very simple nor very technical.
- It should involve some thinking and interpretation on the part of students.
- Teacher should see that every one participates in the discussion. Whole essence of discussion is "Thinking together."
- Teacher should see that the discussion is not dominated by one or two students.
- Teacher should be very careful that the discussion remains a discussion and it does not change into a debate.
- No student should be allowed to put more than one question or answer a question at a time during discussion to avoid irrelevant discussions.
- The teacher should talk to bare minimum and also should not allow any one student to talk much during discussion.
- Teacher should see that the discussion is not stretched away from the main topic.
- Teacher should keep a check on answers of the students and should not allow a student to go beyond the scope of a topic under discussion.
- Teacher has to maintain discipline during discussion.
- Healthy traditions of group discussion should be formed. The arguments or viewpoints of all the students are given due hearing and not ridiculed.
- Any controversial point should be settled by the teacher at the proper time. The points left by a particular group should be supplemented.

3. Problem Solving Method

According to Risk, "Problem-solving may be defined as planned attack upon a difficulty or perplexity for the purpose of finding a satisfactory solution." Risk further elaborates that problem solving teaching procedure is a process of raising a problem in the minds of students in such a way as to stimulate purposeful, reflective thinking in arriving at a National solution.

According to Ross, "Problem-solving method is an educational device whereby the teacher and the pupils attempt in a conscious, planned, purposeful manner to arrive at an explanation or solution to some educationally significant difficulty."

According to Yokam, Gerald and Simpson, "Problem-solving method is a method in which a person uses his ability to solve the problems which confront him, enables a man to exercise control over his activities and his environment. Without it he is at the mercy of nature and cannot make intelligent social progress."

It is obvious that learning environmental education is more than just accumulating knowledge about environment. The methods of discovery learning involve the students in exploration, questioning, problem-solving, inductive reasoning, invention and labelling. However, a guided approach to discovery learning can reduce errors and time. It is important that both the teacher and the students be aware of the steps of problem-solving method.

Steps in problem-solving method

The following steps should be followed to solve a problem. Dewey has outlined this method in the following series of steps:

(i) Identifying and defining the problem,

(ii) Formulating the hypotheses,

(iii) Testing hypotheses by collecting and evaluating data,

(iv) Interpreting results,

(v) Drawing conclusions.

(i) Identifying and defining the problem

Students come across several situations where they can apply skills and knowledge to a problem that motivates them to participate in exploring. These problems can stem from daily life or from the background literature on some topic or from the place of work of the students. The students define their problem in a concise, definite and clear language. The teacher should help the student in stating the problem. The student may be asked to write down the statement of the problem in the light of above criteria and then read it in the class criticism and discussion. The most appropriate statements should be accepted.

(ii) Formulating the hypotheses

The student should focus on hypothesising the relationship between two or more variables or difference between two treatments. A review of literature would give students more content information; various possible causes of the problem may be listed. These possible causes are hypotheses or "educated guesses." Next the students are asked to outline a laboratory procedure to test out their proposed solution.

(iii) Testing hypotheses by collecting and evaluating data

Students are permitted to enter the laboratory to conduct their tests and note down observations. The teacher's job at this juncture is to ensure that the students work carefully and collect accurate data.

(iv) Interpreting results

All inferences bearing on the data at hand must be considered tentatively. This phase of problem-solving demands an unusual amount of guidance from the teacher. Interpretation of data should be based on proper use of techniques and charts; graphs; tables can be used to record the data. At this stage, students can become careless in their work and it is an opportunity to develop skills in constructing tables and graphs.

(v) Drawing conclusions

The students are asked to determine if their results substantiate the expected solution. Conclusions drawn on the basis of data should be accurately reported after proper interpretation. Findings should be reported concisely, and recommendations for further work should be mentioned. The students should be able to make generalisations and apply it to their daily life.

Factors influencing problem-solving

Ausubel identified several factors which influence problem-solving. Some of these are:

- Problem-solvers focus more on the problem on hand then other aspects.
- They are able to relate additional content information with the problem they are working on.
- Problem-solvers, besides being more persistent, possess self-confidence.
- They are objective in their approach to problem-solving.

Criteria for selection of problems

The selection of a problem is very important in investigating thought process. The following criteria should be kept in mind:

- The problem should be stated in a clear and concise way; using words and terms the students are familiar with.
- The problem chosen should be neither too difficult nor too easy. If possible the teacher should select problems based on the daily experiences of the children.
- The problem should preferably be a new one, though the children should possess all the basic information needed to solve the problem.
- Every child in the class should be able to solve at least part of the problem.
- The problem should provide for:
  - Setting up hypotheses and their testing against the data.
  - Inclusion of formal solutions which may lead to generalisations.
  - For gradual development and growth of the solution.

Advantages of problem-solving method

Some of the advantages of problem-solving method are:

- Students learn to find the solution of their problems themselves.
- They develop the power of observation and argumentation.
- It helps the students to develop reflective thinking and increases their intellectual potency.
- It helps students to develop the ability to sense the relevance of variables, make intuitive guesses and define problems concisely.
- It builds a mental attitude for effective learning based on critical thinking.
- It helps students to approach future problems with confidence in their abilities to seek out the solutions, patterns and relationships.
- They are familiar with the process of the collection of data, evaluation and drawing inferences.
- They are capable to generalise.
- They learn to use old facts in new references.
- They develop a feeling of working together.
- This is based on "Learning by doing."
- This is a motivating method.
- It gives enough training to students in techniques of information processing.
- It trains the students to identify and formulate scientific problems.
- It provides the students training in the methods and skills of discovering new knowledge.

Limitations of problem-solving method

Some limitations of this method are as under:

- It is time consuming process. Consequently, the teacher may not be able to complete the syllabus.
- It can never be a full-fledged method of learning environmental education.
- It is not suitable for all students as it suits only bright and creative students.
- Majority of teachers cannot implement it successfully because of this lack of exposure to such a method.
- Not all students are problem-solvers.
- The curriculum cannot be organised according to the problems chosen.
- Reference and resource materials may be difficult to come by.
- Not all school laboratories are equipped to allow this method to be followed.
- This method requires gifted teachers trained in the scientific inquiry approach, with not only tact and patience, but also research skills.
- There is always a doubt of drawing wrong conclusions.

4. Excursion or Field Trips

"Learning by Doing" and "Learning by Living" are the two cardinal principles of teaching environmental education. 'Field Trips' are a rich source of true education. A field trip or excursion is a planned visit to a point outside the regular classroom. It may be in the school, out in the community or it could be a long trip to faraway places. Usually in field trips to places like visits to a factory, observatory, agricultural institute, poultry farms, museums etc. We often see other people doing things. As spectators we are not involved but we directly watch it and get first-hand knowledge. Therefore, field trip is an excellent bridge between the work of the classroom and the work of the outside world. The chief difference between a field trip and other educational experiences is that the students get their experiences in the field and not in the classroom. If the field trips are planned and arranged in such a way that they go beyond observation, for example of a sea beach, on a pond where they can also touch, feel and collect things, it becomes a direct experience for them. As regards to its importance it is said that "Field trips when properly conducted, satisfy two main concepts of educational theory, the motivation of the desire to learn and the actual learning."

Objectives of Field Trips

- To create interest in the students about different subjects.

- To draw conclusions from the exercises conducted in natural environment.
- To exhibit relation between theoretical and practical knowledge.
- To develop the desire among students to understand responsibility and fulfill it.
- To develop the observation power of students.
- To learn the students proper utilisation of vacation or leisure time.
- To provide first hand observation and experience.

Organisation of field trip or excursion

The following procedure is suggested for the organisation of field trip:

1. Planning for field trip.
2. Preparation of students for excursion or field trip.
3. Execution.
4. Follow-up activities.
5. Evaluation of field trip.

1. Planning for field trip

The field trip should be planned well in advance with the active co-operation of teacher and pupils in the light of its purpose. This will include the formation of the purpose of visit, little disturbance to the school time table and regular school work, obtaining permission from the owner in-charge of the place to be visited, route to be travelled, the time schedule, arrangement of transport and lodging facilities, the expenditure to be borne by the pupils, the luggage and other necessary articles to be taken along with etc.

2. Preparation of students for field trip

It is essential to brief students after arriving at the area. This should be as minimum as possible. Students should be divided into small groups appointing a group leader for each group. Activities and responsibilities should be so divided among the students as to be equally shared by all types of students without any feeling that they are slow learners or rapid learners. Students may be advised to take notes and draw diagrams, whenever they think it is necessary.

3. Execution

During the visit the teacher should act as a supervisor. Though the success of a visit depends upon a good planning and preparation yet much of it depends upon the directions of the teacher at the spot. He should see that the pupils are acting according to the instructions given.

4. Follow-up activities

Follow-up activities are very important in field trip such as writing report, discussion about what they have learnt, conservation of energy, preservation of environment, eradication of different types of pollution, classification and displaying of material, making model of a factory etc. they have seen during field trip.

5. Evaluation of field trip

The objectives and their achievement as regards to the field trip should be evaluated through discussion with the students about the field trip. The feedback given by students as regards to the success of the field trip should be counterchecked by a checklist. The students should be asked to submit a report about the field trip.

Role of teacher during field-trip

The teacher's role is very important for a successful field trip. Some of them are listed below:

- Watches students closely and gives specific help as and when needed.
- Recognises student's achievement.
- Avoids frequent interruption in student's work but occasionally if it is justified.
- Does not lecture while in field.
- Avoids loud voiced comments.
- Acts as a guide, resource person or consultant.
- Does the relevant follow-up activities of the trip.

Responsibility of students in the field trip

- The students should have complete knowledge of the objectives of the trip and other aspects of the trip beforehand.
- They should follow the instructions given to them carefully.
- They should follow the safety rules.
- They should behave in a dignified manner.
- After careful observation they should note down their problems and doubts and clarify them during discussion session.
- The field trip should be taken as mean to gain knowledge and keep jotting down important things.
- The students should keep studying after the trip also.

Precautions during field trip

- The organising teacher should gather all relevant information about the meeting place. If possible he should visit the meeting place and find out about the facilities and problems of that place. Accordingly he should make necessary arrangements and prepare instructions.

- A suitable and economical vehicle should be used. A first-aid kit should be taken along in the vehicle.
- If a road-guide is required it should be taken.
- The students should be given necessary instructions to bring torch, megaphone, tape recorder and camera etc.
- Pay proper attention to problematic students.
- The students should be given instructions as regards to their clothes, bedding, writing material etc.

Advantages of field trip

- The students obtain actual knowledge in natural surroundings.
- Field trip permits first-hand study of many things that cannot be brought into the classroom because of size and other inconvenience.
- Field trips tend to be much more meaningful and permit easier transfer of learning to solutions of real life problems.
- The students get a chance to observe, actually experience and describe.
- The students develop the quality of mutual cooperation.
- It teaches the students proper utilisation of leisure.
- It gives an opportunity to the students to perform practical independently which come under theoretical knowledge.
- Field trip awakens many interests that classroom work cannot arouse.
- They get opportunity to collect things and preserve them for the museum.
- It helps to develop a spirit of scientific enquiry and scientific attitude.

Limitations of field trip

- A whole day is required for the field trip, it is not possible to conduct it in few hours.
- It is time consuming.
- There should be enough finances for field trips.
- There can be accidents during field trips.
- Co-operation is required between teacher and students for its success.

11.12 Role of teacher in Environmental Education

Environmental education consists of curricular course that is formal and non-formal. For the first part we already have whole syllabi and other details.

For as the second part, Teacher has to play an important role. This is through co-curricular activities linked with real life situation. An indicative list is given below:

- He should correlate the topics of environmental issues while teaching his own subject matter.
- He should help individuals in providing awareness of and sensitivity to the total environment and its allied problems.
- He should create an awareness regarding renewable and non-renewable resources of environment.
- He should help his pupils to acquire basic understanding of the total environment, its associated problems and humanity's critically responsible presence and role in it.
- He should use play-way techniques to make them understand the significance of food chains and food web on ecological balance.
- He should help his students to acquire social values, strong feelings of concern for the environment and the motivation for active participation it its protection and improvement.
- He should conduct activities like drama on environmental conservation.
- He should help individuals to acquire the skills for solving environmental problems.
- He should organise field trips to zoos, national parks, polluted cities, polluted rivers, birds sanctuaries, etc.
- He should help his pupils to evaluate environmental measures and education programmes in terms of ecological, social and aesthetic factors.
- He should organise seminars and workshops on environmental issues like soil erosion or population explosion etc.
- He should help students to develop a sense of responsibility and urgency regarding environmental problems to ensure appropriate action to solve these problems.
- He should arrange lectures on topic of environmental concerns.
- He should teach the interdependence on living thing as the relationship between the needs of society and the interaction with environment.

- He should discuss environmental issues along with simple teaching activities through which pupils understand the significance of environmental resources.
- He should motivate and train to acquire and spread knowledge and skills that will help society solve interrelated environmental problems and prevent their occurrence.

12

Climate Change

12.1 Introduction

The twenty-first century in this globe has been experiencing many unprecedented natural phenomena causing great threat to human survival. The most popular threat that we are experiencing at this stage is climate change. The impact of the climate change on the earth has adverse effects on the structure and functions of ecosystems. Climate is an integral part of ecosystems and organisms have adapted to their local climate over time. Climate change has potential to alter these ecosystems and the services they provide to each other and to human society at large. The services provided by the ecosystems almost sustain half the human population worldwide.

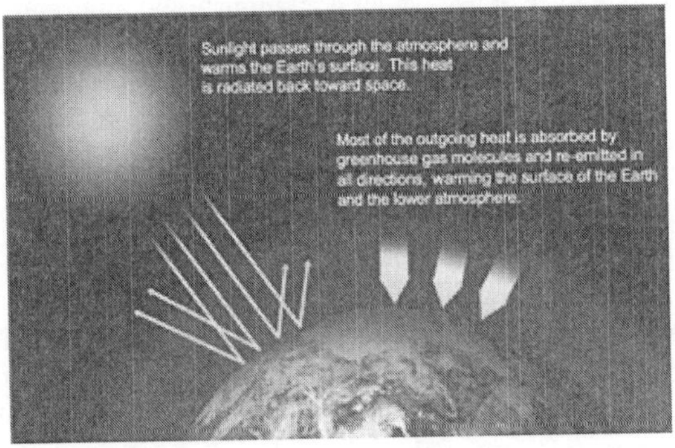

Fig. 12.1: global warming.

It is well known that climate change is taking place globally. The global changes in the temperature, rainfall, etc. are the indications of climate change. The change of weather over a period of time is known as climate. It is important to know the climate and the weather and also the differences between these two. The weather is day to day condition of temperature, rainfall, cold, etc.

while the climate is the average weather of a place over a period of time. Thus, rainfall, sunshine, wind, humidity, and temperature etc. are the factors which determine the climate of a location. While changes in the weather may occur suddenly and noticeably, changes in the climate take a long time to settle and are less obvious. Throughout the earth's history there have been changes in the climate. There have been well-marked cold and hot periods and all life forms adapted naturally to this change. Over the last 150-200 years climate change has been taking place too rapidly and certain plant and animal species have found it hard to adapt. Human activities are said to be responsible for the speed at which this change has occurred and it is now a cause of concern to scientists, policy-makers and the governments across the globe.

12.2 Climate Change: Contemporary View

It is important to examine the phenomenon of global change from a contemporary point of view. The facts are challenging. While in the developing countries, population growth is stressing environment with a consequent deterioration in the capacity to enhance or even sustain a desirable quality of life; in the developed countries, it is economic growth that degrades environmental quality thereby stressing environmental carrying capacity. In both instances, these stresses are beginning to affect the "global commons" of air and water, with consequences that adversely affect both developing and developed countries. Thus, in the industrialised nations when economic production is high, the flow of energy and materials through the manufacturing process had leaks and residues which contaminate the environment. In the developing countries where economic production is relatively low, the stock of environmental resources is being eroded to meet the needs of a rapidly growing population.

A very strange situation has arisen where developing countries are of the opinion that developed countries should own up the responsibility of environment damage leading to climate change; the developed countries feel the developing countries should bear the responsibility. The global climate change is global in impact, not in sources. This is a problem that is absolutely impossible for either a single nation or a single area to resolve. It is unreasonable to blame and expect only a few nations and regions to take up the responsibility for wroughting the change and then finding means of restraining and wiping it from the face of the earth, as is expected by the developing world from the developed world and vice-versa. These climate changes in the wake of already depleting world resources will naturally lead to magnifying the already prevailing problems. In fact, environmental tensions are said to be both a cause and consequence of political tensions and international disputes.

12.3 Climate Change: Causes Thereof

As we know that climate change is a significant and lasting change in the statistical distribution of weather patterns over periods ranging from decades to millions of years. It may be a change in average weather conditions or the distribution of events around that average (e.g., more or fewer extreme weather events). Climate change may be limited to a specific region or may occur across the whole earth. The earth's climate is dynamic and always changing through a natural cycle. What the world is more worried about is that the changes that are occurring today have been speeded up because of man's activities. These changes are being studied by scientists all over the world, who are finding evidence from tree rings, pollen samples, ice cores, and sea sediments. The causes of climate change can be divided into two categories - natural causes and man induced causes.

Natural causes

There are a number of natural factors responsible for climate change. Some of the more prominent ones are continental drift, volcanoes, the earth's tilt, ocean currents, and comets and meteorites. Let's look at them in a little detail.

Continental drift

The climate has been affected by continental drift over decades. The drift of continents is a continuing phenomenon. The drift continues even today. The Himalayan range is rising by about one millimeter every year because the Indian landmass is moving towards the Asian landmass, slowly but steadily. Continents that we are familiar with today were formed when the landmass began gradually drifting apart, millions of years back. This drift also had an impact on the climate because it changed the physical features of the landmass, their position and the position of water bodies. The separation of the landmasses changed the flow of ocean currents and winds, which affected the climate.

Volcanoes

When a volcano erupts it throws out large volumes of sulphur dioxide (SO_2), water vapour, dust, and ash into the atmosphere leading to cooling for a few years. Although the volcanic activity lasts only a few days, yet the large volumes of gases and ash influence climatic patterns for years. Millions of tons of sulphur dioxide gas reach the upper levels of the atmosphere (called the stratosphere) from a major eruption. The gases and dust particles partially block the incoming rays of the sun, leading to cooling. Sulphur dioxide combines with water to form tiny droplets of sulphuric acid. These droplets are so small that many of them can stay aloft for several years.

They are efficient reflectors of sunlight, and screen the ground from some of the energy that it would ordinarily receive from the sun. Winds in the upper levels of the atmosphere, called the stratosphere, carry the aerosols rapidly around the globe causing cooling in atmosphere. The volcanic eruptions at Mount Pinatoba, in the Philippine islands in April 1991 and Tambora in Indonesia in 1815 are the striking example.

Tilting of earth

The earth makes one full orbit around the sun each year. It is tilted at an angle of 23.5 degree to the perpendicular plane of its orbital path. For half of the year when it is summer, the northern hemisphere tilts towards the sun. In the other half when it is winter, the earth is tilted away from the sun. If there was no tilt we would not have experienced seasons. Changes in the tilt of the earth can affect the severity of the seasons - more tilt means warmer summers and colder winters; less tilt means cooler summers and milder winters.

The earth's orbit is somewhat elliptical, which means that the distance between the earth and the Sun varies over the course of a year. We usually think of the earth's axis as being fixed, after all, it always seems to point toward Polaris (also known as the Pole Star and the North Star). Actually, it is not quite constant: the axis does move, at the rate of a little more than a half-degree each century. So Polaris has not always been, and will not always be, the star pointing to the North. When the pyramids were built, around 2500 BC, the pole was near the star Thuban (Alpha Draconis). This gradual change in the direction of the earth's axis, called precession is responsible for changes in the climate.

Ocean currents

The oceans are a major component of the climatic system. They cover about 71 per cent of the earth and absorb about twice as much of the sun's radiation as the atmosphere or the landsurface. Ocean currents move vast amount of heat across the planet - roughly the same amount as the atmosphere does. But the oceans are surrounded by land masses, so heat transport through the water is through channels. Winds push horizontally against the sea surface and drive ocean current patterns. Certain parts of the world are influenced by ocean currents more than others. The coast of Peru and other adjoining regions are directly influenced by the Humboldt Current that flows along the coastline of Peru. The El Niño event in the Pacific Ocean can affect climatic conditions all over the world. Another region that is strongly influenced by ocean currents is the North Atlantic. Ocean currents have been known to change direction or slow down. Much of the heat that escapes from the oceans are in the form of water vapour also contributes to the formation of clouds, which shade the surface and have a net cooling effect. These phenomena can have an impact on the climate, as is believed to have happened at the end of the last Ice Age, about 14,000 years ago.

Man induced causes

The man-made causes include agricultural practices, deforestation, increase in global temperature, green house effect, etc as detailed below:

Agriculture

According to the Intergovernmental Panel on Climate Change, the three main causes of the increase in greenhouse gases observed over the past 250 years have been fossil fuels, land use, and agriculture. Agriculture has been shown to produce significant effects on climate change, primarily through the production and release of greenhouse gases such as carbon dioxide, methane, and nitrous oxide. Agriculture alters the earth's land cover, which can change its ability to absorb or reflect heat and light, contributing to climate change. Land use change such as deforestation and desertification, together with use of fossil fuels, are the major anthropogenic sources of carbon dioxide.

Deforestation

Forests form part of a delicate ecosystem which has evolved over millions of years. These forests help to absorb almost 20 per cent of man-made CO_2 emissions and thus play a major role to control climate. Cutting down forests faster than they can be replaced has a devastating effect on the carbon emission cycle producing an extra 17 per cent of greenhouse gases. Deforestation by means of cutting down and burning these tropical rainforests usually pave the way for agriculture and industry which often produce even more CO_2. It is proved beyond doubt that climate change and forests are interlinked. The increased destruction of the rainforest forming a precious cooling band around the earth's equator is recognised as one of the main causes of climate change. Forests trap and store carbon dioxide and play a major role in mitigating climate change.

Forests reduce greenhouse gas emissions to combat global warming. 20 per cent of global greenhouse gas emissions result from deforestation and degradation of forest, more than all the world's cars, trucks, ships and planes combined. Fossil fuels release carbon dioxide into the atmosphere contributing to global warming and climate change. Forest alleviates this change by converting carbon dioxide to carbon during photosynthesis.

Global temperatures

The most recent assessment report from the Intergovernmental Panel on Climate Change (IPCC) says that the earth's average temperature has risen by 0.74 degrees in the period from 1906 to 2005, and that the average temperature will continue to rise. The greenhouse effect is a natural mechanism that retains

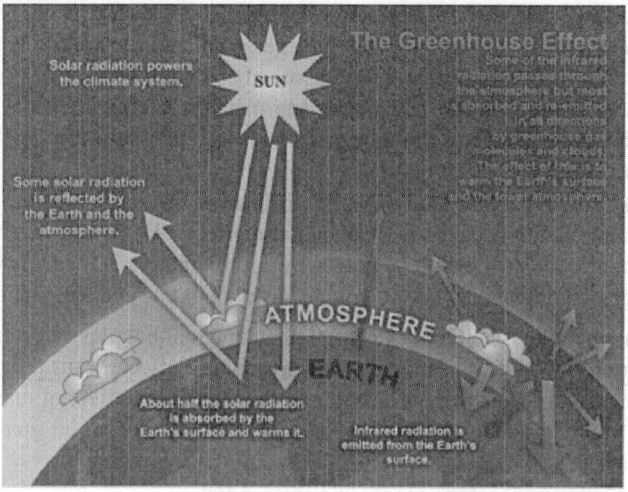

Fig. 12.2: The Greenhouse Effect.

the heat emitted from the earth's surface. The earth's average temperature is at the moment around 14 degrees Celsius (57 degrees Fahrenheit). If the natural greenhouse effect did not exist, the average temperature would be around minus 19 degrees Celsius (minus 2 degrees Fahrenheit).

The greenhouse effect is caused by a range of different gases in the earth's atmosphere. Water vapour makes the most significant contribution to the greenhouse effect, followed by CO_2. At present the concentration of CO_2 in the atmosphere is about 385 ppm (parts per million). Before industrialisation it was about 280 ppm. Analyses of air contained in ice from the Antarctic ice cap show that there is far more CO2 in the air today than at any time in the last 6,50,000 years. The consequence is that the greenhouse effect is becoming stronger, and therefore the earth is becoming warmer. The warming is stronger over land areas than over the sea, and accordingly it is strongest in the northern hemisphere. At the same time occurrences of heat waves and violent downpours have also increased, the oceans have risen, and the ice at the world's poles and on its mountains has begun to melt. All of these effects are predictable in the event of global warming. The IPCC's most recent assessment report concludes that the average temperature will continue to rise. The extent and the duration of this rise, and the severity of its consequences will depend on how quickly and how effectively emissions of greenhouse gases can be restricted and, over time, reduced.

12.4 Green House Effect

Life on earth depends on energy from the sun. About 30 per cent of the sunlight that beams toward earth is deflected by the outer atmosphere and scattered back into space. The rest reaches the planet's surface and is reflected upward again as a type of slow-moving energy called infrared radiation. The heat caused by infrared radiation is absorbed by "greenhouse gases" such as water vapour, carbon dioxide, ozone and methane, which slows its escape from the atmosphere. Although greenhouse gases make up only about one per cent of the earth's atmosphere, they regulate our climate by trapping heat and holding it in a kind of warm-air blanket that surrounds the planet. This phenomenon is called the "greenhouse effect." Without it, the average temperature on earth would be colder by approximately 30 degrees Celsius (54 degrees Fahrenheit), far too cold to sustain our current ecosystem.

The greenhouse effect is a natural phenomenon that plays a central role in determining the earth's climate. The greenhouse effect means progressive warming up of the earth's surface due to the blanketing effect of man-made carbon dioxide in the atmosphere. This mechanism keeps the greenhouse warmer from the outside environment. In a nutshell, greenhouse is the body which allows the shortwave incoming solar radiation to come in but does not allow the long wave outgoing terrestrial infrared radiation to escape. Carbon dioxide and water vapour act as a greenhouse agent. They allow visible light of the sun to reach the surface of the earth but absorb and reflect back the long wave outgoing terrestrial radiation mainly infrared rays and thus held in keeping the earth's surface warmer.

The green house effect is thus caused by gases such as carbon dioxide, water vapour, trace amounts of ozone, methane, nitrous oxide, chlorofluorocarbons and other gases that trap infrared waves that radiates from the earth's surface. Collectively these gases are known as green house. They allow light, infrared radiation and some ultraviolet radiation from the sun to pass through the troposphere. Earth's surface absorbs much of this solar energy and degrades it to longer wave, infrared radiation that is heat which then rises into the troposphere. Some of this heat escapes into space, some is absorbed by molecules of greenhouse gases, warming the air and some radiated back toward earth's surface. This natural trapping of heat in the troposphere is called the green house effect.

12.5 Green House Gases

The primary heat trapping gas in the atmosphere is water vapour. However, its concentration in the atmosphere averages 1-5 per cent and the inputs of water vapour from human activities have little effect on the green house effects. By contrast, because of the concentration of carbon dioxide in the atmosphere is so small (0.036 per cent) the fairly large input of CO_2 from human activities can significantly affect the amount of heat trapped in the atmosphere. As a result of human activity such as the consumption of fossil fuels, the carbon dioxide level has risen more than 20 per cent in the past century. Fossil fuel consumption alone is responsible for the annual release of five billion metric tons of carbon into the air, or roughly one metric ton for each person on earth. Thus, principal green house gases are carbon dioxide CO_2, Methane CH_4, Nitrous Oxide N_2O and Halocarbons. The gases differ in terms of atmospheric concentrations rates of increase of concentration, warming potential per molecule atmospheric lifetime. Their relative contributions to total potential warming depend on the time horizon considered and the emissions scenarios used. CO_2 is the major contributor over a 100 year horizon, it contributes 70 per cent + of the total greenhouse gas radioactive forcing.

12.6 Major Sources of Green House Gases

As we have learnt in the preceding paragraph, the major sources of green house gases are Carbon dioxide, Methane, Nitrous oxide and Halo-carbons. Let us discuss them in little details.

Carbon Dioxide

The most significant greenhouse gas is carbon dioxide which is released to the atmosphere by burning of fossil fuels for different purposes in various ways e.g. electric power stations, numerous factories, transport, deforestation and burning of fire woods. These electric power stations are the most significant and widespread major sources of man-induced carbon dioxide. Numerous factories spread all over the world burn immense quantity of coal, mineral oil and natural gas and spew huge amount of carbon dioxide together with other undesirable gases through their chimneys into the atmosphere. The third major source is the transport sector which includes various types of vehicles run on coal and petroleum. For example, railways are large consumers of coal mainly in the developing countries. Similarly, large fleets of automobiles (trucks, buses, cars and two wheelers – motor cycles, scooters etc.), agricultural implements like tractors, combines etc. and aircrafts all over the world burn immense quantity of diesel and petroleum each year. The fourth major source of the production of carbon dioxide is deforestation and burning of fire woods. The people are acquainted with the first three major sources of carbon dioxide as they directly spew carbon dioxide but the mechanisms of the release of carbon dioxide through deforestation are little understood by common man.

The climatic changes caused by global greenhouse effect due to higher concentration of carbon dioxide in the atmosphere are primarily related to the pattern of energy transfer and uses the world over. The concentration of carbon dioxide into the atmosphere has increased by 25 per cent since the industrial revolution. Detailed measurements since 1958 showed an increase of about 35 parts per million by volume. Both land clearing and fossil fuel combustion has contributed to this rise, but the fossil fuel has dominated in recent years. Carbon-dioxide is increasing at a rate of about 0.4 per cent per year and is responsible for about half of the current increases in the greenhouse effect.

Methane

The concentration of methane has more than doubled during the last four centuries. There is considerable uncertainty about the total emissions from specific sources of methane, but the observed increase is probably due to increases in a number of sources, as well as changes in tropospheric chemistry. Agricultural sources, particularly rice cultivation and animal husbandry have probably been the most significant contributors to historical increase in concentrations. But there is the potential for rapid growth in emissions from landfills, coal seams, permafrost, natural gas exploration and pipeline leakage and biomass burning associated with forest clearings in the future. Methane is increasing at a rate of one per cent per year and is responsible for about 20 per cent of the current increases in the greenhouse effect.

Nitrous Oxide

The concentration of nitrous oxide has increased by 510 per cent since pre-industrial times. The cause of this increase is highly uncertain, but it has been understood that the use of nitrogenous fertiliser, land clearing, biomass burning and fossil fuel combustion have all contributed. Nitrous oxide is over 200 times more powerful, on a per molecule basis, than carbon-dioxide as a greenhouse gas and can also contribute to stratospheric ozone depletion. Nitrous oxide is currently increasing at a rate of 0.25 per cent per year, which represents and in a balance between sources and sinks of about 30 per cent. Nitrous oxide is responsible of about six per cent of the current increases in the greenhouse effect.

Chlorofluorocarbons (CFCs)

CFCs were introduced into the atmosphere for the first time during the twentieth century. The most common species are CFC-12 and CFC-11 which had atmospheric concentrations in 1985 of 380 and 220 parts per trillion by volume respectively. These concentrations are although tiny compared to carbon dioxide, these compounds are about 30,000 times more powerful than carbon dioxide, on a per molecule basis, as a greenhouse gas. These have been increasing very rapidly at the rate of five per cent per year from 1978 to 1983. Of major concern because of their potential to deplete stratospheric-zone, the CFCs also represent about 15 per cent of the current increases in the greenhouse effect.

12.7 Green House Effect and Climate Change

The carbon dioxide is a natural constituent of the earth's atmosphere. It is not necessarily a pollutant at least in the lower atmosphere. Its increased concentration in the atmosphere leaves adverse effects on biological communities through changes in the thermal conditions and global radiation and heat balance. The carbon dioxide is present in gaseous form in the atmosphere. The unique properties inherent in it allow the solar radiation to reach the surface of the earth. It prevents long wave terrestrial radiations (such as infrared heat radiation from the earth) from the earth surface from escaping into outer space. This mechanism results in the increase of temperature of the surface of the earth and the lower atmosphere. About 50 per cent of the total carbon dioxide produced by anthropogenic sources (combustion of fossil fuels and burning of wood) is dissolved into the oceans and fixed by the plants in their biomass whereas the remaining 50 per cent is stored in the atmosphere. Concentration of carbon dioxide in the atmosphere steadily increases. The trend of atmospheric carbon dioxide increases the greenhouse effect which raises the temperature of the earth's surface. This mechanism may be explained in simple term as given below.

The ever increasing proportion of carbon dioxide in the atmosphere through anthropogenic source changes the general composition of the atmosphere and overall heat balance. This is because carbon dioxide is more or less transparent to incoming shortwave solar radiation but it absorbs most of the outgoing long wave radiation emitted from the earth's surface. Thus, the supply of additional amount of carbon dioxide to the atmosphere every year enhances the absorption of radiation of more heat emitted from the earth's surface. This mechanism (absorption of more heat emitted from the earth's surface by the atmospheric carbon dioxide) results in the warming of the lower atmosphere. This warmed lower atmosphere again reradiates heat (counter-radiation) to the earth's surface which further warms the earth's surface. The net result of these mechanisms is the gradual increase of the temperature of the earth's surface and the lower atmosphere which causes several changes in the climatic conditions at local through regional to global levels.

The possible impacts of green house effect and climate change are discussed below:

- According to A. B. Pittock (1972), the change in the global mean temperature by a few degrees Celsius caused by greenhouse effect would greatly affect the human society and agriculture.
- It is believed by some scientists that increased temperature due to increased greenhouse effect would cause decrease in precipitation and soil moisture content in the most developed agricultural regions of the world. The plants, animals and insects may be able to adjust themselves to the changed environmental conditions caused by rise in the air temperature but the whole ecosystems may be adversely damaged.
- If the concentration of carbon dioxide goes on increasing the oceans would be required to absorb more and more carbon dioxide. More absorption and decomposition of carbon dioxide in the oceans

would raise their normal level of acidity. Increased oceanic acidity would decrease biological productivity of the marine ecosystem and the decreased plant cover in the oceanic areas would change the Albedo (more clouds would reflect more solar radiation back to outer space) of the ocean surface.

- The increased surface temperature would cause melting of continental and mountain glaciers and polar ice caps. The resultant melt-water would raise sea-level and thus would cause flooding of coastal areas of lowland countries. According to an estimate on metre rise in sea level may be possible by 2050 A.D. due to warming impact of greenhouse effect. This rise in sea level may cause flooding of 15 per cent of the agricultural lands of UAR bordering the Mediterranean Sea and thus about eight million people would be displaced. Similarly, a major portion of the lower deltaic region of Bangladesh would be submerged under sea water and consequently about eight to ten million people would lose their agricultural lands and homes.
- It may be possible that the concentration of carbon dioxide may increase to such an extent that the total atmospheric pressure would be increased. This increase in the atmospheric pressure would broaden the absorption bands and increase the capacity of the atmosphere to the outgoing long wave terrestrial radiation which would in turn increase the surface temperature to such an extent that all the atmospheric processes which are now responsible for the existence and sustenance of all life in the biosphere would come to grinding half and everything, then, would be over. But this is an extreme situation which is unlikely to occur and this should not occur.
- The impact of greenhouse gases mainly carbon dioxide is also expected to influence rather intensify the depletion of ozone layer which would cause further rise in the temperature of the earth's surface.
- It is also argued by some scientists mainly botanists that the increased concentration of carbon dioxide in the atmosphere would increase plant production. According to an estimate an increase of carbon dioxide between 300 to 600 ppm would increase vegetative productivity by about 30 per cent. It may be pointed out that this positive response of the increased carbon dioxide on the vegetative productivity is only theoretically deduced conclusion because increase in temperature in believed to have serious adverse effects on vegetation communities mainly agricultural crops.

12.8 Remedial Measures

The first and the foremost step to arrest the problem of ever increasing greenhouse effect and expected rise in the global mean temperature is to prevent or to reduce the release of additional carbon dioxide from the combustion of fossil fuels and through deforestation. The following measures may be suggested to decrease the increasing greenhouse effect.

- ***Drastic cut in the consumption of fossil fuels***: There should be drastic cut in the consumption of fossil fuels mainly in the developed and highly industrialised countries. The Toronto World Conference held at Toronto, Canada, in June, 1988 called for 20 per cent voluntary reduction in the emissions of carbon dioxide by the year 2005 so that the greenhouse effect may be minimised or at lease may be stabilised and the possible climatic changes at regional global levels may be prevented.
- ***Alternative sources of energy:*** The scientists must discover and develop alternative sources of energy and power and improved better technologies. For example, more serious researchers are required to assess and evaluate the potentials of methanol, derived from methane, as the major source of fuel to be used in the transport sector. Thus, methanol may be expected to be a substitute for petroleum.
- ***Efficient technologies:*** More advanced and efficient technologies should be developed so that maximum energy may be derived from the use of existing fossil fuels and emissions of carbon dioxide may be minimised. The internal combustion energies should be improved and maintained properly so that maximum benefits may be derived from minimum use of petroleum and emissions of carbon dioxide, nitrous oxides etc. may be reduced to maximum degree.
- ***Solar energy:*** Solar energy may be developed as alternative to the conventional fossil fuel energy at least in those tropical and subtropical countries where sunlight is available during most period of the year.
- ***Large scale afforestation:*** Afforestation and reforestation on a large scale will certainly reduce the greenhouse effect. It is a well known fact that the forests are big natural 'gink' of carbon dioxide. Greenery of the landscape is the only immediate solution of ever increasing greenhouse effect caused by ever increasing concentration of carbon dioxide in the atmosphere.

12.9 Carbon Trading and Clean Energy Concept

It includes carbon footprints, carbon sequestration, carbon credit and audit.

12.9.1 Carbon Footprints

A carbon footprint is historically defined as "the total sets of greenhouse gas emissions caused by an organisation, event, product or person." The total carbon footprint cannot be calculated because of the large amount of data required and the fact that carbon dioxide can be produced by natural occurrences. It is for this reason that Wright, Kemp, and Williams, writing in the journal Carbon Management, have suggested a more practicable definition: A measure of the total amount of carbon dioxide (CO_2) and methane (CH_4) emissions of a defined population, system or activity, considering all relevant sources, sinks and storage within the spatial and temporal boundary of the population, system or activity of interest. Calculated as carbon dioxide equivalent (CO_2e) using the relevant 100-year global warming potential (GWP100).

Greenhouse gases (GHGs) can be emitted through transport, land clearance, and the production and consumption of food, fuels, manufactured goods, materials, wood, roads, buildings, and services. For simplicity of reporting, it is often expressed in terms of the amount of carbon dioxide, or its equivalent of other GHGs, emitted. Most of the carbon footprint emissions for the average US household come from "indirect" sources, i.e. fuel burned to produce goods far away from the final consumer. These are distinguished from emissions which come from burning fuel directly in one's car or stove, commonly referred to as "direct" sources of the consumer's carbon footprint.

The concept name of the carbon footprint originates from ecological footprint, discussion, which was developed by Rees and Wackernagel in the 1990s which estimates the number of "earths" that would theoretically be required if everyone on the planet consumed resources at the same level as the person calculating their ecological footprint. However, given that ecological footprints are a measure of failure, Anindita Mitra (CREA, Seattle) chose the more easily calculated "carbon footprint" to easily measure use of carbon, as an indicator of unsustainable energy use. In 2007, carbon footprints were used as a measure of carbon emissions to develop the energy plan for City of Lynnwood, Washington. Carbon footprints are much more specific than ecological footprints since they measure direct emissions of gases that cause climate change into the atmosphere.

12.9.2 Measuring carbon footprints

An individual's, nation's or organisation's carbon footprint can be measured by undertaking a GHG emissions assessment or other calculative activities denoted as carbon accounting. Once the size of a carbon footprint is known, a strategy can be devised to reduce it, e.g. by technological developments, better process and product management, changed Green Public or Private Procurement (GPP), carbon capture, consumption strategies, carbon offsetting and others. Several free online carbon footprint calculators exist, including a few supported by publicly available peer-reviewed data and calculations including the University of California, Berkeley's Cool Climate Network research consortium and Carbon Story. These websites ask you to answer more or less detailed questions about your diet, transportation choices, home size, shopping and recreational activities, usage of electricity, heating, and heavy appliances such as dryers and refrigerators, and so on. The website then estimates your carbon footprint based on your answers to these questions. A systematic literature review was conducted to objectively determine the best way to calculate individual/household carbon footprints. This review identified 13 calculation principles and subsequently used the same principles to evaluate the 15 most popular online carbon footprint calculators. The research documented significant shortcomings of a majority of the calculators.

The mitigation of carbon footprints through the development of alternative projects, such as solar or wind energy or reforestation, represents one way of reducing a carbon footprint and is often known as carbon offsetting. The main influences on carbon footprints include population, economic output, and energy and carbon intensity of the economy. These factors are the main targets of individuals and businesses in order to decrease carbon footprints. Scholars suggest the most effective way to decrease a carbon footprint is to either decrease the amount of energy needed for production or to decrease the dependence on carbon emitting fuels.

12.9.3 Average carbon emissions per person by country

The Average Carbon Footprint in the United States vs. World: The average US household carbon footprint is about 50 tons CO_2e per year. The single largest source of emissions for the typical household is from driving (gasoline use). Transportation as a whole (driving, flying and small amount from public transit) is the largest overall category, followed by housing (electricity, natural gas, waste, construction) then food (mostly from red meat, dairy and seafood products, but also includes emissions from all other food), then goods followed lastly by services. The carbon footprint of US households is about five times greater than the global average, which is approximately 10 tons CO_2e per household per year. For most US households, the single most important action to reduce their carbon footprint is driving less or switching to a more efficient vehicle.

12.9.4 Direct carbon emissions: The Carbon footprint of energy

The following figures compares, from peer-reviewed studies of full life cycle emissions and from various other studies, the carbon footprint of various forms of energy generation: nuclear, hydro, coal, gas, solar cell, peat and wind generation technology.

Flight: Some representative figures for CO_2 emissions are provided by LIPASTO's survey of average direct emissions (not accounting for high-altitude radiative effects) of airliners expressed as CO_2 and CO_2 equivalent per passenger kilometre:

- Domestic, short distance, less than 463 km (288 mi): 257 g/km CO_2 or 259 g/km (14.7 oz/mile) CO_2e
- Long distance flights: 113 g/km CO_2 or 114 g/km (6.5 oz/mile) CO_2e

Road: Some representative figures for CO_2 equivalent per passenger kilometre for road travel are provided by the Finnish survey LIPASTO (for 2011):

- Average for car travel: 98 g/km CO_2e
- Average for urban bus travel: 58 g/km CO_2e
- Average for highway coach travel: 49 g/km CO_2e

Rail: In 2005, the US company Amtrak's carbon dioxide equivalent emissions per passenger kilometre were 0.116 kg, about twice as high as the UK rail average (where much more of the system is electrified), and about eight times a Finnish electric intercity train.

Sea: Average carbon dioxide emissions by ferries per passenger-kilometre seem to be 0.12 kg (4.2 oz). However, 18-knot ferries between Finland and Sweden produce 0.221 kg (7.8 oz) of CO_2, with total emissions equalling a CO_2 equivalent of 0.223 kg (7.9 oz), while 24–27-knot ferries between Finland and Estonia produce 0.396 kg (14.0 oz) of CO_2 with total emissions equalling a CO_2 equivalent of 0.4 kg (14 oz).

12.9.5 Indirect carbon emissions: the carbon footprints of products

Several organisations offer footprint calculators for public and corporate use, and several organisations have calculated carbon footprints of products. The US Environmental Protection Agency has addressed paper, plastic (candy wrappers), glass, cans, computers, carpet and tires. Australia has addressed lumber and other building materials. Academics in Australia, Korea and the US have addressed paved roads. Companies, non-profits and academics have addressed mailing letters and packages. Carnegie Mellon University has estimated the CO_2 footprints of 46 large sectors of the economy in each of eight countries. Carnegie Mellon, Sweden and the Carbon Trust have addressed foods at home and in restaurants.

The Carbon Trust has worked with UK manufacturers on foods, shirts and detergents, introducing a CO_2 label in March 2007. The label is intended to comply with a new British Publicly Available Specification (i.e. not a standard), PAS 2050, and is being actively piloted by The Carbon Trust and various industrial partners. As of August 2012, The Carbon Trust state they have measured 27,000 certifiable product carbon footprints.

Evaluating the package of some products is the key to figuring out the carbon footprint. The key way to determine a carbon footprint is to look at the materials used to make the item. For example, a juice carton is made of an aseptic carton, a beer can is made of aluminum, and some water bottles either made of glass or plastic. The larger the size, the larger the footprint will be.

Food: In a 2014 study by Scarborough *et. al.*, the real-life diets of British people were surveyed and their greenhouse gas footprints estimated. Average greenhouse-gas emissions per day (in kilograms of carbon dioxide equivalent) were:

- 7.19 for high meat-eaters
- 5.63 for medium meat-eaters
- 4.67 for low meat-eaters
- 3.91 for fish-eaters
- 3.81 for vegetarians
- 2.89 for vegans

Textiles: The precise carbon footprint of different textiles varies considerably according to a wide range of factors. However, studies of textile production in Europe suggest the following carbon dioxide equivalent emissions footprints per kilo of textile at the point of purchase by a consumer:

- Cotton: 7
- Nylon: 5.43
- PET (e.g. synthetic fleece): 5.55
- Wool: 5.48

Accounting for durability and energy required washing and dry textile products, synthetic fabrics generally have a substantially lower carbon footprint than natural ones.

Materials: The carbon footprint of materials (also known as embodied carbon) varies widely. The carbon footprint of many common materials can be found in the Inventory of Carbon and Energy database.

Cement: Cement production and carbon footprint resulting from soil sealing was 8.0 Mg $person^{-1}$ of total per capita CO_2 emissions (Italy, year 2003); the balance between C loss due to soil sealing and C stocked in man-made infrastructures resulted in a net loss to the atmosphere, -0.6 Mg C ha^{-1} y^{-1}.

12.9.6 Schemes to reduce carbon emissions

Carbon dioxide emissions into the atmosphere, and the emissions of other GHGs, are often associated with the burning of fossil fuels, like natural gas, crude oil and coal. While this is harmful to the environment, carbon offsets can be purchased in an attempt to make up for these harmful effects.

The Kyoto Protocol defines legally binding targets and timetables for cutting the GHG emissions of industrialised countries that ratified the Kyoto Protocol. Accordingly, from an economic or market perspective, one has to distinguish between a mandatory market and a voluntary market. Typical for both markets is the trade with emission certificates:

- Certified Emission Reduction (CER)
- Emission Reduction Unit (ERU)
- Verified Emission Reduction (VER)

12.9.7 Mandatory market mechanisms

To reach the goals defined in the Kyoto Protocol, with the least economical costs, the following flexible mechanisms were introduced for the mandatory market:

- Clean Development Mechanism (CDM)
- Joint Implementation (JI)
- Emissions Trading

The CDM and JI mechanisms requirements for projects which create a supply of emission reduction instruments, while Emissions Trading allows those instruments to be sold on international markets.

- Projects which are compliant with the requirements of the CDM mechanism generate Certified Emissions Reductions (CERs).
- Projects which are compliant with the requirements of the JI mechanism generate Emission Reduction Units (ERUs).

The CERs and ERUs can then be sold through Emissions Trading. The demand for the CERs and ERUs being traded is driven by:

- Shortfalls in national emission reduction obligations under the Kyoto Protocol.
- Shortfalls amongst entities obligated under local emissions reduction schemes.

Nations which have failed to deliver their Kyoto emissions reductions obligations can enter Emissions Trading to purchase CERS and ERUs to cover their treaty shortfalls. Nations and groups of nations can also create local emission reduction schemes which place mandatory carbon dioxide emission targets on entities within their national boundaries. If the rules of a scheme allow, the obligated entities may be able to cover all or some of any reduction shortfalls by purchasing CERs and ERUs through Emissions Trading. While local emissions reduction schemes have no status under the Kyoto Protocol itself, they play a prominent role in creating the demand for CERs and ERUs, stimulating Emissions Trading and setting a market price for emissions. A well-known mandatory local emission trading scheme is the EU Emissions Trading Scheme (EU ETS).

New changes are being made to the trading schemes. The EU Emissions Trading Scheme is set to make some new changes within the next year. The new changes will target the emissions produced by flight travel in and out of the European Union. Other nations are scheduled to start participating in Emissions Trading Schemes within the next few years. These nations include China, India and the United States:

12.9.8 Voluntary Market Mechanisms

In contrast to the strict rules set out for the mandatory market, the voluntary market provides companies with different options to acquire emissions reductions. A solution, comparable with those developed for the mandatory market, has been developed for the voluntary market, the Verified Emission Reductions (VER). This measure has the great advantage that the projects/activities are managed according to the quality standards set out for CDM/JI projects but the certificates provided are not registered by the governments of the host countries or the Executive Board of the UNO. As such, high quality VERs can be acquired at lower costs for the same project quality. However, at present VERs cannot be used in the mandatory market.

The voluntary market in North America is divided between members of the Chicago Climate Exchange and the Over The Counter (OTC) market. The Chicago Climate Exchange is a voluntary yet legally binding cap-and-trade emission scheme whereby members commit to the capped emission reductions and must purchase allowances from other members or offset excess emissions. The OTC market does not involve a legally binding scheme and a wide array of buyers from the public and private spheres, as well as special events that want to go carbon neutral. Being carbon neutral refers to achieving net zero carbon emissions by balancing a measured amount of carbon released with an equivalent amount sequestered or offset, or buying enough carbon credits to make up the difference.

There are project developers, wholesalers, brokers, and retailers, as well as carbon funds, in the voluntary market. Some businesses and non-profits in the voluntary market encompass more than just one of the activities listed above. A report by Ecosystem Marketplace shows that carbon offset prices increase as it moves along the supply chain—from project developer to retailer.

While some mandatory emission reduction schemes exclude forest projects, these projects flourish in the voluntary markets. A major criticism concerns the imprecise nature of GHG sequestration quantification methodologies for forestry projects. However, others note the community co-benefits that forestry projects foster. Project types in the voluntary market range from avoided deforestation, afforestation/reforestation, industrial gas sequestration, increased energy efficiency, fuel switching, methane capture from coal plants and livestock, and even renewable energy. Renewable Energy Certificates (RECs) sold on the voluntary market are quite controversial due to additional concerns. Industrial Gas projects receive criticism because such projects only apply to large industrial plants that already have high fixed costs. Siphoning off industrial gas for sequestration is considered picking the low hanging fruit; which is why credits generated from industrial gas projects are the cheapest in the voluntary market. The size and activity of the voluntary carbon market is difficult to measure. The most comprehensive report on the voluntary carbon markets to date was released by Ecosystem Marketplace and New Carbon Finance in July 2007. AEON of Japan is firstly approved by Japanese authority to indicate carbon footprint on three private brand goods in October 2009.

12.9.9 Ways to reduce carbon footprint

The most common way to reduce the carbon footprint of humans is to Reduce, Reuse, Recycle, Refuse. In manufacturing this can be done by recycling the packing materials, by selling the obsolete inventory of one industry to the industry that is looking to buy unused items at lesser price to become competitive. Nothing should be disposed off into the soil; all the ferrous materials which are prone to degrade or oxidise with time should be sold as early as possible at reduced price.

This can also be done by using reusable items such as thermoses for daily coffee or plastic containers for water and other cold beverages rather than disposable ones. If that option isn't available, it is best to properly recycle the disposable items after use. When one household recycles at least half of their household waste, they can save 1.2 tons of carbon dioxide annually.

Another easy option is to drive less. By walking or biking to the destination rather than driving, not only is a person going to save money on gas, but they will be burning less fuel and releasing fewer emissions into the atmosphere. However, if walking is not an option, one can look into car-pooling or mass transportation options in their area.

Yet another option for reducing the carbon footprint of humans is to use less air conditioning and heating in the home. By adding insulation to the walls and attic of one's home, and installing weather stripping or caulking around doors and windows one can lower their heating costs more than 25 per cent. Similarly, one can very inexpensively upgrade the "insulation" (clothing) worn by residents of the home. For example, it's estimated that wearing a base layer of long underwear (top and bottom) made from a lightweight, super insulating fabric like microfleece (aka Polartec®, Capilene®) can conserve as much body heat as a full set of clothing, allowing a person to remain warm with the thermostat lowered by over 5°C. These measures all help because they reduce the amount of energy needed to heat and cool the house. One can also turn down the heat while sleeping at night or away during the day, and keep temperatures moderate at all times. Setting the thermostat just 2 degrees lower in winter and higher in summer could save about one ton of carbon dioxide each year.

Choice of diet is a major influence on a person's carbon footprint. Animal sources of protein (especially red meat), rice (typically produced in high methane-emitting paddies), foods transported long distance and/or via fuel-inefficient transport (e.g., highly perishable produce flown long distance) and heavily processed and packaged foods are among the major contributors to a high carbon diet. Scientists at the University of Chicago have estimated "that the average American diet – which derives 28 per cent of its calories from animal foods – is responsible for approximately one and a half more tonnes of greenhouse gasses – as CO_2 equivalents – per person, per year than a fully plant-based, or vegan, diet." Their calculations suggest that even replacing one-third of the animal protein in the average American's diet with plant protein (e.g., beans, grains) can reduce the diet's carbon footprint by half a tonne. Exchanging two-thirds of the animal protein with plant protein is roughly equivalent to switching from a Toyota Camry to a Prius. Finally, throwing food out not only adds its associated carbon emissions to a person or household's footprint, it adds the emissions of transporting the wasted food to the garbage dump and the emissions of food decomposition, mostly in the form of the highly potent greenhouse gas, methane. The carbon handprint movement emphasises individual forms of carbon offsetting, like using more public transportation or planting trees in deforested regions, to reduce one's carbon footprint and increase their "handprint."

Furthermore, the carbon footprint in the food industry can be reduced by optimising the supply chain. A life cycle or supply chain carbon footprint study can provide useful data which will help the business to identify critical areas for improvement and provides a focus. Such studies also demonstrate a company's commitment to reducing carbon footprint now ahead of other competitors as well as preparing companies for potential regulation. In addition to increased market advantage and differentiation eco-efficiency can also help to reduce costs where alternative energy systems are implemented.

12.10 Carbon Sequestration

Carbon sequestration is the process of capture and long-term storage of atmospheric carbon dioxide (CO_2) and may refer specifically to:

- "The process of removing carbon from the atmosphere and depositing it in a reservoir." When carried out deliberately, this may also be referred to as carbon dioxide removal, which is a form of geoengineering.

- The process of carbon capture and storage, where carbon dioxide is removed from flue gases, such as on power stations, before being stored in underground reservoirs.
- Natural biogeochemical cycling of carbon between the atmosphere and reservoirs, such as by chemical weathering of rocks.

Carbon sequestration describes long-term storage of carbon dioxide or other forms of carbon to either mitigate or defer global warming and avoid dangerous climate change. It has been proposed as a way to slow the atmospheric and marine accumulation of greenhouse gases, which are released by burning fossil fuels.

Carbon dioxide is naturally captured from the atmosphere through biological, chemical or physical processes. Some anthropogenic sequestration techniques exploit these natural processes, while some use entirely artificial processes.

Carbon dioxide may be captured as a pure by-product in processes related to petroleum refining or from flue gases from power generation. CO_2 sequestration includes the storage part of carbon capture and storage, which refers to large-scale, permanent artificial capture and sequestration of industrially produced CO_2 using subsurface saline aquifers, reservoirs, ocean water, aging oil fields, or other carbon sinks.

12.10.1 Biological processes

An oceanic phytoplankton bloom in the South Atlantic Ocean, off the coast of Argentina. Encouraging such blooms with iron fertilisation could lock up carbon on the seabed. Bio sequestration or carbon sequestration through biological processes affects the global carbon cycle. Examples include major climatic fluctuations, such as the Azolla event, which created the current Arctic climate. Such processes created fossil fuels, as well as clathrate and limestone. By manipulating such processes, geoengineers seek to enhance sequestration.

Peat production: Peat bogs are a very important carbon store. By creating new bogs, or enhancing existing ones, carbon can be sequestered.

Reforestation: Reforestation is the replanting of trees on marginal crop and pasture lands to incorporate carbon from atmospheric CO_2 into biomass. For this process to succeed the carbon must not return to the atmosphere from burning or rotting when the trees die. To this end, the trees must grow in perpetuity or the wood from them must itself be sequestered, e.g., via biochar, bio-energy with carbon storage (BECS) or landfill. Short of growth in perpetuity, however, reforestation with long-lived trees (>100 years) will sequester carbon for a more graduated release, minimising impact during the expected carbon crisis of the twenty first century.

Wetland restoration: Wetland soil is an important carbon sink; 14.5 per cent of the world's soil carbon is found in wetlands, while only six per cent of the world's land is composed of wetlands.

Agriculture: Globally, soils are estimated to contain approximately 1,500 gigatons of organic carbon to 1 m depth, more than the amount in vegetation and the atmosphere.

Modification of agricultural practices is a recognised method of carbon sequestration as soil can act as an effective carbon sink offsetting as much as 20 per cent of 2010 carbon dioxide emissions annually.

Carbon emission reduction methods in agriculture can be grouped into two categories: reducing and/or displacing emissions and enhancing carbon removal. Some of these reductions involve increasing the efficiency of farm operations (e.g. more fuel-efficient equipment) while some involve interruptions in the natural carbon cycle. Also, some effective techniques (such as the elimination of stubble burning) can negatively impact other environmental concerns (increased herbicide use to control weeds not destroyed by burning).

12.10.2 Reducing emissions

Increasing yields and efficiency generally reduces emissions as well, since more food results from the same or less effort. Techniques include more accurate use of fertilisers, less soil disturbance, better irrigation, and crop strains bred for locally beneficial traits and increased yields.

Replacing more energy intensive farming operations can also reduce emissions. Reduced or no-till farming requires less machine use and burns correspondingly less fuel per acre. However, no-till usually increases use of weed-control chemicals and the residue now left on the soil surface is more likely to release its CO_2 to the atmosphere as it decays, reducing the net carbon reduction.

In practice, most farming operations that incorporate post-harvest crop residues, wastes and byproducts back into the soil provide a carbon storage benefit. This is particularly the case for practices such as field burning of stubble - rather than releasing almost all of the stored CO_2 to the atmosphere, tillage incorporates the biomass back into the soil where it can be absorbed and a portion of it stored permanently.

12.10.3 Enhancing carbon removal

All crops absorb CO_2 during growth and release it after harvest. The goal of agricultural carbon removal is to use the crop and its relation to the carbon cycle to permanently sequester carbon within the soil. This is done by selecting farming methods that return biomass to the soil and enhance the conditions in which the carbon within the plants will be reduced to its elemental nature and stored in a stable state. Methods for accomplishing this include:

- Use cover crops such as grasses and weeds as temporary cover between planting seasons.
- Concentrate livestock in small paddocks for days at a time so they graze lightly but evenly. This encourages roots to grow deeper into the soil. Stock also till the soil with their hooves, grinding old grass and manures into the soil.
- Cover bare paddocks with hay or dead vegetation. This protects soil from the sun and allows the soil to hold more water and be more attractive to carbon-capturing microbes.
- Restore degraded land, which slows carbon release while returning the land to agriculture or other use.

Agricultural sequestration practices may have positive effects on soil, air, and water quality, be beneficial to wildlife, and expand food production. On degraded croplands, an increase of one ton of soil carbon pool may increase crop yield by 20 to 40 kilograms per hectare of wheat, 10 to 20 kg/ ha for maize, and 0.5 to 1 kg/ha for cowpeas.

The effects of soil sequestration can be reversed. If the soil is disrupted or tillage practices are abandoned, the soil becomes a net source of greenhouse gases. Typically after 15 to 30 years of sequestration, soil becomes saturated and ceases to absorb carbon. This implies that there is a global limit to the amount of carbon that soil can hold.

Many factors affect the costs of carbon sequestration including soil quality, transaction costs and various externalities such as leakage and unforeseen environmental damage. Because reduction of atmospheric CO_2 is a long-term concern, farmers can be reluctant to adopt more expensive agricultural techniques when there is not a clear crop, soil, or economic benefit. Governments such as Australia and New Zealand are considering allowing farmers to sell carbon credits once they document that they have sufficiently increased soil carbon content.

12.10.4 Ocean-related Iron fertilisation

Ocean iron fertilisation is an example of such a geoengineering technique. Iron fertilisation attempts to encourage phytoplankton growth, which removes carbon from the atmosphere for at least a period of time. This technique is controversial due to limited understanding its complete effects on the marine ecosystem, including side effects and possibly large deviations from expected behaviour. Such effects potentially include release of nitrogen oxides, and disruption of the ocean's nutrient balance.

Natural iron fertilisation events (e.g., deposition of iron-rich dust into ocean waters) can enhance carbon sequestration. Sperm whales act as agents of iron fertilisation when they transport iron from the deep ocean to the surface during prey consumption and defecation. Sperm whales have been shown to increase the levels of primary production and carbon export to the deep ocean by depositing iron rich feces into surface waters of the Southern Ocean. The iron rich feces cause phytoplankton to grow and take up more carbon from the atmosphere. When the phytoplankton dies, some of it sinks to the deep ocean and takes the atmospheric carbon with it. By reducing the abundance of sperm whales in the Southern Ocean, whaling has resulted in an extra two million tonnes of carbon remaining in the atmosphere each year.

12.10.5 Urea fertilisation

Ian Jones proposes fertilising the ocean with urea, a nitrogen rich substance, to encourage phytoplankton growth.

Australian company Ocean Nourishment Corporation (ONC) plans to sink hundreds of tonnes of urea into the ocean to boost CO_2-absorbing phytoplankton growth as a way to combat climate change. In 2007, Sydney-based ONC completed an experiment involving one tonne of nitrogen in the Sulu Sea off the Philippines.

12.10.6 Mixing layers

Encouraging various ocean layers to mix can move nutrients and dissolved gases around, offering avenues for geoengineering. Mixing may be achieved by placing large vertical pipes in the oceans to pump nutrient rich water to the surface, triggering blooms of algae, which store carbon when they grow and export carbon when they die. This produces results somewhat similar to iron fertilisation. One side-effect is a short-term rise in CO_2, which limits its attractiveness.

12.10.7 Physical processes

Biochar can be landfilled, used as a soil improver or burned using carbon capture and storage. Biomass-related Bio-energy with carbon capture and storage (BECCS) refers to biomass in power stations and boilers that use carbon capture and storage. The carbon sequestered by the biomass would be captured and stored, thus removing carbon dioxide from the atmosphere. This technology is sometimes referred to as bio-energy with carbon storage, BECS, though this term can also refer to the carbon sequestration potential in other technologies, such as biochar.

Burial: Burying biomass (such as trees) directly, mimics the natural processes that created fossil fuels. Landfills also represent a physical method of sequestration.

Biochar burial: Biochar is charcoal created by pyrolysis of biomass waste. The resulting material is added to a landfill or used as a soil improver to create terra preta. Biogenic carbon is recycled naturally in the carbon cycle. Pyrolysing it to biochar renders the carbon relatively inert so that it remains sequestered in soil. Further, the soil encourages bulking with new organic matter, which gives additional sequestration benefit.

In the soil, the carbon is unavailable for oxidation to CO_2 and consequential atmospheric release. This is one technique advocated by scientist James Lovelock, creator of the Gaia hypothesis. According to Simon Shackley, "people are talking more about something in the range of one to two billion tonnes a year." The mechanisms related to biochar are referred to as bio-energy with carbon storage, BECS.

12.10.8 Ocean storage

River mouths bring large quantities of nutrients and dead material from upriver into the ocean as part of the process that eventually produces fossil fuels. Transporting material such as crop waste out to sea and allowing it to sink exploits this idea to increase carbon storage. International regulations on marine dumping may restrict or prevent use of this technique.

Subterranean injection

Carbon dioxide can be injected into depleted oil and gas reservoirs and other geological features, or can be injected into the deep ocean. The first large-scale CO_2 sequestration project which began in 1996 is called Sleipner, and is located in the North Sea where Norway's Statoil Hydro strips carbon dioxide from natural gas with amine solvents and disposed of this carbon dioxide in a deep saline aquifer. In 2000, a coal-fueled synthetic natural gas plant in Beulah, North Dakota, became the world's first coal-using plant to capture and store carbon dioxide, at the Weyburn-Midale Carbon Dioxide Project.

CO_2 has been used extensively in enhanced crude oil recovery operations in the United States beginning in 1972. There are in excess of 10,000 wells that inject CO_2 in the state of Texas alone. The gas comes in part from anthropogenic sources, but is principally from large naturally occurring geologic formations of CO_2. It is transported to the oil-producing fields through a large network of over 5,000 kilometres (3,100 mi) of CO_2 pipelines. The use of CO_2 for enhanced oil recovery (EOR) methods in heavy oil reservoirs in the Western Canadian Sedimentary Basin (WCSB) has also been proposed. However, transport cost remains an important hurdle. An extensive CO_2

pipeline system does not yet exist in the WCSB. Athabasca oil sands mining that produces CO_2 is hundreds of kilometers north of the subsurface Heavy crude oil reservoirs that could most benefit from CO_2 injection.

12.10.9 Chemical processes

Developed in the Netherlands, an electrocatalysis by a copper complex helps reduce carbon dioxide to oxalic acid. This conversion uses carbon dioxide as a feedstock to generate oxalic acid.

Mineral Carbonation

Carbon, in the form of CO_2 can be removed from the atmosphere by chemical processes, and stored in stable carbonate mineral forms. This process is known as 'carbon sequestration by mineral carbonation' or mineral sequestration. The process involves reacting carbon dioxide with abundantly available metal oxides–either magnesium oxide (MgO) or calcium oxide (CaO)–to form stable carbonates. These reactions are exothermic and occur naturally (e.g., the weathering of rock over geologic time periods). Calcium and magnesium are found in nature typically as calcium and magnesium silicates (such as forsterite and serpentinite) and not as binary oxides.

12.11 Carbon Audit and Carbon Credit

A carbon audit regime is a means of accounting for quantifiable greenhouse gas control efforts. It establishes that the claimed reductions in emissions or enhancements of carbon sinks, has actually occurred and is stable.

A carbon credit is a generic term for any tradable certificate or permit representing the right to emit one tonne of carbon dioxide or the mass of another greenhouse gas with a carbon dioxide equivalent (tCO_2e) equivalent to one tonne of carbon dioxide.

Carbon credits and carbon markets are a component of national and international attempts to mitigate the growth in concentrations of greenhouse gases (GHGs). One carbon credit is equal to one tonne of carbon dioxide, or in some markets, carbon dioxide equivalent gases. Carbon trading is an application of an emissions trading approach. Greenhouse gas emissions are capped and then markets are used to allocate the emissions among the group of regulated sources.

The goal is to allow market mechanisms to drive industrial and commercial processes in the direction of low emissions or less carbon intensive approaches than those used when there is no cost to emitting carbon dioxide and other GHGs into the atmosphere. Since GHG mitigation projects generate credits, this approach can be used to finance carbon reduction schemes between trading partners and around the world.

There are also many companies that sell carbon credits to commercial and individual customers who are interested in lowering their carbon footprint on a voluntary basis. These carbon offsetters purchase the credits from an investment fund or a carbon development company that has aggregated the credits from individual projects. Buyers and sellers can also use an exchange platform to trade, such as the Carbon Trade Exchange, which is like a stock exchange for carbon credits. The quality of the credits is based in part on the validation process and sophistication of the fund or development company that acted as the sponsor to the carbon project. This is reflected in their price; voluntary units typically have less value than the units sold through the rigorously validated Clean Development Mechanism.

13

Ozone Depletion

13.1 Introduction

Planet Earth has its own natural sunscreen that shields us from the sun's damaging ultraviolet radiations. This natural sunscreen is due to ozone. The layer of atmosphere which contains ozone is termed as ozone layer. In other words, the ozone layer is a part of the Earth's atmosphere that has relatively high levels of ozone (O_3). Ozone is a gas that is naturally present in our atmosphere, and it is found primarily in the part of the atmosphere called the stratosphere, which is about 50 kilometers above Earth. The maximum ozone concentration is 10 ppm (parts per million) in the stratosphere at an altitude of 25-30 kilometer. Pure ozone is a pale blue gas.

Human activities have caused a substantial thinning of this protective covering, not only over the North and South Poles, but right over our heads. Primarily, the release of chlorofluorocarbons (CFCs) has depleted the ozone layer. This depletion is measured in Dobson units (DU), 1 DU =0.01 mm of compressed gas at 0°C and 760 mm mercury pressure. The level above 200 DU is considered to be normal. But if ozone level decreases below 200 DU, the situation is generally referred to as ozone hole. The depletion of ozone layer will lead to penetration of more ultraviolet (UV) rays to the earth. Exposure to higher amounts of UV radiation will have serious impacts on human beings, animals and plants. Therefore, reversing the process of ozone layer depletion has become one of the major challenges of the world today. According to a United Nations report, the annual dose of harmful ultraviolet radiation striking the northern hemisphere rose by five per cent during the past decade. During the past 40 years, the world has seen an alarming increase in the incidence of malignant skin cancer; the rate today is tenfold higher than in the 1950s. Although the entire increase cannot be blamed on ozone loss and increased exposure to ultraviolet radiation, there is evidence of a relationship. Scientists estimate that for each one per cent decline in ozone levels, humans will suffer as much as a two to three per cent increase in the incidence of skin cancers.

13.2 Ozone Hole and Ozone Depletion

Ozone Depletion is a slow, steady decline of about three to 4 per cent per decade, in the total amount of ozone in the earth's stratosphere during the past twenty years and a much larger, but seasonal, decrease in stratospheric ozone over the earth's Polar Regions during the same period.

There are two different types of ozone depletion. The first one has been a slow, but steady ozone depletion of three to four per cent per decade of the Earth's stratosphere (ozone layer). This has been happening constantly since the 1970s. The other is a much larger, although seasonal loss of ozone over the Polar Regions (Antarctic). This yearly occurrence is called the ozone hole. The spring-time ozone hole is the result of emissions, mainly in the northern hemisphere, of chlorofluorocarbons (CFCs) and halons. These gases are in widespread use in refrigeration, industrial solvents and fire control. The gases are broken down into their constituents over the tropics, and circulate towards both poles. Only over the Antarctic during winter it is cold enough for clouds to form in the ozone layer, and here chemical reactions on the cloud surfaces convert chlorine into an active form. When the sunlight comes back in the spring, this activated chlorine destroys ozone at about one per cent per day leading to the ozone hole.

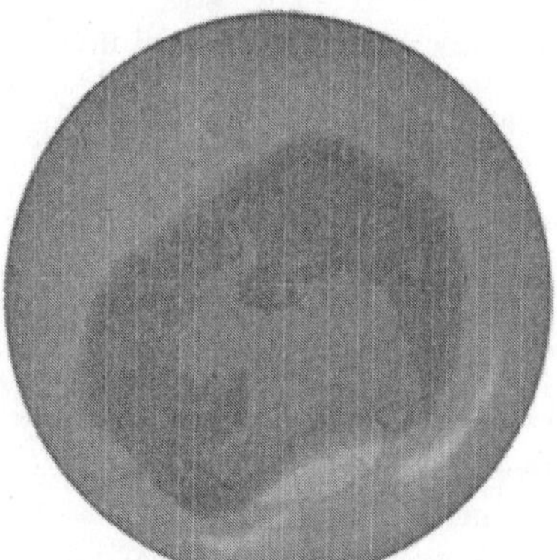

Figure 13.1: Ozone hole.

The discovery by the British Antarctic Survey of the Antarctic ozone hole provided an early warning of the dangerous thinning of the ozone layer worldwide and spurred international efforts to curb the production of CFCs.

The provisions of the Montreal Protocol of 1987 on Substances that Deplete the Ozone Layer have been revised and strengthened and are being followed by virtually all UN Member states. There is a reasonable prospect that the Antarctic ozone hole will permanently repair itself by around 2070.

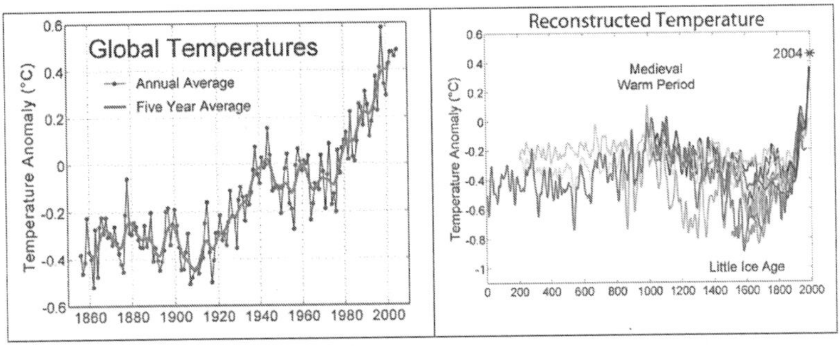

Figure 13.2: According to Scientific Assessment of Ozone Depletion: 2002 reported by scientific assessment panel of World Meteorological Organisation (WMO) and United Nations Environment Programme (UNEP), recovery of the Ozone Layer is expected by mid century provided full compliance to Montread Protocol is ensured by all countries.

13.3 Ozone depletion – Causes

There are many causes for ozone depletion but the most important is the process of catalytic destruction of ozone by atomic chlorine and bromine. Both come from the breaking down of chlorofluorocarbons (Freon) by photons in the atmosphere. Let us discuss chlorofluorocarbons (CFCs) to know the causes of ozone depletion.

Chlorofluorocarbons (CFCs)

Chlorofluorocarbons (CFCs) were discovered by American chemist Thomas Midgley in 1930s and have been used in refrigerators, home insulation, plastic foam and throwaway food containers. Researches by Sherwood Rowland and Mario Molina in 1974, provide that CFCs have the catastrophic effect on the stratosphere. The conclusive proof of damage was discovery of ozone layer hole over Antarctica in 1984. It is estimated that release of CFCs accounted for 80 per cent of all stratospheric ozone depletion. In fact, CFCs are man made chemicals that are very stable in the atmosphere. They take 20 to 120 years to break down and all the while they keep on destroying ozone molecules. CFCs do not fall back to Earth with rain, nor are they destroyed by other chemicals. CFCs rise into the stratosphere due to their relative stability and eventually brake down by ultraviolet rays from the Sun. This leads to release chlorine. The chlorine reacts with oxygen which leads to the chemical process of destroying ozone molecules. The net result is that two molecules of ozone are replaced by three of molecular oxygen leaving. The chlorine then reacts again with the oxygen molecules to destroy the ozone and the process repeats 100,000 times per molecule. While naturally occurring chlorine has the same effect on the ozone layer, it has a shorter life span in the atmosphere and thus it effects are considerably minimal.

13.4 Creation of Ozone Layer

Ozone is defined as 'a three-atom isotope (one of a set of chemically identical species of atom which have the same atomic number but different atomic weight is called ISOTOPE) of oxygen (O_3)' or merely a triatomic form of oxygen (O_3), which is a faintly blue irritating gas with a pungent odour. Ozone is a strong oxidising agent which decomposes high with an explosion at high concentration.

As we know that ozone is present almost at all altitudes in the atmosphere but the bulk of its concentration is present in a layer from 10 to 50 km up in the atmosphere and within this zone the highest concentration of ozone is between the altitudes of 12 and 35 km in the stratosphere. This zone (12-35 km) of ozone is called ozonosphere or ozone layer or stratospheric ozone layer. The ozone gas is unstable because it is created as well as destroyed or disintegrated. In other words, the creation and destruction of ozone gas is gradual and continuous natural process. The oxygen molecules are broken up or separated in the atmospheric layer between the altitudes of 80 to 100 km by ultraviolet solar radiation or by an electric discharge in oxygen or air during a thunderstorm in the troposphere in the following manner –

$O_2 = O + O$ (oxygen breaks up into two separate oxygen molecules)

These separated oxygen atoms (O) are then combined with oxygen molecules (O_2) and thus ozone (O_3) is formed.

$O_2 + O + m = O_3 + m$ (where m denotes energy and momentum balance produced by the collision of oxygen molecules (O_2) with another individual atom or molecule. The collisions of 3 atoms or molecules or the collisions of oxygen (O_2) with the third atom are not very common features of regular occurrence between the altitudes of 80 to 100 km (though O_2 is very frequently broken up into individual atom or molecule in this layer) because of very low density of gases in this part of the atmosphere. Such collisions are very rare in the atmosphere below the altitude of 35 km because most of the solar ultraviolet rays usually get absorbed above this height. Thus, the formation of ozone due to collision of three atoms through the process of Photo Chemical Reaction triggered by the sunlight is more active in the atmospheric zone of 30 to 60 km height from the sea level. The Ozone Mixing Ratio (ozone mixing ratio = mass of ozone per unit + mass of dry air) is maximum at the height of about 35 km but the maximum ozone density (ozone density = mass of ozone per unit volume) is found between the height of 20 km to 25 km. This is because of the fact that ozone is transported to lower height (upto 12 km) by some upper air atmospheric circulation mechanisms which allow the ozone gas to accumulate between the heights of 12 to 35 km.

It is also important to note that most of the stratospheric ozone is formed in the atmosphere over the tropical areas from where some ozone is transported by the atmospheric circulation to the polar areas up in the atmosphere. The ozone is also transformed back into oxygen by further collision of ozone with monatomic oxygen (individual molecule of oxygen, O) in the following manner – Ozone (O_3) + O = oxygen (O_2) + oxygen (O_2).

Ozone is also transformed into oxygen by Photo Chemical Process (by the actions of solar radiation on ozone). In simpler term, the process of formation of ozone may be described as the production of ozone by the actions of ultraviolet rays on ordinary oxygen atoms by the Photo Chemical Process which is responsible for the constant transformation of oxygen through the collision of three atoms of oxygen i.e. (O_2+ O) to ozone and from ozone to back to oxygen. Thus, the constant formations or production and destruction of ozone are natural process which maintains an approximate equilibrium level of ozone in the atmosphere if not interfered by human activities. Though ozone layer contributes only about 3 to 4 mm of thickness to the total atmospheric thickness of 8 m (if the whole of atmosphere may be compressed to sea level temperature and pressure) but this layer is a life saving protective cover for all the biota of the biosphere.

13.5 Factors of Ozone Depletion

Combining of atmospheric oxygen (O_2) with individual oxygen molecule (O) results in the creation of ozone ($O_2 + O = O_3$) whereas the breaking of ozone (O_3) into O_2 and O or recreation of oxygen due to collision of ozone (O_3) with monatomic oxygen (O) results in the depletion or destruction of ozone ($O_3 = O_2 + O$ or $O_3 + O = O_2 + O_2$). The collective process of constant metamorphosis of oxygen into ozone (ozone formation) and ozone back into oxygen (ozone destruction or ozone depletion) is triggered by Photochemical Processes. If this is true, there must be maximum formation of ozone during June near the equator but the distributional pattern of ozone denotes its maximum concentration in the high latitudes (beyond 50° latitudes in both hemispheres) and minimum concentration over the equator. This anomalous distribution of ozone may be explained if we consider transport of ozone by the atmospheric circulation towards the polar areas.

It is believed that ozone having maximum concentration between the altitudes of 30 to 40 km during summer months mainly during June in the low latitudes (equatorial zone) is transported during winter months towards high latitudes (Polar areas) between the altitudes of 20 to 25 km. Thus, the accumulation of ozone in the polar areas during winter season results in the development of rich ozone layer during early spring season. The creation and destruction of ozone is a regular natural process which never disturbs the equilibrium level of ozone in the stratosphere but when the destruction of ozone exceeds the level of ozone creation, serious repercussions are bound to crop up in due to disequilibrium in the level of ozone.

In the beginning there was a lot of controversy about the causes and factors of ozone depletion but now a consensus has been reached that the main culprits of ozone depletion are halogenated gases called Chlorofluorocarbons, Halons and Nitrogen oxides. The World Meteorological Organisation's (WMO) statement on anthropogenic modification of the stratospheric ozone layer issued in 1976 maintained that a continuous release of chlorofluoro methane into the atmosphere may destroy ozone to a considerable extent. Contrary to this, M L Parry maintained in 1977 that the ozone concentration in the stratosphere might be rising and chlorine does not necessarily cause depletion of ozone. The latest NASA report has however set aside the controversy about the factors and causes of ozone depletion and recognised as chlorofluorocarbon (CFCs) and Halons as the main culprits of ozone depletion.

It may be pointed out that the chlorofluorocarbons are neither toxic nor flammable at ground level but on reaching the stratosphere they become potent destroyer of the ozone layer through a set of chemical reactions. The chlorofluorocarbons (popularly known as CFCs) belonging to the category of synthetic chemicals are relatively simple compound of the elements Chlorine, Fluorine and Carbon and are initially stable compounds which do not have any toxic effect on life processes in the biosphere at the ground level. These synthetic chemicals are widely used as propellants in spray can dispenses, as fluids in air conditioners and refrigerators, as blowing agents in insulation foams (popularly known as Styrofoam) and as industrial solvents. It is estimated that about 25 per cent of the total world production of chlorofluorocarbons is used to propel personal care products such as deodorants, hair sprays, shaving creams and numerous other cosmetic products. The most important of the chlorofluorocarbons hydrocarbons are the Trichlorofluoromethane (trade name FREON11) and Dichlorofluoromethane (trade name FREON12). The atmospheric concentrations of CFCs are increasing rapidly at the rate of 13 to 28 per cent (Freon11) per annum.

13.6 Mechanism of Ozone Depletion

The mechanisms of ozone depletion include both: (i) the Natural Processes and (ii) the anthropogenic processes as detailed below:

Natural Processes

The natural process of ozone depletion involves the conversion of atmospheric nitrogen into nitrous oxides by solar activity. This is because of maximum sunspots at the end of every 11 year cycle. According to latest estimate, the level of nitrous oxides rises from 30 to 60 per cent at the end of 11 year cycle in the middle latitudes of the southern hemisphere. This mass of nitrous oxides is transported to the stratosphere of the polar areas during winter season (polar night). These nitrous oxides then deplete the ozone layer through Photochemical Reactions. These nitrous oxides also augment the rate of ozone depletion triggered by chlorine molecule. Ozone (O_3) is also split into oxygen (O_2) and single oxygen molecule because of ultraviolet solar radiation. The natural mechanisms of ozone depletion do not necessarily upset the ozone equilibrium in the atmosphere because the loss of ozone caused by natural processes is suitably compensated by the creation of ozone through natural processes. The Dynamic Mechanism involves the redistribution of ozone by the atmospheric circulation. The upper air atmospheric circulation transports ozone from over South Pole and accumulates it in a belt from 60 to 70. This transport of ozone from over South Pole results in the thinning of ozone layer and thus the formation of Ozone hole.

Anthropogenic processes

The anthropogenic mechanisms of ozone depletion include a few processes viz. (a) chlorine hypothesis; (b) sulphate hypothesis; and (c) nitrogen oxides hypothesis.

Chlorine Hypothesis: The chloro fluorocarbon and halon gases are released during the maintenance or operation of several devices using these synthetic chemicals (such as refrigerators, air conditioners, spray-can dispenses etc.), shredding of foam insulation and fire fighting into the atmosphere. Initially, these gases are chemically inert and non-toxic at the ground level and in the troposphere. These gases also do not break down in the troposphere. These are transported upward into the stratosphere. The transport of chlorofluorocarbons and halons by vertical atmospheric circulations to the stratosphere normally take six to eight years or even ten years. These gases are further transported to the south polar stratosphere. The depletion of ozone due to chlorofluorocarbons and halons involves the following steps:

- A swirling polar vertex is formed over the south pole (in the atmosphere) during long Antarctic winter (from March to September).
- This Swirling South Polar Antarctic Vertex causes considerable lowering of temperature.
- The meager amount of vapour present in the dry upper atmosphere is frozen due to markedly low temperature below freezing point. This frozen upper atmospheric moisture forms upper atmospheric or stratospheric clouds.
- The chlorine and bromine of chlorofluorocarbons and halon are converted from their initial non-reactive form to reactive from

because of the chemical reactions on the ice crystals. It may be mentioned that CFCs and halons are transported to the stratosphere by vertical atmospheric circulation. Thus, the transformed form of non-reactive chlorine and bromine, as reactive molecules, becomes very much sensitive to sunlight.

- The nitrogen oxides generally inactivate chlorine but he lowering of stratospheric temperature because of Polar Antarctic Swirling Vortex transforms nitrogen oxides into frozen form which then becomes non-reactive nitric acid.
- During the next spring sunlight breaks down CFCs halon through the mechanism of photochemical processes and thus chlorine and bromine are released to the atmosphere. These halogen molecules then disintegrate ozone (O_3) into ordinary oxygen (O_2 + O) and thus the process of destruction or depletion on ozone starts.

Sulphate Hypothesis: In 1986, it was established by the scientists that the chemistry of cloud surface is of paramount significance in the destruction of ozone. It is believed that the sulphate aerosols emitted through volcanic eruptions (natural) and numerous constantly active human volcanoes (chimneys of factories) accumulate in the atmosphere at all latitudes between the altitudes of 15 km to 22 km. It has been discovered that the concentration of sulphate aerosols is most prevalent over the populated and industrialised areas of the northern hemisphere. This trend further validates the belief that most of the sulphate aerosols present in the atmosphere are contributed by human (industrial) activities. These sulphate aerosols catalyse the transformation of ozone to ordinary oxygen (O_2+ O). If this sulphate hypothesis of ozone depletion is accepted, the destruction of the ozone layer thus becomes global phenomenon and the depletion of ozone would be accelerated more than anticipated on the basis of chlorine hypothesis (depletion of ozone due to chlorine molecules released from the breakdown of chlorofluorocarbon).

Nitrogen Oxides Hypothesis: The Supersonic Transport Aircrafts (SST) flying at the speed of more than twice the speed of sound at the altitude of 18 to 20 km release significant amount of nitrogen oxides from their exhausts. Harold H. Johnson, an atmospheric scientist at the University of California, Berkeley (USA), studied the impact of exhaust of Supersonic Transport (SST) aircrafts and demonstrated that 'a fleet of 500 Boeing SSTs would reduce global ozone by a value between 3 and 237 over all the earth's surface, and by as much as 50 per cent near areas of intensive air travel'. The Climatic Impact Assessment Programme (CIAP) by the US Department of Transportation (DOT) also confirmed considerable impact of nitrogen oxides released from the exhausts of supersonic transport aircrafts on ozone. The US National Academy of Sciences and the US National Academy of Engineering have also confirmed the potential impact of Nitrogen oxides on ozone depletion.

13.7 Effects of Ozone Depletion

The most important function of the stratospheric ozone is to protect the troposphere and the earth's surface from most of the ultraviolet solar radiation by absorbing ultraviolet rays. Thus the ozone layer serves as an umbrella or shield against the ultraviolet solar radiation and saves the earth's surface from becoming too hot. The most dangerous effect of ozone depletion would be substantial increase in the ultraviolet solar radiation reaching the earth's surface. The increased ultraviolet solar radiation in turn would raise the temperature of the earth's surface and the lower atmosphere. This would trigger a chain of effects and counter effects which would adversely affect the life forms in the biosphere in a variety of ways.

Effects on Climates

It is believed that the depletion of ozone layer would result in 5 to 20 per cent more ultraviolet radiation reaching the populated areas of the world. The substantial increase in the surface temperature of the earth would cause global warming and climate changes at regional and global levels. The overall warming of the environment would cause melting of continental glaciers and ice sheets such as those of Antarctica and Greenland. This would in turn cause rise in sea level and consequent submergence of coastal low lands. Chlorofluoromethanes besides depletion of ozone layer are also supposed to enhance the greenhouse effect of carbon dioxide. This is because these halogen gases are effective absorbers in the 8-13 micros wave length band but water vapour and carbon dioxide may not effectively absorb these radiation waves. Thus, the increased temperature would induce several climatic changes in various parts of the globe. It is also believed that the depletion of ozone in the stratosphere would result in the increase of the amount of hydrogen peroxide in the troposphere which would ultimately induce Acid rain. Ozone depletion and increased ultraviolet solar radiation would also increase photochemical processes which in turn would create poisonous urban smog.

Effects on Human and Animal Health

The increase in UV radiation associated with stratospheric ozone depletion is likely to have a substantial impact on human health. Potential risks include increases in the incidence of morbidity from eye diseases, skin cancer and infectious diseases. UV radiation has been shown in experimental systems to damage the cornea and lens of the eye. Chronic exposure to UV (resulting in a high, cumulative, lifetime dose) is one of several factors associated with the risk of cataract of the cortical and posterior sub-capsular forms. Some components of the immune system are present in the skin, making the immune system accessible to UV radiation. Experiments on animals show that UV exposure decreases the immune response to skin cancers, infectious agents and other antigens, and can lead to infectious. Studies on human subjects indicate also that exposure to UV radiation can suppress the induction of some immune responses.

In susceptible (light-skinned) populations, UV radiation is a key risk factor for development of non-melanoma skin cancer (NMSC). Using information derived from animals experiments and human epidemiology, it is estimated that a sustained one per cent decrease in stratospheric ozone will result in an increase in NMSC incidence by about two per cent. The relationship between UV exposure and melanoma skin cancer is less well understood and appears to differ fundamentally from that of NMSC.

Effects on Terrestrial Plants

Physiological and development processes of plants are affected by UV radiation, even by the amount of UV in present day sunlight. Plants also have several mechanisms to ameliorate or repair these effects and may acclimate to a certain extent to increased levels of UV. Nevertheless plant growth can be directly affected by UV radiation.

Response to UV also varies considerably among species and also cultivars of the same species. In agriculture, this will necessitate using more UV tolerant cultivars and breeding new ones. In forests and grasslands, this is likely to result in changes in species composition; therefore, there are implications for the biodiversity in different ecosystems.

Indirect changes caused by UV (such as changes in plant form, biomass allocation to parts of the plant, timing of developmental phases and secondary metabolism) may be equally, or sometimes more important than damaging effects of UV. These changes can have important implications for plant competitive balance, herbivore, plants pathogens and biogeochemical cycles. These ecosystem level effects can be anticipated, but not easily predicted or evaluated. Research at the ecosystem level for solar UV is barely beginning. Other factors, including those involved in climate change such as increasing CO_2, also interact with UV. Such reactions are not easily predicted, but are of obvious importance in both agriculture and in non-agriculture ecosystems.

Effects on Aquatic Ecosystems

More that 30 per cent of the world's animal protein for human consumption comes from the sea and in many countries, particularly the developing countries, this percentage is significantly higher. As a result, it is important to know how increased levels of exposure to solar UV radiation might affect the productivity of aquatic systems. Solar UV radiation has been found to cause damage in the early developmental stages of fish, shrimp, crab, amphibians and other animals. The most severe effects are decreased reproductive capacity and impaired development. Even at current levels, solar UV radiation is a limiting factor, and even small increases in UV exposure could result in significant reduction in the size of the population of consumer organisms.

Effects on Biogeochemical Cycles

Increase in solar UV radiation could affect terrestrial and aquatic biogeochemical cycles, thus altering both sources and sinks of greenhouse and chemically important trace gases for example, carbon dioxide, carbon monoxide and carbonyl sulfide and possibly other gases, including ozone. These potential changes would contribute to biosphere atmosphere feedbacks that attenuate or reinforce the atmospheric build-up of these gases.

In terrestrial ecosystems, increased UV may modify both the production and decomposition of plant matter with concomitant changes in the uptake and release of atmospherically important trace gases. Decomposition processes can be accelerated when UV photo degrades surface litter or retarded when the dominant effects is one of the chemical composition of living tissues resulting in reduced bio-degradability of buried litter. Primary production can be reduced by enhanced UV with variable effect between species and crops. Solar UV radiation stimulates the degradation of aquatic dissolved organic matter (DOM), resulting in loss of UV absorption and formation of dissolved inorganic carbon (DIC) and organic substrates that are readily mineralised or taken up by aquatic micro-organisms.

Aquatic nitrogen cycling can be affected by enhanced UV through inhibition of nitrifying bacteria and photo-decomposition of simple inorganic species such as nitrate. The marine sulphur cycle may be affected by UV radiation, resulting in possible changes in the sea to air emissions of carbonyl sulphide (COS) and dimethylsulphide (DMS), two gases that are degraded to sulphate aerosols in the stratosphere and troposphere, respectively.

Effects on Air Quality

Reduction to stratospheric ozone and the consequent increase of UV radiation penetrating to the lower atmosphere result in higher photo dissociation rates of key trace gases that control the chemical reactivity of the troposphere. This can increase both production and destruction of ozone (O_3) and related oxidants (such as hydrogen peroxide H_2O_2), which are known to have adverse effects on human health, terrestrial plants and outdoor materials. Changes in atmospheric concentration of hydroxyl radical (OH) may change the atmospheric lifetimes of climatically important gases such as methane (CH_4) and the CFC substitutes.

In polluted regions (High NO_x), tropospheric O_3 is expected to increase, reaching potentially harmful concentrations earlier in the day and leading to more frequent violation of oxidant standards for air quality in urban areas where O_3 levels are routinely near such air quality thresholds. Increase of

OH concentrations cause a nearly proportionate decrease in the steady state tropospheric concentrations of CH_4 and CFC substitutes such as the HCFCs and HFCs. Thus, the measured reductions in the ozone column are likely to have moderate CH_4 increases over the past decade and may account for about one-third of the slowing of the global CH_4 trends. Increased tropospheric reactivity could also lead to increased production of particulates such as cloud condensation nuclei, from the oxidation and subsequent nucleation of sulphur of both anthropogenic and natural origins (e.g. carbonyl sulphide and dimethyl sulphide). While these processes are still not fully understood, they exemplify the possibility of complex feed-backs between stratospheric ozone reductions, tropospheric chemistry and ultimate change.

Effects on Materials

Synthetic polymers, naturally occurring bio-polymers, as well as some other materials of commercial interest are adversely affected by solar UV radiation. Application of these materials, particularly plastics, in situations which demand routine exposure to sunlight is only possible through the use of light stabilisers and/or surface treatments to protect them from sunlight. Any increase in solar UV content owing to partial ozone depletion will therefore accelerate the photo degradation rates of those materials, limiting their service lifetime outdoors.

The nature and extent of such damage from increased UV radiation in sunlight is quantified in action spectra. In spite of the several polymer action spectra available in research literatures the information is often inadequate to make reliable estimates of the increased damage. However, it is clear from available data that shorter UV wavelength processes are mainly responsible for photo damage ranging from discolour action to loss of mechanical integrity. The molecular level interpretation of such UV-induced. Changes remain unclear in many instances.

13.8 Protection and Maintenance of Ozone Layer

The depletion of ozone layer and consequent imminent danger to biological communities in general and human society in particular have become a matter of serious environmental concern to governments, scientific communities and general public at local, regional and global levels. Serious attempts are being made at international level to heal the already wounded stratosphere by protecting and maintaining the precious ozone layer. The Montreal Protocol, 1987 has been signed to reduce the production and consumption of chlorofluorocarbons. The organisation of international conference known as London Conference hosted by the British Government with collaboration of the United Nations Environment Programme (UNEP) during March 5-7, 1989 at London indicated the level of seriousness of the problem and keenness of the world communities to protect the gradually depleting precious ozone layer. The remedial measures of ozone depletion at international level are being taken at two levels viz. (i) to promote reduction in the production and consumption to emissions of ozone depleting chemicals and (ii) to make serious efforts to produce and propagate the use of alternative chemicals which do not deplete ozone in the stratosphere.

Reduction in the production and consumption of CFCs, Halons

The emissions and spread of CFCs and halons do not care for any international boundary as about 95 per cent emissions of these ozone depleting chemicals occur in the northern hemisphere (because of the location of all the developed countries in this hemisphere) whereas the concentration of these chemicals is only five to ten per cent less in the southern hemisphere because of their rapid spread through the troposphere by the atmospheric circulations. According to a survey conducted in 1976, the concentrations of Freon 11 and Freon 12 in the southern hemisphere were 12 ppm and 220 ppm respectively which were expected to increase to 700 ppm and 900 ppm by the turn of the twentieth century. It is reported that the major world producers of CFCs excluding socialist countries produced 10,00,000 tons of CFCs in 1987. Most of the world production of CFCs is consumed in the developed countries such as the USA, European countries and Japan.

The first and foremost task before the world communities is to stop or markedly reduce the production and consumption of ozone depleting synthetic chemical compounds like CFCs and halons. The Montreal Protocol on Substances that deplete the Ozone signed in September 1987 at Montreal, Canada, by 35 developed countries of the world is the first concrete step in this regard. The signing of this Montreal Protocol was made possible because of continued efforts and negotiations made by the United Nations Environment Programme (UNEP).

The aforesaid Montreal Protocol suffered from certain lacunae viz. (i) the provisions for Phase Out reduction in the production of CFCs and Halons, (ii) the provisions of exemption to developing countries to implement the reduction programme from 1999. It was argued that the phase out programme of the reduction of CFCs and halon production by 50 per cent by the end of 1998 was inadequate to stop the depletion of ozone as reduction by 50 per cent could at best slow down the pace of ozone depletion. Secondly, there are also some other chemical compounds which contain chlorine and bromine such as methyl chloroform and carbon tetrachloride which contribute to the depletion of ozone layer but these chemicals are not covered by the Montreal Protocol. The Montreal Protocol also granted exemption to developing countries to implement the phase out programme of the deduction of ozone depleting chemicals say CFCs and halons 10 years later i.e. from

1999. Although per capital consumption of CFCs and halons in the developing countries aggregating to 16 per cent of the total world consumption is very low, which however, is expected to increase enormously in the coming days, in view of the large populations. The developing countries were expected to freeze the production of CFCs and halon with effect from 1999 and reduce its production by 50 per cent in a phased manner.

The eight major developing countries e.g. China, India, Brazil, Indonesia, Iran, Mexico, Saudi Arabia and South Korea did not sign the Montreal Protocol and not participated in the phase out programme of the production and consumption of CFCs initially. Later some countries including India signed the protocol in 2003.

Search for Alternative Technology and substitute chemicals

Besides reducing the level of production and consumption of ozone depleting CFCs and halon, attentions are focused on improving the use and maintenance of existing CFCs and halon and on searching substitute chemicals which can replace dangerous CFCs and halons. New techniques should be developed so that leakage of these gases may be stopped and new efficient equipments may be used to handle these gases. A few substitutes chemicals claimed to be chlorine free have been developed. For example, a US-based Petroleum Company has developed Bioact EC 7, a bio-degradable, non-toxic and non-corrosive chemical known as HFC 134 (a trade name) which may be used in place of FREON 12 in air conditioners and refrigerator. This chemical is claimed to be free from chlorine. A new chemical called CFC 22 has been developed in the USA as a substitute for FREON 11 and FREON 12. But the researchers on the use and effects of CFC 22 conducted by the US scientists have revealed that the CFC 22, a monochlorofluoromethane considered to be best among the fluorocarbons, also depletes ozone more than CFC 11 (FREON 11) and CFC 12 (FREON 12). The research laboratories of some companies have discovered that HCFs or CFCs with an added extra hydrogen atom may be used in air conditioners. Attempts are also being made in the developed and the industrialised countries to search for chlorine-free substances that do not have ozone depletion potential but can be used in refrigerators.

13.9 The Montreal Protocol and India's Commitment

In the year 1980, as scientific knowledge of ozone depletion grew, the international response to the issue also grew. In 1987, leaders from many countries came together to sign the Montreal Protocol on Substances that Deplete the Ozone Layer.

The Montreal Protocol was signed in September 1987 by 35 developed countries of the world at Montreal, Canada. It is an international agreement to address the causes of ozone depletion. While several substances were addressed, CHCs and HCFCs were the main ones that the international community agreed to phase-out of production.

The following provisions were commonly agreed by the countries which signed the said protocol.

- To freeze the production of CFCs at 1986 level by 1989;
- To decrease the production of these synthetic chemical compounds by 20 per cent by the end of 1993;
- To allow further 30 per cent cut in the production of these chemicals by 1998;
- To freeze the production of halons at 1986 level starting from 1992;
- Thus, the total production of ozone depleting chemicals (mainly CFCs and halons) would be reduced, according to the Montreal Protocol, by 50 per cent by the beginning of 1999.

The protocol also developed a fund to help underdeveloped countries to find other methods of production so that they could stop using CFCs and HCFCs, also.

The Montreal Protocol established legally binding controls on the national production and consumption of Ozone Depletion Substances (ODS). Today, 191 countries are signatories to the treaty. These countries are committed to taking action to reduce and eliminate ODS to protect the ozone layer. Production and consumption of all principal ODS by developed and developing countries will be significantly phased out before the middle of the twenty first century. The Montreal Protocol has been successful because of scientific accuracy, effective public policy, and market-based, flexible, innovative approaches to ensuring ozone layer protection and developing alternatives. The year 2007 marked the twentieth Anniversary of the Montreal Protocol, and was taken as an opportunity to emphasise the commitment to completing the worldwide phase-out of CFCs.

Indian commitment to Montreal Protocol

India signed the Montreal Protocol along with its London Amendment on 17th September 1992 and also ratified the Copenhagen, Montreal and Beijing Amendments on 3rd March 2003. Thereafter, Government of India, as a Party to the Montreal Protocol has taken a number of initiatives for precautionary measures, continues its action, measures and adoption of necessary regulations with the sole objective of protection of Ozone Layer.

Regulatory Measures

Committee on Subordinate Legislation, Parliament (Rajya Sabha) has examined the Ozone Depleting Substances (Regulation and Control) Rules, 2000. In compliance with certain recommendations of the Committee in order to specify a time limit for completing the process of registration, renewal and cancellation under various provisions of these Rules, necessary amendments to the ODS Rules were notified in August 2003.

Ratification of all four amendments to the Montreal Protocol

The London Amendment (1990) to the Montreal Protocol mandates to phase out CFCs and Halons by January 2010 with the intermediate reduction schedule of 50 per cent by January 2005. The use of CTC is also to be phased out by January 2010 with the intermediate reduction of 85 per cent by January 2005. HCFCs have been introduced as transitional substances/ immediate substitutes to CFCs and can be used till 2040. India ratified this Amendment in June 1992.

The Copenhagen Amendment (1992) to the Montreal Protocol introduced HCFCs, HBFCs and Methyl Bromide as controlled substances. India did not ratify the Copenhagen Amendment immediately on its adoption in 1992 due to several uncertainties such as lack of adequate policy decisions for phasing out of ODS in consumption and production sector but ratified the Amendment on 3rd March 2003.

The Beijing Amendment (1999) to the Montreal Protocol introduced control measures applicable to the production of HCFCs for developed countries with a provision of 15 per cent additional allowance to meet the domestic needs of developing countries. India being a producer of HCFC-22 has the advantage of exporting it to develop and developing countries and it is necessary to import HCFC-14 lb and HCFC-123 as substitute to CFC- 11 as these are not produced in the country. Moreover, the technology for manufacturing these two substances are not easily available and the requirements do not attract the industry houses to establish an economically viable production facility. The import of these substances will continue. India ratified this Amendment on 3rd March, 2003.

The Enterprises who are recipients of financial assistance from the Multilateral Fund

The Ministry of Environment and Forests has established an Empowered Steering Committee which is supported by four Standing Committees, namely– (i) Technology and Finance Standing Committee; (ii) Standing Committee for Small Scale, Tiny and Unorganised Industries; (iii) Standing Committee on Implementation of ODS phase out projects; and (iv) Monitoring and Evaluation Committee. As on 31 August 2003, 349 projects in the consumption and production sector have been approved and funded by the Multilateral Fund. Of these 272 are ODS phase out investment projects while 77 are non-investment and support activities. A total amount of about US$ 138 million has been approved by the Executive Committee of the Multilateral Fund Secretariat for the phasing out of 12,405 ODP tons.

Fiscal Incentives extended for phasing out of ODS

In order to meet the obligation of the Montreal Protocol, Government of India is granting full exemption from payment of Customs and Central Excise Duties for import of goods designed exclusively for non-ODS technology. The duty exemption scheme has been followed for Multilateral Fund (MLF) projects for about nine years and for non-MLF projects and new investment projects for about five years. The maximum number of duty exemption certificates so far have been availed by the small and medium enterprises in ODS consumption sector.

Important Trade issues and the Government stand

The Directorate General of Foreign Trade (DGFT), Ministry of Commerce and Industry under its Exim Policy included CFCs, Halon, CTC and HCFC as restricted items for the purpose of trade since March 1996. Thereafter, export and import of CFCs and Halon were made under license issued by DGFT based on the recommendations of Ozone Cell. The guidelines for recommending issuance of license for export and import of CFCs and Halon were developed during June 1996.

Subsequently, the Ozone Depleting Substances (Regulation and Control) Rules, 2000 mandated provision of trade with parties and export and import to be made by obtaining license issued by the authority.

Illegal trafficking of ODS

Illegal trade in ODS in the South East Asian Region seems to have occurred since 1996, as the licensing system is under implementation in this region. Illegal trade in ODS in India is attributed to the following reasons:

- Imports by Mislabelling/Misdeclaration at various Inland Container Depots;
- Infiltration through porous land borders of neighbouring countries of India;
- Ship-breakers selling the ODS locally in India by manipulating documents and misappropriating ODS placed in the Bonded warehouse, meant for re-exports to Foreign Going Vessels only.
- The gravity of the menace of illegal trade in ODS can be gauged by the large quantities of ODS being infiltrated in the country and some of which are being intercepted and seized by the various Enforcement Agencies such as Border Security Force (BSF), Customs Police etc.
- Importers have been misdeclaring the consignment as Refrigerant Tubs, Refrigerant Gas, Refrigerant-21/22, Gas Cans etc. and the Customs Authorities are unaware about the illegality of such imports

as import is permitted only by actual users against a license, from a country which is party to the Montreal Protocol.

- Taking advantage of the lack of background information, it has been observed that importers have brought many consignments in the country and invading the markets with product which is illegally imported and being sold in packing which is banned in the country as per Gas Cylinder Rules, 1981.

14

Acid Rain

14.1 Introduction

Acid rains have of late assumed one of the grave global ecological problems. Acid precipitation is a mixture of strong mineral acids such as sulphuric, nitric and hydrochloric acids having less than 5.6 pH, the value of distilled water in equilibrium with atmospheric carbon - dioxide. The term acid rain refers to the fall of acids mixed with rain and snow. The phenomenon of "acid rain" (more correctly acid deposition) was identified in Manchester, England, way back in 1852 and described more thoroughly in 1872 by Robert Angus Smith, a scientist working in Manchester. Modern scientific research however commenced as late as mid 1950s. Public concern about this devastating problem began much later - in the late 1960s. The problem of acid rain is hence not a new one but the nature of the problem has changed from being a local problem for towns and cities to an international problem. In Smith's time, acid rain fell both in towns and cities whilst today pollutants can be transported thousands of kilometers due to the introduction of tall chimneys dispersing pollutants high into the atmosphere.

Acid is a substance with a sour taste that will react with a base to form a salt. Acids turn blue litmus paper (also called pH paper) red. Strong acids can burn your skin. A pH scale is used to measure the amount of acid in a liquid like water. The acid content is based on the concentration of hydrogen ions and is expressed as "pH." This scale is used to measure the acidity of rain samples.

14.2 Formation of Acid Rain

The oxides of sulphur and nitrogen are important gaseous pollutants of air. These are produced mainly by combustion of fossil fuels, smelters, power plants, automobile exhausts, domestic fires, etc. Swept up into the atmosphere these oxides can travel thousands of kilometers. The longer they stay in the atmosphere, the more likely they are to be oxidised into acids. Sulphuric acid and nitric acid are the two main acids, which dissolve in water in the atmosphere and fall to the grounds as acid rains or may remain in atmosphere in clouds and fogs as shown in figure below:

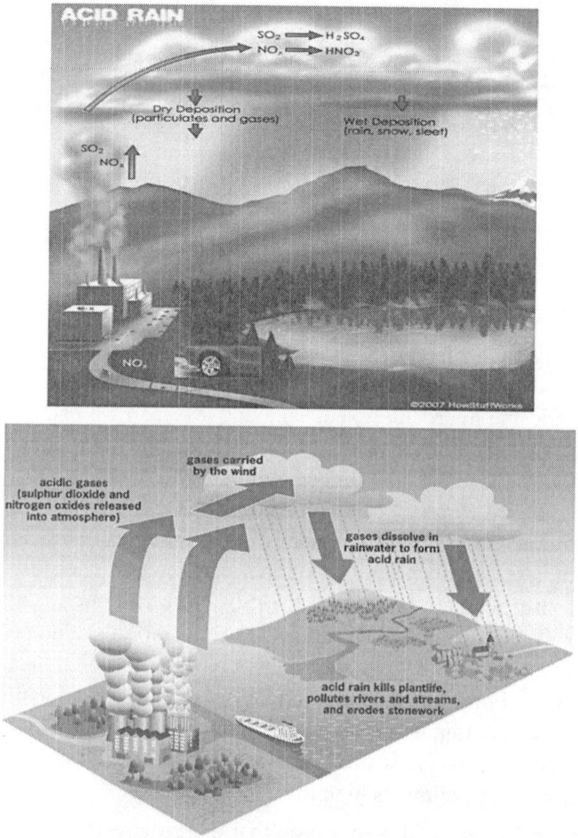

Figure 14.1 and 14. 2: Acid Rain.

As would be seen from above, the process that results in the formation of acid rain generally begins with emissions into the atmosphere of sulfur dioxide and nitrogen oxide. These gases are released by automobiles, certain industrial operations (e.g., smelting and refining), and electric power plants that burn such fossil fuels as coal and oil. The gases combine with water vapour in clouds to form sulfuric and nitric acids. When precipitation falls from the clouds, it is highly acidic, having a pH value of about 5.6 or lower. The term pH is defined as the negative logarithm of the hydrogen ion concentration in kilograms per cubic meter. The pH scale ranges from 0 to 14, with lower numbers indicating increased acidity. At several locations in the eastern United States and Western Europe, pH values between 2 and 3 have been recorded. In areas such as Los Angeles, San Francisco, and Whiteface Mountain in New York, fog is often 10 or more times as acidic as the local precipitation. This phenomenon is further described through the diagrammatic representation below:

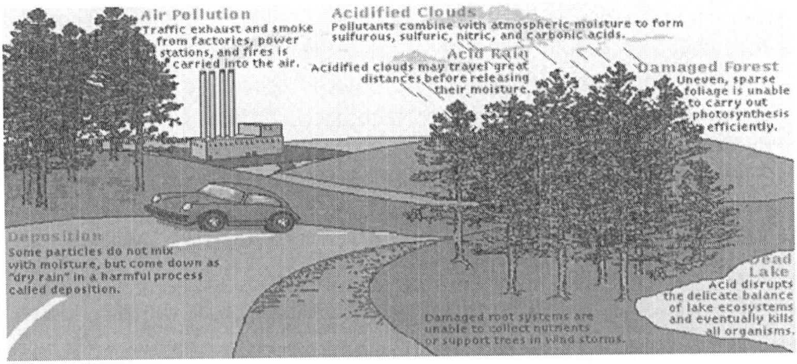

Figure 14.3: Phenomenon of Acid Rain.

14.3 Causes of Acid Rain

Acidification of environment is man-made phenomenon. The acid rain is a cocktail of H_2SO_4 and HNO_3. The ratio of the two may vary depending on the relative quantities of oxides of sulphur and nitrogen emitted. On an average 60-70 per cent of the acidity is ascribed to H_2SO_4 and 30-40 per cent to HNO_3. Figure below depicts the causes of acid rain.

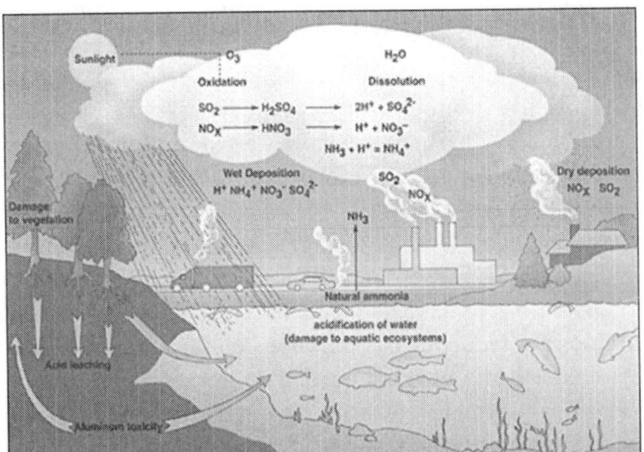

Figure 14.4: Causes of Acid Rain.

As would be noticed, causes of acid rains are: (i) Rapid industrialisation (ii) Burning of fossil fuels for power generation contributes to almost 60-70 per cent of total SO_2 emitted globally, (iii) Anthropogenic sources- emission of NO_x from anthropogenic sources ranges between 20-90 million tonnes annually over the globe. As oxides travel a long distance and during their journey in atmosphere they may undergo physical and chemical transformation to produce more hazardous products. Acid deposition is the accumulation of potential acid - forming particles on the surface; (iv) Natural causes- such as vegetation, volcanoes and geyzers which contribute SO_x and NO_x, the most significant is formic acid; (vi) Forest fires- Biomass burning due to forest fires causes emissions of formic acid (HCOOH) and formaldehyde gets oxidized to formic acid in the atmosphere; (vii) Millions of metric tons of sulphuric acid and nitric acid fall in rain on earth each year, principally on the United States, Canada and Europe. The concentrations of these acids are too weak to cause burns, but they do produce other severe effects. Thus, acidification results from emission and deposition of airborne primary pollutants such as sulphur dioxide, nitrogen oxides, volatile organic compounds and particulates given off by power plants, industry and vehicles and of ammonia produced by agriculture. Reactions among these can produce Secondary Pollutants such as Nitrogen oxide, formed mainly by a reaction between Nitric Oxide and Oxygen. These primary and secondary pollutants can be converted in the atmosphere, on the surface of buildings, inside plants and animals, or below ground, into sulphuric acid and nitric acids. The mechanism of formation of atmospheric sulphuric acid and nitric acid droplets are shown in figures above.

14.4 Acid Rain: Problem and Impacts

In the 1970s and 1980s, Scandinavian countries began to notice the effects of acid deposition on trees and freshwaters. Much of the pollution causing this damage was identified as being transported from other more polluting countries and accordingly acid rain became an international concern. Acid rain became particularly prominent as a media issue during the 1980s. However, during the 1970s many countries started to notice changes in fish populations in lakes and damage to certain trees. By the late 1970s concern led to international efforts to identify the causes and effects of long-range (trans-boundary) transport of air pollutants, and thus during the 1980s much research was conducted in Europe and North America. International legislation during the 1980s and 1990s has led to reductions in sulphur dioxide emissions in many countries but reductions in emissions of nitrogen oxides have been much less. Although media attention has shifted towards other environmental issues such as global warming, etc. acid rain continues to be a problem at the beginning of the twentyfirst century. Acid rains create complex problems, their impacts are far reaching. They increase soil acidity, affecting land flora and fauna. They cause acidification of lakes and streams affecting aquatic life, crop productivity and human health, corrode buildings, monuments, statues, bridges, fences, railings, etc. Due to acidity, levels of heavy metals as aluminum, manganese, zinc, cadmium, lead and copper in water increases beyond the safe limits. Over 10,000 lakes in USA, Canada, Norway have become unproductive due to acidity.

Precipitation and fog of high acidity contaminate and are particularly harmful to fish and other aquatic life in regions with thin soil and granitic rock, which provide little buffering to acidic inputs. It also has been discovered that aluminum is leached from the soil in such regions subjected to acid precipitation, and that dissolved aluminum seems to be extremely toxic to aquatic organisms. All forms of acid precipitation have been found to damage various kinds of vegetation, including agricultural crops and trees, chiefly by inhibiting nitrogen fixation and leaching nutrients from foliage. In addition, these pollutants can corrode the external surfaces of buildings and other man-made structures.

The effects of acid rain are summarised below:

- **Effects on Trees and Soils:** One of the most serious impacts of acid precipitation is on forests and soils. Great damage is done when sulphuric acid falls onto the earth as rain. Nutrients present in the soils are washed away. Aluminium also present in the soil is freed and these toxic elements are absorbed by the roots of trees. Thus, the trees are starved to death as they are deprived of their vital nutrients such as calcium and magnesium. The entire sulphur dioxide is not converted to sulphuric acid. A substantial amount can float into the atmosphere, move over to another area and return to the soils unconverted. As this gas returns back to earth, it clogs up the stomata in the leaves, thus hindering photosynthesis. Research has been made where red spruce seedlings were sprayed with different combinations of sulphuric and nitric acid of pH ranging from 2.5 to 4.5. The needles of these seedlings were observed to develop brown lesions. Eventually, the needles fall off. It was also found that new needles grew more slowly at higher concentrations of acid used. Because the rate at which the needles were falling was greater than the rate at which they were replenished, photosynthesis was greatly affected, and the actual way in which these needles were killed is still not yet known. However, studies have shown that calcium and magnesium nutrients are washed away from their binding sites when sulphuric acid enters the system. They are replaced by useless hydrogen atoms and this inhibits photosynthesis. In addition, severe frosts may also further aggravate this situation. With sulphur dioxide, ammonia and ozone present in the air, the frost-hardiness of trees are reduced. Ammonia oxidises with sulphur dioxide to form ammonium sulphate. This product forms on the surface of the trees. When ammonium sulphate reaches the soils, it reacts to form both sulphuric and nitric acid. Such conditions also stimulate the growth of fungi and pests like the ambrosia beetle.

Figure 14.5 and 14.6: Effects of Acid Rain on trees and soils.

When trees are under such stress, they release chemicals such as terpenes which attract the ambrosia beetle. Nitrogen oxide and nitric oxide, also components of acid rain, can force trees to grow even though they do not have the necessary nutrients. As well, the trees are sometimes forced to grow well into late autumn when it is actually time for them to prepare for severe frosts in the winter.

- ***Effects on Lakes and the Aquatic Ecosystems:*** One of the direct effects of acid rain is on lakes and its aquatic ecosystems. There are several routes through which acidic chemicals can enter the lakes. Some chemical substances exist as dry particles in the air while others enter the lakes as wet particles such as rain, snow, sleet, hail, dew or fog. In addition, lakes can almost be thought of as the "sinks" of the earth, where rain that falls on land is drained through the sewage systems eventually make their way into the lakes. Acid rain that falls onto the earth washes off the nutrients out of the soil and carries toxic metals that have been released from the soil into the lakes.

Another harmful way in which acids can enter the lakes is spring acid shock. When snow melts in spring rapidly due to a sudden temperature change, the acids and chemicals in the snow are released into the soils. The melted snow then run off to streams and rivers and gradually makes its way into the lakes. The introduction of these acids and chemicals into the lakes causes a sudden drastic change in the pH of the lakes - hence the term "spring acid shock."

The aquatic ecosystem has no time to adjust to the sudden change. In addition, springtime is an especially vulnerable time for many aquatic species since this is the time for reproduction for amphibians, fish and insects. Many of these species lay their eggs in the water to hatch. The sudden pH change is dangerous because the acids can cause serious deformities in their young or even annihilate the whole species since the young of many of such species spend a significant part of their life cycle in the water.

Subsequently, sulphuric acid in water can affect the fish in the lakes in two ways: directly and indirectly. Sulphuric acid (H_2SO_4) directly interferes with the fish's ability to take in oxygen, salt and nutrients needed to stay alive. For freshwater fish, maintaining osmoregulation is the key in their survival. Osmoregulation is the process of maintaining the delicate balance of salts and minerals in their tissues. Acid molecules in the water cause mucus to form in their gills and this prevents the fish to absorb oxygen as well. If the buildup of mucus increases, the fish would suffocate. In addition, a low pH will throw off the balance of salts in the fish tissue. Salts levels such as the calcium (Ca_2) levels of some fish cannot be maintained due to pH change. This result in poor reproduction, their eggs produced would be damaged; they are either too brittle or too weak. Decreased Ca_2 levels also result in weak spines and deformities. For example, crayfish need Ca_2 to maintain a healthy exoskeleton; low Ca_2 levels would mean a weak exoskeleton. Another type of salt N^+ also influences the well-being of the fish. As nitrogen-containing fertilisers are washed off into the lakes, the nitrogen stimulates the growth of algae, which would mean an increase in oxygen production, thus benefitting the fish. However, because of increased deaths in the fish population due to acid rain, the decomposition process uses up a lot of the oxygen, which leaves less oxygen for the surviving fish to take in.

Indirectly, sulphuric acid releases heavy metals present in soils to be dissociated and released. For example, aluminium (Al_2) is harmless as part of a compound, but because acid rain causes Al_2 to be released into the soils and gradually into the lakes, it becomes lethal to the health of the fish in the lakes. Al_2 burns the gills of the fish and accumulates in their organs, causing much damage. So, although many fish may be able to tolerate a pH of approximately 5.9, this acid level is high enough to release Al_2 from the soils to kill the fish. This effect is further augmented by spring acid shock. The effect of acid rain can be dynamically illustrated in a study done on Lake 223 which started in 1976. Scientists monitored the pH and aquatic ecosystem of Lake 223. They observed that as the pH of the lake decrease over the years, a number of crustaceans died out because of problems in reproduction due to the acidity of the lake caused by acid precipitation. At a pH of 5.6, algae growth in the lake was hindered and some types of small died out. Eventually, it was followed by larger fish dying out with the same problem in reproduction; there were more adult fish in the lake than there were young fish. Finally, in 1983, the lake reached a pH of 5 and the surviving fish in the lake were thin and deformed and unable to reproduce. This indicates the significant effect of acid rain on lakes and its aquatic ecosystem.

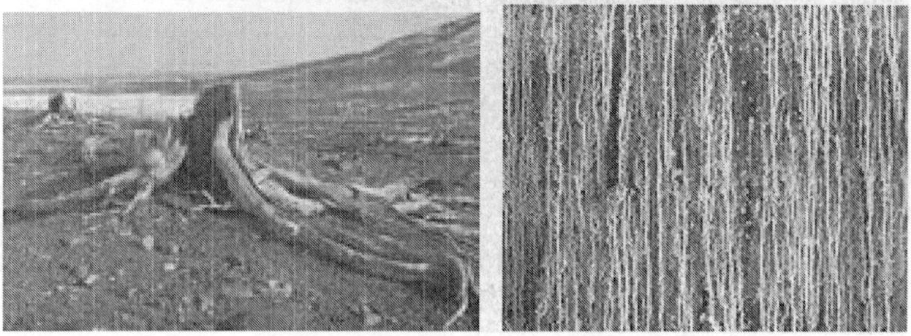

Figure 14.7 and 14.8: Effects of Acid Rain on Aquatic Ecosystem.

- ***Effects on Materials:*** Acid rain also damages materials such as fabrics. For example, flags that are put up are being "eaten away" by the acidic chemicals in the precipitation. Books and age-old art that are centuries old are also being affected; the ventilation systems of the libraries and museums that hold them do not prevent the acidic particles from entering the buildings and so, they get in and circulate within the building, affecting and deteriorating the materials.
- ***Effects on Humans:*** Among one of the serious side effects of acid pollution on humans is respiratory problems. The Sulphur Dioxide and Nitrogen Oxide emissions give rise to respiratory problems such as asthma, dry coughs, headaches, eyes, nose and throat irritations. An indirect effect of acid precipitation on humans is that the toxic metals dissolved in the water are absorbed in fruits, vegetables and in the tissues of animals. Although these toxic metals do not directly affect the animals, they have serious effects on humans when they are being consumed. For example, mercury that accumulates in the organs and tissues of the animals has been linked with brain damage in children as well as nerve disorders, brain damage and death. Similarly, another metal, Aluminum, present in the organs of the animals, has been associated with kidney problems and recently, was suspected to be related to Alzheimer's disease.
- ***Effects on the Atmosphere:*** Some of the constituents of acid pollution are sulphates, nitrates, hydrocarbons and ozone. These exist as dry particles in the air and contribute to haze, affecting

visibility. This makes navigation especially hard for air pilots. Acid haze also interferes with the flow of sunlight from the sun to the earth and back. In the Arctic, this affects the growth of lichens which in turn, affect the caribou and reindeer which feed on it.

Figure 14.9: Effects of Acid Rain on the Atmosphere.

- ***Effects on the Architecture:*** Acid particles are also deposited on to buildings and statues, causing corrosion. For example, the Capitol building in Ottawa has been disintegrating because of excess sulphur dioxide in the atmosphere. Limestone and marble turn to a crumbling substance called gypsum upon contact with the acid, which explains the corrosion of buildings and statues. Another example of effect of Acid Rain is the British parliament building which suffered damage due to H_2SO_4 rains. In addition, bridges are corroding at a faster rate, and the railway industries as well as the airplane industries have to expend more money in repairing the corrosive damage done by acid rain. In 1967, the bridge over the Ohio River collapsed killing 46 people due to corrosion caused by acid rain. Not only is this an economically taxing problem caused by acid rain, but also a safety hazard to the general public.

14.5 Acid Rain: An overarching Concern

As mentioned above, acid rains have assumed international problem and have of late become a major political issue. Acid rains are carried away by prevailing winds to elsewhere where precipitation takes place. Thus, oxides may be produced at one place, and these affect elsewhere by turning into acids. The two such victims are Canada and Sweden. Canada gets acid rains from petrochemical units in North America. Some of the studies conducted by the environmentalists have shown that heavy winds pick up acid rain from factories in Britain and France to Sweden. Equally grim are the acid rains in

Norway, Denmark and West Germany. 90 per cent of the acid rain of Norway and 75 per cent of Sweden are due to drifted acid rain oxides.

Though acidity of rain water is yet to be adequately monitored, developing countries like ours may soon have to face the acid rain problem. The acid rain is fast spreading to developing world where tropical soils are even more vulnerable than those of Europe. It appears that acid rain problem is on the anvil in India. Due to Sulphur dioxide from coal-based power plants and petroleum refinery, industrial areas with the pH value of rain water below or close to the critical value have been recorded in Delhi, Nagpur, Pune, Mumbai and Kolkata. According to a study made by Bhava Atomic Research, Air monitoring section; the average pH value of acid rain at Kolkata is 5.80, Hyderabad 5.73, Chennai 5.85, Delhi 6.21 and Mumbai 4.80. The situation may even worsen in future due to increased installation of thermal power plants by NTPC and consequent increase in coal consumption. According to one estimate total emission of SO_2 in India from fossil fuel burning has increased from 1.38 million tons in 1980 to 3.20 million tons in 1996, a 21 per cent increase as compared to corresponding increase to only 8.4 per cent in USA during the same period. There is urgent need for proper regular monitoring to provide timely warnings about acidification of our environment.

The phenomenon of acid rain is fast becoming grave global ecological problem, threatening forests, farms, human health and aquatic life. Dying forests in West Germany, barren lakes in North America, despoiled monuments in India and degrading farmlands in Brazil – all point out to the rapidly expanding menace of acid rain caused by the pollutants emitted by fossil fuel based industries. Scientists say that acid rain is made up of 65 per cent sulphuric acid, 30 per cent nitric acid and 5 per cent hydrochloric acid. Sweden was first to recognise the threat of acid rain in the mid 1960. Acid rain was first raised as an international problem at the UN conference on Human Environment in Stockholm in 1972. Since then, it has developed into a major environmental issue. The sulphur dioxide, coming from coal and oil fired power plants and industrial smelters, on reaching the upper atmosphere gets transformed into sulphuric acid through a complex chemical reaction. Similarly, oxides of Nitrogen coming from automobile exhaust and high temperature combustion engines are converted into nitric acid in the upper reaches of the atmosphere.

Though many industrialised countries in Europe are now going in for higher mode stacks in the hope that it would obviate the problem of acid rain, the menace nevertheless persists. For after all what has gone up has to come down. The atmosphere has its own mechanism of dumping back unwanted pollutants through rain and wind. Acid rain fallout is one of the channels through which the atmosphere keeps itself free of pollutants. Sweden and Canada are perhaps the worst victims of acid rain. Both these countries are victims of the industrial pollutants released into the atmosphere from neighbouring countries. While, Canada gets acid rains as a result of pollution caused by gigantic petro-chemical units in Northern America, Sweden blames factories in Great Britain and Northern France. After all, pollutants are not expected to respect national boundaries. Around 10,000 fresh water lakes in Sweden are decaying due to unchecked acid rain. The result is telling – decimation and malformation of fish in acidified lakes and a substantial decrease in the number of bacteria and other beneficial micro-organisms sustaining life forms in aquatic habitats. Equally grim is the acid rain crisis in neighbouring Norway where about 500 sq. miles of Lakeland have become barren. Other countries have passed on their problems to Norway. About 90 per cent of pollution in Norway comes from United Kingdom, Central Europe and Eastern Europe-one-third from each region. Denmark's lime rich earth is said to be acting as a cushion, absorbing the ill effect of acid rain. Both Sweden and Norway dumped thousands of tonnes in their lakes and water bodies to counteract the menace of acid rain.

14.6 Acid Rain: Control Measures

Effects of acid rain especially on fish and wild life resources cannot be directly countered without reducing or eliminating the sources of pollution. However, some measures may be taken locally to counter acidification of streams, soil, and rest of the environment. Some of the measures are: (i) *Buffering* through adding a neutralising agent - such as lime in the form of calcium oxide and calcium carbonate to the acidified water to increase the pH; (ii) *breeding of hatching fish in acidified waters* replenishes fish population that would otherwise decline thus helping to maintain an ecological balance within acidified lakes; (iii) *prevention of the emission of excess SOx and NOx from industries* through Legislation by the Government to regulate the emission towards decreasing emissions of SO_2 from power stations by burning less fossil fuel, using alternate energy sources like tidal, wind, hydropower etc, (iv) Using low sulphur fuel, (v) desulphurisation, (vi) decrease in emission of NOx from power stations, and (vii) modification of engines; etc.

Every day we need energy to heat and light our homes, and to drive our cars. Most of the energy we use for this comes from the burning of fossil fuels which release pollutant gases, such as sulphur dioxide and nitrogen oxides, into the atmosphere. Through international protocols and the use of emission control technology introduced since the end of the 1980s, countries have witnessed reductions in acidic emissions from power stations and road vehicles. Nevertheless, it is only by reducing our dependence on fossil fuels and energy consumption that a long-term reduction in acid deposition can be maintained. The individual has little influence on how his/her energy is produced, for example by coal or gas fired power stations, or alternatively by wind or solar power. However, the individual does have control on how he or she uses that available energy. Through the implementation of simple measures we can all effectively bring about a reduction in energy consumption, and help to reduce the amount of emissions which may lead to acid rain. Using less energy also means savings on fuel bills. Energy-saving light bulbs are now widely available in markets. The initial cost of energy saving light bulbs are relatively high compared to standard light bulbs, but the lower running costs and longer lifetimes mean that the initial cost can be recouped within a couple of years. The energy use and efficiency of household appliances, such as fridges, freezers, cookers, washing machines and televisions depends on the age, model and manufacturer. In the UK, 20 per cent of electricity is used by domestic appliances. Retailers in Europe are required to label all new fridges and freezers with an eco-label.

Transport is the fastest growing energy-consumption sector and the number of cars on the road is projected to increase considerably in coming years. It is therefore an area that requires great attention to reduce fuel consumption and hence pollution. Transport pollution is emitted at ground level from a mobile source, and is therefore a larger problem than other pollution sources. As an alternative to driving the car, walk, cycle or use public transport where it is suitable and safe for you to do so, particularly for short trips where using the car is not really necessary and an alternative exists. Where walking or cycling is impractical, consider taking public transport if it is available and convenient to use. A bus full of passengers is more than twice as fuel-efficient as a family car. In addition, if you and your friends drive to work consider the option of car sharing. Everyone contributes to national and global emissions of pollutant gases, but it is not only governments that can take action to reduce the environmental damage caused. For their policies to work effectively and for their targets to be achieved the actions of the individual are required. The cumulative energy reductions by individuals would reduce the need for energy consumption, conserve stocks of raw materials such as coal, oil and gas, and bring about a reduction in pollutant gas emissions which cause acid rain.

14.7 International Agreements

We all know that acid deposition has become an international problem precisely because pollutants can be carried many hundreds of kilometers away by winds and thus acid pollutants emitted in one country may be deposited as acid rain in other countries. This problem is highlighted by the fact that emission of a particular pollutant from one country does not equal the deposition of that pollutant in the same country. Some countries emit small quantities of pollutants yet deposition can be several times greater. Other countries emit more pollution than is deposited in their country because of prevailing wind directions.

In 1979, the United Nations Economic Commission for Europe (UNECE) implemented the Convention on Long-Range Trans-boundary Pollution. In 1985, most UNECE members adopted the Protocol on the Reduction of Sulphur Emissions, agreeing to reduce sulphur dioxide emissions by 30 per cent (from 1980 levels) by 1993 popularly known as ***'30** per cent **club'***. All of the countries that signed the Protocol achieved this reduction, and many of those that did not sign, have met these reductions. In June 1994, a number of European countries signed the Second Protocol for sulphur. Most of the western European countries agreed to reduce sulphur emissions by between 70 and 80 per cent by the year 2000 (against 1980 levels) whilst eastern European countries generally have a lower target of between 40 and 50 per cent (against 1980 levels). Overall, emissions of sulphur dioxide in Europe are estimated to have fallen by 25-30 per cent between 1980 and 1990, and by 40 per cent by the year 2000. Further falls in sulphur dioxide emissions are expected over the next decade. The ***Sofia Protocol*** for reducing nitrogen oxide emissions was adopted in 1988. This required all countries that signed the Protocol to stabilise emissions of nitrogen oxide (against 1987 levels), although some countries committed themselves to 30 per cent reductions by 1998 (against levels of any year between 1980 and 1986). However, many of these countries are have not met these targets, due to increases in road traffic, despite European Union legislation requiring cars built after 1993 to be fitted with a catalytic converter. In 1988, a Directive was introduced for European Community (EC) countries which required power stations to reduce emissions of sulphur dioxide and nitrogen oxides. The most recent UNECE Convention on Long Range Transboundary Air Pollution protocol was signed by 27 countries in December 1999. The ***Gothenburg Protocol***, designed to Abate Acidification, Eutrophication and Ground-level Ozone aims to cut emissions of four pollutants: sulphur dioxide (SO_2), nitrogen oxides (NO_x), volatile organic compounds (VOCs), and ammonia (NH_3), by setting country-by-country emission ceilings to be achieved by the year 2010.

15

Deforestation

15.1 Introduction

Forests are invaluable property of a nation because they provide raw materials to modern industries; timber for building purposes; habitats for numerous types of animals and micro-organisms; good friable and nutrient-rich soils having high content of organic matter; offer protection to soils by binding the soils through the network of their roots and by protecting the soils from direct impact of falling raindrops; they encourage and increase infiltration of rainwater and thus allow maximum recharge of groundwater resources; minimize surface runoff and hence reduce the frequency, intensity and dimension of floods; they help in increasing the precipitation; they are natural 'sink of carbon dioxide' because they use carbon dioxide to prepare their food during the process of photosynthesis; they provide firewood to millions of people all over the world, and food and shelter to innumerable humans and animals. In fact, forests are 'life line' of a nation because prosperity and welfare of the society directly depends on sound and healthy forest cover of a nation concerned. Forests are main component of the biotic components of the natural environmental system and the stability of the environment and ecosystem/ ecological balance largely depend on the status of the forests of the region concerned. Many of the developing countries of the tropical and Subtropical regions have lost substantial portions of their forest covers due to conversion of forested land into agricultural land in order to feed the teeming millions. India has also not been exception to the present global trend of rapid rate of deforestation. According to the Report of the Forest Survey of India, the following is the present status of different land uses under forest covers in India.

Ecologically required forest cover =33 per cent of the total geographical area of the country.

Actual forested cover = 20.4 per cent of the total geographical area of India.

Net required forested cover = 12.6 per cent of the total geographical area of India.

15.2 Causes of Deforestation

The major causes of deforestation at global and regional levels are:-

(i) Conversion of forest land into agricultural land
(ii) Shifting or Jhuming cultivation
(iii) Transformation of forests into pastures
(iv) Overgrazing of forests
(v) Forest fires
(vi) Lumbering
(vii) Multi-purpose river projects
(viii) Biological factors

(i) Conversion of forest land into agricultural land

Increasing population growth at fast rate mainly in the developing countries has put enormous pressure on forested land because it became necessary to clear the virgin forest covers and convert them into agricultural land so that agricultural production may be substantially increased and food may be provided to hungry human population. This trend has resulted into large-scale destruction of savanna vegetation in the Subtropical regions. Rich and extensive grasslands of Russian 'Steppes', American 'Prairies', South American ' Pampas', south African 'Velds' and New Zealandean 'downs' have been extensively converted into agricultural farms and these areas have now become major granaries of the world. Extensive forest covers of the Mediterranean areas have been converted into horticultural farms. The same is the story in the majority of the countries of South and South-East Asia.

(ii) Shifting or Jhuming cultivation

It is a major cause of forest Loss in the hilly and mountainous areas of South and South-East Asia. The loss of virgin forest cover due to shifting cultivation is increasing every year in the different parts of India.

(iii) Transformation of forests into pastures

This has been responsible for rapid rate of loss of virgin forests in the Mediterranean and temperate areas mainly in North America, South America and Africa. The main factor behind large-scale conversion of woodland into pasture land is expanding dairy farming and cattle ranching for meat. Extensive areas of original forest stands in New England region, Michigan and mountainous states of the western USA; Canada, South American countries and African Savannas have been converted into pasture for cattle ranching.

(iv) Overgrazing of forests

Overgrazing of forests of moderate cover by animals mainly in the tropical and subtropical and arid and semi-arid areas has resulted into large-scale degradation of natural vegetation if not the complete destruction of forests. Very low yielding (low per capita yield of both meat and milk) but large numbers of cattle in the developing countries of the world have consumed most part of the ground cover and bushes and herbaceous plants. The deforested areas have been worst affected by grazing animals because no fresh regeneration of plant has been allowed by large heads of grazing animals. The savanna grasslands have been completely destroyed partly by conversion of grasslands into agricultural forms by man and partly by overgrazing.

(v) Forest fires

Forest fires whether natural or man-made are effective destroyers of forest covers. Atmospheric lightning is the major source of natural forest fires. Besides, man causes forest fires through his intentional/advertent and unintentional actions. He burns forests and grasses for cultivation. Deliberate burning of vegetation to get rich and fresh grasses next season leads to several types of changes in the surface materials. The herdsmen also throw burning 'bidies' (Smoking Sticks used mostly in South Asian countries particularly in India, Pakistan, Bangladesh and Sri Lanka) inadvertently which causes forest fires. Besides destroying vegetations, forest fires harden the ground surface which decreases the porosity of the soils and consequently there is little infiltration of rainwater. Thus, most of the rainwater becomes effective surface runoff which accelerates the rate of soil erosion. Secondly, the frequent forest fires destroy the leaf litters on the ground and thus the soil nutrients and humus contents are markedly reduced and sometimes are completely destroyed. Besides, forest fires kill all of the micro-organisms living in the leaf litters mainly decomposers and in the soils and plant roots. Thus, forest fires not only destroy natural vegetation and retard and taboo regeneration of trees but also cause tremendous damage to the biological communities and thus cause ecological imbalance.

(vi) Lumbering

Lumbering for domestic and commercial purposes is the real cause of large-scale destruction of forest covers. Ever increasing demand of timber for various purposes due to industrial expansion, urban growth and rapidly increasing human population has done great damage to natural forest covers all over the world. Inspite of the provision of forest policy in force since 1894 and implementation of National Forest policy since 1952 and despite the guidelines issued by the union government of India for not diverting the forest area to non-forestry uses there has been remarkable loss of 91,70,000 hectares of good forest area in India between 1972 and 1980.

(vii) Multipurpose river projects

It requires larger areas to be submerged for the storage of huge volume of water in the reservoirs constructed behind the dams. Thus, submergence of forested riverine areas completely destroys the natural forests. Tehri Dam project on the head-waters of the Ganga and Narmada River project in Madhya Pradesh and Gujarat, India, are under serious public protests. Tehri Dam on the head-waters of the sacred Ganga river, in Garhwal Himalaya, Uttar Pradesh, India, is meant to generate hydroelectricity to meet out the growing demand of power in Uttar Pradesh and adjoining states and Union Territory of Delhi but its construction is frequently stopped because of protest by noted environmentalist and Chipko Movement leaders, Bhat and Sunder Lal Bahuguna. It is feared that storage of millions of acre feet of water in the reservoirs behind the Tehri Dam will submerge hundreds of square kilometers of forested land which will destroy rich forest cover and displace local inhabitants. Similarly, there is strong protest from general public to abandon the proposed projects of Sardar Sarovar and Indira Sagar on Narmada river in the states of Madhya Pradesh and Gujarat, India. The ecologists believe that the submergence of thousands of square kilometers of areas will destroy regional forest covers and animal community and thus will cause serious environmental and ecological problems.

(viii) Biological factors

It also helps in destroying the natural vegetation. Conversion of forest areas into agricultural farms has resulted into marked shrinkage in the forest covers and thus tremendous pressure of animals on existing forests. Furthermore, application of chemical fertilisers, pesticides and herbicides in the agricultural fields nearer to the forests has driven out micro-organisms such as insects and termites towards the adjoining forests where these cause serious damages to the plants.

15.3 Adverse Effects of Deforestation

The adverse effects of deforestation are discussed in following paragraphs:

Adverse effect on productivity

Destruction of biotic potential of land is the result of over-grazing, indiscriminate felling of trees and overexploitations of land resources. The devastating effects of deforestation in India include soil, water and wind erosions, estimated to cost over 16,400 crores every year. Deforestation has a major impact on the productivity of our croplands in two ways:

- Soil erosion increases manifold and the soil actually gets washed, leading to an accentuated cycle of floods and drought.
- But equally important is the impact of the shortage of firewood on the productivity of our croplands.

When firewood becomes scares, people begin to use cow-dung and crop wastes as fuel, mainly for cooking. Thus, every part of the plant gets used up gradually and nothing goes back to soil. Over a period of time, this nutrient drain affects crop productivity due to loss in soil fertility.

Land Erosion and Landslides

Deforestation and over-grazing have been causing tremendous land erosion and landslides. On an average India is losing about 6,000 million ton of top soil annually due to water erosion in the absence of trees. The loss worked out from the top soil erosion in 1973 was Rs 700 crore, in 1976, 1977 and 1978 it was Rs 889 crore, Rs 1,200 crore and Rs 1,091 crore respectively.

Low per capita forest land

India today is the poorest in the world as per capita forest land is concerned. The per capita forest land in India is 0.10 hectare compound to the world average of one hectare, Canada 14.2 hectare, Australia 7.6 hectare and USA 7.30 hectare. India is losing about 1.5 million hectares of forest cover each year. If this trend continues India may in the next 20 years or so reach to Zero forest value. During a period of 25 years (1951-1976) India has lost 4.1 million hectares of forest area. Large-scale deforestation has been done for fuel, fodder, valley projects, industrial uses, road construction etc. Nearly one per cent of the land surface of India is turning barren every year due to deforestation. In the Himalayan range, the rainfall has declined three to four per cent due to deforestation.

Thus, deforestation gives birth to several problems encompassing environmental degradation through accelerated rate of soil erosion, increase in the sediment load of the rivers, siltation of reservoirs and river beds, increase in the frequency and dimension of floods and droughts, changes in the pattern of distribution of precipitation, intensification of greenhouse effects, increase in the destructive force of the atmospheric storms etc; economic loss though damages of agricultural crops due to increased incidence of floods and droughts, decrease in agricultural production because of loss of fertile top soils, decrease in the supply of raw materials to the industries and building materials (timber) to the urban and rural areas, marked decrease in fodder to animals etc. and social problems in the form of economic poverty, crimes and increased legal litigation.

15.4 Conservation Measures of Deforestation

The protection and conservation of forest resources are not only desirable but are also necessary for the economic development of a nation and maintenance of environmental and ecological balance from local though regional to global levels. Forest conservation measures include: (i) Protection of remaining forest covers and (ii) Increase in the forest cover so as to cover

33 per cent of the total geographical area of a country by forests through afforestation in the open wasteland and reforestation of already deforested areas particularly in those deforested arcas which are not suitable for cultivation such as mountainous and hilly areas.

Integrated Conservation Research (ICR), an ecological group of USA, has launched massive programmes of forest conservation in collaboration with UNESCO's Man and Biosphere (MAB) programme. The ICR has demonstrated that the rainforests are more valuable if used on a sustainable basis than if they are cut down for immediate short-term profit of a few selected elites and affluent class of society. The findings of ICR have shown that about 50 per cent of the world's tropical and sub-tropical forests have already disappeared because of unchecked reckless felling of trees. The main goals of the ICR's programme of forest conservation in the developing countries of the tropical and subtropical areas are– (a) to protect the species diversity that exist in the tropical and sub-tropical forests and (b) to expand the forest land under government protection. The first and foremost task to conserve forest is to protect the existing forests from merciless, reckless cutting of trees by greedy economic man. This task may be achieved through government legislation and by arousing public interest in the importance of the forest resources. Majority of the countries have their national polices on forests and there are provisions for some legislations against deforestation but even then forests are being destroyed at faster rates. This is because of the fact that the contractors achieve their selfish ends in connivance with the government officials.

The National forest policy of India has also laid down certain basic principles for proper management and conservation of the forest resources of the country such as:

- Classification of forests according to functional aspects into protected forests, reserved forests, village forests etc.
- Expansions in the forest cover by planting trees in order to ameliorate the physical and climatic conditions for the welfare of the people.
- Provision for ensuring progressive increasing supplies of fodder for animal and timber for agricultural implements and firewood to local inhabitants nearer to the forests.
- Opposition to reckless extension of agricultural land at the cost of forest land.
- Extension of forested area by massive plan of tree plantation on a large-scale at war-footing so as to bring 33 per cent of the country's geographical area under forest etc.

It appears that directive principles and laws alone cannot guarantee safeguard of forests from their destruction but mass public opinion against the adverse effects of mass felling of trees is also necessary to check onslaught of the forests. Relentless efforts of Sundarlal Bahuguna, a noted environmentalist from the hills of the Uttaranchal Himalaya (India) and his followers Culminating into the Chipko Movement (Sticking to the trees while contractors try to chop the trees) and the movement of domestic women of Reni, Uttaranchal (India) are a few examples of mass awakening of public opinion in favour of economic and environmental significance of natural forests and their concern against adverse effects of their destruction.

Similar movements are being organised by several groups of environmentalists of voluntary organisations and some forceful and effective environmental Slogans have awakened the local public such as 'Save the Western Ghats' 'Save the Ganga and the Himalayas' (launched by Sundarlal Bahuguna against the construction for Tehri Dam on the upper reaches of the Ganga at Tehri town), 'Save the Narmada watersheds and their ecology' (launched by Baba Amte) against the implementation of Narmada Valley project and the construction of Sardar Sarovar (reservoir) and India Sarovar in Madhya Pradesh and Gujarat, India. It is evident that the people themselves may become environmental mediators, guardians and protectors of natural forests if their sentiments are aroused for the conservation and protection of natural forests.

The second important measure of effective conservation of natural forest is to adapt scientific and judicious method of cutting of trees by following selective approach. In other words, only mature and desired trees should be cut and unwanted trees of low economic value should be avoided. It may be pointed out that cutting of mature trees is also ecologically desirable because the old saying 'use them or lose them' holds good because if mature trees are not removed they will automatically perish and may damage other trees.

The third significant measure of forest conservation is to cover more and more wasteland and already deforested land with forests through vigorous planning of afforestation. The afforestation programme must be based on the principle of plantation of multi-species of trees rather than single species of trees because biotic diversity is ecologically more significant than monoculture. Secondly, ecologically sound trees should be given more preference than the commercial trees at least in the areas of fragile environment. For example, deforested areas of the Himalayas are being planted with more pine saplings than oak because of commercial purposes. Thirdly, only those trees should be given preference under the scheme of afforestation which are suitable for the local environmental conditions. For example, planting of eucalyptus trees (an exotic species) on large-scale almost in all parts of India is not advisable because eucalyptus is suitable for certain combinations of environmental conditions only such as 'tarai' region of India. Furthermore, eucalyptus is not of much ecological and environmental significance because of less branching, small size of leaves, fewer numbers of leaves and long roots. Fourthly, forests should not be replaced by commercially important fruit orchards. For example, cultivation of apples in many parts of the Himalayas in general and Himachal Pradesh (India) in particular has done great damage to the original stands of natural forests. Apple cultivation causes deforestation in two ways viz. (i) Apple cultivation requires clearance of land from vegetal cover and (ii) Huge quantity of wood is required for packing of apples every year. According to an estimate the clearance of forest for apple cultivation accelerates the rate of soil erosion by 250 times of normal rate of soil erosion. It has been estimated that one hectare of apple farm damages seven to ten hectares of forests.

The Integrated Conservation Research, a US ecological research group, has suggested elaborate programmes for the betterment of forests. These programmes include: (i) agroforestry, (ii) ethno botany and (iii) natural history oriented tourism.

Thus, deforestation is one of the most serious and widespread environmental problems which India is facing. The country is losing its forest cover steadily because of clearing of forests is done for agricultural purpose, cattle grazing and plantation crops such as tea, coffee etc. India was one of the first countries in the world to have introduced a social forestry programme to introduce trees in non-forested areas along road sides, canals and railway lines.

15.5 Forest Conservation Act, 1980

The Parliament has enacted the Forest (Conservation) Act, 1980, to check further deforestation and conserve forests and to provide for matters connected therewith or ancillary or incidental thereto.

- This Act has five sections which deal with conservation of forests.
- The Act was enacted with the twin objectives under Section 2 of restricting the use of forest land for non-forest purposes, and preventing the de-reservation of forests that have been reserved under the Indian Forest Act, 1927. However, in 1988 the Act was further amended to include two new provisions under Section 2, where it sought to restrict leasing of forest land to private individuals, authority, corporations not owned by the government, and to prevent clear felling of naturally grown trees.
- The Act empowers the Central Government to constitute a committee to advise the government with a grant of approval under Section 2, as also on any other matter connected with the conservation of forest and referred to it by the Central Government.

- The Act provides for the punishment of imprisonment, extendable to fifteen days for the contravention of the provisions of the Act.
- The Act provides for punishment of offenders from the Government Departments, including Head of the Departments and authorities. However, these persons can escape criminal liabilities if they can prove that:
  - The offence was committed without their knowledge,
  - They had exercised all due diligence to prevent the committing of such offence.

15.6 Desertification

Desertification is diminution or destruction of the biological potential of the land which ultimately leads to the formation of desert. The land that has lost its productivity is called a desert. A desert landscape supports a very limited growth of sparse vegetation and stunted growth of plants. Substantial part of earths 132.4 million sq. km of terrestrial area is facing desertification due to over exploitation and mismanage of land resource for human activities.

The arid and semi-arid areas where climate is dry, restoration is very slow, mining and overgrazing etc. adds to several other desertification pressures. Desertification is a systematic phenomenon resulting from excessive felling of trees which manifests itself in the loss of soil fertility, high wind velocity, low precipitation, increasing aridity and extremes of temperatures in the affected areas.

Desert supports very little vegetation and animals which are especially adapted to extremely unfavourable conditions. Although desertification can develop from natural causes along in a majority of instance human intervention promoted arid conditions in an already dry areas. This can happen in any climatic zone or ecosystem resulting from exploitative interaction of man with the natural ecosystem. Most of the deserts of recent origin have resulted from any one or more on the following human activities:

- Uncontrolled and overexploitation of grazing land, indiscriminate cutting of trees and forest resources leading to drought, soil erosion, deterioration of soil fertility which results in stunted plant growth.
- Excessive mining in arid and semi-arid regions for extractions of minerals, cost on limestone resulting in loss of trees and green cover and leading to total destruction of conditions conducive to vegetation growing.
- Uneconomic land use for agriculture by cultivation on marginal lands affecting adjacent fertile lands and causing soil erosion.

- Intensive and uneconomic exploitation of water resources leading to fall in water table, seepage and problems of excessive salinisation of soil.

15.6.1 Causes of Desertification

Some of the principal causes, which promote desertification, are:

- Over cultivation
- Over grazing
- Deforestation, and
- Salt accumulation due to irrigation.

(a) **Over cultivation:** Every cycle of cultivation is preceded by ploughing to remove weeds. The ploughed land turns soil upside down thus exposing rich sub soil to wind and water erosion. Such land may remain barren for most part of the year and in turn lose more soil due to erosion. Such erosion is most pronounced on slopes. Moreover, in regions where rainfall is low, the soil is often dry and is more susceptible to erosion. Ploughed soil loses more water by evaporation.

(b) **Overgrazing:** Deserts received less rainfall. Deserts have sparse vegetation mostly consisting of grasses and herbs less and best used for grazing. Overgrazing by goats, domestic cattle remove the protective vegetation and expose the soil. Further the movements of grazing animals loosen the soil surface by their hoofs. Unprotected loose soil becomes highly susceptible to erosion by wind and water. Such conditions lead to progressive desertification due to series of events.

(c) **Deforestation:** Forests and vegetation prevent soil erosion and to hold water in soil. Plants roots absorb and recycle nutrients released from the decaying organic matter. Forests are often cleared to agriculture, timber, construction wood, firewood, raw material for paper etc. All this leads to barrenness of the land leading to desertification.

(d) **Salt accumulation due to irrigation:** With demand for more land for agriculture, crops are grown in areas that have little access to natural water bodies. The water is supplied to these growing areas by artificial means and improved irrigation methods. Such water brings salts dissolved in it. Even the best quality of irrigation water contains 200-500 ppm of salts. Water used for irrigation is lost from agriculture field through evaporation and transpiration by crop plant. The water gets evaporated but the dissolved salt keeps on accumulating which makes the soils more salty. Saline accumulation of excessive soils prevents retards plant growth. Land devoid of plant cover easily becomes desertified. Accumulation of excessive salt in soil or salinisation makes the soil unfit for agriculture.

Table 15.1: Extent and causes of land degradation of the world

Area	*Causes of land degradation*
580 million hectare	**Deforestation** – vast reserves of forests have been degraded by large scale logging and clearance for farm and urban use. More than 200 million ha of tropical forests were destroyed mainly for food production.
680 million hectare	**Overgrazing** – about 20 per cent of the world pasture and range lands have been damaged. Recent losses have been most severe in Africa and Asia.
137 million hectare	**Fuel wood consumption** – about 1730 million of fuel wood are harvested annually from forests and plantations. Wood fuel is the primary source of energy in many developing regions.
550 million hectare	**Agricultural mismanagement** – loss of soil due to water erosion is estimated at 25,000 million tonnes annually. Soil salinisation, water logging, chemical degradation and desertification affect about 40 million ha of land globally.
195 million hectare	**Industrialisation and urbanisation** – urban growth, road construction, mining and industry are major factors in land degradation in different regions. Valuable agricultural land is often lost.

15.6.2 Extent of desertification

About 76.15 per cent of the total Indian desert area has resulted from man-made desertification process. Another 19.5 per cent of the total area is subjected to medium or slight desertification. This area is concentrated mostly along the eastern Rajasthan in the north-east to south-west zone parallel to the foothills of Aravalis.

Most of the deserts, in India are found in the states of Rajasthan and Western Gujarat where about 23.8 mha areas has been affected by desertification. About 4.34 per cent of this area lies in the extreme west of Rajasthan in Jaisalmer district. This desert is concentrated along a belt in Ganganagar, Churu, Bikaner, Jaisalmer, Barmer, Jodhpur, Jalore, Jhunjhunu and Nagaur districts. The predominant processes of desertification in this belt are the expansion of sand cover and shifting sand dunes by wind erosion.

Desertification adversely affects agriculture, the health and the very survival of humans and livestock, and economic activities such as ecotourism. Agriculture is the mainstay of good economy of many countries. If the process of desertification and deforestation is not contained, the world shortage of food will further increase. Dry land desertification can be arrested and even reversed by using appropriate land management techniques, and monitoring. Desertification aggravated by unsustainable development and resultant climate change, call for strong and urgent measures to avoid mass migration of environmental refugees. These migrants, driven by degraded homelands will move to greener pastures thereby adding pressure on those areas that may already be busting at the seams. It is therefore imperative that we combat desertification and adopt sustainable agricultural practices to preserve our natural land resources for sustenance of economy for benefit of generations still to come.

16

Biodiversity

16.1 Introduction

Biodiversity is the short form of biological diversity which denotes variety of life on earth. This includes all organisms, species, and populations; the genetic variation among these; and the complex assemblages of communities and ecosystems. It also refers to the inter-relationship of genes, species, and ecosystems and their interactions with the environment. Biodiversity exists at three main levels- Genetic, species and ecosystem diversity. Genetic diversity is all the different genes contained in all individual plants, animals, fungi, and micro-organisms. It occurs within a species as well as between species. Species diversity is the variety of species on earth and ecosystem diversity denotes the variety of the earth's habitats, ecosystems and ecological processes.

It is believed that biodiversity is as old as the planet itself. The evolution of bio-diversity has been traced over the last 3.8 billion years. The word 'bio-diversity' was coined by Water Rosen in the National Forum at Smithsonian Institute, Washington in 1986. The importance of biodiversity has been recognised over last 25 years, especially after the report of the World Commission on Environment and Development, commonly known as 'Brundtland Commission (1987)'.

16.2 Bio-diversity: Meaning and Definitions

Biodiversity is the quantity and variability among living organisms within species (genetic diversity), between species and between ecosystems. Biodiversity is not itself an ecosystem service but underpins the supply of services for cultural ecosystem service called "ethical values."

Biodiversity is the variety of life on Earth. It includes diversity at the genetic level, such as that between individuals in a population or between plant varieties, the diversity of species, and the diversity of ecosystems and habitats. It includes diversity in abundance - such as number of genes, individuals, populations or habitats in a particular location, distribution - across locations and through time and in behaviour, including interactions among the components of biodiversity, such as between pollinator species and plants, or between predators and prey. Biodiversity also incorporates human cultural diversity, which can be affected by the same drivers as biodiversity, and which has impacts on the diversity of genes, other species and ecosystems. Biodiversity is thus the variety and variability among living organisms and the ecological complexes in which they occur.

Some of the definitions are given below:

'Biological diversity is the variety and variability among living organisms and the ecological complexes in which they occur.
– *US office of Technology Assessment (1987)*

The Bio-diversity is the totality of genes, species and ecosystems in a region.-*IUCN and UNEP*

The ensemble and interaction of genes, species and ecological diversity at given place and time is known as bio-diversity.- *De Castri (1996)*

Biodiversity is often defined as the variety of all forms of life, from genes to species, through the broad scale of ecosystems.-*Gaston (1996)*

The bio-diversity can be defined as "the diversity of life, which includes the full range of variety and variability within and among living organisms and the ecological complexes in which they occur, and encompasses ecosystem or community diversity, species diversity, and genetic diversity."

The variety of organisms conveys the simplest idea of biodiversity. The sources of plants as sources of food, help, wild life and human resource efficiencies along with variation pattern in the microbial world represent biodiversity.

In simple terms, biological diversity is the variety of life and its process; and it includes the variety of living organisms, the genetic differences among them, and the communities and ecosystems in which they occur.

16.3 Levels of Biodiversity

There are various levels of bio-diversity such as genetic, species, ecosystem diversity as detailed below:

Genetic Diversity

Genetic diversity refers to the variation of genes within species. This covers distinct populations of the same species (such as the thousands of traditional rice varieties in India) or genetic variation within populations, both among geographically separated populations and among individuals within single population.

Genetic diversity is the combination of different genes found within a population of a single species, and the pattern of variation found within different populations of the same species. Coastal populations of shrimp are genetically different from freshwater populations. Genetic adaptations to local climatic conditions such as the seasonal zones in time and space in the two regions result in genetic differences between the two populations of the same species.

Species Diversity

Species diversity is the variety and abundance of different types of individual organisms which inhabit an area. At its most basic level biodiversity includes the full range of species on earth, from micro-organisms such as viruses, bacteria and protozoa to multi-cellular kingdoms of plants, animals and fungi.

Ecosystem Diversity

On a wider scale, biodiversity includes variations in the biological communities in which species live, the ecosystem in which communities exists and the interactions among these levels.

16.4 Importance of Biodiversity

It is not easy to define the importance of biodiversity and very often difficult to estimate it. The value of biodiversity is commonly classified into direct and indirect values. Biodiversity has direct consumptive value in agriculture, medicine and industry. The indirect values imply the functions performed by biodiversity which are not of any direct use such as ecological processes etc.

The examples of direct consumptive value include obtaining of considerable part of daily food from the wild plants by tribal communities in rural areas; as 67 per cent–70 per cent of modern medicines, etc. Further, sacred values are attached to entire ecosystems, for example patches of forests were believed to be the abode of gods, and are used only for prayers and rituals. Many sacred groves still exist in different parts of India (Ministry of Environment and Forest, Government of India's report, 1999).

The indirect values include a broad concept such as ecology and focuses on the conservation of all species. Biodiversity performs a number of ecological services for mankind that have economic, aesthetic or recreations value and therefore there is a need to conserving ecologically. Human responses to biodiversity can generally be grouped into the following categories:

Consumptive use

The general consumptive, productive uses of bio-diversity are of great significance. The diversity of organisms provide food, clothing, shelter, medicines, proteins, enzymes, papers, sports goods, musical instruments, beverages, narcotics, pets, zoo specimens, tourism, raw material for business prospects. Biodiversity in association with latest bio-technology helped in mitigation of disastrous diseases, environmental pollution, drug designing, industrialisation and expediting green revolution.

Productive Use

The biodiversity has provided us with many benefits. Some of these benefits come in the form of goods that can be directly valued and coasted while there are many which provide indirect benefits. The directly valued goods include everything from agricultural crops that form the basis of the world's food supply to medicines that protect and cure us to the fibers that make up the cloths we wear. Thus, biodiversity is widely valued as food pantry and genetic storehouse for biotechnology.

Biodiversity also provides critical indirect benefits to humans that are difficult to quantity because it cannot be valued and coasted. These benefits encompass ecosystem services, such as air and water purification, climate regulation, and the generation of moisture and oxygen.

Social Value

Economists and others have attempted to estimate the social value of biodiversity but met with little success as it cannot be valued easily as in case of economic terms. Biodiversity is a direct source of pleasure and aesthetic satisfaction- its contribution to quality of life, outdoor recreation, and scenic enjoyment; to preserving a sense of place; and to preserving refuges of wildness (Wild lands and wild habitats). Social value of biodiversity is likely to motivate habitat conservation.

Ethical Value

The biodiversity also possesses ethical values. In many places, a cultural value is attached to the biodiversity preservation. It is based on presume that eco-system provide us food, shelter, etc. to survive and therefore must be respected and preserved. Many people and organisation claim that people are duly bound to preserve and protect biodiversity based on high moral principles. This has to be achieved by motivation and explaining the masses about the importance of biodiversity.

Aesthetic Value

Bio-diversity is important as it has aesthetic value. The natural and wild landscapes are aesthetically pleasing and provide solace to the eyes from human dominated landscapes. They also provide opportunities for recreational activities such as hiking, canoeing, bird watching and nature photography, the essence of ecotourism. Horticultural species, wildlife conservation, national parks, zoological and botanical gardens, snake, crocodile, butterfly parks, and curious species add to the aesthetics. The aesthetic value of biodiversity at an undisturbed natural paradise has prompted the ideas of ecotourism which in turn is helpful in preserving natural eco-wealthy conditions and natural biodiversity.

Optional Value

While there are hundreds of examples of known economic and aesthetic benefits of biodiversity, biologist and other scientists have frequently outlined that more is unknown than known. Important ecosystem services and uses for plants and animals are still unknown and await discovery. The optional value includes the co-friendly effort and bio-technology advances that can come up only with the existing bio-diversity.

16.5 Bio-diversity at Global, National and Local Levels

India contains a great wealth of biological diversity in its forest, its wetlands and in its marine areas. This richness is shown in absolute numbers of species and the proportion they represent of the world total.

Table 16.1

Comparison between the number of species in India and the World

Group	*Number of species in India (SI)*	*Number of species in the world (SW)*	*SI/SW* (per cent)
Mammals	350 (1)	4,629 (7)	7.6
Birds	1224 (2)	9,702 (8)	12.6
Reptiles	408 (3)	6,550 (9)	6.2
Amphibians	197 (4)	4,622 (10)	4.4
Fishes	2546 (5)	21,730 (11)	11.7
Flowering Plants	15,000 (6)	250,000 (12)	6.0

Source: Biodiversity profile of India by Centre for Ecological Sciences, Bangalore, India.

Inventories of birds, mammals, trees, fish and reptiles are only moderately complete and are steadily improving through collaboration of domestic scientists with those from overseas.

16.6 India as a Mega Diversity Nation

India has a great diversity of natural ecosystems from the cold and high Himalayan ranges to the sea coasts, from the wet northeastern green forests to the dry northwestern acid deserts, different types of forests, wetlands, islands and the oceans. India consists of fertile river plains and high plateaus and several major rivers, including the Ganges, Brahmaputra and Indus.

The climate of India is determined by the Southwest monsoon between June and October, the northeast monsoon between October and November and dry winds from the north between December and February. From March the climate is dry and hot. India, being a vast country, shows great diversity in climate, topography and geology and hence the country is very rich in terms of biological diversity. India's biological diversity is one of the most significant in the world, since India has only two per cent of the total landmass of the world containing about six per cent of the world's known wildlife.

Diversity in Vegetation and Wildlife

India is a land of great natural contrasts. It has a great variety of natural vegetation. Himalayan heights are marked with temperate vegetation; the Western Ghats have tropical forests and mangroves, and the desert and semi-desert areas in Rajasthan.

Indian forests can be classified into: (i) Mountain Forests; (ii) Tropical Evergreen Forests; (iii) Tropical Dry Deciduous Forests; (iv) Semi-arid and Desert Forests; (v) Wetlands, Littoral and Swamp Forests; and (vi) Grasslands. The details are given below:

- **Mountain forests**

Mountain vegetation is found in the mountainous regions. In India they are mainly of two types: Himalayan Mountain Forests; and Peninsular Mountain Forests.

Himalayan Mountain Forests: The Himalayan vegetation is classified as tropical, subtropical, temperate and alpine, mainly on the basis of altitude and rainfall.

Tropical evergreen mountain rain forests are confined to the humid foothills of the Eastern and Central Himalayas. These forests consist of a group of timber and resin producing trees of different species. Greenwood is found on porous soils, bamboo on steep slopes, oaks and chestnuts on littoral covering the sandstone all the way from Arunachal Pradesh westward to central Nepal at altitudes ranging from 1200 to 1300 m. Alder trees are found along the watercourses on the Steeper slopes. Besides these trees, some 4,000 species of flowering plants are also found in moist region of Nepal, Uttarakhand and Uttar Pradesh. Lower regions have several species including bamboo, cane etc. Abundantly found trees in this region are sal, ber, gular, jhingal, semal, amla, jamun etc. In these forests several species of insects, birds and butterflies are found. Tree climbers such as monkeys are also found along with tree frogs, rhino, tiger etc.

Temperate forests are found at altitudes between 1,500 and 3,500 m. They contain conifers and broad leaved temperate trees. Evergreen forests of oaks and conifers are specially seen on the outer slopes of Pir Panjal range in

Kashmir. Pines, Deodar are also predominant plant species of this region. Common animals in the region are wild goats and sheep, Himalayan black bear etc. Some other animal species which are found in the region are snow leopard, Hangul, Himalayan brown bear, musk deer, Himalayan wolf etc.

Alpine zone begins above the tree line, at an altitude of 3200 to 3500 m and extends upto 3900 m in the Western Himalayas and 4450 m in the eastern Himalayas. This zone is marked by wet and moist alpine vegetation. These include shrubs, rhododendrons mosses, lichens and wild flowers.

Peninsular Mountain Forests are located in Western Ghats, Vindhyas and the Nilgiris. As they are closer to the tropics and only 1500 m above sea level, vegetation in their higher region is temperate while subtropical vegetation is found in lower regions. Some trees found in the region are magnolia, laurel, eucalyptus, cinchona and wattle etc. These are important sources of oil and have medicinal value. Animal species found in these areas are tiger, leopard, sambar, pigmy, hog, lion, tailed macaque etc.

- **Tropical Evergreen Forests**

Evergreen forests grow in the high rainfall areas between 25 cm to 130 cm and temperature ranging from 22°C to 27°C. These forests grow in areas where the monsoon period lasts for several months. Areas of Western Ghats, Northeastern India and Andaman and Nicobar islands have such forests. Even some places of South India which gets two monsoons, show tropical evergreen forests. Tropical evergreen forests can be classified into three types: (i) The **Wet evergreen forests** which are mainly confined to tropical evergreen forests of Western Ghats, Peninsular parts along Arabian Sea and Andaman and Nicobar Islands; (ii) **Semi evergreen forests** that are confined to eastern side of Western Ghats which fall in rain shadow zone; (iii) **Moist deciduous forest** that are mostly found in parts of Madhya Pradesh, Kerala, South Coimbatore area of Tamil Nadu, Uttar Pradesh, Osisha, Bihar, West Bengal and Assam. The total forest area covered by these types of forests is around 49 per cent. There are substantial differences in both flora and fauna of all the above forests. In Northeastern part of India e.g. Assam, Nagaland, Meghalaya, Mizoram and Manipur, there are evergreen forests with wide biodiversity. Several species of bamboo and sal, and animals such as rhinoceros are also found in these forests.

- **Tropical dry deciduous forests**

These forests are found in Ganga plain, central part of the peninsula and the Coimbatore plateau in Tamil Nadu. These forests are found in regions with a moderate amount of seasonal rainfall approximately 60 cm to 120 cm that lasts for only a few months. The deciduous trees shed their leaves during the winter and hot summer months. In March or April monsoon, they grow vigorously in response to the rains. Dominant trees species are the teak, tamarind, cassia, khair and the bamboo. Tiger, chital, barking deer, animals are found in these areas.

- **Semi-arid and desert forests**

These forests are a mixture of grassland and shrubs. Areas of eastern Rajasthan, Southwest Punjab, Western Haryana, Bundelkhand region of Madhya Pradesh and Uttar Pradesh, Southern Karnataka and adjoining Andhra Pradesh have this type of vegetation. Semi-arid and desert forests are found in dry areas having annual rainfall ranging from 30 to 60 cm.

Thorny plants are the main characteristic of this area. They are called as X-xerophytes plants and are able to conserve water. Some of these trees have small leaves, while other species have thick, waxy leaves to reduce water loss during transpiration. Roots of trees are long and fibrous which make water reach at great depths. Many of these plants have thorns, which reduce water loss and protect them from herbivores. Other vegetation includes wild date palms which grow in the valleys. Along the river and in the sand dunes grow the khair (Acacia catechu) and Sissoo, papal (ficus religiossa) and babul (Acacia arbica).

- **Wet lands, littoral and swamp forests**

India has a rich variety of wetland habitats. Wetlands of mangrove forest grow along the coast especially in the river deltas. In India, the mangrove forests spread over 6740 sq. kilometers which is seven per cent of the world's total mangrove forests. They are highly developed in Andaman and Nicobar Islands and Sundarbans of West Bengal. Other areas of significance are the Mahanadi, the Godavari and Krishna deltas. Two sites – Chilka Lake (Odisha) and Keoladeo National Park (Bharatpur) are protected water bound habitats under the convention of wetlands of International Importance. Plants of these regions are uniquely adapted to grow in a mix of saline and fresh water. They grow luxuriantly in muddy areas covered with silt, brought down by the rivers. The mangrove trees have breaking roots that emerge from the mud banks. Plants of Aricenia species are found in these areas. Animals include crocodiles, **share birds – sand – pipers, poovers, fish, crustaceans, water monitor lizards etc.**

- **Grasslands**

A wide range of landscapes, in which the vegetation is predominantly grasses and small annual plants, are specifically adapted to India's varied climatic conditions. There are about 60 species of perennial grasses which are exclusively found in India. Pastures and grasslands are products of dry semi-deserts but they have often resulted from degradation and destruction of forests into savannas. These pastures are found only in the sub-alpine and alpine areas in the higher altitudes of the Himalayas. Himalayan pastures have a great variety of grasses and herbs. Himalayan slopes are covered with thousands of colourful flowering plants as well as a large number of medicinal plants.

Terai region of Uttar Pradesh consists of patches of tall grasslands interspersed with Sal forest. The semi - arid plains of western and central India and the Deccan are covered by grass tracts with patches of thorn forest. Several mammals such as the wolf, the black buck, the chinkara and birds such as bustards and horicans are adapted to these arid conditions. These areas show diverse insect life on which the insectivorous birds feed.

Diversity in aquatic life

The aquatic ecosystems comprise the marine environments of the seas and the freshwater systems in lakes, rivers, ponds and wetlands. India is blessed with wide network of rivers and scattered presence of ponds and is found in these freshwater ecosystems. One such strange creature is Gangetic Dolphin. It lives in the Ganga river. It is born blind and lives sightless for the rest of its life. Marine ecosystems around peninsular India constitute the Indian Ocean, the Arabian Sea and the Bay of Bengal. Several kinds of plant and animal species are found in these marine ecosystems. Some parts of our coastal area are one of the best fishing zones in the world. In the coastal area, where sea is shallow we find phytoplankton and large seaweeds. There are millions of zooplanktons and a large variety of invertebrates on which fish, turtles and other mammals feed on. The shallow areas near Kutch and around the Andaman and Nicobar Islands are some of the most incredible coral reefs of the world. These coral reefs are very rich in species diversity. Several species of fish – crustaceans, starfish, jellyfish and polyps – are found in these areas.

16.7 Hot-spot of Biodiversity

"Hot-Spots" are biologically rich areas with high diversity and a large percentage of endemic species. For example, 20 per cent of the world's plants are found on 0.5 per cent of the earth's surface. Biological hot - spots include the western Amazon (Colombia, Ecuador, Peru), Madagascar, North and Eastern Borneo, Northeastern Australia, West Africa, and the Brazilian Atlantic forest. All of these areas have high diversity and many are threatened by human activities.

Global biodiversity hot-spots

The Tropical Andes (Venezuela, Colombia, Ecuador, Peru and Bolivia), Madagascar, Brazil's Atlantic Forest Region, The Philippines, Meso – American forests, Wallacea (eastern Indonesia), Western Sunda (in Indonesia, Malaysia and Brunei), South Africa's Cape floristic region, The Antilles,

Brazil's Cerrado, The Darien and Choco of Panama, Colombia and Western Ecuador, Polynesia and Micronesian Island complex, including Hawaii, South Western Australia, The Eastern Mediterranean region, The Western Ghats of India and the island of Sri Lanka, The Guinean forests of West Africa, New Himalayas, Eastern Himalayas, and Southeastern Australia and Tasmania.

Hot-spots in India

Hot-spots are areas that are extremely rich in species, have high endemissism, and are under constant threat. Among the 25 hot spots of the world, two are found in India extending into neighbouring countries – the Western Ghats/ Sri Lanka and the Indo - Burma region (covering the Eastern Himalayas). These areas are particularly rich in floral wealth and endemision, not only in flowering plants but also in reptiles, amphibians, swallow - tailed butterflies, and some mammals.

Eastern Himalayas

The area comprises Nepal, Bhutan and neighbouring states of northern India. Here tropical forests are found between altitudes of 1780 m to 3500 m. Many deep and semi - isolated valleys are exceptionally rich in endemic plant species. Of the 5150 native plant species, 3500 are found in the Himalayas and adjoining regions.

Western Ghats

Of the 5150 native plant species, the remaining 1600 plant species are found in the 17,000 sq. km strip of forest along the coastal areas of Western Ghats in Maharashtra, Karnataka, Tamil Nadu and Kerala. There are two main centres of diversity; the Agastyamalai Hills and the Silent Valley Reserve basin.

World Heritage Sites

The world heritage list has been maintained by UNESCO since 1972 based on Conservation Treaty Known as World Heritage Conservation that has been ratified by 160 countries. Areas around the world that are magnificent due to their cultural traditions or their unique natural beauty or ecological importance were designated as World Heritage Sites. India ratified the World Heritage Conservation in 1977. There are five World Heritage sites in India, for protecting the biodiversity, viz; Kaziranga National Park, Keoladeo National Park, Manas Wildlife Sanctuary, Sunderbans, and Nanda Devi National Park.

16.8 Loss of Biodiversity

We are living in the age of science. Every day we are exploring and discovering new things. Presently, science has recognised about 1.8 million species of plants and animals. But still the number of unknown species is more than the species known to us which collectively constitute our ecosystem. Human greed and profit making tendency lead to overuse or misuse of most of these natural ecosystems. Unsustainable use of resources has slowly turning the productive forests and grasslands into deserts and wastelands all over the world. Mangroves have been cleared for fuel wood, prawn farming led to decrease in the habitat essential for the breeding of marine fish. Such destruction of natural resources on a wide scale has endangered diversity of life on the earth. Many species of plants and animals are on the verge of extinction. Scientists have estimated that human activities are likely to eliminate approximately 10 million species by the year 2050. Present rate of extinction is so high that within next twenty or thirty years about 25 per cent of world's species will be exterminated. Much of this mega extinction species is related to human population growth, industrialisation and changes in land use patterns. A major part of this extinction will occur in bio rich areas, such as tropical forests, wetlands and coral reefs.

16.9 Threats to Biodiversity

Following types of species tend to disappear in due course of time. They are: (i) Species with a very narrow geographical range; (ii) Species with only one or small population; (iii) Species in which population size is small; (iv) Species with low population density; (v) Species with need a large home range; (vi) Species that have large body size; (vii) Species with low rate of population increase; (viii) Species that are not effective disperses; (ix) Species that migrate; (x) Species with little genetic variability; (xi). Species with specialised requirements; (xii) Species that characteristically found in stable environments; (xiii) Species that form permanent or temporary aggregations; and (xiv) Species that hunted or harvested by people.

16.10 Causes of Loss of Biodiversity

Human activity is the major threat to biodiversity. The chief causes of human led extinction of species are discussed below:

Over Population

The ever increasing human population is the chief cause of loss of diversity. Over population calls for increased demands for agricultural land, housing, etc. These demands are met through encroachment on forests which in turn adversely affects the habitat of plants and animals. Over population can also be held responsible for deforestation, pollution and global warming and other climatic changes.

Deforestation

Population explosion of twentieth century and heavy industrialisation created unsustainable burden on ecosystem. Forests are first to face this attack caused by large scale deforestation to meet the requirement of timber and agricultural land. This has created great loss not only to plant species but also to several animal species living in the forest. They have lost their habitat. Survival for them became impossible.

Agricultural Expansion and Overgrazing

Agricultural expansion necessitated due to ever increasing population is one of the requirements for deforestation. Overgrazing in forest areas by adjoining villagers has created additional competition for wild herbivorous animals. This may result in decline in the number and species of herbivorous animals affecting the forest food chain.

Indiscriminate Hunting

Hunting animals had been a matter of entertainment and pride for feudal class of society which is prevented by law. But still hunting is carried out for trade and commercial purposes to obtain hides, skins, fur, leather, feathers, horns, ivory, meat etc. Indiscriminate hunting for commercial and recreational purposes has been threatening bio-diversity and many wild species have come to the verge of extinction.

Urbanisation and Human Development Works

Twentieth century saw rapid industrialisation and urbanisation. There is migratory trend from rural to urban areas. Several development activities are, therefore, carried out to provide sustenance to urban population and industrialisation process. Development works such as tall buildings, big factories, large over bridges, dams, reservoirs, roads, railway lines, mines etc. cause hindrances to natural discourse. Dams block spawning and migration of fishes, construction of road, railway lines and mines leads to deforestation. Construction of artificial posts and tidal power generators disturb life in coastal areas and coral reefs, etc. The list is endless.

Environmental pollution

Rapid industrialisation and urbanisation in the past century led to environmental pollution. Emission of carbon dioxide, carbon monoxide and certain other dangerous gases cause air pollution. Sewage disposal, urban waste and harmful chemicals release in rivers cause water pollution. Entry of such pollutants in the natural cycles creates devastating effects on diverse aquatic life existing in that area. Soil erosion and soil pollution turn fertile land into barren land thereby making diverse plants life difficult.

Habitat Loss

The primary cause of the loss of biodiversity is not direct human exploitation but the habitat destruction which results from expansion of human and livestock population and human activities. Most of the original habitats have been destroyed in the regions of high population density. Vast areas of habitat are lost every year as forests are cut down. Rain forests, tropical dry forests, wetlands, mangroves and grasslands are threatened habitats and leading to desertification.

In many cases, the factors causing habitat destruction are the large industrial and commercial activities, associated with a global economy, such as mining, cattle ranching, commercial fishing, forestry, plantation, agriculture, manufacturing and dam construction, initiated with the goal of making a profit.

Habitat Fragmentation

Habitat that formerly occupied wide areas are now often divided into pieces by roads, fields, towns, canals, power lines, etc. Habitat fragmentation is the process where a large, continuous area of habitat is both, reduced in area and divided into two or more fragments. When habitat is destroyed there is often a patchwork of habitat treatments left behind. These fragments are often isolated from one another by a highly modified or degraded landscape. Habitat fragmentation may limit the potential of species for dispersal and colonisation. It also reduces the foraging ability of animals. Habitat fragmentation causes such edge effects micro climatic changes in light, temperature, wind, etc.

Habitat Degradation

Some activities may affect the other species of a community instead of dominant species. For example, physical degradation of forest due to uncontrolled fire might not destroy trees but the rich store of wild plants and insects on the forest floor would be greatly affected. Boating and diving in coral reef areas degrade the fragile species.

Introduction of Exotic Species

The widespread introduction of exotic species by humans is a potent threat to local species. Exotic species are the species which are not native of given area but have been brought there from the place of their origin. Water hyacinth is an example of exotic species and is today widely affecting the aquatic ecosystems in India, as weed.

All the exotic species do not flourish in new places. Some species are able to adopt themselves and flourish in new areas. These species may hunt native species to the point of extinction or to such an extent that many native species may not be able to survive.

Disease

Human activities may increase the incidence of disease in wild species. The extent of the disease increase when animals are confined to a nature reserve rather than being able to disperse over a large area. Also, animals are more prone to infection when they are under stress. Animals held in captivity are also more prone to higher level of disease.

Overexploitation

Increasing human population has escalated the use of natural resources. Methods of harvesting have been dramatically modified to have maximum gains. In traditional societies, there were some controls to prevent over exploitation in several ways. In contrast to this, in today world resources are exploited as rapidly as possible. Overexploitation threatens about one - third of the endangered vertebrates in the world, as well as other species. Growing rural poverty, increasingly efficient methods of harvesting and the globalisation of the economy combine to exploit species to the point of extinction. Even if a species is not completely eliminated by overexploitation the population size may become so low that the species is unable to recover.

Shifting or Jhum cultivation

The local farmers often have no choice except to move to remote underdeveloped areas and attempt for their livelihood through shifting cultivation. In many countries, the practice of shifting cultivation is in vogue even today. In this, a community is forced to leave one place and go to another place, mostly to the remote places, to practice agriculture. Even, in our country, the practice is prevalent, where a community practices farming and other activities by shifting their base; from one place to another. This practice endangers the species or different places. This commonly practiced agricultural system is known as Sweden agriculture, slash - and - burn agriculture and jhum cultivation. This greatly affects forest structure and species composition by creating a mosaic of forest patches of different ages as the trees are cut down; the fallen material is burnt, and crops are planted in nutrient - rich ash. After two or three harvests, the nutrients are washed out of soil by the rain. The farmer then abandons this patch and cuts down a new patch of forest trees elsewhere for crop production.

Lack of Government Initiatives

Rapid loss of biodiversity is not the problem of any specific country. Across the world, the concerns have been raised. World organisations, namely, United Nations and other regional groups of countries like EU (European Union) and SAARC etc. have already framed regulations regarding protection of biodiversity and environment conservation. On same lines many governments in the world including Indian government have framed laws for environment protection. For example, Environment (Protection) Act, Wildlife (Protection) Act etc. However, we observe official laxity in implementation of such laws. Government officials, bureaucrats and even judiciary many a time fail to punish culprits. Illegal trade in musk, ivory and rhino horn encourages mass killing of animals.

Lack of Awareness

Environment education and awareness regarding wildlife protection is lacking amongst general population. Education system, mass media and government departments can play vital role in increasing the awareness among the people. Increased awareness and mass environment education will help to protect diverse wildlife on this earth.

17

Biodiversity Conservation

17.1 Introduction

As we have learnt in previous chapter, biodiversity is fundamental to the fulfillment of human needs. In fact, biodiversity is part of our daily lives. Biological diversity offers the broadest array of options for sustainable economic activity and sustainable human welfare. Biodiversity is important for ensuring food security, safeguarding human health, providing recreational opportunities, arrest unprecedented rates of species extinction and global economy. In short, biodiversity provides 'life support system' and therefore its conservation is important. Conservation of biodiversity means the management of human use of the biosphere so that it may give maximum benefit to the present generation while maintaining its potential to meet the needs and aspirations of the future generations.

The word 'Conservation' is derived from the Latin words, '*Con*' which means 'together' and '*servare*' which means 'guard'. Considering the fact that biodiversity provides life support system in earth, it is necessary to begin enormous conservation efforts to arrest loss of biodiversity and its restoration. It is the responsibility of all of us to conserve, restore and sustainably use the biological diversity for sustainable future.

17.2 Objectives of Biodiversity Conservation

The primary objective of the biodiversity conservation is to stop further damage to the environment so that climate change, changes to the aquatic environment and water flows, fragmentation and degradation of habitat, unsustainable use of natural resources, etc. are checked. Some of the sub-objectives are given below:

Maintain ecological processes

Ecological processes are the interactions and connections between living and non-living systems. These processes include nutrient cycling; seasonal flow patterns of rivers; dispersal of animals and seeds; local adaptations by species to changing environmental conditions; ecological disturbance by wildfire, flooding and storms; and functional interactions between soils, plants and animals such as pollination, decomposition, predation and competition. Ecological processes are fundamentally important to sustaining life and its diversity. The loss of biodiversity is damaging this natural process. Report on 'Millennium Ecosystem Assessment 2005' also indicated ecological processes as crucial to human survival and wellbeing, and economic activity. These ecosystem services are generally not valued or are undervalued, and are taken for granted until they break down. It is therefore one of the important objectives to maintain ecological processes at its most natural state as far as possible for human survival and maintaining economic growth.

Preserve the diversity of species

The existing diversity of species in the natural habitats is complimentary to survival of one another and also for maintaining the diversity of species. The world's renowned conservation biologists have estimated that human interference on the environment is causing species to vanish at a rate that is hundreds of times faster than the natural rate. Considering the importance of diversity of species of plants and animals for human life's necessities- food, clothing, medicine; economic growth through use of natural products by industry to produce everyday goods; etc. it is necessary to preserve the diversity of species. Preservation of the diversity of life acts as trustee for the planet, and preserving genetic capital for use by future generations. It is therefore, one of the important objectives of biodiversity conservation to preserve the diversity of species for maintaining the ecological balances and sustainable development.

Retention of natural environments

Natural environment is god gifted which has in-built natural balances within it to support ecosystem. This natural environment provide basis for economic growth. The natural environment and economic development are mutually compatible provided it is used judiciously. Owing to excessive extraction of natural environment (resources) for fast paced economic growth, the natural balances are disturbed. The deterioration is more than its natural regeneration, taking a toll on natural processes and thereby affecting the ecosystems. Retention of natural environment, protection and improvement is therefore one of the core objective within the planning system for sustainable economic growth and human survival.

Manage biodiversity conservation

Biodiversity refers to the variety and variability among living organisms, the ecological complexes in which they occur, and the ways in which they interact with each other and their environment. Extinction is a natural process.

The geological record indicates that hundreds of plant and animal species have disappeared over time as they failed to adapt to changing conditions due to geological events like continental drift, massive volcanic eruptions or asteroid impacts. The rapidly escalating human demand for natural resources is causing genes, species and habitat to disappear at an unprecedented rate. Conservative estimates indicate that human activity has increased the extinction rates of plants and vertebrates to between 10 and 100 times the normal rate. Considering the contribution and importance of diversity in genes, species and ecosystems in productivity of agriculture, forestry, fisheries and industry in terms of security in income, employment and livelihood and farming systems to the local communities, the proper management of biodiversity is one of the primary objectives of biodiversity conservation.

Improvement in delivery mechanism

We all know that the ecosystem is important for our survival and well being. With the passage of time, natural balances of biodiversity is deteriorating at a very fast pace. While a number of species have been extinct, many others are facing threat of extinction. The loss of biodiversity will affect life forms and its survival. It is therefore necessary to realise the loss and attempt to arrest the process, if not reverse it. The countries world over are trying to save ecosystems by conservation efforts. It is equally important to improve delivery mechanism for knowledge sharing on extent of loss of biodiversity, causes, techniques of biodiversity conservation, etc. to maintain the current level of natural balances. Thus, improvement of delivery mechanism to enable all stakeholders to know about this is one of the key objectives of biodiversity conservation.

17.3 Strategies for Conservation

India has always been in the forefront in safeguarding environmental degradation and biodiversity conservation. The country has vowed to protect threatened, endangered and vulnerable wildlife species, care and protection of exotic species, conservation of all the possible varieties of old or new food, forage and timber plants, livestock, aquaculture animals and microbes, identification and conservation of economically important and commercially viable flora and fauna, identification and safeguard of critical habitats for each species, regulated international trade in wildlife products with proper trade rules and regulations, preservation of proper ecosystems on priority basis, development of reserves or protected areas, framing of proper legislation and legal provisions for wildlife protection, and increasing public awareness.

The Ministry of Environment and Forests (MoEF), Government of India has been designated the Nodal Agency with the responsibility of implementing Conservation of Bio-Diversity (CBD) in the country. MoEF involves a number of other ministries, departments, institutions and NGOs as major partners for developing and implementing national strategies on conservation and sustainable use of biodiversity. MoEF has initiated a number of plan and programmes for biodiversity conservation as detailed below.

Conservation of biological diversity

Our county is committed for conservation of biological diversity within its territory. The strategy for its conservation includes identification of all biological diversity and its threat, management plans and execution process for their conservation, conservation within protected areas, conservation outside protected areas, wildlife conservation, threatened biological diversity, and ex-situ conservation, etc. Various acts and rules framed for the purpose delineate the strategy for biodiversity conservation. Some of the important acts are - The Indian Forest Act, 1927; The Wildlife (Protection) Act, 1972 (amended upto 1991); The Forest (Conservation) Act, 1980 (amended in 1988); The Environment (Protection) Act, 1986; The Biological Diversity Act, 2002; etc.

Integrating biological diversity conservation

The issue biodiversity conservation assumes lot of importance in present day world. Its unprecedented importance and the necessity of conservation cut across many sectors and fields. The national strategy, therefore, attempted to develop synergy between various fields and sectors with due integration for adequate and effective biodiversity conservation. The strategy includes integrated policies at national level for proper resource management in the field of agriculture, fisheries, forestry, wildlife, water, tourism and recreation, etc. and its effective execution.

Managing threatening processes

Many species have already been lost, while existence of some of the other species- both plants and animals are threatened. The national strategy through various plans and programmes stipulates identification of threatening species including threatening processes and activities. Impacts of climate change on biological diversity, environmental assessment and the rehabilitation of threatening species and their processes are also studied and measures to manage them are also indicated in the strategy for biodiversity conservation.

Improving our knowledge

Recognising the fact that knowledge and understanding is primarily important to know the usefulness of biodiversity conservation for sustainable development on earth, strategy of biodiversity conservation emphasises on improving the knowledge base of every individuals, political leaders, educators and all others. The improvement of knowledge will help in initiating various measures for bio-conservation and pave way for greater partnership between the government and the civil society.

17.4 Types of Biodiversity Conservation

The conservation of biodiversity is of two types:

- In-situ conservation, and
- Ex-situ conservation.

In-situ conservation

The in-situ conservation is also known the on-site conservation. It involves conservation of species in their natural habitat. The natural surrounding is protected and restored so that all the species unknown or known to man are preserved. This is a better way of conservation as the biodiversity can best flourish in the natural habitat as organisms get favourable environmental conditions.

Institutionalised management of biodiversity in-situ started with the establishment of the first National Park in the country, the Hailey National Park (now Corbett National Park) in 1935. Following this, more than 300 protected areas were set up representing a wide range of ecosystems. The strategy of in-situ conservation lays stress on the establishment of protected areas of different sizes which were meant exclusively for wildlife preservation. Keeping this in view, a variety of protected areas are developed which differed from one another in their size, purpose and degree of human interference. These protected areas are biosphere reserve, national parks, wildlife sanctuaries, and sacred forests and lakes. Institutionalised efforts at conservation of endangered animals were initiated in the country about 40 years ago with the launching of Project Tiger, followed by swamp deer, elephant, rhino and wild buffalo.

Biosphere Reserves

Fig. 17.1: Biosphere Reserves.

These are large areas where both plants and animals are conserved and protected in their natural habitats to enable them lead a natural life. The guidelines for establishment of biosphere reserves was issued by Man and Biosphere (MAB) programme in 1974. The guidelines provide areas for ecological and environmental research and facilities for education and training.

The Biosphere Reserves programme was launched by MoEF in 1986. The primary objective of this programme was to identify representative ecosystems which are still in pristine condition and strengthen the conservation efforts keeping in view the livelihood needs of the people. The various implications and facets of the issue are being debated through a consecutive proccss.

Natural Zone is the innermost part of the biosphere reserve which is completely protected from all human activities. Buffer zone is the area next to the natural zone where activities related to education and research along with some resource management activities are carried out. Transitional zone is the outermost area where local people and management are interrelated. Human activities which cause no harm to biodiversity are allowed in the region.

Till date there are 14 biosphere reserves established by the Government of India, of which four biosphere reserves are part of the International Network of Biosphere reserves. They are Nilgiri biosphere reserve (Tamil Nadu, Kerala, Karnataka); Nanda Devi biosphere reserve (Uttarakhand), Sunderban biosphere reserve (West Bengal), Gulf of Mannar biosphere reserve (Tamil Nadu), Dihang Dibang (Andhra Pradesh), Pachmarhi (Madhya Pradesh), Simlipal (Orissa), Achanakamar - Amarkantak (Madhya Pradesh, Chhattisgarh), Manas (Assam), Kanchanjunga (Sikkim), Agasthyamalai (Kerala), Great Nicobar (Andaman and Nicobar Islands), Nokrek (Meghalaya), and Dibru Saikhowa (Assam).

National Parks

It is a reserve of land that is usually owned and declared by the Union Government. A national park is normally located in undeveloped area and is protected from human developmental activities and pollution. It is a reserve of land to save exceptional native animals and plants, scenic beauty of landscape, geological formations, etc. Most national parks attract tourists who can view wildlife in exceptional locations. A national park may also be declared in some developed area with the objective of returning the area to its original state. Every national park has a set of rules which the public must abide by. Activities like hunting of animals, grazing, mining, cutting of trees, construction activity etc. are totally banned. In some countries, like UK, the areas designated as national parks are not wilderness, nor owned by the government and can include several settlements and land uses which are integral parts of the landscape.

The first national park of the world was the Yellowstone national park in USA. It was established in 1872 with an area of 8,983 sq. km. At present there are around 4,000 national parks throughout the world.

In our country, the Wildlife Protection Act, 1972 provides for the creation of National Parks in India. In 1970, India had only five national parks but today the number has reached to 92. Some important national parks of India are Kaziranga national park (Assam), Ranthambore National Park (Rajasthan), Bandipur National Park (Karnataka), Jim Corbett National Park (Uttar Pradesh), Gir National Park (Gujarat), Kanha National Park (Madhya Pradesh), and Tandoba National Park (Maharashtra).

Wildlife sanctuaries

These are comparatively large protected areas usually meant for protection of endangered species and their habitats. The boundaries of the wildlife sanctuaries are often not well defined controlled human interference is permitted in sanctuaries. India has 500 wildlife sanctuaries till date. Some popular sanctuaries are: Sultanpur Bird Sanctuary (Haryana); Periyar Sanctuary (Kerala); Chilka Lake bird sanctuary (Orissa); and Manas wildlife sanctuary (Assam).

Sacred forests and lakes

These are traditionally protected areas by virtue of religious and cultural beliefs. The sacred forests are protected by tribal communities due to religious sanctity accorded to these forests. These forests have been free from all disturbances. In India, many states such as Maharashtra, Kerala, Karnataka, Meghalaya etc. possess sacred forests. Similarly, aquatic flora and fauna is also protected in sacred water bodies. For instance, Khecheopalri Lake in Sikkim has been declared sacred by the people to save aquatic life from degradation.

Ex-situ conservation

The ex-situ conservation is also known as the off-site conservation. It involves maintenance and breeding of endangered plant and animal species in partially or fully controlled conditions, away from their natural habitats under human supervision. Human care eliminates the stress which organism experience in natural habitats and conditions necessary for a secured life and breeding. Man has been breeding plants and animals under his care from time immemorial for various purposes, which is the strategy of ex-situ conservation. However, these captive breeding were rarely done at that time for the purpose of wildlife conservation. Today, captive breeding has become a very important method of conserving biodiversity.

Fig. 17.2: Captive breeding.

Captive breeding

It is a process of breeding endangered animals by capturing them from their natural environment and then breeding them in favourable condition. Later, they are released back to their natural habitat when threats to the animals is lessened or removed. This activity is being practiced in many parts of the world with great success. This technique is difficult to apply for those species which are highly mobile like migratory birds and fishes.

Captive breeding helps to maintain viable and healthy species in the conservation facilities. It also helps in supplementing current populations with new stock. For any captive breeding programme to be successful and of conservational value it is essential that the origins and genetic purity of the animals within that programme are known.

Zoological gardens

These are the places where different species of fauna are conserved. The main objectives behind the maintenance of zoological gardens are the preservation and breeding of endangered species and to enable the population of these species to be reintroduced in natural habitats. Zoos can help in creating public awareness of conservation of wildlife. Zoos have made excellent contribution by replenishing and re-strengthening the natural population of a large number of species. An example is Indira Gandhi Zoological Park in Andhra Pradesh.

Botanical gardens

These are the places where different species of flowering and fruit giving plants, trees and vegetables are conserved. Since time immemorial man has been cultivating plants for various purposes. Today, botanical gardens cultivate several exotic species for the purpose of exhibition and education. Apart from nurturing specimens of plants from all over the world, many of these gardens also maintain preserved samples. Many of these botanical gardens are doing excellent work in preserving, propagating and reintroducting plants in their natural habitats. Currently, there are more than 1500 botanical gardens and arboreta gardens with trees and shrubs having more than 80,000 species including 12,000 threatened plant species.

Seed bank or gene banks

These are also called as germplasm banks. The germplasm of a plant refers to a living organ or a part of it from which new plants can be generated seeds which are to be stored for a few years are dried in sun and kept in sealed containers at a temperature of 5°C or even at room temperature. If seeds are to be maintained for several decades or even longer they are dried to reduce the moisture content to about 4.5 per cent and kept in sealed containers at temperatures between 10°C and 20°C.

Cryopreservation

Plants which cannot be preserved by traditional methods are preserved in the form of tissue cultures in liquid nitrogen where the temperature is as low as about – 19°C.

Preservation plots

Many states like Uttar Pradesh and Uttarakhand, have forest preservation plots. These are important means to conserve and protect the important floral species. It also helps in assessing ecological changes occurring in such areas over a period of time. These plots have to be demarcated and actively maintained.

Controlling wildlife trade

The increased demand for some body parts of wild animals, especially bones, lead to the involvement of illegal traffickers. Though India has made great efforts to save the wild animals but the recent threat of wildlife trade would need to be tackled through better enforcement and effective implementation of the wildlife protection act. To tighten the enforcement of the existing wildlife law the following steps are recommended:

- Setting up of a central task force having an intelligence unit, a legal cell, an investigation wing and an operation cell to carry out undercover operations.
- Creation of special courts in states for adjudicating on wildlife crimes.
- To create a central wildlife crime databank to collect and analyse data on wildlife trade.

- To activate state forest vigilance cells and creating a legal cell within each state forest department, and
- Formation of enforcement cell by the state chief wildlife wardens.

Information networking

There are several government controlled and private agencies that are involved in the generation and the dissemination of data. In the absence of such system there is often huge wastage of money and efforts in recreating such data. They are helpful in effective sourcing and pooling of information promoting networking and sharing of information is very much essential for an informed and inexpensive approach to biodiversity conservation.

Geographical Information System (GIS)

Utilisation of GIS and remote sensing also help in determining the rates, causes and scale of biodiversity loss. These systems and technology blend information obtained from different sources like Survey of India topographical sheets, remote sensing imagery, vegetation maps and other archival material. After utilising this information it provides a clear picture of the state and extent of loss of resource over time. Information on deforestation and land use change can also be integrated with data on the distribution of biodiversity, soils, topography, climate etc. it helps to obtain a comprehensive picture. The tool of GIS must be used extensively in the policy and landscape level planning.

17.5 Wildlife Protection Act, 1972

The most significant legislation on wildlife protection which is based on the ecosystem approach and a regulatory regime of command and control is the Wildlife Protection Act, 1972 (No. 53 of 1972). The objective of this enactment was three-fold, i.e., to have a uniform legislation on wildlife throughout the country, to establish a network of protected areas, i.e., national parks and sanctuaries and to regulate illicit trade in wildlife and its products. The Wildlife Protection Act, 1972 (No. 53 of 1972) has 66 Sections and has been divided into seven chapters relating to: (i) Preliminary, (ii) Authorities to be Appointed or Constituted under the Act, (iii) Hunting of Wild Animals, (iiiA) Protection of Specified Plants, (iv) Sanctuaries, National Parks (Omitted 1991) and Closed Areas, (ivA) Central Zoo Authority and Recognition of Zoos, (v) Trade or Commerce in Wild Animals, Animal Articles and Trophies, (vA) Prohibition of Trade or Commerce in Trophies, Animal Articles, etc., derived from Certain Animal, (vi) Prevention and Detection of Offences, (viA) Forfeiture of Property Derived from Illegal Hunting and Trade, and (vii) Miscellaneous, and Schedules:- I, II, III, IV, V, VI. The salient features of the Act include:

- "Animal" includes mammals, birds, reptiles, amphibians, fish, other chordates and invertebrates and also includes their young and eggs.

- "Animal Article" means an article made from any captive animal or wild animal, other than vermin, and includes an article or object in which the whole or any part of such animal has been used, and ivory imported into India and an article made therefrom.
- "Captive Animal" means any animal specified in Schedules I, II, III and IV, which is captured or kept or bred in captivity.
- "Circus" means an establishment, whether stationary or mobile, where animal are kept or used wholly or mainly for the purpose of performing tricks or manoeuvres.
- "Dealer" in relation any captive animal, animal article, trophy, uncured trophy, meat or specified plant, means a person, who carries on the business of buying or selling any such animal or article, and includes a person who undertakes business in any single transaction.
- "Habitat" includes land, water or vegetation which is the natural home of any wild animal.
- "Hunting", with its grammatical variations and cognate expressions, includes:
  (a) killing or poisoning of any wild animal or captive animal and every attempt to do so,
  (b) capturing, coursing, snaring, trapping, driving or baiting any wild or captive animal and every attempt to do so,
  (c) injuring or destroying or taking any part of the body of any such animal or, in the case of wild birds or reptiles, disturbing the eggs or nests of such birds or reptiles.
- "Land" includes canals, creeks and other water channels, reservoirs, rivers, streams and lakes, whether artificial or natural, marshes and wetlands and also includes boulders and rocks.
- "Livestock" means farm animals and includes buffaloes, bulls, bullocks, camels, cows, donkeys, goats, sheep, horses, mules, yaks, pigs, ducks, geese, poultry and their young but does not include any animal specified in Schedules I to V.

17.6 Biological Diversity Act, 2002

The Biological Diversity Act, 2002 is an Act of the Parliament of India for preservation of biological diversity in India, and provides mechanism for equitable sharing of benefits arising out use of traditional biological resources and knowledge. The Act was enacted to meet the obligations under Convention on Biological Diversity (CBD), to which India is a party.

(a) "benefit claimers" means the conservers of biological resources, their byproducts, creators and holders of knowledge and information relating to the use of such biological resources, innovations and practices associated with such use and application;

(b) "biological diversity" means the variability among living organisms from all sources and the ecological complexes of which they are part, and includes diversity within species or between species and of eco-systems;

(c) "biological resources" means plants, animals and micro-organisms or parts thereof, their genetic material and by-products (excluding value added products) with actual or potential use or value, but does not include human genetic material;

(d) "bio-survey and bio-utilisation" means survey or collection of species, subspecies, genes, components and extracts of biological resource for any purpose and includes characterisation, inventorisation and bioassay;

(e) "Chairperson" means the Chairperson of the National Biodiversity Authority or, as the case may be, of the State Biodiversity Board;

(f) "commercial utilisation" means end uses of biological resources for commercial utilisation such as drugs, industrial enzymes, food flavours, fragrance, cosmetics, emulsifiers, oleoresins, colours, extracts and genes used for improving crops and livestock through genetic intervention, but does not include conventional breeding or traditional practices in use in any agriculture, horticulture, poultry, dairy farming, animal husbandry or bee keeping;

(g) "fair and equitable benefit sharing" means sharing of benefits as determined by the National Biodiversity Authority under Section 21;

(h) "local bodies" means Panchayats and Municipalities, by whatever name called, within the meaning of clause (1) of Article 243B and clause (1) of Article 243Q of the Constitution and in the absence of any Panchayats or Municipalities, institutions of self-government constituted under any other provision of the Constitution or any Central Act or State Act;

(i) "member" means a member of the National Biodiversity Authority or a State Biodiversity Board and includes the Chairperson;

(j) "National Biodiversity Authority" means the National Biodiversity Authority established under Section 8;

(k) "prescribed" means prescribed by rules made 1 under this Act;

(l) "regulations" means regulations made under this Act;

(m) "research" means study or systematic investigation of any biological resource or technological application, that uses biological systems, living organisms or derivatives thereof to make or modify products or processes for any use;

(n) "State Biodiversity Board" means the State Biodiversity Board established under Section 22;

(o) "sustainable use" means the use of components of biological diversity in such manner and at such rate that does not lead to the long-term decline of the biological diversity thereby maintaining its potential to meet the needs and aspirations of present and future generations;

(p) "value added products" means products which may contain portions or extracts of plants and animals in unrecognisable and physically inseparable form;

(q) No person referred to in sub-section (2) shall, without previous approval of the National Biodiversity Authority, obtain any biological resource occurring in India or knowledge associated thereto for research or for commercial utilisation or for bio-survey and bio-utilisation.

(r) The persons who shall be required to take the approval of the National Biodiversity Authority under sub-section (1) are the following, namely:

   (a) a person who is not a citizen of India;

   (b) a citizen of India, who is a non-resident as defined in clause (30) of Section 2 of the Income-tax Act, 1961;

   (c) a body corporate, association or organisation—

      (i) not incorporated or registered in India; or

      (ii) incorporated or registered in India under any law for the time being in force which has any non-Indian participation in its share capital or management.

(s) No person shall, without the previous approval of the National Biodiversity Authority, transfer the results of any research relating to any biological resources occurring in, or obtained from, India for monetary consideration or otherwise to any person who is not a citizen of India or citizen of India who is non-resident as defined in clause (30) of Section 2 of the Income-tax Act, 1961 or a body corporate or organisation which is not registered or incorporated in India or which has any non-Indian participation in its share capital or management.

18

Ecotourism

18.1 Introduction

Ecotourism is a form of tourism involving visiting fragile, pristine, and relatively undisturbed natural areas, intended as a low-impact and often small scale alternative to standard commercial (mass) tourism. Its purpose may be to educate the traveller, to provide funds for ecological conservation, to directly benefit the economic development and political empowerment of local communities, or to foster respect for different cultures and for human rights. Since the 1980s ecotourism has been considered a critical endeavour by environmentalists, so that future generations may experience destinations relatively untouched by human intervention. Several university programmes use this description as the working definition of ecotourism.

Generally, ecotourism deals with living parts of the natural environments. Ecotourism focuses on socially responsible travel, personal growth, and environmental sustainability. Ecotourism typically involves travel to destinations where flora, fauna, and cultural heritage are the primary attractions. Ecotourism is intended to offer tourists insight into the impact of human beings on the environment, and to foster a greater appreciation of our natural habitats.

Responsible ecotourism programmes include those that minimise the negative aspects of conventional tourism on the environment and enhance the cultural integrity of local people. Therefore, in addition to evaluating environmental and cultural factors, an integral part of ecotourism is the promotion of recycling, energy efficiency, water conservation, and creation of economic opportunities for local communities. For these reasons, ecotourism often appeals to advocates of environmental and social responsibility.

The term 'ecotourism', like 'sustainable tourism', is considered by many to be an oxymoron. Tourism in general depends upon and increases air transportation, contributing significantly to greenhouse gas emissions from combustion placed high into the stratosphere where they immediately contribute to the heat trapping phenomenon behind global warming and climate change.

The involvement of local communities in the tourism (called 'eco-tourism' herein after) would support their livelihood needs and consequently create their direct stake in conservation of local culture, ecology and environment........ "This concept of 'community based eco-tourism' would go a long way in providing better income generation options to the rural people. This would also mean less dependence upon the natural resources in as far as it amounts to removal of produce from these areas. There would be, moreover, greater incentive in conservation of local traditions, culture, heritage and environs, as these would be seen as aiding in local economy rather than an impediment to it."

Ecotourism is "Responsible travel to natural areas that conserves the environment and improves the well-being of local people." (TIES, 1990)

18.2 Characteristics of Ecotourism

- Involves travel to natural destinations
- Minimises impact
- Builds environmental awareness
- Provides direct financial benefits for conservation
- Provides financial benefits and empowerment for local people
- Respects local culture
- Supports human rights and democratic movements such as:
  - conservation of biological diversity and cultural diversity through ecosystem protection;
  - promotion of sustainable use of biodiversity, by providing jobs to local populations;
  - sharing of socio-economic benefits with local communities and indigenous peoples by having their informed consent and participation in the management of ecotourism enterprises;
  - Tourism to unspoiled natural resources, with minimal impact on the environment being a primary concern;
  - minimisation of tourism's own environmental impact;
  - affordability and lack of waste in the form of luxury;
  - local culture, flora and fauna being the main attractions;
  - local people benefit from this form of tourism economically, often more than mass tourism.

India is recognised as one of the 12 mega diversity centres of the world. India has two out of the 18 Biodiversity hot-spots in the world, which are in the Western Ghats and Eastern Himalayas. Sikkim, covering just 0.2 per cent of the geographical area of the country, has tremendous biodiversity and has been identified as one of the Hot-Spot in the Eastern Himalayas. The Sikkim Himalayas falls under the Himalayan (2) Bio-geographic Zones and Central Himalaya (2C) Biotic Province. As per the Champion and Seth, 1968 new classification of Forests Types about nine Types of Major Forests Types are found in the State. Sikkim Himalayas has more than 26 per cent of flowering plants of the country and is very important phyto-geographical reserve of the country.

- There are 10 bio-geographic zones and 25 biotic provinces— which have 16 major forests types and > 200 sub-types as per (Champion and Seth, 1968).
- Sikkim falls under "Himalayan (2) Biogeographic zone and Central Himalaya (2c) biotic province——having about nine types of forests types (Champion and Seth).

18.3 Forest Lands, Areas, Locations and Ecotourism

For promotion and development of eco-tourism in forest areas, it is not required that entire forest area would be used in any location. Only a small degraded or barren land may be put to the use along with the landscaping, plantation, regeneration and protection components which would be jointly managed by the Tourism Department and Forest Department for which no specific diversion may be required. For specific project only diversion may be considered. The areas which are reserved for any specific conservation programme would not be proposed. There would be no major construction programme other than which is minimum required for Tourism and Forest management as well may only be taken up. Reserve Forests, Khasmal Forests, Goucharan Forests, National parks, Sanctuaries, Biosphere reserve, Lakes/ water bodies and other forest lands may be involved only in limited under the joint management concept. There would be no felling of any trees while the plantation would be an integrated part of the programme. For each location and area the impact assessment shall be done on annual basis and necessary corrective and improvement programme shall be taken up immediately.

18.4 Important Components of Eco-Tourism Projects

For the promotion and development of Eco-tourism, the activities to be taken up would be eco-friendly and they would be also used for management, conservation, regeneration of Forests, Environment and Wildlife in the area and in the State as well. Some of the important components of eco-tourism programme are: Improvement of surroundings of the destination. This would include activities like landscaping, development of parks, fencing, compound wall etc., Illumination of the Tourist destination, Providing for improvement in solid waste management and sewerage management, Public Conveniences etc., Improvement of road connectivity leading to the tourist sites, especially from the National Highways/State highways and other entry points, Construction of Wayside Public Conveniences, Construction of Budget Accommodation, Restaurant and Wayside Amenities, Procurement of equipments directly related to tourism, like Water Sports, Adventure Sports, Eco-friendly modes of transport for moving within the Tourism Zone, Refurbishment of the Monuments, Signages and display boards showing Tourist Area Maps and documentation on places of Interest at the locations, Tourist Arrival Centres, Reception Centres, Interpretation Centres, and Improvement of municipal services directly related to Tourism, Other work/ activities directly related to tourism, Improvement of the surroundings of the village. This would include activities like landscaping, development or parks, fencing, compound wall etc., Improvements to roads within the Panchayat limits. This shall not include any major road which connects the village, Illumination in the village, Providing for improvement in solid waste management and sewerage management, Construction of Wayside Amenities, Procurement of equipments directly related to tourism, like Water Sports, Adventure Sports, Eco-friendly modes of transport for moving within the tourism zone, Refurbishment of the Monuments, Signages, Reception Centres, Other work/activities directly related to tourism. Tourist Accommodation, Trekking route, mountain biking, skiing, Adventure in general.

18.5 Tourist Facilities

Develop rules and Regulations in consultation with the Division level Coordination Committee. These rules will be site-specific (a FRH/camp site in remote area may have different set of rules as compared to the FRH/camp site located on the roadside). The rules will incorporate items such as FRH/ camp-site/film-shooting fee, Do's and Don'ts in nature, and other locality specifics. Display the rules and regulations at the prominent points in English and Local language- Conduct regular surveys for the tourists coming to a popular 'Heritage FRH'/forest trails/other FRH/camp-sites/film-shooting grounds. They may be Backpackers who rely mostly on local availability of food, shelter and other services, such as school children, NCC cadets, trekkers from Youth Hostel of India, some tight-budget foreigners; Do-it-yourself Trekkers who come prepared with own food, tents, etc. A number of foreigners are in this category and Pre-planned Trekkers with pre-planned, organised trips, which are executed by a trekking agency. Develop plans to cater to these trekkers, accordingly. Ensure safeguards/regulations to various activities are followed earnestly and the Laws/rules/regulations in this respect are followed:

- Invest timely in infrastructure e.g. timely repairs/maintenance of FRH, trekking routes, bridle paths, etc. Conduct regular scouting trips arranged by the Division level Coordination Committee on different routes through the forest/Wildlife areas (PAs) and report back on trail conditions, wildlife, forest use, littering by trekking groups, etc.

- Improve the waste disposal around 'Heritage FRH'/forest trails/ other FRH/camp-sites/film shooting grounds.
- Wherever needed, use alternative energy sources e.g. Indane cooking gas, solar lights, solar geysers, green houses. Introduce fuel sufficiency rule, whereby LPG will be used in the kitchen and firewood will be provided for the fire-places in FRH rooms (which is in good demand from the tourists).
- Let there be dedicated firewood plantations in association with the HPFD (about 10,000 trees of fast growing firewood species per hectare to be planted in three to ten hectares for each FRH, and develop a rotation so that the wood is available on annual basis) for the selected / prioritised FRHs and camping sites. Let tourists pay for this facility. Till it happens, make alternative arrangements.
- Create herbal gardens of local medicinal plants with information about plants, their uses. A well maintained medicinal plant nursery is part of nature conservation education and a big attraction for the tourists.

18.6 Revenue and Investment in Site for Development

Since, the objectives are clear like: minimise impact, build environmental and cultural awareness and respect, provide positive experiences for both visitors and hosts, provide direct financial benefits for conservation and to local people and hence the revenue sharing model for each project may be worked out on case to case basis and location to location basis which shall be used for site in question only. The government may be approached to create the specific budget head for all such locations and the revenue received shall be utilised for such sites only.

18.7 The Responsibilities of Eco-Tourists and of the Host Community

If a community wants to host ecotourism, it has a central role to play. The host community's success in bringing ecotourism to it and ensuing that the level and type of tourism is compatible with the community's aspirations are matters the community can control.

- Help conserve habitats of flora and fauna as well as any site, natural feature or culture, which may be affected by tourism.

- Make no open fires and discourage others from doing so. If water has to be heated with scarce firewood, use it as little as possible. Where feasible, use kerosene or fuel-efficient wood stoves. Remove litter, burn or bury paper and carry back all non-degradable litter.
- Keep local water clean and avoid using pollutants such as detergents in streams or springs. If no toilet facilities are available, relieve yourself at least 30 metres away from water sources and bury or cover the waste.
- Leave plants to flourish in their natural environment and avoid taking away cuttings, seeds and roots.
- Leave campsites clean after use.
- Help guides and porters to follow conservation measures.
- Do not allow cooks/porters to throw garbage in streams or rivers.
- Respect the natural and cultural heritage of the area and follow local customs.
- Respect local etiquette and do not wear tight fitting clothes. Remember that kissing in public is disapproved of in India.
- Respect privacy of individuals and ask permission to take photographs of local inhabitants.
- Respect holy places; do not touch or remove religious objects.
- Strictly follow the guidelines for personal safety and security and always take your own precautions and safety measures.
- Realise and respect the value of the environment, the flora and fauna, the monuments and your cultural heritage.
- Practice conservation of nature and culture as a way of life.
- Establish guidelines to protect valuable local resources and foster tourism management.
- React to the potential threat of investors who see opportunities in development but lack sensitivity to local values.
- Become effective nature guides and conservationists of natural areas by utilising practical and ancestral knowledge of the natural features of the area.
- Be friendly to the visitors and help them to practice ecotourism principles.

Finally there is a role for others, such as scientific and research institutions and non-government organisations, in promoting ecotourism. The things they can do include: (i) create awareness, among all concerned, about the importance of sound eco-practices in tourism development; (ii) motivate the local community to increase their involvement in sustainable tourism activities;

and (iii) organise training programmes to prepare the local people to take up various vocations related to ecotourism.

18.8 Motivations for Involvement in Ecotourism

Hotel and travel companies in our country function in a relatively free environment. The country is slowly but surely moving towards a market economy where commercial considerations dictate motivation for the private sector to take up various activities. Crass commercial considerations have, however, to be controlled by the government on behalf of the public. The environment has to be protected through awareness generation, legislation, policy and administrative action.

The travelling public is also becoming conscious of the need to protect the environment, to some extent at least. As a result, many enterprises in the hospitality sector have adopted environment-friendly practices like conserving energy and water and recycling unutilised hotel outputs. These can be powerful marketing tools for hotel groups. Furthermore, with the increase in cost of vital inputs like energy, water etc. companies are motivated to conserve limited resources by adopting practices which reduce levels of consumption. Many hotel companies advise their clients to be careful in the use of lights, water and other hotel services. Civil society has also begun to exercise control over the environment.

Many non-governmental organisations have been generating awareness about environmentally destructive practices. Individuals have taken recourse to public interest litigation to stop environmentally destructive practices. The print and electronic media have been very active in India in investigating environmentally injurious activities by highlighting such issues and creating public opinion for environmentally compatible practices.

The Ministry of Tourism has issued ecotourism guidelines for adoption by all concerned introduced an ecotourism pledge which requires their members to adopt environment-friendly practices.

18.9 Globalisation and Tourism

Globalisation is the buzzword of the new millennium. It is a summary term for the increasingly complex interactions between individuals, enterprises, institutions and markets across national borders. The term 'globalisation' has also been referred as the increasing interconnectedness of economic, political, social and cultural practices worldwide. It also refers to the movement of people *i.e.* labour, knowledge and technology across international borders. In short, the world will be borderless and would turn into 'Global Village'.

The unification and re-shaping of the world into a global village and the description of the dynamics of political and economic relations within it constitute the essence and the development of the new phenomenon globalisation. Usually people believe that globalisation has opened up new and extensive opportunities for worldwide development. However, this is not "progressing evenly" as some countries (especially in Europe and East Asia) are becoming integrated into the global economy more rapidly than others with the evidence of fast growth and reduced poverty; while others (Latin America and Africa) have suffered from economic stagnation or deteriorating socio-economic conditions leading to poverty and high inflation. This has raised a number of questions and increasing debate on the subject and in many ways has actually become the source of confusion and controversy. While the proponents of globalisation believe that globalisation promotes information exchange, greater understanding of other cultures, raises living standards, increases purchasing power; the opponents feel that the West's gain at the expense of developing countries that too not everyone in the West.

According to United Nations Report (2000), increasing globalisation of the world economy is a threat to poorer and developing countries. In order words, the poorer countries are in danger of further falling behind more development competitors in an increasingly globalise economy. The United Nations Secretary General Kofi Annan's Millennium report also acknowledged that although globalisation will lead to faster economic growth, higher standards of living, accelerated innovation and diffusion of technology and management skills; globalisation has "begun to generate a backlash" because the benefits resulting from it remain highly concentrated among a relatively small number of countries and are spread unevenly within them."

The globalisation is rooted in the belief that the globalisation will create enormous opportunities, through greater trade and the flow of capital to where it is most productive, and that its benefits typically outweigh the costs. But the net effect being positive does not mean that it has no negative effects. Globalisation does have a tendency to marginalise some people and regions. Since the effect of globalisation is not always positive and at times throws a challenge for the local trade and businesses due to the specificity of local conditions and balances, the challenge require individually defined approaches in every region according to the wider socioeconomic and political environment within which local policy is formulated. While the federal government is important in providing a national strategy, it is too distant from local areas to play a major role in development and hence the role of local government, public and the stakeholders are crucial.

Through this article, we will attempt to trace how globalisation has a concurrent tendency to marginalise people and regions especially in mountain tourism to enable the policy-makers to devise suitable policy measures to counter the process and spread the benefits of globalisation to all without exception.

18.10 Mountain Tourism and Marginalisation

Tourism is recognised as one of the largest global industries. Tourism industry is growing exponentially especially after globalisation as the people have access to information about various tourist places hitherto scarcely known owing to frequent movement of people and development of information technology. Even in our country, the tourism industry is substantial and vibrant; employing around 20 million people and the country is fast becoming a major global destination. India's travel and tourism industry is one of the most profitable industries in the country, and also credited with contributing a substantial amount of foreign exchange of US $ 8.9 billion from 04 million foreign tourists in 2006. Tourist arrivals are projected to increase by over 22 per cent per year with 33 per cent increase in foreign exchange earnings. Mountain tourism is equally important to our country as it accounts for 15 to 20 per cent of total tourism in the country and generates about US $ 80 billion.

Tourism industry occupies a very important place for Sikkim as the State has earned a reputation of one of the hotspot of major tourist destination in the world. It is also one of the substantial employment provider and revenue earners marked by the fact that tourist arrivals touched almost five lakhs in 2007-08 of which five per cent constituted foreign tourist. In terms of tourist arrivals as a proportion of population, Sikkim ranked 12th across states in India. The overall earnings from the tourism sector were estimated around Rs 127 crores in the year 2007-08, which is close to ten per cent of the Gross Domestic Product of the state. Tourism has made an indelible impression on the economical, ecological, environmental and social lifestyle of Sikkim.

Tourism business being an industry with rapidly changing demands, fashions and requirements characterised by globalisation of demand and supply also invites globalised competition, where mountain areas not only compete among themselves, but also with other major tourism destinations. Tourism is thus particularly vulnerable at the local level owing to globalisation and marginalisation threats. The primary product of tourism is often the heritage, wealth, and expected legacy of the community that serves as the tourist destination.

Tourism related consumption has three stages of impact. First, prior to departure, tourists purchase travel related clothing and equipment, which may be produced under conditions that undermine the social and ecological sustainability of the producing communities. Second, when tourists travel long distances to tourist destinations, they create considerable atmospheric pollution and other impacts on the global environment. Third, upon arrival at the tourist destination, tourists often continue their accustomed habits of consumption, even though these destinations may not have the infrastructure required to manage those consumption patterns. Tourist activities fundamentally involve the transportation and hosting of the tourism consumer in a local community (tourist destination) impacting upon the local tourist community, including the interruption of local customs and lifestyles, the spread of infectious diseases, changes in local demographics, housing and labour markets and a host of other threats owing to globalisation are discussed below:

Stiff competition: The globalisation has twin effect. On the one hand it facilitates better opportunity for the various mountain regions as sought after tourist destination owing to better and improved access, barrier free entry, ease of availability of required facilities for comfortable stay; one the other hand it triggers off stiff competition among various tourist places. This stiff competition puts a lot of pressure on tourism business and affect revenue generation thereby drop in income level of tourism dependent families. This is especially true for foreign tourists as they have liberty to visit places of their choices based on latest information available and lifting of restriction on movement. In the process the tourist destinations with less developed infrastructure is slowly and steadily marginalised owing to globalisation.

Strain on existing infrastructure: Following arrival at tourist destinations, the tourism industry strives to host tourists according to the standards and amenities of their country of origin. These hospitality standards mimic and encourage the high consumption lifestyles of developed countries. For instance, luxury hotel rooms, with high levels of energy and water consumption, are given the highest rankings or "stars" in international hotel rankings. These "luxury" consumption standards, using current technologies, are themselves globally unsustainable (i.e., in an equitable world). The most immediate observable impacts of introducing these high consumption practices into lower consumption communities are: degradation of local water and soil quality, with direct impacts on local health and economies, as a result of the lack of adequate water, drainage, waste water, and waste management infrastructure to manage the higher volumes of waste produced by higher levels of consumption; reduced access by local residents to land, housing and marine resources through, among other things, reallocation of these community resources to foreign tourist residents and inflation of local prices; destruction of traditional sources of income. The local community is not only outnumbered during peak tourist season but also have to compromise with the available civic facilities. At times, they are faced with contradictory situations. While on the one hand, increased tourist inflow have catalyst role leading to spurt in economic activities thereby enhancing revenue generation for persons associated with tourism industry; on the other hand, it leads to compromise in available infrastructure.

Interruption of local customs and lifestyles: An ever increasing tourist inflow affects the local customs and traditions to some extent. The modern and notion free lifestyles of the visiting tourists attracts the local community especially the youngsters. This at times leads to interruptions in local customs and traditions as the youngsters steadily develop less interest towards their own tradition and local customs.

Spread of infectious diseases: The visiting tourist hail from different part of the globe in the era of globalisation. Many tourists suffer from some or the other kind of infectious diseases and the local community runs the risk of acquiring such diseases from the visiting tourists. Cases have come to notice that tourists suffering with infectious skin diseases taken dip in the hot spring water have afflicted the diseases to local community through the contaminated water in Sikkim.

Changes in local demographics and moral values: The intrusion of large numbers of uninformed foreigners into local social system also undermine pre-existing social relationships and values, and at times become source of degradation of local ecological, economic and social systems, and economic losses which encourages socially deleterious economic activities such as prostitution, crime, and migrant and child labour. These business activities degrade the community's heritage and wealth and as a result the community suffers more directly than the tourists who can return to their own community without responsibility for or awareness of the impacts of his tourist activities. Tourism activities can, in particular, degrade the social and natural wealth of a community.

Negative local environmental impacts: In addition to high altitude emissions from long distance air travel, air travel produces considerable negative local environmental impacts, including ground level emissions of VOCs and particulates, disposal of fuel, hazardous chemicals and solid waste, noise pollution, and wildlife and habitat disruption. Marine dumping of wastes from cruise ships is an increasing concern. However, very little public information is available on the environmental and social impacts of long distance travel.

18.11 Local Responses to Threat

For many mountain communities, tourism is now the great hope of reversing the process of marginalisation. This hope is based on the attractiveness of the tourist business. Tourist businesses can make a significant voluntary contribution to resolving the social costs of tourism by providing local resident employment and training opportunities, including in traditional trades and crafts; establishing purchasing guidelines that favour local goods and services procurement; making donations and investments in local recreational facilities, parks, cultural facilities, etc.

In sum, the locally intricate system of mountain development is confronted with all the opportunities but also all the risks of tourism as a global business. This contrast produces key challenges for sustainable development in mountain regions. At the core of solutions lies the mountain community themselves. They need to take advantage of opportunities, but also to diversify their activities. Tourism planning should be done in such a way that encompasses planning for residents as well as for visitors to make tourism a positive force in the lives of local residents and elicit appropriate local response, involvement and support. Governments play an important role in managing and regulating these interactions and relations between local communities and global tourism. The core triangle of communities, tourism industry, and government can further be supported and guided by development agencies, NGOs, and research, all of which may play a facilitating and moderating role.

Mainstream economic thought promises that globalisation would lift the poor above poverty, dissolve dictatorships, protect the environment, integrate cultures, and most importantly, reverse the growing economic gap between rich and poor countries of the world. The frequent observation that globalisation is not global, meaning that processes and benefits associated with globalisation are uneven throughout the world, is reinforced in this backlash. In other words, a large percentage of the world's population feels excluded from the benefits of globalisation. Statistics abound showing how globalisation is increasingly polarising the world into two different camps impoverishment and prosperity. This differentiation holds true for all sectors including tourism. To foster and promote "win-win" situation for all, it is imperative on the tourism stakeholders to develop appropriate policy suitable to promote local tourism, put some restriction on unbridled exploitation of local natural resources (environment, water etc), ban on unethical lifestyle to suit the sentiments and customs of local community, etc. Solutions to adverse tourism impacts are to be found in the shared interest of local communities, tourism businesses, and tourism consumers to maintain the natural wealth and social heritage of the tourist destination. The local government may sensitise people on the ill effects of globalisation (marginalisation) on tourism industry and take benefits of globalisation through appropriate policy measures, regulated use of natural resources, restricted openness and lifestyle, etc.

18.12 Conclusion

Tourism has proved to be an engine of growth in many economies in the world. It provides for the generation of income, wealth and employment, and helps in the sustainable development of remote areas. In Sikkim, tourism provides direct employment to more than 40,000 people (minimum) and indirect employment is substantial. Its contribution to the Economy of state is significant.

19

National Environmental Issues

19.1 Population Growth: Introduction

Population is defined as a group of individuals living in the same given area and capable of interbreeding and sharing genetic material. The large human population issue is one of the most important issues of the environment. The human populations pose danger to the environment through two main factors: (i) the number of people and (ii) the impact of each person on the environment. We know that in last 40 years world human population has doubled from 2.5 billion to more than 6 billion. In the same period in our country it has risen from 431 million to 1027 million.

On economic terms, population can be categorised as follows: if the resources of a region are more than adequate for its people, the region is called: (i) under populated – if these are just enough, then the region is said to have, (ii) optimum population. However, if the resources get overused and it is not possible to produce the same amount of goods or services for every individual of the region, the region is termed and (iii) over populated. Therefore, it is not only the number of individuals but also the quality of life of each of them in a region is very important. Disparities in such qualities are quite often the cause of social tension/imbalances. On economic terms a population constitutes both consumers as well as producers. Its study helps us to:

- Provide data on the total manpower available now and in future.
- Estimate the total amounts of goods/services required currently and in future.
- To promote cultural/regional/linguistic harmony.

19.2 Major Periods of Human Population Growth

Through history, four major periods of human population growth worldwide can be traced:

- **An early period of hunters and gatherers:** At that time the total population was less than a few million.

- **The period of rise of agriculture:** This period led to greater density of people and caused the first major rise in the human population.
- **The industrial revolution:** This resulted in better food supply, improved healthcare which, in turn, led to rapid rise in the population, and
- **The present:** When the population is slowing down in the wealthy and industrialised nations but is still growing rapidly in poorer and developing and underdeveloped nations.

19.3 Demographic Features

The study of various aspects of a population is called demography. The major parameters used for study of demography are size, growth, age structure, demographic transactions, fertility, birth rate, death rate, standard of living and growth rates and migration.

(i) **Size:** The size of the population is measured in terms of the number of persons of a region/country. The population count by census 2011, by the Registrar General of India shows that India's population is 120 crores. The absolute rise in the last decade 2001-2011 has been more than 18 crores. Are we as a Nation providing every individual essential goods/services? This is a very important environmental issue that our country faces today.

(ii) **Growth of the population:** The growth of population at different times can be expressed in terms of growth rates. The growth rate, that is the rate of change per 1000 individuals, determines the changes in population.

Calculation of growth rate of population

For the calculation of growth rates, we have to first calculate the birth rate and death rate. We can calculate them as follows:

Birth Rate: Rate at which births occur in a population

Let N = total number of individuals in the population, B = Number of births per unit time by the total population 'N', b = birth rate

Then, b = Birth rate of Total no. of individual added in the population-N = number of births per unit time by the total population

$$b = B/N$$

Death rate: Rate at which death occur in population

Let N = Total number of individuals in the population

D = Total number of deaths per unit time in the population 'N'

d = death rate

Then, d = death rate – total number of individual in the population
N = Total number of deaths per unit time in the population

$$d = D/N$$

(iii) Growth rate: The growth rate (g) is the result of the number of births, minus the number of deaths per unit time divided by the total number of individuals in the population.

To calculate the growth rate,

Let B = Total number of births per unit time

D = total number of deaths per unit time

G = the difference between the total births and the deaths of the individuals per unit time

N = the total number of individual in the population

g = growth rate for that per unit time

Then, $g = (B–D)/N$ i.e. $g = G/N$

i.e. $g = G/N$ or the difference between the total births and the deaths of the individuals per unit time and the total number of individual in the population.

(iv) Mortality: Mortality refers to the death of individuals. In a population, members die due to various causes, such as, malnutrition, disease, old age, accidents, natural calamities and war etc. It is equal to death rate.

(v) Natality: Natality is an expression of the addition of new individual in a population. It is equivalent to birth rate.

(vi) Migration: Migration means the movement of individuals of a population. The movement of the individuals out of one's own country is called emigration. Emigration may occur because of various reasons, viz: better job opportunities elsewhere; better education facilities elsewhere; illegal transfer; war; natural calamities; internal disturbances in the host country, for example, emigration of youth of our country to USA, New Zealand, Australia and other country. The movement of individual from one region of a country into another region of the same country is called internal immigration. Does internal immigration affect the population of the country? The internal migration within the country is usually from rural areas to urban sector. The population in rural areas rises sharply as compared to urban areas. Lack of demand for labour for agriculture, increased job opportunities in cities and better education facilities in cities, better healthcare in cities, better living conditions are some of the key factors deciding internal migration from rural areas to urban areas. Why do you think that internal emigration from rural area to cities is a very important environmental concern in our country?

19.4 Exponential Growth Rate

Whenever something increases in such a way that the increase is a fixed proportion of its own size at any time, the increase is called exponential. Population growth of human beings also follows the same pattern as seen for bacteria, you would find similar J-shaped curved in both bacteria and human growth rates. You shall also note the decrease in time it took to add each additional billion in human population. It took thousands of years to reach a billion of human population. It took, further, 130 years to reach two billion, only 30 years to reach three billion, and only 11 years to add another billion. When the population approaches the full carrying capacity, the growth rate decreases and the growth changes from J-shaped curve to S-shaped curve (Sigmoid curve).

If we know the growth rates in percentage for years, we can easily calculate/predict the time 't' in years for a population to double by using formula.

t= 70 / annual growth rate in percentage

For example, if a population is growing at the rate of 2 per cent annually, the population shall double in 70/2 = 35 years.

19.5 Structure of Population

In population studies, the structure of a population is determined by certain characteristics such as population density, dispersion, age structure and sex ratio. Let us understand these terms.

Density

Density represents the number of individuals of a species inhabiting a unit area. If reflects the success of a population. The complete count of the individuals in an area is called census. Such censuses have been regularly conducted in our country. The last census was completed in the year 2011.

The problems arising out of increase in population density are very alarming. Some of them are:

- Per capita income decreases;
- Basic needs of life can become limited;
- Available natural resources such as water, land, fuel decreases;
- Shortage of essential goods results in rise of prices;
- Non-availability of essential goods leads to disparity/interest;

- Land mass used for housing/industry;
- Agricultural space decreases;
- Fall in farm output as well as decreased forest cover;
- Lack of balanced diet to all the members of the family; leading to malnutrition; loss of efficiency, increased susceptibility to disease;
- Increased demand for healthcare services;
- Fall in job ratio leading to unrest;
- Lack of adequate educational facilities, lowering of standards, increased number of uneducated people;
- Severe stress on sanitation; increased pollution of air, water and soil, and
- Overall harmful effects on human health.

Dispersion

Dispersion pattern of a population is the dispersion of its individual members relative to one another in a given area. For example, human population, it is not uniformly dispersed, only one third of the total land area is inhabitated by humans. Even out of this one-third, some areas are thinly and others are very heavily populated. The distribution variation depends on availability of the requirements of life. About 56 per cent of world population resides in Asia.

Age structure

In a population, individuals are different ages. The proportion of individuals in each age group is called age structure of that population.

Study of age structure is important because it provides:

- Current and future status of age profile;
- Possible effects on environment;
- Insights into population history;
- Available and future work force (15-59 years)/manpower;
- Status of elderly people needing social support, now and in future;
- Projection for current, future educational needs;
- Projection for job needs;
- Projection for medical/social/housing/healthcare needs; and
- Economic status of the society.

Sex ratio

Ideally there should be a balance in number of males and females in a population. However, in Nature, there are more male births than female birth. If there is no discrimination on the part of the society, the sex ratio of a population should remain more or less constant or balanced. Any deviation from this balance is not desirable for the population. In our country, there were 972 females per every 1000 male (i.e. sex ratio is 972) in 1901. By 2001, the sex ratio has fallen to 933 to every 1000 male. There are, however, very sharp regional differences. For example, in Kerala and Puduherry, the sex ratio is 1058 and 1001 respectively; it is very poor in Delhi (821), Haryana (861), Punjab (874), Chandigarh (773). What is a poor sex ratio with much fewer women compared to men suggestive of?

19.6 Human Population and the Environment

Human beings are part of the environment and important components of biosphere. Like any other living organism humans exchange materials with the surroundings. Besides this give and take from the environment, human influence on other life forms and ability to change and control the environment to some degree, has affected the global environment drastically. Hence, one can say that human population and human activity has immense impact on the environment.

Impact on environment

Human activities have had lasting impact on the environment. Some of such activities that have modified or degraded the environment are:

- Ability to produce food through agriculture.
- Transfer excess food to regions of food shortage.
- Store excess food in warehouses, cold storage and canneries, thereby preventing food deterioration.
- Impressive and innovative efficiency of energy utilisation has caused shift from wood energy to fossil energy to electric energy to atomic energy.
- Ability to provide shelter for self, elderly and the young, protection against for unfavourable weather or enemies.
- Ability to destroy animal enemies' e.g. lions, tigers, wolves, snakes, rats, mice, household insects etc.
- Ability to reduce competition from other animals by fencing crops and live stock.
- Reducing the mortality rate by controlling a number of life threatening diseases through proper sanitation, medication, immunisation etc.

Inspite of all the intelligence at its source, human beings have not been able to conquer the environment completely. Natural as well as human made modifications in the environment have, through various periods offered fatal blows to the human population. Some such problems confronting us are:

- **Food shortage or famine:** It could be because of less agricultural production; transfer of agricultural land for utilisation; improper and inadequate storage, transport facilities; economic poverty to purchase food etc.

- **Inadequate shelter:** Every individual is not provided with safe shelter and is exposed to extremes of high and cold temperatures of atmosphere, and falling prey to tigers, lions, wolves, leopards, rats, snakes etc.
- **Diseases:** Malnutrition, inadequate sanitation, lack of medical facilities, increased susceptibility to disease especially among young and old as well as invasion and mutation of the pathogens leads to epidemic / fatal attacks of bubonic plague, malaria, yellow fever, typhoid, tuberculosis, HIV-AIDS, dengue, influenza etc.
- **Calamities:** Natural calamities such as floods, cyclones, earthquakes, volcanoes, tsunami, avalanches etc. uproot human settlements and damage property.
- **Miscellaneous:** Various mostly human made, accidents involving explosions, fire, pollution, ship wrecks, air and road accident wipe out lives.

Thus, you should be able to imagine the tussle between man to change environment to his liking and the environment striking back in one form or the other. If, humans are able to interact with the environment judiciously, an environment friendly life can be led by them.

Standard of living

A population is also characterised by certain parameters, such as:

- Life expectancy (should be high),
- Infant mortality rate (should be low),
- Income per head (should be high),
- Literacy (maximum of individuals be literate),
- Consumption of food, natural resources (should be balanced),
- Kind of energy used (eco-friendly),
- Eco-friendly activity.

Such parameters decide the standard of living of a population. The developed rich countries have better standard of living and underdeveloped, poor countries have a poor standard of living.

19.7 Urbanisation and Environmental Problems

With economic development comes urbanisation and with urbanisation comes destruction of the environment. Urbanisation causes environmental and social upheaval, some of them are listed below:

19.7.1 Urbanisation and Environmental Degradation

- Since cities are located near rivers, along coastlines, the expanded urban inhabitants often overtake the good agricultural land for housing, industry etc.
- Loss of such an important and delicate habitat effects many rare and endangered species.
- Forest are cut.
- Wetlands are filled with soil.
- Soil is removed from productive use.
- Many hazardous materials are released into surroundings.
- Air, water and soil are polluted.

19.7.2 Urbanisation and Socio-Economic Factors

- Population is redistributed,
- Peasant society changes to factory/business dependent community,
- Automobiles/industries pollute air,
- Civic amenities are unable to cope with increased sewage disposal,
- Poor sanitation leads to water and soil pollution,
- Poor sanitation breed pathogens/vectors resulting in rise of communicable diseases,
- Overcrowding and unemployment lead to unbalanced urban life which causes in turn a number of social evils.

The urban population in our country has grown 11.1 times over the last century from 254 lakh in 1901 to 2850 lakh in 2001. In relative terms the rural and urban population ratio has decreased from 8.1:1 to 2.6:1. During the period 1991-2001, 678 lakhs people were added to the urban population.

19.7.3 Urbanisation and limited energy resources

Energy is a critical input for most of the production processes and consumption activities. With urbanisation comes increased need for energy sources. In last sixty years we have had more than four-fold increase in total energy use for less than one-third rise in the population. However, the commercial activity has shown a 10-fold rise during the same period. This shows that the bulk of non-commercial energy use has had shifted to commercial use (mostly due to urbanisation). Of the various sectors that use commercial energy around 70-75 per cent is consumed by industry and transport.

Our country has three major kinds of generating plants: hydroelectric, thermal and nuclear. They roughly contribute about 21 per cent, 75 per cent and four per cent of our energy requirement. As of now, in conventional resources of energy such as solar, garbage, winds are negligible and significant.

With growing population and increasing rural migration to cities, our country must cope with increased energy requirement. Production of energy is very costly. At individual levels prevention of wasteful expenditure of energy can contribute to national use.

India is world's sixth largest energy consumers accounting for 3.4 per cent of global energy consumption. This demand is growing at an average of 3.6 per cent per year over past 30 years. Although India generated 680 billion kWh of power during the year 2006 about 5000 million Indians still have no access to electricity. As compared to the world's average of 1200 kWh per capita power consumption, in our country the per capita power consumption in about 600 kWh. The total demand for electricity in India is expected to cross 9,50,000 MW by the year 2030. If we have to succeed as a nation, we must attain the capability to either generate or purchase the required per capita power consumption comparable to a developed, industrialised country. In the mean time, we must optimise the use of the power available and minimise the wasteful expenditure.

19.7.4 Urbanisation and scarcity of water

Regular supply of water on earth is maintained through its circulation in the atmosphere. Precipitation of water vapour, in the form for rain, snow, dew, hail etc. is the main source of water in the environment. Water vapours present in the atmosphere, in turn, come from the water bodies such as lakes, streams, oceans, ponds, moist earth as well as from living organisms. Of the total water present on the earth, oceans have 97 per cent and only three per cent of total water is available as fresh water. Water on earth is classified into following three types:

- **(i) Fresh water:** It is inland water and its salt content is less than 5 ppt or 0.05 per cent.
- **(ii) Marine water:** It occurs in seas, oceans and its salt content is more than 35 ppt or 3.5 per cent
- **(iii) Brackish water:** Its salt content is more than 5 ppt but less than 35 ppt. It is present in estuaries, salt marshes and salt lakes. A lot of underground water in Rajasthan, Gujarat, Haryana and Punjab is brackish.

With rapid population growth and rising migration from villages to cities, expectation for use in life, the natural resources of our earth face even increasing pressure. Along with air and land, water especially the fresh water resource is the one that we must protect for own survival. Of all the three per cent fresh water resources that we have glaciers and ice account for about two per cent. The rest of the fresh water is beneath the earth surface. Rivers and lakes contain only one-fifth of the total one per cent of earth's fresh water.

The ultimate source of the water is rainfall. India receives about 2750 km of rainfall every year. About 600 km of its seeps into the ground and about 9000 km evaporates water vapour back into environment.

As per 2001 census, India's population is 1027 million. It is expected to rise and stabilise around 1640 million by the year 2050. The gross per capital water availability in year 2000 was 1820 m^3/year. By the year 2050 the per capita availability of water is expected decline to as low as 1140 m^3/year. The total water requirement of the country for various activities around the year 2050 has been assessed to be 1459 km^3/yr. The current availability is about 500 km^3/yr. It is apparent that by the year 2050 our water availability has to be trebled.

The scarcity of urban water is due to:

(i) **Careless attitude:** Release of untreated sewage and other waters into rivers and lakes.

(ii) **Lowering of water table:** Due to excessive pumping of ground water.

(iii) **Waste in agriculture:** Water is losing due to seepage or evaporation during irrigated and poor water management practices.

(iv) **Increase in water demand:** Due to increased urbanisation and increased population and increase in per capita water consumption.

(v) **Water pollution:** Pollution of ground water by nitrates, fertilisers, toxic chemical sewage, industrial effluents, domestic wastes etc.

To meet the growing requirements of water, it is imperative not only to develop the net water resources but also to conserve, recycle and reuse water whenever or wherever possible. It has also been shown that conservation of water through rain water harvesting and artificial ground water recharge can generate about 125 km^3/yr. of additional water. Augmentation of existing water supply through desalination of sea water is an additional possibility. Similarly, recycling of municipal and industrial waste water can generate 177 km^3/yr water. How does the water get polluted? Can you imagine? Drinking, bathing, swimming, recreation, irrigation, all required good, uncontaminated, potable water, domestic effluent too cause water pollution. It develops foul smell and creates unhygienic condition in the surrounding affecting our health. In most of our cities and towns, the liquid waste product in kitchen, bathroom and toilet are discharged directly or indirectly without any treatment into rivers or any other water bodies. Even in our cities only half of the population has access to sewage system. Therefore, raw sewage affluent are discharged into fresh water bodies. The conditions in the villages are not better. Such domestic wastes contain pathogens that cause various viral, bacterial and the parasite diseases. Cholera, dysentery, typhoid, jaundice, worm-related diseases affect the health of the population. Household effluents are also rich in nitrates and phosphates. These deteriorate the water quality and promote growth aquatic organism making water for human consumption.

Therefore, India as a nation has to now initiate action on all fronts for developing its water resource. Can you imagine the consequences for not meeting this challenge in the next few decades? Our well being depends on combined efforts of all citizens of the nation.

19.8 Flood and Drought

Flood and drought are also important events connected with water that affect our lives.

Flood: Flood is a body of water that covers normal dry lands. Consequences of most lands are as follows: They

- Destroy homes and valuable property,
- Carry top fertile soil, leaving the land barren,
- Destroy both food and cash crop,
- Cause huge losses to human lives and cattle,
- Cause landslide in the hilly areas,
- Cause dam burst.

Floods occur when there is too much rain. Heavy rains cause with floods. Sudden melting of ice also results in flood. In deserts, the floods are caused by thunderstorms. Certain human activities such as deforestation and over intensive farming are also the causes of flood. Thus, along the sea coasts are caused by hurricane, cyclones or development of low pressure zones in the atmosphere. Floods can be controlled by building dams to store water, planting trees on eroded land and by building dams, flood walls, hurricane barriers during the coast line.

Thus, however, can be controlled by proper planning involving (a) storage of water; (b) migrating people from the affecting areas; (c) storing plentiful stocks of food and fodder during good times; (d) cloud seeding; (e) proper and effective water shed / catchment area management; (f) afforestation etc.

Drought

Drought is the condition that results when the average rainfall for an area drops below the normal amount for a long time. The consequences of drought are:

- Streams/pond/well dry up
- Water supply for agriculture, industry, personal use is greatly reduced
- Dry top soil is blown away by hot dry winds

- Livestocks die
- Increase susceptibility to vulnerable diseases especially diarrhoea

19.9 Urbanisation and Pollution

With urbanisation population gets unevenly dispersed. This results in unbalanced demand for resources and even unbalanced release of harmful matter into the surroundings, sub-harmful and often hazardous material comes from industrial, domestic, transport, vehicle etc. when released, they severely affect the soil, water and air. The management of pollution is discussed in detail in less 10 pollutants can prove to be dangerous to human beings and other organisms.

19.10 Environmental Economics

- Environmental economics is a subfield of economics concerned with environmental issues. Quoting from the National Bureau of Economic Research Environmental Economics programme: Environmental Economics undertakes theoretical or empirical studies of the economic effects of national or local environmental policies around the world. Particular issues include the costs and benefits of alternative environmental policies to deal with air pollution, water quality, toxic substances, solid waste, and global warming.

  Environmental economics is distinguished from Ecological economics that emphasises the economy as a subsystem of the ecosystem with its focus upon preserving natural capital. One survey of German economists found that ecological and environmental economics are different schools of economic thought, with ecological economists emphasising 'strong' sustainability and rejecting the proposition that natural capital can be substituted by human-made capital.

Concept of Environmental Economics

Central to environmental economics is the concept of market failure. Market failure means that markets fail to allocate resources efficiently. As stated by Hanley, Shogren and White (2007) in their textbook *Environmental Economics*: 'A market failure occurs when the market does not allocate scarce resources to generate the greatest social welfare. A wedge exists between what a private person does given market prices and what society might want him or her to do to protect the environment. Such a wedge implies wastefulness or economic inefficiency; resources can be reallocated to make at least one person better off without making anyone else worse off.' Common forms of market failure include externalities, non-excludability and non-rivalry.

Externality: The basic idea is that an externality exists when a person makes a choice that affects other people that are not accounted for in the market price. For instance, a firm emitting pollution will typically not take into account the costs that its pollution imposes on others. As a result, pollution in excess of the 'socially efficient' level may occur. A classic definition influenced by Kenneth Arrow and James Meade is provided by Heller and Starrett (1976), who define an externality as 'a situation in which the private economy lacks sufficient incentives to create a potential market in some good and the nonexistence of this market results in losses of Pareto efficiency'. In economic terminology, externalities are examples of market failures, in which the unfettered market does not lead to an efficient outcome.

Common property and non-exclusion: When it is too costly to exclude people from access to an environmental resource for which there is rivalry, market allocation is likely to be inefficient. The challenges related with common property and non-exclusion have long been recognised. Hardin's (1968) concept of the tragedy of the commons popularised the challenges involved in non-exclusion and common property. 'Commons' refers to the environmental asset itself, common property resource' or 'common pool resource' refers to a property right regime that allows for some collective body to devise schemes to exclude others, thereby allowing the capture of future benefit streams; and 'open-access' implies no ownership in the sense that property everyone owns nobody owns.The basic problem is that if people ignore the scarcity value of the commons, they can end up expending too much effort, over harvesting a resource (e.g., a fishery). Hardin theorizes that in the absence of restrictions, users of an open-access resource will use it more than if they had to pay for it and had exclusive rights, leading to environmental degradation.

Public goods and non-rivalry: Public goods are another type of market failure, in which the market price does not capture the social benefits of its provision. For example, efforts to mitigate climate change would be a public good since the risks of climate change are both non-rival and non-excludable. Such efforts are non-rival since climate mitigation provided to one does not reduce the level of mitigation that anyone else enjoys. They are non-excludable actions by one will have global consequences from which no one can be excluded. A country's incentive to invest in carbon abatement is reduced because it can "free ride" off the efforts of other countries. Over a century ago, Swedish economist Knut Wicksell (1896) first discussed how public goods can be under-provided by the market because people might conceal their preferences for the good, but still enjoy the benefits without paying for them.

Valuation

Assessing the economic value of the environment is a major topic within the field. Use and indirect use are tangible benefits accruing from natural resources or ecosystem services. Non-use values include existence, option, and bequest values. For example, some people may value the existence of a diverse set of species, regardless of the effect of the loss of a species on ecosystem services. The existence of these species may have an option value, as there may be possibility of using it for some human purpose (certain plants may be researched for drugs). Individuals may value the ability to leave a pristine environment to their children.

Use and indirect use values can often be inferred from revealed behaviour, such as the cost of taking recreational trips or using hedonic methods in which values are estimated based on observed prices. Non-use values are usually estimated using stated preference methods such as contingent valuation or choice modelling. Contingent valuation typically takes the form of surveys in which people are asked how much they would pay to observe and recreate in the environment (willingness to pay) or their willingness to accept (WTA) compensation for the destruction of the environmental good. Hedonic pricing examines the effect the environment has on economic decisions through housing prices, travelling expenses, and payments to visit parks.

Solutions

Solutions advocated to correct such externalities include:

Environmental regulations: Under this plan, the economic impact has to be estimated by the Regulator. Usually this is done using cost-benefit analysis. There is a growing realisation that regulations (also known as "command and control" instruments) are not so distinct from economic instruments as is commonly asserted by proponents of environmental economics. E.g. 1: regulations are enforced by fines, which operate as a form of tax if pollution rises above the threshold prescribed. E.g. 2: pollution must be monitored and laws enforced, whether under a pollution tax regime or a regulatory regime. The main difference an environmental economist would argue exists between the two methods, however, is the total cost of the regulation. "Command and control" regulation often applies uniform emissions limits on polluters, even though each firm has different costs for emissions reductions. Some firms, in this system, can abate inexpensively, while others can only abate at high cost. Because of this, the total abatement has some expensive and some inexpensive efforts to abate. Environmental economic regulations find the cheapest emission abatement efforts first, then the more expensive methods second. E.g. as said earlier, trading, in the quota system, means a firm only abates if doing so would cost less than paying someone else to make the same reduction. This leads to a lower cost for the total abatement effort as a whole.

Quotas on pollution: Often it is advocated that pollution reductions should be achieved by way of tradable emissions permits, which if freely traded may ensure that reductions in pollution are achieved at least cost. In theory, if such tradable quotas are allowed, then a firm would reduce its own pollution load only if doing so would cost less than paying someone else to make the same reduction. In practice, tradable permits approaches have had some success, such as the US's sulphur dioxide trading programme or the EU Emissions Trading Scheme, and interest in its application is spreading to other environmental problems.

Taxes and tariffs on pollution/Removal of "dirty subsidies": Increasing the costs of polluting will discourage polluting, and will provide a "dynamic incentive", that is, the disincentive continues to operate even as pollution levels fall. A pollution tax that reduces pollution to the socially "optimal" level would be set at such a level that pollution occurs only if the benefits to society (for example, in form of greater production) exceed the costs. Some advocate a major shift from taxation from income and sales taxes to tax on pollution- the so-called "green tax shift."

Better defined property rights: The Coase Theorem states that assigning property rights will lead to an optimal solution, regardless of who receives them, if transaction costs are trivial and the number of parties negotiating is limited. For example, if people living near a factory had a right to clean air and water, or the factory had the right to pollute, then either the factory could pay those affected by the pollution or the people could pay the factory not to pollute. Or, citizens could take action themselves as they would if other property rights were violated. The US River Keepers Law of the 1880s was an early example, giving citizens downstream the right to end pollution upstream themselves if government itself did not act (an early example of bioregional democracy). Many markets for "pollution rights" have been created in the late twentieth century.

Relationship to other fields

Environmental economics is related to ecological economics but there are differences. Most Environmental economists have been trained as economists. They apply the tools of economics to address environmental problems, many of which are related to so-called market failures-circumstances wherein the "invisible hand" of economics is unreliable. Most ecological economists have been trained as ecologists, but have expanded the scope of their work to consider the impacts of humans and their economic activity on ecological systems and services, and vice-versa. This field takes as its premise that economics is a strict subfield of ecology. Ecological economics is sometimes described as taking a more pluralistic approach to environmental problems and focuses more explicitly on long-term environmental sustainability and issues of scale.

Environmental economics is viewed as more pragmatic in a price system; ecological economics as more idealistic in its attempts not to use money as a primary arbiter of decisions. These two groups of specialists sometimes have conflicting views which may be traced to the different philosophical underpinnings.

Another context in which externalities apply is when globalisation permits one player in a market who is unconcerned with biodiversity to undercut prices of another who is creating a race to the bottom in regulations and conservation. This in turn may cause loss of natural capital with consequent erosion, water purity problems, diseases, desertification, and other outcomes which are not efficient in an economic sense. This concern is related to the subfield of sustainable development and its political relation, the anti-globalisation movement.

Environmental economics was once distinct from resource economics. Natural resource economics as a subfield began when the main concern of researchers was the optimal commercial exploitation of natural resource stocks. But resource managers and policy-makers eventually began to pay attention to the broader importance of natural resources (e.g. values of fish and trees beyond just their commercial exploitation; externalities associated with mining). It is now difficult to distinguish "environmental" and "natural resource" economics as separate fields as the two became associated with sustainability. Many of the more radical green economists split off to work on an alternate political economy.

Environmental economics was a major influence for the theories of natural capitalism and environmental finance, which could be said to be two sub-branches of environmental economics concerned with resource conservation in production, and the value of biodiversity to humans, respectively. The theory of natural capitalism (Hawken, Lovins) goes further than traditional environmental economics by envisioning a world where natural services are considered on par with physical capital.

The more radical Green economists reject neoclassical economics in favour of a new political economy beyond capitalism or communism that gives a greater emphasis to the interaction of the human economy and the natural environment, acknowledging that "economy is three-fifths of ecology"- *Mike Nickerson.*

These more radical approaches would imply changes to money supply and likely also a bioregional democracy so that political, economic, and ecological "environmental limits" were all aligned, and not subject to the arbitrage normally possible under capitalism.

Professional bodies

The main academic and professional organisations for the discipline of Environmental Economics are the Association of Environmental and Resource Economists (AERE) and the European Association for Environmental and Resource Economics (EAERE). The main academic and professional organisation for the discipline of Ecological Economics is the International Society for Ecological Economics (ISEE) and The Green Economics Institute for Green Economics is its international professional body.

20

Environmental Impact Assessment

20.1 Introduction

Every country strives to progress ahead one aspect of progress is economic development though manufacturing and trading. Every country builds industries which provide employment, serve the consumer's needs and help to generate revenue. Development projects in the past were undertaken without any consideration to their environmental consequences. As a result, rivers and lakes got polluted; air pollution reached at threatening level and pilling of industrial wastes resulted in land degradation. Industrialisation and economic growth provided material comforts and luxuries of life but at the same time deteriorated the quality of life.

In view of the colossal damage to environment by developmental activities people are now concerned about the environmental impact of developmental projects. Environmental Impact Assessment (EIA) enables the decision-makers to analyse the effect of developmental activities on the environment, if any well before the developmental project is implement.

The probable impact of anthropogenic activities regarding the use of environmental resources on natural environment is termed as environmental impact and the assessment and evaluation of environmental effects of human activities are collectively called as environmental impact assessment (EIA). The possible effects of human activities during the exploitation and processing of natural resources on natural environment are called as environmental impact Statement. According to K.J. Gregory and D.E. Walling (1981), environmental impact assessment and environmental impact statement (EIS) together refer to studies which firstly attempt to suggest the estimates of future environmental changes attributable to a proposed action and secondly, attempt to suggest the likely impact of environmental changes due to human activities, on man's future wellbeing.

Thus, environmental impact assessment is a method of evaluating environmental consequences (i.e. environmental changes which are likely to be caused by the proposed human activities related to land use changes, construction of dams, roads, rails, bridges etc. industrial location, urbanisation etc.) and the possible detrimental environmental changes (environmental degradation and pollution resulting into ecological imbalance and ecosystem disequilibrium).

In 1969, United States of America introduced on Act for environmental impact assessment, which is known as National Environmental Policy Act (NEPA). This Act had four major objectives.

- To declare a national policy to encourage productive and enjoyable harmony between environment and man.
- To promote efforts to prevent or eliminate damage to the environment and its biosphere, and stimulate health and welfare of the human beings.
- To increase understanding of ecological system and natural resources important to nation.
- To establish a Council on Environmental Quality (CEQ).

20.2 Concept of EIA

EIA was introduced in India in 1978, with respect to river valley projects. Later the EIA legislation was enhanced to include other developmental sections since 1941. EIA is now mandatory for 30 categories of projects, and these projects get environmental clearance only after the EIA requirement are fulfilled. EIA is a tool which helps to evaluate environmental impact of proposed developmental projects or programmes are visualised clearance accorded after mitigation strategies are included in the Plan. EIA thus proves to be a tool which improves decision-making and ensures that the project under construction is environmentally sound and within limits of the capacity of assimilation and regeneration capacities of the ecosystem. Environmental clearance of developmental projects is mandatory for the new project.

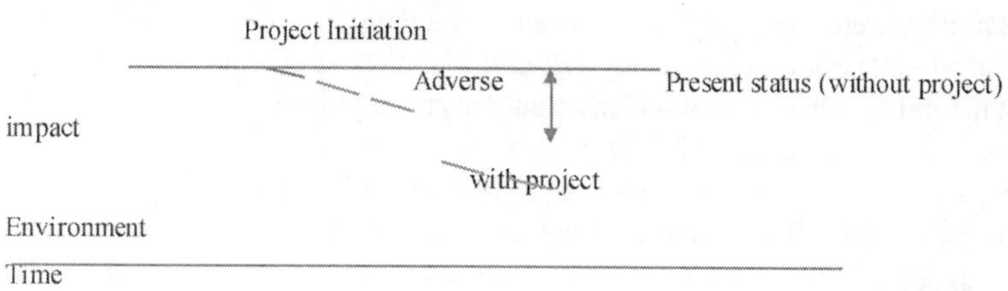

Figure 20.1: Anticipated environmental impact of developmental project.

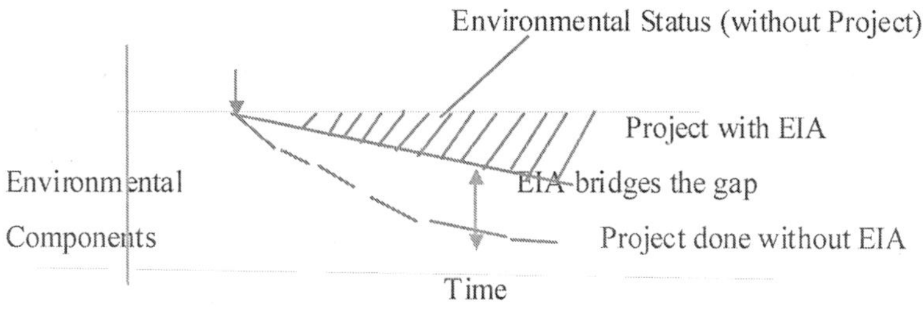

Figure 20.2: Environmental impact rectification after EIA.

The objective of environmental impact assessment is to achieve sustained development with

- Minimal environmental degradation, and
- Prevention of long-term environmental adverse effects by incorporating suitable mitigating measures.

Environmental impact assessment process, therefore, involves evaluation of environmental implications and incorporation of necessary safeguards for those activities having a bearing on environmental quality.

The important aspects of EIA are:

- Risk assessment
- Environmental management and
- Post-product monitoring.

EIA provides a cost-effective method to eliminate or minimise the adverse impact of development projects. Environmental appraisal of projects is an important responsibility of the Department of Environment (DoE), Government of India. Accordingly, questionnaires and guidelines have been evolved for development projects in selected sectors such as industry, river-valley, hydel, thermal and atomic power, ports and harbours, mining etc. The questionnaires and guidelines are updated periodically to facilitate relevant data collection necessary for critical analysis of the project from environmental angle. Guidelines for setting of industries have also been brought out. Presently the DoE have environmental appraisal committees for following sectors of development project/activities:

- River valley projects/irrigation hydel power and multipurpose
- Mining projects
- Industrial projects and
- Thermal power projects.

Special expert groups/Committees and task forces are constituted for assessment of other major projects referred to the DoE from time to time.

20.3. Legal Bases of Environmental Impact Assessment

The EIA process will be designed such that its guidelines follow basic legal and policy equipments. For example, EIA is to-

- Serve as a primary environmental tool with clear provisions.
- Apply consistently to all proposals with potential environmental impacts.
- Use scientific practice and suggests strategies for mitigation.
- Address all possible factors such as short-term, long-term, small scale and large scale effects.
- Consider sustainable aspects such as capacity for assimilation, carrying capacity, biodiversity protection.
- Lay down a flexible approach with and provides for public involvement.
- Have in-built mechanism of follow up and feedback for comply into mandatory requirements.
- Include mechanisms for monitoring, auditing and evaluation.

EIA appraises the environmental health and social implications of planned developmental projects. It thus links environment with development. The goal of EIA is to ensure environmentally safe and sustainable development.

20.4 Goals of EIA Process

Environmental goals may fall into three categories: clean up, controlled land use and social welfare.

The first goal is to set straight the mistake of the past- cleaning up our air and water recovering and recycling wastes, and controlling pesticides and toxic substances. Generally, we know what needs to be done. We have much of the necessary technology and we are working to develop that which we do not yet have.

Secondly, for decades this country has been squandering its land and water resources. We have been developing land which should not be developed- food plains and wetlands, ravines and stream banks- and we have been using five acres to do work of one. Plainly we can no longer afford to have key decisions shaped largely by market forces. We must move toward some form of land use control.

Thirdly, the rapid physical deterioration of our cities and the critical human problems accompanying this decline pose an enormous challenge to the stability of our nation. Indeed, the essence of quality urban living lies in its diversity and complexity. As such, achieving a better environment for our cities will involve not only providing for physical needs such as litter-free streets, clean air and water, houses, free of rats and lead-based paint, and maintenance of natural surroundings, but much more. The goal must include adequate health, housing, education, jobs, recreation, cultural opportunities, and means of transportation. It also demands, particularly for the people of our inner cities, a sense of personal dignity, self-respect, community involvement, and participation indecisions which affect their lives.

Increasing demand for environmental quality and cleaner surroundings places a high priority on the quality of natural surroundings as it affects human wellbeing. Protection of scenery, clean air and water, minimisation of noise, congestion and monotonous city-scapes, and open space for active outdoor recreation have all taken on new importance. There is great concern for man's health and a desire to live work, and play in more pleasant surroundings. For the planner and impact analyst these have proved to be very important considerations.

20.5 Environmental Impact Statement

The Environmental Impact Statement (EIS) is a document written in the format as specified by DoE (Department of Environment). The EIS represents a summary of the environmental inventory and the findings of the environmental assessment.

There are two categories of EISs: draft Statements and final statements. The draft statement is the document prepared by an agency proposing an action; it is circulated for review and comment to other federal agencies, State and local agencies, and public and private interest groups. The final statement is the draft statement modified to include a discussion of problems and objections raised by reviewers. The final statement must be on file with DoE for at least a 30 day period prior to initiation of construction on project participants, the various participants in the EIA process should be clearly identified. Following is a list of those that are normally involved.

Decision maker: Can be a head of state, a group of ministers, an elected body, or a single designated individual.

Assessor: Is the person, agency, or company having responsibility for preparing the EIS.

Proponent: Can be a government agency or a private firm wishing to initiate the project.

Reviewer: Is the person, agency, or board with responsibility for reviewing the EIS and assuring compliance with published guidelines or regulations.

Other agencies of government: Are agencies with a special interest in the project; they may be associated with provinces, states, cities or villages.

Expert advisors: Are persons with the specialised knowledge required to evaluate the proposed action; they may come from within or outside the government service.

Public at large: Includes citizens and the media.

Special-interest groups: Includes environmental organisations, labour unions, professional societies, and local associations.

20.6 EIA Process and Procedures

It includes steps in EIA process, methods of carrying out EIA, composition of the expert committees for EIA and main participants of EIA.

20.6.1. Steps in EIA process

EIA involves the steps mentioned below. However, EIA process is cyclical with interaction between the various steps.

- **Screening:** The project plan is screened for scale of investment, location and type of development and if the project needs statutory clearance.
- **Scoping:** The project's potential impacts, zone of impacts, mitigation possibilities and need for monitoring. The EIA agency has to follow the published guidelines by the Ministry of Environment and Forest (MoEF) of Government of India.
- **Collection of baseline data:** Baseline data is the environmental status of study area.
- **Impact prediction:** Positive and negative, reversible and irreversible and temporary and permanent impacts need to be predicted which presupposes a good understanding of the project by the assessment agency.
- **Mitigation measures and EIA report:** The EIA report should include the actions and steps for preventing, minimising or by passing the impacts or else the level of compensation for probable environmental damage or loss.
- **Public hearing:** On completion of the EIA report, public and environmental groups living close to project site may be informed and consulted.
- **Decision making:** Impact Assessment (IA) authority along with the experts consult the project-in-charge along with consultant to take the final decision, keeping mind EIA and EMP (Environment Management Plan).
- **Monitoring and implementation of environmental management plan:** The various phases of implementation of the project are monitored.

- **Risk assessment:** Inventory analysis and hazard probability and index also form part of EIA procedures.

20.6.2 Methods of carrying out EIA

Preparation of EIA report comprises the following steps:

- Collection of baseline data from primary and secondary sources;
- Prediction of impacts based on past experience and mathematical modelling;
- Evolution of impacts versus evaluation of net cost benefit; preparation of environmental management plans to reduce the impacts to the minimum;
- Quantitative estimation of financial cost of monitoring plan and the mitigation measures;
- Preparation of environmental management plans to reduce the impacts to the minimum;
- Quantitative estimation of financial cost of monitoring plan and the mitigation measures.

20.6.3 Composition of the expert committees for EIA

- The committees will consist of experts in the following disciplines:
  - Eco-system management
  - Air/water pollution control
  - Water resource management
  - Flora/fauna conservation and management
  - Land use planning
  - Social Sciences/ rehabilitation
  - Project appraisal
  - Ecology
  - Environmental Health
  - Subject Area Specialists
  - Representatives of NGOs/ persons concerned with environmental issues.
- The chairman will be an outstanding and experienced ecologist or environmentalist or technical professional with wide managerial experience in the relevant development.
- The representative of Impact Assessment Agency will act as a Member-Secretary.
- Chairman and members will serve in their individual capacities except those specifically nominated as representatives.
- The membership of a committee shall not exceed 15 members.

20.6.4 Main Participants of EIA

EIA applies to public and private sections. The six main players are:

- Those who propose the project.
- The environmental consultant who prepare EIA on behalf of project proponent.
- Pollution Control Board (State or National).
- Public has the right to express their opinion.
- The Impact Assessment Agency.
- Regional centre of the Ministry of Environment and Forest.

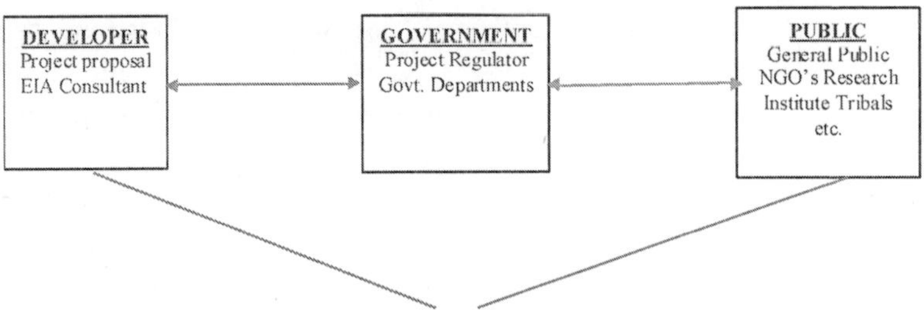

Figure 20.3.: Participants for EIA.

20.7. Environmental Clearance

Environmental clearance or the 'go ahead' signal is granted by the Impact Assessment Agency in the Ministry of Environment and Forests, Government of India. All projects that require clearance from central government can be broadly categorised into the following:

- Industries
- Mining
- Thermal Power Plants
- River valley projects
- Infrastructure and CRZ (Coastal Regulation Zone)
- Nuclear power projects

20.7.1 Issues of Environmental clearance/rejection letter Single Window clearance

When a project requires both environmental clearance as well as approval under the Forest (Conservation) Act, 1980 proposals for both are required to be given simultaneously to the concerned divisions of the Ministry. The processing is done simultaneously for clearance or rejection, although separate letters may issue. If the project does not involve diversion of forestland, the case is processed only for environmental clearance.

Time Frame

Once all the requisite documents and data from the project authorities are received and public hearings (where required) have been held, assessment and evaluation of the project from the environment angle is completed within 90 days and the decision of the ministry shall be conveyed within 30 days thereafter.

Post-Project Monitoring

It is to be noted that whenever a project is given environment clearance, a set of recommendations and conditions are stipulated by the appraisal committee on a case to case basis, which have to be complied with by the project proponent once the project is commissioned. The project authorities are required to submit a half-yearly compliance report to the Ministry about the compliance of conditions stipulated in the environmental clearance order by the Ministry. To monitor the implementation of the recommendations and conditions stipulated by the appraisal committee subject to which the environmental clearance has been given. The six regional offices of the Ministry located at Shillong, Bhubneshwar, Chandigarh, Banglaru, Lucknow and Bhopal, help the Ministry in post-project monitoring of the cleared projects. Cases of non-compliance of the recommendations and conditions by cleared projects/units are brought to the notice of the Ministry which may then initiate action against the project authorities.

20.8 Environmental Components of EIA

The EIA process looks into the following components of the environment:

Air Environment

- Quality of ambient air
- Wind speed, direction, humidity etc.
- Quantity of emission likely from project
- Impact of the emission on the area
- Pollution control desires/air quality standards

Noise

- Levels of noise present and predicted
- Strategies for reducing noise pollution

Water Environment

- Existing ground and surface water resources, their quality and quantity within the zone.
- Impact of proposed project on water resources.

Biological environment

- Flora and fauna in impact zone.
- Potential damage (likely) due to project, due to effluents, emissions and landscaping.
- Biological stress (prediction).

Land Environment

- Study of soil characteristics land use, and drainage pattern, and the likely adverse impact of the project.
- Impact on historical monuments and heritage site.

Assessment of expected economic benefits arising out of the project have to be compared to the all the above mentioned factors. Thus, we can say that environmental concerns have to be made a part of the decision to set up a project.

20.9 Conclusion

An effective EIA exercise is focused, time bound, cost effective and makes assessment understandable. The sole objective is to erase any situations of environmental damage during construction and implementation of the developmental project. It should also be keep in mind the general public and people in the local and neighbourhood of the project. The evaluation of EIA is possible only when there is public awareness of those responsible for protecting environmental quality and enforcement and the EIA report and information contained therein is reliable.

21

Solid Waste Management

21.1 Introduction

Solid waste means any garbage, refuse, sludge from a wastewater treatment plant, water supply treatment plant, or air pollution control facility and other discarded materials including solid, liquid, semi-solid, or contained gaseous material, resulting from industrial, commercial, mining and agricultural operations, and from community activities.

Waste management is the collection, transport, processing or disposal, managing and monitoring of waste materials. The term usually relates to materials produced by human activity, and the process is generally undertaken to reduce their effect on health, the environment or aesthetics. Waste management is a distinct practice from resource recovery which focuses on delaying the rate of consumption of natural resources. The management of wastes treats all materials as a single class, whether solid, liquid, gaseous or radioactive substances, and tried to reduce the harmful environmental impacts of each through different methods.

Waste management practices differ for developed and developing nations, for urban and rural areas, and for residential and industrial producers. Management for non-hazardous waste residential and institutional waste in metropolitan areas is usually the responsibility of local government authorities, while management for non-hazardous commercial and industrial waste is usually the responsibility of the generator.

21.2 Solid Waste Management Programme

The purpose of the Solid Waste Management Programme is to ensure solid waste is managed in such a way that protects both public health and the environment. The Solid Waste Management Programme works hard to help all people better manage their solid wastes. Through the cooperative efforts of citizens, businesses, industry and government, people can continue to increase material reuse and recycling from all solid waste sources. Reducing the amount of solid wastes generated remains the programme's primary goal.

People living in homes, businesses and industry generate millions of tons of solid waste annually. While landfill disposal continues to be an option, new disposal facilities face strong public examination and are costly to site, build and operate. The department is constantly seeking alternatives to landfill disposal that are both environmentally protective and cost-effective for the consumer. Solid waste management permitting, monitoring and enforcement efforts can prevent illegal dumping and other factors that may cause long-term social, economic and environmental problems.

21.3 Urban Waste Management Issues

The conditions, issues and problems of urban waste management in the industrialised and developing worlds are different. Though the developed countries generate larger amounts of wastes, they have developed adequate facilities, competent government institutions and bureaucracies to manage their wastes. Developing countries are still in the transition towards better waste management but they currently have insufficient collection and improper disposal of wastes. Clear government policies and competent bureaucracies for management of solid wastes are needed urgently especially in countries where there is rapid population growth through urbanisation into peri-urban areas. Services and programmes that include proper waste disposal for management of hazardous biological and chemical wastes, minimisation and recycling will be needed. Disposal of wastes is commonly done by dumping (on land or into water bodies), incineration or long-term storage in a secured facility. All these methods have varying degrees of negative environmental impacts with adverse environmental and health risks if wastes are improperly disposed or stored.

21.4 Methods of Waste Disposal

1. Landfill

Fig. 21.1: Landfill area

Fig. 21.2: Incineration

Disposing of waste in a landfill involves burying the waste, and this remains a common practice in most countries. Landfills were often established in abandoned or unused quarries, mining voids or borrow pits. A properly designed and well-managed landfill can be a hygienic and relatively inexpensive method of disposing of waste materials. Older, poorly designed or poorly managed landfills can create a number of adverse environmental impacts such as wind-blown litter, attraction of vermin, and generation of liquid leach ate. Another common byproduct of landfills is gas (mostly composed of methane and carbon dioxide), which is produced as organic waste breaks down an aerobically. This gas can create odour problems, kill surface vegetation, and is a greenhouse gas.

Design characteristics of a modern landfill include methods to contain leach ate such as clay or plastic lining material. Deposited waste is normally compacted to increase its density and stability, and covered to prevent attracting vermin (such as mice or rats). Many landfills also have landfill gas extraction systems installed to extract the landfill gas. Gas is pumped out of the landfill using perforated pipes and flared off or burnt in a gas engine to generate electricity.

2. Incineration

Incineration is a disposal method in which solid organic wastes are subjected to combustion so as to convert them into residue and gaseous products. This method is useful for disposal of residue of both solid waste management and solid residue from waste water management. This process reduces the volumes of solid waste to 20 to 30 per cent of the original volume. Incineration and other high temperature waste treatment systems are sometimes described as "thermal treatment." Incinerators convert waste materials into heat, gas, steam and ash.

Incineration is carried out both on a small scale by individuals and on a large scale by industry. It is used to dispose of solid, liquid and gaseous waste. It is recognised as a practical method of disposing of certain hazardous waste materials (such as biological medical waste). Incineration is a controversial method of waste disposal, due to issues such as emission of gaseous pollutants.

Incineration is common in countries such as Japan where land is scarcer, as these facilities generally do not require as much area as landfills. Waste-to-energy or energy-from-waste is broad terms for facilities that burn waste in a furnace or boiler to generate heat, steam or electricity. Combustion in an incinerator is not always perfect and there have been concerns about pollutants in gaseous emissions from incinerator stacks. Particular concern has focused on some very persistent organics such as dioxins, furans, PAHs which may be created which may have serious environmental consequences.

3. Recycling

Fig. 21.3: Recycling.

Steel crushed and baled for recycling

Recycling is a resource recovery practice that refers to the collection and reuse of waste materials such as empty beverage containers. The materials from which the items are made can be reprocessed into new products. Material for recycling may be collected separately from general waste using dedicated bins and collection vehicles, or sorted directly from mixed waste streams. Known as kerb-side recycling, it requires the owner of the waste to separate it into various different bins (typically wheelie bins) prior to its collection.

The most common consumer products recycled include aluminum such as beverage cans, copper such as wire, steel food and aerosol cans, old steel furnishings or equipment, polyethylene and PET bottles, glass bottles and jars, paperboard cartons, newspapers, magazines and light paper, and corrugated fiberboard boxes.

These items are usually composed of a single type of material, making them relatively easy to recycle into new products. The recycling of complex products (such as computers and electronic equipment) is more difficult, due to the additional dismantling and separation required.

The type of material accepted for recycling varies by city and country. Each city and country has different recycling programmes in place that can handle the various types of recyclable materials. However, variation in acceptance is reflected in the resale value of the material once it is reprocessed.

The management of waste is a key component in a business' ability to maintaining certain accreditation. Companies are encouraged to improve their environmental efficiencies each year. One way to do this is by improving a company's waste management with a new recycling service. (such as recycling: glass, food waste, paper and cardboard, plastic bottles etc.)

4. Biological reprocessing

(*Composting, Home composting, and Anaerobic digestion*)

Fig. 21.4: Biological reprocessing.

Waste materials that are organic in nature, such as plant material, food scraps, and paper products, can be recycled using biological composting and digestion processes to decompose the organic matter. The resulting organic material is then recycled as mulch or compost for agricultural or landscaping purposes. In addition, waste gas from the process (such as methane) can be captured and used for generating electricity and heat (CHP/cogeneration) maximising efficiencies. The intention of biological processing in waste management is to control and accelerate the natural process of decomposition of organic matter.

There is a large variety of composting and digestion methods and technologies varying in complexity from simple home compost heaps, to small town scale batch digesters, industrial-scale enclosed-vessel digestion of mixed domestic waste. Methods of biological decomposition are differentiated as being aerobic or anaerobic methods, though hybrids of the two methods also exist.

Anaerobic digestion of the organic fraction of municipal solid waste (MSW) has been found to be in a number of LCA (life cycle analysis) studies to be more environmentally effective, than landfill, incineration or pyrolisis. The resulting biogas (methane) though must be used for cogeneration (electricity and heat preferably on or close to the site of production) and can be used with a little upgrading in gas combustion engines or turbines. With further upgrading to synthetic natural gas it can be injected into the natural gas network or further refined to hydrogen for use in stationary cogeneration fuel cells. Its use in fuel cells eliminates the pollution from products of combustion.

An example of waste management through composting is the Green Bin Programme in Toronto, Canada, where Source Separated Organics (such as kitchen scraps and plant cuttings) are collected in a dedicated container and then composted.

5. Energy Recovery

Fig. 21.5: Anaerobic digestion component of Lübeck mechanical biological treatment plant in Germany, 2007.

The energy content of waste products can be harnessed directly by using them as a direct combustion fuel, or indirectly by processing them into another type of fuel. Thermal treatment ranges from using waste as a fuel source for cooking or heating and the use of the gas fuel, to fuel for boilers to generate steam and electricity in a turbine.

Pyrolysis and gasification are two related forms of thermal treatment where waste materials are heated to high temperatures with limited oxygen availability. The process usually occurs in a sealed vessel under high pressure. Pyrolysis of solid waste converts the material into solid, liquid and gas products. The liquid and gas can be burnt to produce energy or refined into other chemical products (chemical refinery). The solid residue (char) can be further refined into products such as activated carbon. Gasification and advanced Plasma arc gasification are used to convert organic materials directly into a synthetic gas composed of carbon monoxide and hydrogen. The gas is then burnt to produce electricity and steam. An alternative to pyrolisis is high temperature and pressure supercritical water decomposition (hydrothermal monophasic oxidation).

6. Resource Recovery

Resource recovery (as opposed to waste management) uses LCA (life cycle analysis) attempts to offer alternatives to waste management. For mixed

MSW (Municipal Solid Waste) a number of broad studies have indicated that administration, source separation and collection followed by reuse and recycling of the non-organic fraction and energy and compost/fertiliser production of the organic waste fraction via anaerobic digestion to be the favoured path.

7. Avoidance and reduction methods

An important method of waste management is the prevention of waste material being created, also known as waste reduction. Methods of avoidance include reuse of second-hand products, repairing broken items instead of buying new, designing products to be refillable or reusable (such as cotton instead of plastic shopping bags), encouraging consumers to avoid using disposable products (such as disposable cutlery), removing any food/liquid remains from cans, packaging, and designing products that use less material to achieve the same purpose (for example, light weighting of beverage cans).

8. Waste handling and transport

(Waste collection vehicle, Dustbin, and Waste sorting)

Fig. 21.6: Molded plastic, wheeled waste bin in Berkshire, England.

Waste collection methods vary widely among different countries and regions. Domestic waste collection services are often provided by local government authorities, or by private companies in the industry. Some areas, especially those in less developed countries, do not have a formal waste-collection system. Examples of waste handling systems include:

- In Europe and a few other places around the world, a few communities use a proprietary collection system known as Envac, which conveys refuse via underground conduits using a vacuum system. Other vacuum-based solutions include the MetroTaifun single-line and ring-line systems.

- In Canadian urban centres curbside collection is the most common method of disposal, whereby the city collects waste and/or recyclables and/or organics on a scheduled basis. In rural areas people often dispose of their waste by hauling it to a transfer station. Waste collected is then transported to a regional landfill.
- In Taipei, the city government charges its households and industries for the volume of rubbish they produce. Waste will only be collected by the city council if waste is disposed in government issued rubbish bags. This policy has successfully reduced the amount of waste the city produces and increased the recycling rate.
- In Israel, the Arrow Ecology company has developed the Arrow-Bio system, which takes trash directly from collection trucks and separates organic and inorganic materials through gravitational settling, screening, and hydro-mechanical shredding. The system is capable of sorting huge volumes of solid waste, salvaging recyclables, and turning the rest into biogas and rich agricultural compost. The system is used in California, Australia, Greece, Mexico, United Kingdom and in Israel. For example, an Arrow-Bio plant that has been operational at the Hiriya landfill site since December 2003 serves the Tel Aviv area, and processes up to 150 tons of garbage a day.

While waste transport within a given country falls under national regulations, trans-boundary movement of waste is often subject to international treaties. A major concern to many countries in the world has been hazardous waste. The Basel Convention, ratified by 172 countries, deprecates movement of hazardous waste from developed to less developed countries. The provisions of the Basel convention have been integrated into the EU waste shipment regulation. Nuclear waste, although considered hazardous, does not fall under the jurisdiction of the Basel Convention.

Fig. 21.7: Waste disposalsite.

21.5 Alternatives to Land Filling

There is a strong movement in many countries to reduce the volume of wastes to be dumped. The increase of composting sites is an indication that organic fraction of garbage can be converted into a useful and commercial product with a higher value. For immobile materials, technologies are needed to use wastes as raw materials to produce new products. Development of new materials from recycled materials will also encourage sorting of solid wastes. "Zero Waste" movement also targets industries and waste exchange. 40 per cent of land filled wastes in industrialised countries come from building materials and this suggests that such wastes can be avoided by developing long-lasting materials and dwellings to reduce wastes from need to rebuild. Advocates of long-lasting materials and buildings say that any new waste recycling projects is not going to increase the knowledge base appreciably. Instead funds for research and development should be diverted to redesigning dwellings that can last longer and that will facilitate higher levels of wastes-handling efficiencies. Conventional thinking will provide small gains only. Other alternatives and efforts indicate that:

- Onsite treatment and utilisation will reduce need for transport.
- Waste minimisation is a socially desirable goal.
- Subsidy on products generated from recycled materials will encourage socio-economic changes.
- Centres with technologies that use collected waste materials are needed.
- Wastes that have severe risks and excessive problems in disposal should be identified and those which cannot be neutralised may need to be restricted at the point of creation or entry.
- A database on wastes that are available will provide information to possible users of wastes.

21.6 Consumer and Human Lifestyles

A change to less waste-generating with the use of less polluting products and cultivating habits with broad and deep educations are encouraged to understand the extent of the interdependent ecological problems. Producer Take-Back Campaigns and "Customer service" marketing strategy will also foster change in lifestyles. Waste is not just garbage and includes mis-prioritising limited financing or limited productivity so that unimportant things get done but important ones Never gets done. Why don't we tackle and sort those Wastes? The Waste of Anecosystem is petro-pollution which should have been obsolete and displaced over two decades ago with non-pollution alternatives.

Fig. 21.8: Mismanagement of Waste.

There is increasing evidence that community-based approaches to waste management can promote a more sustainable development. Grassroots efforts can be more successful than top-down programmes created by bureaucrats or experts with little or no community participation. During most of human history, the approach to waste management in many cultures and civilisations was the recovery of materials. Only around the turn of the twentieth century the emphasis shifted from recovery to disposal. During the nineteenth century there were pioneering efforts in England to minimise wastes as a way to improve industrial competitiveness.

21.7 Hazardous Waste

Any substance that is present in the environment or released into the environment causing substantial damage to public health and welfare of the environment is called hazardous substance.

Any substance that could have serious irreversible health effects from a single exposure is called very hazardous substance. Any hazardous substance could exhibit any one or more of the following characteristics:

- Toxicity
- Ignibility
- Corrosivity
- Reactivity (explosive)

Thus, any waste that contains hazardous or very hazardous substance is called hazardous waste.

Hazardous wastes can originate from various sources such as: household, local areas, urban, industry, agriculture, construction activity, hospitals and laboratories, power plants and other sources.

Problem related to dumping of hazardous waste

The hazardous waste per se or when disposed off release a number of environmentally unfriendly substances. Some of them are given below:

Hazardous wastes, its disposal and effect

Sources	*Disposed/ used as*	*Polluting agent*	*Effect*
Industrial waste	Incineration of waste	Toxic fumes e.g. chlorine polyvinylchlorine	Chlorine could cause acid rain
	Incomplete combustion	Dioxins/organo chlorides	Carcinogenic
	Release into water bodies	Chlorophenol, fluorine compounds aldehydes, SO_2, CO	Cause environmental pollution
	Plastic	Polythene, poly propylene, polyesters etc. on burning release gases	Toxic, ecological pollution
Nuclear waste	Hospital Laboratories	Slow/sustained in medical/ agriculture	Health hazard, carcinogenic, mutation
Agricultural waste	Forms of nitrogen wastes	Manure/dung rich in NO_3/NO_2	Accumulate in vegetables, causes methanoglobenemia cyanosis
		Nitrosamines / NO_3/NO_2	Carcinogenic contribute to acid rain
		N_2O	Green house effect
		NH_3^+ (from livestock breeding)	Affect aquatic life: stimulate fungal growth; epiphytes, causes weathering of forests
	Phosphates		Eutrophicastion of aquatic environment
	Phyto sanitary product	Insecticides/pesticides/ fungicide/herbicides	Enter soil as run off, polluted water table affect aquatic life, carcinogenic renal failure
	Methane	Ruminating cattle, fermentation of organic matter	Powerful green house effect

21.8 Conclusion

There are a number of concepts about solid waste management which vary in their usage between countries or regions. Some of the most general, widely used concepts include: Waste hierarchy - The waste hierarchy refers to the **"3 Rs" reduce, reuse and recycle,** which classify waste management strategies according to their desirability in terms of waste minimisation. The waste hierarchy remains the keystone of most waste minimisation strategies. The aim of the waste hierarchy is to extract the maximum practical benefits from products and to generate the minimum amount of waste.

Trash and garbage is a common sight in urban and rural areas of India. It is a major source of pollution. Indian cities alone generate more than

100 million tons of solid waste a year. Street corners are piled with trash. Public places and sidewalks are despoiled with filth and litter, rivers and canals act as garbage dumps. In part, India's garbage crisis is from rising consumption. India's waste problem also points to a stunning failure of governance.

In the last fifty years the destruction and havoc caused to the environment by the push for ever increasing economic development is astounding. Most of the natural forest and wilderness has been lost and with it many species of plants and animals are now extinct or in danger of becoming extinct. So many rivers, lakes and the oceans have been contaminated with toxic wastes and in many places no longer are able to support life.

This style of living has not left us unscarred either. Now we are facing more and more disease; anxiety, stress and violence are increasing alarmingly; and we don't feel safe anymore. Now, one has to think twice before going out on the street at night almost anywhere in the world dumping waste and garbage, which may cause greater harm to all living being as a whole.

22

Disaster Management

22.1 Introduction

Nature is bountiful of resources used by the living organisms use for their survival and well being. But nature has its own control systems. Resources used up are replenished excesses are checked, all naturally through the biogeochemical cycles, the food chains and webs and other natural phenomena. Thus, equilibrium is maintained in nature. This is called ecological balance and has in recent times been disturbed by human activities. In nature catastrophes such as floods, drought, earthquake, tsunami, happen from time to time causing immense damage to life and property. It is important to devise means and methods to manage and minimise from natural disasters as far as possible. Disasters caused by human activities such as fires, accidents, epidemics are no less sudden than natural disasters and may be equally devastating. Over the last decades, the world has become increasingly vulnerable to natural disasters. Population growth and the increased concentration of physical assets in high risk areas are leading to increased exposures to adverse natural events. Unplanned and unregulated land use, lack of environmental controls, and the poor application of building standards contribute significantly to asset losses in the region. The trend toward increased vulnerability is likely to continue and when coupled with increased climatic variability, resulting from global climate change and future loss from natural disasters like earthquakes are expected to rise. The acceptance of disaster-preparedness, where international financial institutions, national governments and large development agencies see mitigation strategies as an important part of their work, is now recognised as crucial by experts on disaster-risk reduction. GIS provides an opportunity to civilian authorities and international agencies to enhance their preparedness for coping with natural disasters in general and earthquakes in particular. Poor people in developing countries are particularly vulnerable to disasters because of where they live. Research shows that they are more likely to occupy dangerous locations, such as flood plains, river banks, steep slopes, reclaimed land and highly populated settlements of flimsy shanty homes. The earthquake that devastated Bam in Iran in December, 2003 killed more than 40,000 people mainly because their housing was not designed to handle a major tremor. The availability of a probabilistic risk assessment tool may have better prepared the government to handle the situation.

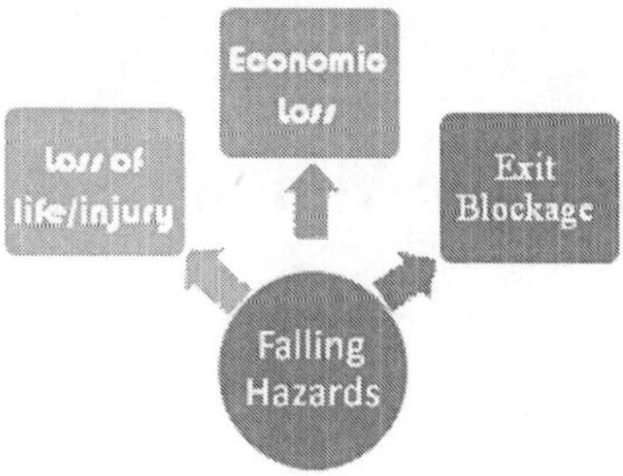

Figure 22.1: Effects of Hazards.

22.2 Type of Disasters

There are two types of disasters namely, natural disasters and man-made disasters. Natural disasters are earthquake, cyclone, volcanic eruption, flood, drought, forest fire, landslides, tsunami, avalanche etc. and man-made disasters are fire, accidents (road, rail or air), industrial accidents or epidemics etc. both natural and man-made disasters which have devastating input resulting loss of human life, loss of livelihoods, property and environmental degradation. Disasters disrupt normal functioning of society and leave long lasting impact.

22.3 Natural Disasters

The Indian subcontinent is highly prone to natural disasters. Floods, droughts, cyclones and earthquake are recurrent phenomena in India. Susceptibility to disease is compounded by frequent occurrences of man-made disasters such as fire. The changing topography due to environmental degradation is also increasing vulnerability to natural disasters. In 1988, 11.2 per cent of total land area was flood prone, but in 1998 floods inundated 37 per cent geographical area. The major disasters that India and neighbouring countries have experienced in the recent past are the earthquake in Latur (Maharashtra in 1993), Gujarat (2001), most parts of India (2006), Sikkim (2011), Nepal and most parts of India (2015), super cyclone in Odisha (1999, 2014), tsunami in Tamil Nadu and Andhra Pradesh (2004), floods in Jammu and Kashmir (2014), Bihar and Assam almost every year. Frequent disasters lead to enormous loss of life and property. Physical safety-especially that of the vulnerable groups is routinely threatened by hazards. Natural disasters cannot be prevented but their damaging impact can be reduced through better forecast, and preparedness to take up effective rescue measures. The four major disasters mentioned above have very clearly illustrated that we need multi-hazard prevention, response and recovery plans for natural hazards so that threat to human life and property is minimised. Disaster risk management is essentially a development problem. Preparedness and planning for disaster management have to be taken up along with environmental concerns that the country is facing today.

Natural disasters are changes which are so great they may cause damage to the shape of the land or to the lives of people and other living things. Great changes happen deep inside the Earth and on its surface. The changes on the outer part of the Earth happen because of different kinds of weather. Natural disasters are disasters which are caused by natural forces. These disasters occur in nature without human provocation and wreck life and property when they strike. Some of the major natural disasters are described below:

22.4 Earthquakes

An earthquake is a natural disaster which causes the surface of the earth to shake and tremble. It is a sudden release of energy accumulated in deformed rocks of earth crust causing the ground to tremble and shake. It is a violent shaking of the ground. Sometimes it is so strong that the ground splits apart. When parts of the earth, called plates, move against each other giant shock waves move upwards towards the surface causing the earthquake. It can occur suddenly any time of the year without any warning causing severe loss of life and property. This may result in minor or sometimes major disasters such as loss of human life and animals lives, collapsing of buildings, bridges and roads breaking or uprooting of trees, etc. The intensity of an earthquake is related to the amount of energy released when rocks give way to the forces within the earth. It is measured with the help of an instrument known as seismograph. The intensity is measured on Richter scale. Scientists assign a magnitude rating to earthquakes based on the strength and duration of their seismic waves. A quake measuring 3 to 5 is considered minor or light; 5 to 7 is moderate to strong; 7 to 8 is major; and 8 or more is great. On average, a magnitude 8 quake strikes somewhere every year and some 10,000 people die in earthquakes annually. Collapsing buildings claim by far the majority of lives, but the destruction is often compounded by mud slides, fires, floods, or tsunamis. Smaller temblors that usually occur in the days following a large earthquake can complicate rescue efforts and cause further death and destruction. Loss of life can be avoided through emergency planning, education, and the construction of buildings that sway rather than break under the stress of an earthquake.

India is highly vulnerable to earthquakes, with more than 60 per cent of the land being prone to tremors of Richter Intensity 7.0 and greater, that can cause structural damage. Earthquakes continue to cause large-scale human fatalities, most of which are due to collapse of man-made structures. Recent earthquakes have revealed the under-preparedness of the country in facing its impacts. Earthquakes are a common occurrence, rumbling below Earth's surface thousands of times every day. But major earthquakes are less common. Earthquakes, also called temblors, can be so tremendously destructive; it's hard to imagine they occur by the thousands every day around the world, usually in the form of small tremors. Some 80 per cent of all the planet's earthquakes occur along the rim of the Pacific Ocean, called the "Ring of Fire" because of the preponderance of volcanic activity there as well. Most earthquakes occur at fault zones, where tectonic plates—giant rock slabs that make up the Earth's upper layer—collide or slide against each other. These impacts are usually gradual and unnoticeable on the surface; however, immense stress can build up between plates. When this stress is released quickly, it sends massive vibrations, called seismic waves, often hundreds of miles through the rock and up to the surface. Other quakes can occur far from faults zones when plates are stretched or squeezed.

Figure 22.2: Earthquake.

22.4.1 Understanding Earthquakes and their characteristics

Illustration of the key characteristics of earthquake ground motion records: Intensity (MMI/MSK): Measure of damage

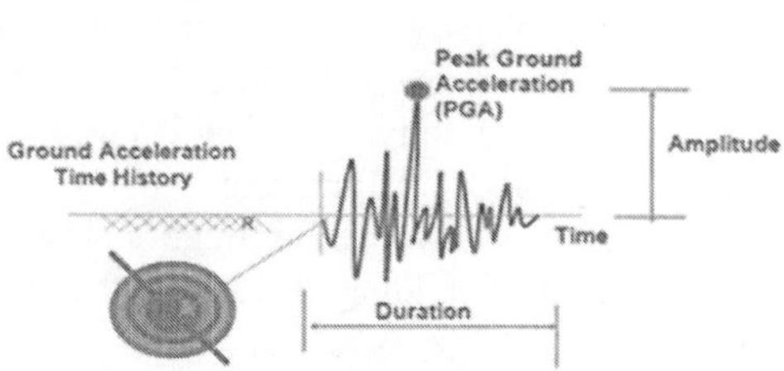

Figure 22.3: Peak Ground Acceleration: Largest acceleration amplitude (high frequency) Spectral Acceleration: Measure of energy for all frequencies.

Local site response to an earthquake is measured by recording the magnitude of ground motion at that site. Ground motion direction is comprised of varying degrees of vertical, horizontal, and oblique ground movement depending upon the type of fault movement. As an example, if you experience ground motion in northern California due to an earthquake on the Hayward Fault, which is a strike-slip fault producing predominantly lateral motion, then you would feel a strong component of side-to-side motion as well as some vertical motion. There are two types of measures of ground motion, a subjective measure of the felt effects of ground motion, and instrumental measures. Instrumental measures provide us with objective measures of the strength (wave amplitude measures), the frequency, and the duration of ground motion.

Three specific ground motion measures used in earthquake measurement:

- **Modified Mercalli Intensity (MMI):** MMI is a subjective measure of felt effects and damage in an earthquake. It is used in products for regions with less instrumental data, and for calibration using historical earthquake data gathered prior to instrumentation.
- **Peak Ground Acceleration (PGA):** PGA is the most common instrumental measure of ground motion. It is a measure of ground motion amplitude, and represents the highest acceleration of the ground motion. PGA is measured relative to the acceleration of gravity (or "g"), so that if the vertical ground motion exceeds "1 g", free standing objects can be thrown vertically into the air. PGA can be correlated to subjective intensity measures like MMI for purposes of comparison and analysis.
- **Spectral Acceleration (SA):** Spectral Acceleration is a relatively new instrumental measure of ground motion that includes building response. SA differentiates the response of structures by building height and structural type, both of which help to classify the building's "natural period," or its natural tendency to respond to wave motions of differing frequencies.

Using these techniques and tools we can plot fairly accurate figures of the likely impact and losses due to any given type of earthquake. Now, come to the role of GIS where we use mapping capabilities to best utilise the information learned above. This can result in effective relief planning and preparedness in the event of a real earthquake.

22.4.2 Causes of an Earthquake

Most earthquakes are caused when there is a build-up of great pressure inside the earth. Earthquakes are natural ways of releasing energy by earth. An earthquake occurs in certain pockets of the earth which has geological faults. The surface of the earth is made up of interlocking plates of rock, which float on the semi-liquid layer called the mantle. When two floating plates collide, the vibrations or tremors pass to the earth's surface as earthquakes. The shaking of the earth is sudden and devastating. The area inside the earth where rocks bend and break is the focus of the earthquake. The point on the earth's surface directly above the point of origin of the earthquake is the epicentre, where the effect or tremor is the greatest. The effects spread around the epicentre in a circular motion and become weak as they move away. So the place which is the epicentre suffers extensive damage. In a matter of seconds thousands of people die and entire cities are damaged. Houses are destroyed, roads get damaged and cracks appear on the ground.

22.4.3 Effects of an Earthquake

Earthquakes may cause physical damage to the buildings, roads, dams and monuments. High rise buildings or building built on weak foundations are especially susceptible to earthquake damage. Household articles including electronic goods and furniture get damaged. Human and livestock deaths and serious injuries from collapsing of buildings are common followed by outbreak of epidemics like cholera, diarrhoea, and infectious diseases. Utilities such as water supply, sewerage, communication lines, power-lines, transportation network, and railways get damaged.

22.4.4 Management and Precautions

It is very difficult to predict when an earthquake will occur. But geographers have tried to study the pattern and have marked out earthquake-prone areas. Japan is the most earthquake-prone country in the world. Thousands of quakes hit it each year. The Japanese people are well aware of the fact and take all necessary precautions, such as building light houses made of wood, to combat such a disaster. While constructing buildings, bridges, flyovers and dams proper norms should be followed. Old buildings should be strengthened. If one is indoors during an earthquake, one should get under a study table or desk. If outside one should stand in an open space away from tall structures. Various studies are being carried out to try and predict earthquakes.

Safety Tips

- Have an earthquake readiness plan.
- Consult a professional to learn how to make your home sturdier, such as bolting bookcases to wall studs, installing strong latches on cupboards, and strapping the water heater to wall studs.
- Locate a place in each room of the house that you can go to in case of an earthquake. It should be a spot where nothing is likely to fall on you.

- Keep a supply of canned food, an up-to-date first aid kit, 3 gallons (11.4 liters) of water per person, dust masks and goggles, and a working battery-operated radio and flashlights.
- Know how to turn off your gas and water mains.

If Shaking Begins

- Drop down; take cover under a desk or table and hold on.
- Stay indoors until the shaking stops and you're sure it's safe to exit.
- Stay away from bookcases or furniture that can fall on you.
- Stay away from windows. In a high-rise building, expect the fire alarms and sprinklers to go off during a quake.
- If you are in bed, hold on and stay there, protecting your head with a pillow.
- If you are outdoors, find a clear spot away from buildings, trees, and power lines. Drop to the ground.
- If you are in a car, slow down and drive to a clear place. Stay in the car until the shaking stops.

22.5 Cyclone

Cyclones are violent storms, often of vast extent, characterised by strong and high winds rotating about a calm centre of low atmospheric pressure. This centre moves onwards, often with velocity of around 50 km/hr. Cyclones strike suddenly though it takes time for them to build up. Cyclone is generally followed by heavy rains causing floods. Satellite tracking can predict on possible affected areas and inhabitants fore-warned can be made for warning. Warning and evacuation is done along the projected path. During a cyclone trees can be uprooted, buildings can be destroyed and cars can be overturned. It is caused by winds which travel at great speed, flattening and destroying everything in their path. The coastal areas are more prone to cyclones than others. Cyclones uproot trees and electric poles and destroy houses.

22.5.1 Effects of Cyclone

Light weight structures built of mud, wood, old buildings with weak walls and structure without proper anchorage to the foundation are at risk. The settlements located in low lying areas of coastal regions are directly vulnerable. Settlements in adjacent areas are vulnerable to floods, mudslide or landslide due to heavy rain. Telephone and electricity poles and wires, fences, light building structures such as thatched, tin shed roofs, signboards, hoardings, fishing boats and trees are most vulnerable to cyclone damages. Due to heavy rains people and their property might be washed away in floods or blown away by cyclone itself. The cyclone along in the coastal areas may cause sea waves to enter on land and flood it. This may cause saline water contamination of soil and water in the affected area, affecting water supply and severely affecting agricultural crops.

22.5.2 Management and Precautions

It is important to identify the cyclone prone areas. No development should be permitted in cyclone-prone areas. People leaving in cyclone-prone areas should make sure that the roofs of their houses are in good condition. The building should be designed to withstand forces of wind and floods. All the elements holding the structures need to be properly anchored to resist the uplift. The branches of trees near a house should be trimmed near the house and an emergency kit, containing a portable radio with batteries, a torch, some food and water, a first aid kit and essential medicines, should be ready. Coastal green belt has been found very effective in minimising the effects of cyclones. Such green belts (trees growing along the coast) need to be developed along the coasts.

22.6 Tsunami

A tsunami is a series of waves that are created when water is an ocean is rapidly displaced. Tsunami is also called seismic sea wave, or tidal wave, catastrophic ocean wave, usually caused by a submarine earthquake occurring less than 50 km (30 miles) beneath the seafloor, with a magnitude greater than 6.5 on the Richter scale. Volcanic eruptions, underwater explosions, underwater or coastal landslides or underwater earthquakes can all generate a tsunami. The effects of a tsunami are devastating.

In a tsunami a train of simple, progressive oscillatory waves is propagated to great distances at the ocean surface in ever-widening circles, much like the waves produced by a pebble falling into a shallow pool. The observation has enormous practical value, enabling seismologists to issue warnings to endangered coasts immediately after an earthquake and several hours before the arrival of the tsunami. As the waves approach the continental coasts, friction with the increasingly shallow bottom reduces the velocity of the waves. This results in increased wave height up to 50 meter and above. Three to five major oscillations generate most of the damage. The effects of tsunami however, vary widely from place to place.

22.6.1 Effects of Tsunami

The effects of tsunami are quite similar to those of cyclones or floods. Huge waves of sea water enters with great force and floods the land and washes away human settlements, agricultural crops and other properties. The famous tsunami of December 2004 has had devastating effects in many countries particularly in Indonesia, Malaysia, Sri Lanka, India etc. one large area of coastal districts of Andhra Pradesh and Tamil Nadu. More than two lacks people died in eight Asian countries including India.

22.6.2 Management and Precautions

If a tsunami warning is sounded one should immediately move to higher ground. People near the sea or at the beach should rush to higher places. One should stay away from the ocean till it is considered safe by authorities.

22.7 Droughts

Drought is an event that results from lower than normal expected rainfall over a season or period. The low rainfall is insufficient to meet the needs of human beings, plants, animals and agriculture. Short fall in rain results in drying of rivers, lakes, reservoirs and drying of wells due to excessive withdrawal and poor recharge of ground water and loss of crop yield due to shortage of water are some of the main indicators of drought. India is an agricultural country and farmers depend on the monsoon rains. When rainfall is delayed or scarce it leads to drought, which causes scarcity of food. Droughts lead to starvation and death of a large number of people. India has quite a few drought-prone regions. Some parts of Maharashtra, Karnataka, Andhra Pradesh, Gujarat, Odisha, and Rajasthan are particularly prone to drought. A large number of people die every year because of drought.

22.7.1 Causes of Drought

Drought occurs due to shortage of rainfall. As per Meteorological Department if rainfall is deficient by more than 10 per cent of the annual average rainfall, the condition is said to be that of drought. The severity of drought is determined by the extent of deviation of rainfall from the average. In the recent past frequency of periods of drought have increasing due to deforestation and environmental degradation.

22.7.2 Effects of Drought

Drought has severe effects on agriculture. To start with drought affects mostly rain fed crops and subsequently the irrigated crops. The herdsman, landless labours, subsistence farmers, women, children and farm animals are most affected.

- Crop failure or food shortage leading to large scale starvation and death.
- Affects dairy activities, timber and fisheries.
- Increases unemployment.
- Depletion of ground water.
- Increases energy consumption for pumping water from deep aquifers.
- Reduces energy production in hydro-electric power plants.

- Loss of biodiversity, and reduced landscape quality.
- Causes health problems, increased poverty, reduced quality of life and social unrest leading to migration.

22.7.3 Management and Precautions

The adverse effects of drought can be minimised if some measures are taken. A regular monitoring of rainfall, water availability in reservoirs, lakes and rivers as well as in comparison it with the demand is checked regularly. When water availability decreases than demand, water consumption needs to be reduced by adopting various water conservation measures. These include economising water consumption, by increasing water use efficiency, reducing wastage, reusing the wastewater for inferior uses. Use of efficient methods irrigation and sowing low water-consuming crops are some important measures to overcome drought. Rain water harvesting increases water availability. Water harvesting is done by either allowing the run-off water from all the catchment areas to a common point and storing it in a reservoir or allowing it to percolate into the ground so far recharging groundwater. Reservoirs and water tanks should be built to store water. Farmers should be educated to avoid overgrazing. Rainwater harvesting which involves collecting rainwater falling on rooftops and on the ground for future use can be very useful. This will help farmers in case there is no rain.

22.8 Floods

Floods are sudden and temporary inundation of large areas as overflowing of rivers or reservoirs. A flood occurs when the amount of water in a river or stream exceeds its capacity to carry water. In India flooding is common during the monsoon season when rivers overflow and almost submerge the areas surrounding them. A flood causes huge damage to life and property. Huts are washed away, as are livestock and human beings. Once the flood water recedes, those who survive get various diseases due to unhygienic conditions and spread of water-borne diseases. Clean drinking water becomes a scarcity as water gets contaminated. There could also be a shortage of food. In India some areas get flooded every year due to their proximity to the big rivers. Bihar, West Bengal and Assam experiences floods every year because the rivers Ganga and the Brahmaputra overflow. In August 2005, Mumbai and its surroundings areas experienced severe flooding and over 1,000 people died. One of the reasons, apart from very heavy rainfall, was the destruction of its mangrove swamps, to accommodate new construction of buildings as well as the city's inadequate drainage system.

22.8.1 Causes of Floods

Floods are caused by rains, high winds, cyclones, tsunami, melting snow or dam burst. Flood can happen gradually or can happen suddenly due to heavy rains, breach of the water storage and control structures, spill over, siltation of the rivers and reservoirs and this can enhance the incidence and magnitude of floods.

22.8.2 Effects of floods

Various effects of floods are given here:

Casualties: Human and livestock death due to drowning, serious injuries and outbreak of epidemics like diarrhoea, cholera, jaundice or viral infections are common problems faced in flood affected areas. Even wells, other source of drinking water get submerged resulting in acute shortage of safe drinking water during floods. Consequently often people are forced to drink the contaminated floodwater, which may cause serious diseases.

Structural damage: During floods mud huts and buildings built on weak foundations collapse endangering human lives and property. Damage may also be cause to roads, rail, dams, monuments, crops and cattle. Floods may uproot trees and may cause landslides and soil erosion.

Material loss: Household articles including eatables, electronic goods, beds, clothes, furniture get submerged in water and get spoilt all materials mounted on ground e.g. food stock, equipment, vehicles, livestock, machinery, salt pan and fishing boats can be submerged and spoilt.

Utilities damage: Utilities such as water supply, sewerage, communication lines, power-lines, transportation network and railways are put at risk.

Crop loss: Apart from the loss of human and cattle life, floods cause severe devastation of standing agricultural crops. Floods water spoils the stored food-grains or harvested crop. Floods may affect soil characteristics and may turn them infertile due to the erosion of the top soil or in coastal areas agricultural lands may turn saline due to flooding by sea water.

22.8.3 Management and Precautions

The flood damage can be considerable reduced and loss of human lives can prevented through proper planning of flood control and management measures.

Flood control: Flood control can be achieved through various means. The floodwater can be reduced by reducing the run-off water through afforestation. Forests promote rainwater percolation in the ground, thus recharging the groundwater and reducing the run-off water. Construction of dams also reduces flood water through storage. Dams can store water, which cannot be accommodated in the river downstream may cause floods. Water can be released in a controlled manner from the dam. Desilting, deepening and increasing embankment increase the capacity of a river, channel, drain.

Identification of flood prone areas: A rational planning for flood management involves identification the flood prone areas and frequency and magnitude of flooding in these areas.

Flood forecasting: Normally there is a reasonable timely warning by alerting people and moving them to safer area well in time. Measurement of intensity of rainfall in the catchment area provide sufficient clue to hydrology engineers to calculate the possible submergence area along a river well before the flooding occurs. Accordingly expected run-off volume people can be warned to evacuate the likely areas to be flooded and advise to go to safer places along with their belongings including livestock. India has a large network of rain measuring stations. Flood warnings are issued by the Central Water Commission (CWC), Irrigation and Flood Control Department and Water Resources Department.

Land use planning: Land use planning is very important for all the developmental activities. No major development should be permitted in flood prone areas. If construction is unavoidable it should be able to withstand the flood forces. Building should be constructed on elevated areas. Afforestation should be encouraged. Deforestation in the catchments areas should be discouraged because deforestation results in excessive runoff water and cause soil erosion, which is the main cause of river siltation resulting in floods. Any construction, which causes obstruction in drainage flow, should not be permitted. Encroachment of the storm water drains should not be allowed.

This reduces the risk of floods. Some precautionary measures are as follows:

- Build houses away from flood prone area.
- Before building a house one needs to check the history of flooding in the area.
- Garbage should not be thrown into drains and rivers. If the banks of rivers have broken, they should be repaired.
- Keep yourself alert and updated to weather and flood forecasting information.
- In case evacuation warnings are issued, immediately go to the shelters provided.
- When you are moving to a shelter, move your valuable articles to safer elevated places so that they are not destroyed by flood water.
- Store extra food, such as rice, pulses etc. for emergency.
- Do not touch any loose electric wire to avoid electrocution.
- All electrical equipment should be disconnected if there is a danger of flood.
- Do not spread rumours or listen to them.

- Make provision for adults and children who need special diet.
- After the flood is over, get yourself and your family members inoculated against diseases and seek medical care for injured and sick.
- Clear the house and dwellings of debris.
- Report any loss to the revenue authorities.

22.9 Volcanic Eruptions

The word 'Volcano' is derived from the name of Vulcano, a volcanic island in the Aeolian Islands of Italy whose name in turn originates from Vulcan, the name of a God of fire in Roman mythology. The study of volcanoes is called volcanology. A volcano is a rupture on the crust of a planetary-mass object that allows hot lava, volcanic ash, and gases to escape from a magma chamber below the surface. Volcanic eruptions take place when magma-molten rocks inside the earth-comes to the surface of the earth through openings called vents. The molten magma which flows out through the vent is called lava. Gases and ash also escape with lava. After the volcanic eruption has cooled it forms a mountain or a volcano and a bowl-shaped hollow is formed at the top called a crater.

22.9.1 Causes of Volcanic Eruptions

Earth's volcanoes occur because its crust is broken into 17 major, rigid tectonic plates that float on a hotter, softer layer in its mantle. Therefore, on earth, volcanoes are generally found where tectonic plates are diverging or converging. For example, a Mid-Oceanic Ridge, such as the Mid-Atlantic Ridge, has volcanoes caused by divergent tectonic plates pulling apart; the Pacific Ring of fire has volcanoes caused by convergent tectonic plates coming together. Volcanoes can also form where there is stretching and thinning of the crust's interior plates, e.g., in the East African Rift and the Wells Gray-Clearwater Volcanic Field and Rio Grande Rift in North America. This type of volcanism falls under the umbrella of 'plate hypothesis' volcanism. Volcanism away from plate boundaries has also been explained as Mantle Plumes. These so-called 'hotspots', for example, Hawaii, are postulated to arise from upwelling diapirs with magma from the core-mantle boundary, 3,000 km deep in the earth. Volcanoes are usually not created where two tectonic plates slide past one another.

Erupting volcanoes can pose many hazards, not only in the immediate vicinity of the eruption. One such hazard is that volcanic ash can be a threat to aircraft, in particular those with jet engines where ash particles can be melted by the high operating temperature; the melted particles then adhere to the turbine blades and alter their shape, disrupting the operation of the turbine. Large eruptions can affect temperature as ash and droplets of sulphuric acid obscure the sun and cool the earth's lower atmosphere (or troposphere), however, they also absorb heat radiated up from the earth, thereby warming the upper atmosphere (or stratosphere). Historically, so called volcanic winters have caused catastrophic famines.

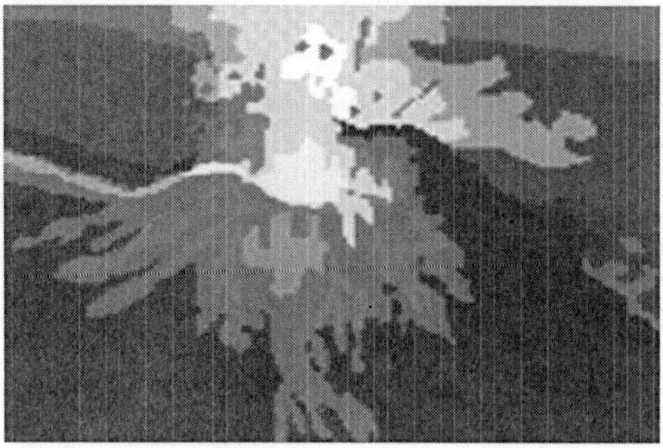

Figure 22.4: Volcano.

22.9.2 Classification of volcanoes

A popular way of classifying magnetic volcanoes is by their frequency of eruption, with those that erupt regularly called active, those that have erupted in historical times but are now quiet called dormant or inactive and those that have not erupted in historical times called extinct.

Thus, Volcanoes are of three types. The first type extinct or dead volcanoes have not erupted for thousands of years and probably never will, for example, Mt Kilimanjaro in Africa. The second type, dormant or sleeping volcanoes have not erupted for many years but have chances of erupting again. When a vent becomes blocked by a hardened lava plug, it becomes a dormant volcano, for example, Mt Fujiyama in Japan. The most dangerous are the active volcanoes which make up the third type. These erupt often and lead to destruction, for example, Mt Etna in Italy.

However, we should never forget that an extinct volcano may, in some cases, become active. For example, Mt Vesuvius in Italy was an extinct volcano but it erupted after many years and destroyed Pompeii in 79 CE. Barren Island, located in the Andaman Sea, is the only confirmed active volcano in South Asia. It erupted very recently on 2nd May 2006.

Active volcano

There is no consensus among volcanologists on how to define an 'active volcano'. The lifespan of a volcano can vary from months to several million years, making such a distinction sometimes meaningless when compared to the lifespan of humans or even civilisations. For example, many of earth's volcanoes have erupted dozens of times in the past few thousand years but are not currently showing signs of eruption. Scientists usually consider a volcano to be erupting or likely to erupt if it is currently erupting, or showing signs of current such as unusual earthquake activity or significant new gas emissions. Most scientists consider a volcano active if it has erupted in the last 10,000 years (Holocene times)-the Smithsonian Global volcanism programme uses this definition of active. Most volcanoes are situated on the Pacific Ring of fire. An estimated 500 million people live near active volcanoes. Historical time is another timeframe for active. The catalogue of the Active volcanoes of the world, published by the International Association of Volcanology, uses this definition, by which there are more than 500 active volcanoes. However, the span of recorded history differs from region to region. In China and the Mediterranean, it reaches back nearly 3,000 years, but in the Pacific Northwest of the United States and Canada, it reaches back less than 300 years, and in Hawaii and New Zealand, only around 200 years. Examples of active volcano are Mount Yasur, Vanuatu, Mount Etna, and nearby Stromboli, two Mediterranean volcanoes, Kilauea, Hawaiian volcano, Mount Nyiragongo, Nyamuragira, Africa.

Extinct volcano

Extinct volcanoes are those that scientists consider unlikely to erupt again, because the volcano no longer has a magma supply. Examples of extinct volcanoes are many volcanoes on the Hawaiian- Emperor Seamount chain in the Pacific Ocean, Hohentwiel, Shiprock and the Zhidwal volcano in the Netherlands. Edinburgh castle in Scotland is famously located atop an extinct volcano. Otherwise, whether a volcano is truly extinct is often difficult to determine. Since 'Supervolcano' calderas can have eruptive lifespan sometimes measured in millions of years, a caldera that has not produced an eruption in tens of thousands of years is likely to be considered dormant instead of extinct. Some volcanologists refer to extinct volcanoes as inactive, though the term is now more commonly used for dormant volcanoes once thought to be extinct.

Dormant volcano

It is difficult to distinguish an extinct volcano from a dormant (inactive) one. Volcanoes are often considered to be extinct if there are no written records of its activity. Nevertheless, volcanoes may remain dormant for a long period of time. For example, Yellowstone has a repose/ recharge period of around 700,000 years, and Toba of around 380,000 years. Vesuvius was described by Roman writers as having been covered with gardens and vineyards before its eruptions of AD 79, which destroyed the town of Herculaneum and Pompeii. Before its catastrophic eruption of 1991, Pinatubo was an in conspicuous volcano, unknown to most people in the surrounding areas. Two other examples are the long-dormant Sonfriere Hills volcano on the island of Montserrat, thought to be extinct before activity resumed in 1995 and Fourpeaked Mountain in Alaska, which, before its September 2006 eruption, had not erupted since before 8000 BC and had long been thought to be extinct. Narcondan Island, India, is classified as a dormant volcano by the Geological Survey of India.

22.9.3 Effects of volcano

There are many different types of volcanic eruptions and associated activity: Phreatic eruptions (Steam-generated eruptions), explosive eruption of high silica lava (e.g., rhyolite), effusive eruption of low-silica lava (e.g. basalt), pyroclastic flows, lahars (debris flow) and carbon dioxide emission. All of these activities can pose a hazard to humans. Earthquake, hot springs, fumaroles, mud pots and geysers often accompany volcanic activity.

Volcanic gases: The concentrations of different volcanic gases can vary considerably from one volcano to the next. Water vapour is typically the most abundant volcanic gas, followed by carbon dioxide and sulphur dioxide. Other principal volcanic gases include hydrogen sulphide, hydrogen chloride and hydrogen fluoride. A large number of minor and trace gases are also found in volcanic emissions, for example, hydrogen, carbon monoxide, halocarbons, organic compounds and volatile metal chlorides. Large, explosive volcanic eruptions inject water vapour, H_2O, CO_2, SO_2, HCl, HF and ash (pulverised rock and pumice) into the stratosphere to heights of 16-32 kms above the earth's surface. The most significant impacts from these injections come from the conversion of SO_2 to H_2SO_4, which condenses rapidly in the stratosphere to form fine sulphate aerosols. It is worth mentioning that the SO_2 emissions alone of two different eruptions are sufficient to compare their potential climatic impact. The aerosols increase the earth's albedo-its reflection of radiation from the sun back into space-and thus cool the earth's lower atmosphere or troposphere, however, they also absorb heat radiated up from the earth, thereby warming the stratosphere. Several eruptions during the past century have caused a decline in the average temperature at the earth's surface of up to half a degree (Fahrenheit scale) for periods of one to three years- SO_2 from the eruption of Huaynaputina probably caused the Russian Famine of 1601-1603. The 1815 eruption of Mount Tambora created global climate anomalies that became known as the 'year without a summer' because of the effect on North America and European weather. Agricultural crops failed and livestock died in much of the Northern Hemisphere, resulting in one of the worst famines of the nineteenth century. The freezing winter of 1740-41, which led to widespread famine in Northern Europe may also owe its origins to a volcanic eruption.

22.9.4 Management and Precautions

In many places where volcanoes are active, people are taken to safe places by authorities till the volcanoes have stopped erupting. People keep food and water stored for such times. All electronic gadgets are switched off in such times.

22.10 Avalanche

An Avalanche is a rapid flow of snow down a slopping surface. It is a movement of snow, ice and rock down a mountainside. Avalanches happen very suddenly and can move as fast as a racing car up to 124 mph. Avalanches are typically triggered in a starting zone from a mechanical failure in the snowpack when the forces on the snow exceed its strength but sometimes only with gradually widening. After initiation, avalanches usually accelerate rapidly and grow in mass and volume as they entrain more snow. If the avalanche moves fast enough some of the snow may mix with the air forming a powder snow avalanche, which is a type of gravity current. Slides of rocks or debris, behaving in a similar way to snow, are also referred to as avalanches. Avalanches can be caused by snow melting quickly, snow freezing, melting then freezing again, someone skiing and a loud noise or an earth tremor. The load on the snowpack may be only due to gravity, in which case failure may result either from weakening in the snowpack or increased load due to precipitation. Avalanches that occur in this way are known as spontaneous avalanches. Avalanches can also be triggered by other loads such as skiers, snowmobilers, animals or explosives. Seismic activity may also trigger the failure in the snowpack and avalanches. A popular myth is that avalanches can be triggered by loud noise or shouting, but the pressure from sound is orders of magnitude too small to trigger an avalanche.

Although primarily composed of flowing snow and air, large avalanches have the capability to entrain ice, rocks, trees, and other material on the slope, and are distinct from mudslides, rockslides and serac collapses on an icefall. Avalanches are most common during winter or spring but glacier movements may cause ice and snow avalanches at any time of year. In mountainous terrain, avalanches are among the most serious objective natural hazards to life and property, with their destructive capability resulting from their potential to carry enormous masses of snow at high speeds. Avalanches can be described by their size, their destructive potential, their initiation mechanism, their composition and their dynamics. An avalanche in the Siachen Glacier in the Himalayan Mountains buried at least 124 Pakistani soldiers and 11 civilians in April 2012. Avalanche due to Himalayan earthquake epicentred in Nepal on 25th April 2015, have killed at least 10 and injuring 30 Everest climbers.

22.10.1 Formation and type

Most avalanches occur spontaneously during storms under increased load due to snowfall. The second largest cause of natural avalanches is metamorphic changes in the snowpack such as melting due to solar radiation. Other natural causes include rain, earthquakes, rock fall and icefall. Artificial triggers of avalanches include skiers, snowmobiles and controlled explosive work.

Avalanche initiation can start at a point with only a small amount of snow moving initially; this is typical of wet snow avalanches or avalanches in dry unconsolidated snow. However, if the snow has sintered into a stiff slab overlying a weak layer then fractures can propagate very rapidly, so that a large volume of snow, that may be thousands of cubic meters, can start moving almost simultaneously.

Slab avalanches

Slab avalanches form frequently in snow that has been deposited by wind. They have the characteristic appearance of a block (slab) of snow cut out from its surroundings by fractures. Elements of slab avalanches include the following; a crown fracture at the top of the start zone, flank fractures on the sides of the start zones, and a fracture at the bottom called the staunch wall. Slab avalanches account for around 90 per cent of avalanche-related fatalities in backcountry users.

Powder snow avalanches

The largest avalanches form turbulent suspension currents known as powder snow avalanches or mixed avalanches. These consist of a powder cloud, which overlies a dense avalanche. They can form from any type of snow or initiation mechanism, but usually occur with fresh dry powder. They can exceed speeds of 300 km/h, and masses of 10,000,000 tonnes, their flows can travel long distances along flat valley bottoms and even uphill for short distances.

Wet snow avalanches

In contrast to powder snow avalanches, wet snow avalanches are a low velocity suspension of snow and water, with the flow confined to the track surface. The low speed of travel is due to the friction between the sliding surface of the track and the water saturated flow. The body of the flow of a wet snow avalanche can plough through soft snow, and can scour boulders, earth, trees and other vegetation leaving exposed and often scored, ground in the avalanche track.

22.10.2 Management and Prevention

Preventive measures are employed in areas where avalanches pose a significant threat to people, such as ski resorts, mountain towns, roads, and railways. There are several ways to prevent avalanches and lessen their power and destruction; active preventative measures reduce the likelihood and size of avalanches by disrupting the structure of the snowpack, while passive measures reinforce and stabilise the snowpack in situ. The simplest active measure is repeatedly travelling on a snowpack as snow accumulates; this can be by means of boot-packing, ski-cutting, or machine grooming. When there is a sufficient density of trees, they can greatly reduce the strength of avalanches. They hold snow in place and when there is an avalanche, the impact of the snow against the trees slows it down. Trees can either be planted or they can be conserved, such as in the building of a ski resort, to reduce the strength of avalanches.

22.11 Forest Fire or Bush Fire

Fires can burn out of control in areas of forest or bush land. It is an uncontrolled fire in an area of combustible vegetation that occurs in the countryside area. Forest fires are characterised in terms of the cause of ignition, their physical properties such as speed of propagation, the combustible material present, and the effect of weather on the fire. Bushfires in Australia are a common occurrence; because of the generally hot and dry climate, they pose a great risk to life and infrastructure during all times of the year, though mostly throughout the hotter months of summer and spring. Fires are caused by lightning, sparks of electricity or careless people. Wind may blow a bushfire to areas where people live.

Forest fires can cause extensive damage, both to property and human life, but they also have various beneficial effects on wilderness areas. Some plant species depend on the effects of fire for growth and reproduction, although large wildfires may also have negative ecological effects.

22.11.1 Causes of Forest fire

Forest fires are 'quasi-natural' hazards, meaning that they are not entirely natural features. This is because they are caused by human activity as well. The four major natural causes of forest fire ignitions are lightning, volcanic eruption, sparks from rock falls and spontaneous combustion. The most common human sources of forest fires are arson, discarded cigarettes, sparks from equipment and power line arcs.

22.11.2 Effects of forest fire

The most noticeable adverse effect of forest fires is the destruction of property and biomass. However, the release of hazardous chemicals from the burning of forest fire fuels significantly impacts health in humans. Wildfire smoke is composed primarily of carbon dioxide and water vapour. Other common smoke components present in lower concentrations are carbon monoxide, formaldehyde, acrolein, polyaromatic hydrocarbons and benzene. Small particulates suspended in air which come in solid form or in liquid droplets are also present in smoke. Despite carbon dioxides high concentration in smoke, it poses low health risk due to its low toxicity. Carbon monoxide and fine particulate matter, particularly 2.5 micrometer in diameter and smaller, have been identified as the major health threats. Fire fighters are at the greatest risk for acute and chronic health effects resulting from forest fire smoke exposure. Residents in communities surrounding forest fires are exposed to lower concentrations of chemicals, but they are at a greater risk for indirect exposure through water or soil contamination. Vulnerable persons such as children, the elderly, smokers and pregnant women are at an increased risk due to already compromised body systems, even when the exposures are present at low chemical concentrations and for relatively short exposure periods.

22.11.3 Management and prevention

Forest fire prevention refers to the pre-emptive methods of reducing the risk of fires as well as lessening its severity and spread. Effective prevention techniques allow supervising agencies to manage air quality, maintain ecological balances, protect resources, and to limit the effects of future uncontrolled fires. Forest fire prevention programmes around the world may employ techniques such as wild land fire use and prescribed or controlled burns. Wild land fire use refers to any fire of natural causes that is monitored but allowed to burn. Controlled burns are fires ignited by government agencies under less dangerous weather conditions. Controlled burns are reportedly 'the most effective treatment for reducing a fire's rate of spread, fire line intensity, flame length, and heat per unit of area' according to Jan Van Wagtendonk, a biologist at the Yellowstone Field Station. Additionally, while fuel treatments are typically limited to smaller areas, effective fire management requires the administration of fuels across large landscapes in order to reduce future fire size and severity. Building codes in fire-prone areas typically require that structures be built of flame-resistant materials and a defensible space be maintained by clearing flammable materials within a prescribed distance from the structure.

22.12 Man-made or Anthropogenic Disasters

Certain disasters occur in nature by humans activities. They are described below:

22.12.1 Fires

Fires are events of burning something. They are often destructive taking up toll of life and property. It is observed that more people die in a fire than in a cyclone, earthquake, floods and other natural disasters combined. Fires are a great threat to forests and wildlife because they spread speedily and cause tremendous damage in a short time. In cities fires break out in home, jhuggis, buildings specially godowns and factories. Fire can spread to a large area. Many people may die of burns and asphyxiation. It may also cause contamination of air, water and soil, which may affect the crops, plants and animals, and soil fertility.

Causes of Fires

During summer months such fires results in casualties and enormous economic losses. There are numerous causes of fires. Some important ones are given here-

- Throwing burning matchsticks or cigarettes irresponsibility.
- Heating sources can cause fire in houses e.g. clothes may catch fire while cooking on kerosene stove or gas stove.
- Cooking accidents are a major cause of fire at home. Fire can result due to unattended cooking.
- A short circuit in an electric wiring can cause fire. Overheating of electric appliances, poor wiring connections, use of sub-standard quality appliances can also result in a fire.
- Rubbish and waste materials often lying on roadsides or near houses may catch fire when people throw burning matchstick or cigarette butt.
- Storage and transportation of inflammable material or explosive chemicals without proper precautions may cause fires.
- Forest fires may result from human negligence or carelessness.

Effects of Fires

Death of humans and livestock may occur due to burning or serious injuries from fire. In rural areas often the entire harvested crop stored in securely may catch fire and burn to ashes resulting in heavy loss to the owner.

Management and Precautions

- Obey fire safety rules and remember the evacuation route in case of fire.
- Keep and handle inflammable materials with utmost care.
- Keep a fire extinguisher in the house and learn how to use it.
- When you leave home, make sure to shut off all electric and gas appliances.
- Do not plug several devices into one socket.
- Keep matches away from children.
- Do not block access routes by cupboards or any furniture.
- In the event of a fire call the fire department immediately.
- In the smoke filled corridor, crawl on all floors or on your belly as the smoke is less on the floor.

- Find at least two ways to escape from your home.
- Make sure that you remove all the waste material from work place and home on regular basis.
- Hazardous materials such as paints, solvents, adhesives, chemicals or gas cylinders should be kept in separate storage, well away from fire.
- Fire crackers on Diwali are a major cause of fire in our country. Use them carefully under supervision of elders.

22.12.2 Road, rail and air traffic accidents

Road accidents

Road networks are developed for better connectivity and service. Increased number of vehicles, violation of traffic rules, speeding, drunken driving and poor maintenance of vehicles as well as of roads are some of the main causes of road accidents. In order to avoid accidents following safety measures can be adopted:

- Look on either side of the road before crossing.
- Use zebra-crossing while crossing the road by foot.
- Wear helmet while riding a two-wheeler.
- Use seat belt provided in your car.
- Drive only if you possess a proper driving license.
- Be familiar with road markings and honour them.
- Maintain a safety distance from the vehicle in front.
- Do not jump lanes. It becomes difficult for other vehicles, on the road to anticipate your move.
- Do not be rash and do not try to overtake unnecessarily.
- The best way to be safe on roads is to follow "lane driving."
- While driving avoid sudden acceleration and deceleration.
- Replace the worn tyres and faulty headlamps.
- Check the tyre pressure, radiator water, brake oil and fuel frequently.
- Dip your beam whenever you spot an oncoming vehicle.
- Follow the maintenance schedule prescribed by the manufacturer.
- Overcome impatience, anger and intoxication during driving. Road rage is dangerous.
- In case a mishap occurs stay calm.
- In case of fire, try to get out as early as possible and do not worry about the baggage.

Rail accident

The most common type of rail accident is derailment due to human error, sabotage or natural landslide in a hilly track, or fire. Rail accidents lead to large number of casualties and material damage. Indian Railways incur heavy loss due to such accidents every year. Some of the common safety measures are:

- At railway crossings pay attention to the signal and the swing barrier. Do not get underneath and try to get across.
- In case of an unmanned crossing, get down from the vehicle and look at either sides of the track before crossing.
- Do not stop the train on a bridge or tunnel where evacuation is not possible.
- Do not lean out of a moving train.
- Do not smoke in train.
- Do not pull the emergency cord unnecessarily.

Air accidents

Air accidents may occur due to technical problems, fire, poor landing and take-off, weather conditions, hijacking, bombing etc. some of the common safety measures are:

- Pay attention to the flight crew safety demonstration.
- Carefully read the safety card in the pocket.
- Know where the nearest emergency exit is and learn how to open it.
- Always keep your seatbelt fastened when seated.
- Stay calm, listen to the crew members and follow their instructions.
- Before you try to open any emergency door yourself, look outside the window. If you see a fire outside the door, do not open it or the flame may spread into the cabin. Try to use an alternate route for escape.
- Remember, smoke rises. So try to stay down if there is smoke in the cabin.
- If you have a cloth, put it over your nose and mouth.

22.12.3 Industrial accidents

Industrial accidents can be due to explosion, fire and leakage of toxic or hazardous chemicals and lead to heavy loss of life and material. Leakage of chemicals and explosion may be due to human error, technological failure or geological hazards like earthquakes, flood etc. Fire in an industry may result from human error or electrical faults (short circuit).

Effects of Industrial accidents

The industrial premises and immediate surroundings are at high risk in the event of an industrial accident. Employees and residents of nearly localities and their live-stock and crops in nearby areas are severely affected. The environment over a large area gets polluted. Hazardous chemicals released into the atmosphere or into a water body may travel long distances and may even damage the entire ecosystem around the industrial area. This is what has happened in Bhopal in the year 1984, when about 45 tonnes of Methyl Isocyanides (MIC) gas leaked into the atmosphere killing more than 2500 people.

Explosion or fire or leakage of corrosive chemicals severely damage structures. If the chemical is in gaseous form the geographical spread is fast and wide. Many people may die either due to mechanical damage from explosion or fire or due to toxicity of the poisonous chemicals. The routes of exposure to chemical released from accidents are from inhalation, eye exposure, skin contact and ingestion. The polluting agents can have both immediate and long term effects. The immediate effects include death or other symptoms like dizziness, headache, irritation etc. The long-term effects may include cancer, heart failure, and brain damage, dysfunction of immune system, deformation, genetic disorders or congenital (by birth) disorders in children.

Management and Precautions

Inventory of hazardous chemicals

It is important to have an inventory of hazardous chemicals along with their quality, storage locations, characteristics along with possible hazard associated with hazardous chemicals and this informed all employees and people living in the neighbourhood should informed about the potential risk. The inventory as far as possible high risk areas demarcated and displayed along with indicating affected zone and safe routes for evacuation in the event of emergency.

Location of industries

Industries should not be sited in residential areas. A large buffer zone in form of a green belt is used for separating an industrial area from residential areas.

Community preparedness

The community should be aware of the hazardous installations and know how to combat the situation. Some members of the community should monitor the potential risk and participate in safety training organised by industries.

Other measures

Limit storage capacity of the toxic chemicals. Improve firefighting capability, warning systems and measures for preventing pollution dispersion. Develop emergency relief and evacuation planning for employees and nearby settlements. Adopt insurance for employees and surrounding population which is mandatory under the law.

22.13 Nuclear Disasters

Nuclear energy offers an alternative to many of environmental and social problems. But, it also introduces serious problems of its own. Though environments friendly, it is not yet economically affordable. Nuclear plants pose potential danger of accidents that may release hazardous radioactive materials into the environment. The problems are two-fold: (i) nuclear disasters and fall out and (ii) safe disposal of nuclear waste generated by nuclear plants. Some of the major nuclear disasters are given below:

Table 22.1: List of some major nuclear disasters

Year	*Nuclear power plants*
December, 1952	Chalk River, Toranto, Canada
October, 1957	Windscale Plutonium Production Centre, U.K.
April 26, 1986	Chernobyl Nuclear Reactor, Kiew, Chernobyl, USSR
November, 1995	Monju, Japan

Impact of nuclear disasters on the environment

The detrimental effects of nuclear leakage could be quick or slow. The quick devastating and immediate effects of nuclear radiations are well known as witnessed following Hiroshima and Nagasaki in Japan during World War II. Therefore, military use of nuclear energy is always fraught with unimaginable consequences.

The slow nuclear radiations can also emanate from a variety of sources viz. nuclear reactors, laboratories, hospitals, and direct exposure to radiation for diagnostic purposes (e.g. X-rays).

Such low dose radiations could have substantial impact on life forms and ecosystems. It is now established that continued small dose exposure to nuclear radiation is very harmful. It can cause: childhood leukemia, miscarriage; underweight babies; infant deaths; increased susceptibility to AIDS and other immune disorders and increased criminalities.

Underground bomb testing releases radiations in very small doses of radicals that enter water in the soil. This radioactive water is taken by plants through roots. The radioactivity enters food chain when such plants are eaten by animals and humans. Such radioactivity has been detected even in the milk.

22.14 Community Level Disaster Management

At the time of disaster, various agencies such as government, NGOs and community plays an important role for disaster management. These are preparedness, response, recovery and prevention details are on follows: Disaster management has four basic components:

Preparedness: Measure to ensure that communities and services are capable of coping with the effect of disaster. It has the following main elements:

- Community awareness and education;
- Preparation of disaster management plans for community, school, individual;
- Mock drill, training and practice;
- Inventory of resources both material resources and human skill resources;
- Proper warning systems;
- Mutual aid arrangements;
- Identifying the vulnerable groups.

Response: Measures taken in anticipation of, during and immediately after a disaster for minimising its adverse impact. It has following main elements:

- Activate the emergency operation centres (control room);
- Deployment of search and rescue teams;
- Issuing updated warning;
- Setting up community kitchens using local groups;
- Set up temporary living accommodation and toilet facilities;
- Set up medical camps; mobilising resources.

Recovery: Measures are initiated to undertake reconstruction of the physical infrastructure and restoration of economic and emotional well being. The main elements are as follows:

- Community awareness on health and safety measures;
- Counselling programme for those who have lost the near and dear ones;
- Restoring the essential services-roads, communication links, electricity etc;
- Providing shelters;
- Collecting usable materials for construction from rubble;
- Providing financial support;

- Finding employment opportunities;
- Reconstructing new buildings.

Prevention: Measures to eliminate or reduce the incidence of severity.

- Land use planning;
- Preventing habitation in risk zones;
- Disaster resistant buildings;
- Finding ways to reduce risk even before the disaster strikes;
- Community awareness and education.

The first few hours before and after a disaster are critical and precious for saving lives and reducing further injury. Often external help may take time to reach the disaster site. In any disaster, often the neighbours are first to respond. The first responders are people who act first in a disaster situation, usually lack basic response skills to deal medical or other emergencies. The aim of community level management is to train the individuals and the members of local community to deal with emergency situation effectively. Trained community members are life saving assets in such situations. Thus, community level management involves people's participation.

Government initiatives on disaster management

The Government of India has set up a National Committee on Disaster Management (NCDM) under the Chairmanship of the Prime Minister. The recommendations of this National Committee would form the basis of national disaster risk management programme and strengthening the natural disaster management and response mechanisms. United Nations Development Programmes (UNDP) has also been supporting various initiatives of the government to strengthen disaster management capacities.

The programme components would include the following:

- Development of state and district disaster management plans.
- Development of disaster risk management and response plans at Village/ Ward, Gram Panchayat, Block/ Urban local body levels.
- Constitutions of Disaster Management Teams and Committees at all levels with adequate representation of women in all committees and team. (Village/ Ward, Gram Panchayat, Block/ Urban local body, District and State.)
- Capacity Building of Disaster Management Teams at all levels. Special training for women in first aid, shelter management, water and sanitation, rescue and evacuation, etc.
- Capacity Building in cyclone and earthquake resistant features for houses in disaster prone districts, training in retrofitting and construction of technology demonstration units.

- Integration of disaster management plans with development plans of local self governments.

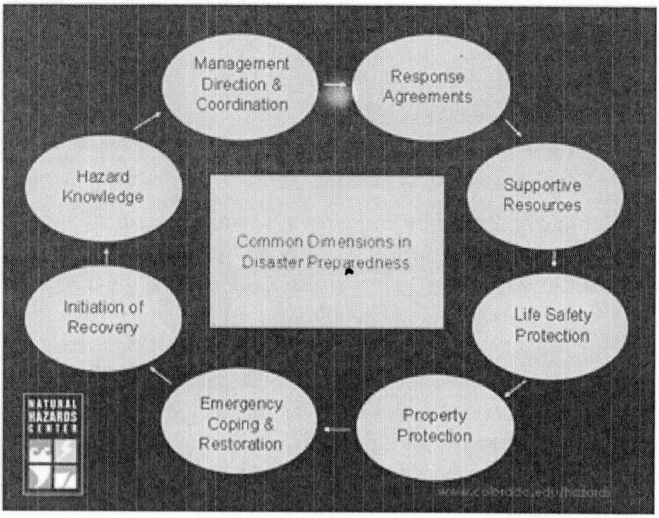

Figure 22.5: Dimensions in Disaster preparedness.

22.15 Conclusion

Disaster preparedness includes all of the activities that are carried out prior to the advance notice of a catastrophe in order to facilitate the use of available resources, relief, and rehabilitation in the best possible fashion. Disaster preparedness starts at the local community level; if local resources were insufficient, it would branch out to the national level, and if needed, the international level. Disaster mitigation is the ongoing effort to lessen the impact disasters have on people and property. Fewer people and communities would be affected by natural disasters with the use of this process. Because of the varying degree of each natural disaster, there are different mitigation strategies for each. Disaster management is the process of addressing an event that has the potential to seriously disrupt the social fabric of the community. Disaster management is similar to disaster mitigation; however it implies a whole-of-government approach to using community resources to fight the effects of an event and assumes the community will be self-sufficient for periods of time until the situation can be stabilised. Through disaster management, we cannot completely counteract the damage but it is possible to minimise the risks through early warning, provide developmental plans for recuperation from the disaster, generate communication and medical resources, and aid in rehabilitation and post-disaster reconstruction. The exchange of correct information following the event is important, in order to ensure the resources necessary to support response and recovery activities. The 72 hours following a major event is the most difficult time because of a lack of coordination among relief organisations. Problems that interrupt rather than coordinate the rescue efforts of all groups involved often occur because of hasty decision-making under complicated circumstances and the large number of organisations, which are unsure of their roles during operations. Disaster prevention is concerned with policies and programmes to prevent the recurrence of natural disasters and covers the long-term aspect of such disasters. The small price to pay for any method of prevention and protection pays off in the long run. In 1994, an earthquake whose epicenter was 12 miles away from the facility hit, however because of the prevention the company took, it saved an estimated $ 300 million in damages.

Programmes that follow and track disasters have improved throughout the years. In the 1970s, only the specialised departments of large companies, universities, and the government covered disasters. Desktop systems and computer communications emerged as a technology for linking emergency professionals on a global basis in the eighties. With the 1990s, computer equipment became more powerful and is now an essential component of disaster operations worldwide. Today Earth observation satellites provide basic support in pre-disaster preparedness programmes: in-disaster response, monitoring activities, and post-disaster reconstruction.

23

Environmental Management

23.1 Introduction

Human actions have already done irreparable damage to the environment. It is high time we start striving for striking a balance between our technological development and its negative effects. We need to understand that we are a part and parcel of the environment and we will suffer if we continue to overlook the need to conserve our degrading resources. Disruption of hydrological cycle, greenhouse effect, global warming, ozone hole and disposal of toxic wastes in oceans are only few of the environmental issues. There are several other issues linked with environment and development.

The global concern of the problems led to the first UN Conference on Human Environment from 5 June to 10 June 1972 at Stockholm, which laid foundation of the ongoing United Nations Environment Programme (UNEP). The United Nations Conference on Environment and Development (UNCED) or the Earth Summit at Rio de Janeiro, the capital of Brazil from 3 June to 14 June 1992 marked the 20th anniversary of the Stockholm Conference. This was the first ever UN sponsored 11 day Earth Summit, attended by more than 160 countries was the first gathering of its kind in the post-cold war era for global unity to ensure growth, without harming the environment. These conferences helped in creating awareness about the need of environmental management.

Man's desire for ultimate joy and comfort has led him to exploit nature's "free" goods to the extent of reducing its natural capacity for self-stabilisation. As a consequence of this outright disregard of the impact of these activities on the environment, numerous environmental problems have arisen. It is an empirically established fact that there exists a vital link between the environment and life. The history of evolution of life has taught us that through the different ages, various forms of life appeared or became extinct in response to the prevailing environmental conditions. Man, in his pursuit of ever faster economic growth, is upsetting the environmental equilibrium and destroying his life support system.

23.2 Concept of Environmental Management

Man's capability to transform his environment can bring the benefits of economic development and an opportunity to enhance the quality of life. But this same power, incorrectly applied, can also cause incalculable harm to the natural environment and consequently to human life. There should be no delay in tackling the task of solving these environmental problems, as these problems have a cumulative impact. Delayed remedial action will cost considerably more and the damage will become irreversible. There is only one world to pollute; if this is ruined, there is no other. Man will survive only as long the earth survives.

Hence, environmental management must regulate the demands and activities of man in such a way that the ability of the environment to sustain future development remains unimpaired. Efficient environmental management is a pre-requisite for sustained economic development.

Environment management and sciences employ the following three key concepts:

- **Systems approach:** A procedure which recognises the relationship between natural and man-made systems, between systems and analysis and management techniques, and the critical role of the human factor.
- **Systems analysis:** A technique of problem formulation, issue definition, and part insight. Systems analysis concerns itself with finding solutions to a problem and does not concern itself with applying those solutions. It consists of techniques that can be used to find solutions.
- **Systems management:** Consists of actual techniques of management for solving problems such as CAM/PERT, PUBS, CSPCS SE and others. These techniques prescribe a measurable path to achieve stated environmental objectives with milestones along the way to chart progress.

To deal with environmental problems, environmental managers and scientists must relate to hierarchical prescription by human society, which can impede achievement of optimum decisions. Environmental managers and scientists have to remove the subjectivity by dealing with natural and man-made systems at equal intensity.

Some related descriptions of environmental management can be defined as follows:

- Environmental management aims at the development of the environment for human benefit, it is the process of balancing the socioeconomic, technological and ecological forces in the development and allocation of resources in order to fulfill the needs and aspirations of present and future generation. In doing so, environmental management should work to preserve the maximum evolutionary potential of the biosphere.
- Environmental management is the integrative ecological, cultural, economic and social process by which the environment is developed in a holistic and systematic manner through the optimal use of existing and potential resources in the biosphere, for the ultimate improvement of human well-being. It aims at the maintenance of the long-term sustained yield from the biosphere, and should be designed to provide greater personal and social opportunities for present and future generations.
- Environmental management consists of the set of activities aimed at choosing appropriate institutional arrangements, technologies and incentives for achieving whatever goals are specified as "environmental quality" targets.
- Environmental management as an operational concept might best be defined as describing the actions of those involved in decision-making that make a deliberate and systematic attempt to understand how their activities affect the environment and how their concerns about the environment will affect their activities.

Thus, environmental management is a positive concept, not a negative "halt progress" or "back to nature" concept. Some of the key aspects involved are:

- Identification of the "needs" and "wants" of man in his individual and social development.
- Identification of the resources that are needed for such development.
- Identification of how meeting some of needs and wants will inhibit or increase the ability to meet others as a result of destruction, degradation, or enhancement of resources.
- Identification of the actors who have a stake in the conflicts that may arise between meeting needs and protecting resources.
- Resolution of these conflicts.

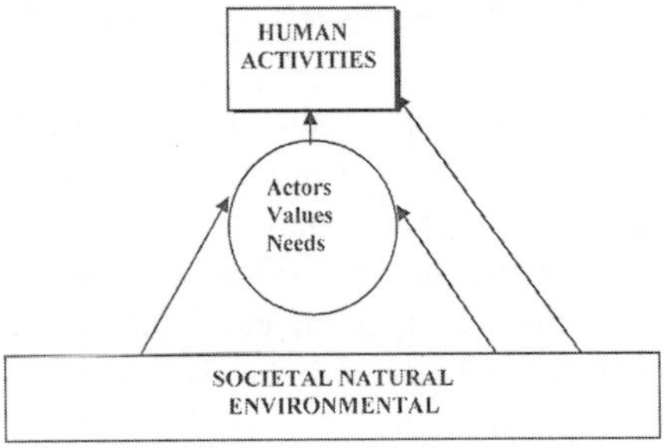

Figure 23.1: Process of environmental management.

No matter how the concept of environmental management is defined, the attainment of its objectives will necessarily require significant changes in the values, attitudes and behaviour of those concerned with the maintenance of society. In many cases, it will also require deep and radical changes in present structures of management. Institutions for environmentally sound management need to be developed, and these need to be based on concerns other than the traditional monetary values.

23.3 Objectives of Environmental Management

The main objectives of environmental management are:

- Maintenance of environmental quality;
- Balancing the ecosystem;
- Restricting and regulating the exploitation of natural resources;
- Protecting the environment from degradation;
- Renewing natural resources and reducing natural disasters;
- Adopting technologies without creating adverse effect on the environment; and
- Formulating laws and regulations to control pollution.

23.4 Components of Environmental Management

The main components of environmental management are:

- Environmental perception and public awareness;
- Control of environmental degradation and pollution;
- Develop technologies to reduce emission and waste generation;
- Environmental Impact Assessment (EIA) to review the existing technology;
- Environmental education and training; and
- Control overpopulation and over-consumption.

Although all the components are of primary importance, yet it is quoted,

"If you plan for one year, plant rice, if you plan for 10 years, grow trees and if you plan for 100 years, educate people."

Environmental management can be achieved through mutual cooperation of general public. Educating the public is of much benefit to bring awareness of environmental issues. The non-governmental organisations as well as governmental organisations are playing a leading role in this regard. Thus, it is important to make environmental management a part and parcel of our lives if we want to improve the quality of environment.

23.5 Concerns for Environmental Management in Five-year Plans

In India, concerns for environmental management have emerged and are reflected in the successive five-year plans.

- The emphasis of the first three five-year plans (1950 to 1966) was on economic development, particularly on developing basic industries.
- In the fourth and fifth five-year plans, an equal emphasis was placed on employment generation, reducing inequalities in income and wealth distribution and satisfying the basic needs of the weaker section.
- The sixth five-year plan (1980 to 1985) for the first time had a specific environmental objective. This was expressed in the following words:

"Bringing about harmony between the short and the long-term goals of development by promoting the protection and improvement of ecological and environmental assets."

- The approach of the Seventh Plan 1985-90, also recognised the ecological and environmental conservation as one of its principal objectives. In terms of integrating environmental considerations with national economic planning, the seventh five-year plan emphasises that:
  - "The environment must not be considered as just another section of national development. It should form a crucial guiding dimension for plans and programmes in each sector. This becomes clear only if the concern for environmental protection is understood in proper context. Environmental problems in India can be classified into two broad categories:
  - Those arising from conditions of poverty and under-development.
  - Those arising as negative effects of the very process of development.

- The first category has to do with the impact on the health and integrity of natural resources (land, soil, water, forests, wildlife etc.) as a result of poverty and the inadequate availability, for a large section of the population of the means to fulfill basic human needs. The second category has to do with the unintended side effects of efforts to achieve rapid economic growth and development. Thus, it is clear that the concern for the environment is essentially a desire to see that national development proceeds along rational sustainable lines. Environmental conservation is, in fact, the very basis for all development."

- The Eighth Five-Year Plan (1992-1997) put emphasis on human development as a main focus of planning.
- The Ninth Five-Year Plan (1997-2002) had the main objective of ensuring environmental sustainability of development through participation of people.
- The targets for Tenth, Eleventh and Twelfth Five-Year Plan (2002-2017) are to provide safe drinking water to all, increase the forest area to 33 per cent of geographical area, clean the major rivers which are polluted and reduce population growth rate to 1.62 per cent per year. The plan would seek to better the quality of life on all fronts.

For environmental management to be effective and systematic, it must: Consistently, be within the existing limitations of knowledge;

- Visualise all processes (natural or artificial) in total perspective;
- Recognise and understand any processes or problems in the structure and its components, interrelationships;
- Be able to manipulate, or otherwise deal with, the inter-dependencies characterising the process or operation as a whole; and
- Be able to design, build and operate the management system which would serve as a means to manage the whole.

The activities of man affecting the equilibrium between him and the environment can be arbitrarily classified as unbalancing and compensating factors. In examining the stress-anti-stress patterns, it can be seen that advances in higher level technology with improved medicine have reduced the death rate and lengthened human life span. The increased population and the resulting demands have imposed a variety of stresses on the dynamic equilibrium between man and the environment.

23.6 Determinants of Priorities in the Framework of Environmental Management

Environmental components can be considered as including both individual items and the systems that link these items together:

- Physical components (water, air, land, minerals and fossil fuels, tidal processes, climate, chemical and geological processes, etc.);
- Biological components or resources (animals, wildlife, vegetation, flora, etc.; food-webs, specific ecosystems, etc.);
- Man-made components (towns, roads, fields, etc.; urban infrastructure, transport and communication systems, agricultural economy, etc.);
- Social components or resources (social groups, political groups, cultural groups, social and political structure, legal structure, etc.);

In relation to each component, there are at least four major roles which people can assume:

- Exploiter or developer (and hence egocentric user/protector/manager),
- Neighbour and appreciator (and hence exocentric user/protector/manager),
- Scientist or other observer, and
- Student or follower.

23.7 Environmental Priorities

The uses of each of the many environmental components are manifold. In practice, of course, the use of certain resources takes priority over others. The setting of environmental priorities is thus a process involving the comparison of two principal variables. The first is the environment itself and the other is human value(s) system, both of which are changing.

The lack of understanding of these interactions means that the identification of environment priorities can only be achieved in a totally empirical way by looking at the system as a whole and working backward from the actors, while at the same time working forwards from the environmental components. Priorities will change from time to time and from place to place. The environmental manager should be very careful about the imposition of his own value system on the people and groups who are, or will be, directly affected by the proposed activities.

23.8 Aspects of Environmental Management

In our society, economy is the system of exchange of goods and services worked out by the members of society. These goods and services are produced, distributed and consumed as people exploit natural resources. This overexploitation of natural resources has resulted in a deterioration of environment on the earth. The environmental problems like ozone layer depletion, global warming, increasing pollution level, loss of biodiversity are the results of deteriorating environment caused by human activities. There exists a strong relationship between the level of development of a nation and exploitation of natural resources. This is because the rich nations have more technology to tap the resources while poor nations have limited technology to tap the resources for meeting their basic needs. Prior to Industrial Revolution, most of the human population survived on subsistence agriculture. That is, families lived on the land and produced sufficient food for their own consumption as well as barter.

This system was sustainable for a small and stable population. But after Industrial Revolution, the death rates declined and population growth was rapid thus resulting in overexploitation of natural resources. Environmental management is one of the best options to solve these problems. There are four main aspects which should be involved in the environmental management. The four aspects of environmental management are:

- Ethical aspect
- Economic aspect
- Technological aspect
- Social aspect.

23.8.1 Ethical Aspects of Environmental Management

Ethics refers to the study of the moral principles of duties which should be remembered while solving any problem. There are four components of ethics.

- **Cases:** These refer to specific acts and question whether a particular act is morally justified or not. The answer must be based on moral rules.
- **Moral rules:** These are general guidelines that can be applied to various areas of concern. For example, the rules that govern how we should treat endangered species.
- **Moral Principles:** These are more general concepts and are considered to be valid in all cases. For instance distributive justice, which states that all persons should be treated equally.
- **Basis:** Ethical principles are justified by reference to some philosophical basis. This is the foundation of an ethical system.

The ethical aspects are fundamental to the environmental management. They are related in a way to the rights of the people as well as to other living creatures of the environment.

- In many countries specially in India, people value their mountains, rivers, forests, trees, animals and several other places. Many forests and mountains have been named after the names of gods and goddesses. Peepal tree is a respected tree and is not cut down by the people in India. In many regions the Banyan tree is respected by tying a thread around it as a symbol of respect. Similarly, the plant of *tulsi* is also highly respected in India. It is planted in most of the homes.
- The patches of forests are regarded as sacred groves. In many cases they have been dedicated to a deity in many societies of India. Many such patches have remained undisturbed and therefore depict the true nature of the forests. A number of plant species therefore have been protected by the sentiments of the local people.
- Several trees and plants are protected or managed for their flowers or fruits. The mango tree is protected for its fruit. The Mahua tree is protected by many tribes as it provides edible flowers. Its seeds are crushed to obtain valuable oil. Similarly, several plants are protected for their medicinal values.
- Some animals are respected as being the '*vahan*' or vehicle of different gods. It is believed that they travelled through cosmos on these animals. Many other animals are also linked to different gods. Elephant is linked to Ganesha and Ganesha is linked to rat. Vishnu is associated with eagle and Rama to the monkeys. In Hindu mythology, the monkey god Hanuman rendered invaluable help to the lord Rama during his travels to Lanka. Similarly, the Sun god Surya rides a horse with a chariot on which he moves in the sky. The blackbuck is linked to the Moon goddess and lion is linked to Durga. The cow is linked with Krishna, snake with Shiva and swan with Saraswati.
- An environmental ethics concerns right and wrong with reference to taking care of natural world and the species in it. As far as human interest is concerned ethical principles and rules are fairly well established, even if they are violated by public and private activities. Though there are no firmly established ethics that deal with the care for environment for its own sake. Most of our ethics concerning environment deal with how those things serve human purposes.
- For example, an ethical principle from U.N. Declaration on Human Rights and the Environment is as follows, "All persons have the right to a healthy, secure and ecologically sound environment."
- All the natural resources found on the earth are required to be used in a sustained manner, so that environmental degradation is reduced to a great extent. Environmental ethics involves the management of

environmental components in a manner that anthropogenic activities cause minimum harm to the environment and are in perfect harmony with nature.

- Man has the prime responsibility to safeguard the various components of the environment comprising flora, fauna, water, air and land. It should be the duty of every individual on the earth to provide sufficient and clean natural resources to the future generations.

"Man's needs but not his greed can be supported by our earth."–*Mahatma Gandhi*

Some of the major issues which can be of good help in environmental management and should be kept in mind are as follows:

Equitable Distribution of Natural Resources

All the countries on the earth have unequal economic growth. It has been observed that developing nations use natural resources only to fulfill basic needs while the developed nations exploit resources for luxury goods. However, the ethical aspect of environmental management favours equal distribution of resources between the rich and the poor countries, so that quality of life in underdeveloped and developing countries can be improved. It will also reduce the increasing stress of resource export and reduce the disparity between the rich and the poor nations.

Welfare of Rural Population

Since Industrial Revolution and urbanisation migration of people to urban areas has increased significantly. The high standards of living, better medical and educational facilities are mainly responsible for this. This has resulted in increase in the urban population this increasing stress on resources in urban areas. To provide for housing facilities, more land near the cities is being encroached thus disturbing the environment.

People in rural areas are devoid of all the basic and essential facilities available in urban areas. The people in rural areas on the other hand work hard to meet the food requirements of urban sector. Thus, efforts should be made for the welfare of rural population so as to provide them all the essential facilities, because they have the right to use all natural resources available in urban areas.

Protection of other species

All the species on the earth have an equal right to exploit natural resources found on the earth. But today man has completely ignored this principle. He has adversely affected many other species found on the earth by his activities. Besides, poaching and hunting of animals have led to the extinction of species.

So it is high time that we should start environmental management to protect organisms and respect their existence in the environment.

Secure Natural Resources for Future

All men on the earth are born free and have equal right to exploit natural resources. But man is excessively using natural resources like fossil fuels and raw materials to the extent that they might disappear in the near future. We should not forget to secure these natural resources while keeping pace with growth and development.

This is important because future generations have an equal right to use the resources. We should handover the natural environment to the future generation in a better condition than we had received from our ancestors.

23.8.2 Economic Aspects of Environmental Management

Today, increasing number of people put increasing demands on the environment both through demand for resources like food, energy and water and through the production of wastes. However, it should be clear that the demand each individual makes depends on how much and what that individual consumes. Every additional purchase represents an additional demand of resources for its production as well as additional waste produced in the course of its production, use and disposal. Therefore, negative effects on the environment also increase dramatically as consumption rises. The economic aspects are equally important. They are related to the economic life of the people and the country.

Increasing prices of several commodities compel the people to make minimum use of them that eventually protect the environment. Petroleum product is one of the major sources of air pollution. The prices of all petroleum products are soaring high resulting into their limited use. It therefore saves the environment. In order to save money, people make little use of petroleum which ultimately helps in cleaning the air. Nowadays, people prefer to go to their place of work on ride sharing basis. It not only saves petrol but also safeguards the environment. Likewise many other household things are also consumed less in order to save money which ultimately is beneficial for the environment. Limited use of electricity is a big step towards environment management. Most of the electricity is generated by polluting the environment.

EPR or extended producer Responsibility is a big step towards environment management. As per EPR, it is the responsibility of producer for environmental impact of their products to the entire life cycle of product especially for recycling and disposal. For example, battery companies take back all the batteries after the life of battery is over. Major world pollution problems including the depletion of ozone layer, the impact of global climate change and the accumulation of toxic wastes in the environment are largely the consequence of high consumption associated with affluent lifestyle. It is the people who drive cars and create energy with fossil fuels that contribute most significantly to the increasing level of carbon dioxide in the atmosphere. Similarly, global deforestation and loss of biodiversity is a consequence of consumer demands in all the nations.

Economic aspects of environmental management have a two way benefit:

Reduces Stress on Natural Resources

This is economically an important aspect as overexploitation of natural resources will reduce. This reduced use of natural resources will help the poor nations by avoiding export of the resources. They can then efficiently use the resources for the development and welfare of their own country through this.

Reduces Cost of Managing the Environment

Fewer environmental problems will require less funds for the solution. Hence more capital can be directed for the developmental work as no problem means no need for solution. This will help in monetary development of poor nations.

Environmental Accounting

Accounting of natural resource, i.e. incorporating environmental criteria in economic analysis is gaining importance day by day in the world. The environmentalists are particularly concerned about the depletion and degradation of natural resources as well as about the harmful impacts of economic activities. A few countries are already preparing the Integrated Accounts focusing on the depletion, degradation and harmful consequence of economic activities.

It is well known that natural resources are much more important than the man-made resources, as they will not be available to future generations for further production. Day by day the need to have a set of accounts which provides information on the utilisation of these natural resources in a proper way is being increasingly felt. Several countries have hence initiated the exercise of preparing estimates which take into account the details of utilisation of natural resources.

However, the conventional system of national accounting suffers from two main drawbacks:

- Neglect of recent scarcity of natural resources which threaten the sustained productivity of the economy.
- Degradation of environmental quality mainly from pollution and effects on human health and welfare.

In addition, some expenditure for maintaining the environmental quality are counted as increase in national income and product, despite the fact that such outlays could be considered as a maintenance cost to society, rather than social progress. In Natural Resource Accounting, attempt is made to attach monetary value to the effects. Thus, National Resource Accounting, if done properly, may present a completely different picture of the economy. This means that an economy which might have been considered as a progressive economy may turn out to be an economy with negative growth if the depletion, degradation and other harmful impacts of economic activities are taken into account. Thus, it is important to include environmental costs and issues in the planning.

23.8.3 Technological Aspects of Environmental Management

Environmental management can be ideally done through the use of some technical aspects with it. Use of technology in the traditional systems will provide for an improved environment. There are a large number of measures which should be taken into consideration before proper management practices are to be formulated for maintaining the environment. Such measures may either help in reducing the use of natural resources or in combating the pollution of environment.

The technology and environment management are closely associated with each other. The technological aspects affect the lifestyle as well as the economy. With the help of technology, the people make different tools and machines so that they gain control over the environment. The technology grows with the civilisation. The technology can be creative as well as destructive to the environment. After the industrial revolution the technological development touched new heights. The research did not consider the aspect of environment at all. As a result, the damage to the environment continued. In the last few decades when the environmental damage started becoming visible the efforts started to develop technologies that are environment friendly. Such a technology is also called eco-friendly technology. It is being used in a number of ways.

- **Energy production:** Every work is accomplished with the help of some energy. Nowadays, the fossil fuels are the major source of energy. They are also the major source of pollution. Moreover, they are not renewable sources. There are many renewable sources of energy like hydropower, wind power, biogas, solar power, tidal power, geothermal power etc. All these sources of energy do not generate any environmental pollution. Therefore, they are called eco-friendly.
- **Synthetic fuel:** Synthetic fuel is the liquid or gaseous fuel which is extracted from the solid earth material. This material is rich in

hydrocarbons. These types of fuels are commonly extracted from coal, tar sands, oil shale, natural gas and biomass. Production of synthetic fuel is yet to be demonstrated successfully but in future further research in this field can bring fruitful results.

- **Ethanol:** Ethanol can serve as an effective alternative source of energy in future. It is a type of alcohol derived by fermentation of sugar. Starch from potatoes and cereals are also used in fermentation.
- **Hydrogen fuel cell:** The hydrogen fuel cell is a device in which chemical reaction is converted into electricity. This fuel cell is another alternative source of energy. It does not run down like ordinary cell and keeps on functioning as long as fuel and oxidant are supplied to it. Research is going on to replace the conventional internal combustion engine of automobiles. It consists of positive end of circuit i.e. anode and negative end of circuit. i.e. cathode. Both are separated by electrolyte. In a hydrogen fuel cell the hydrogen is supplied to the anode and oxygen to the cathode. When electrons move from anode to cathode it generates current that can be tapped to provide energy. The only difficulty is that hydrogen cannot be supplied in abundance to all the people.
- **Gas to liquid fuel:** Technology to convert gas into liquid holds a promising future and has already been developed in many countries. The natural gas can easily be converted into liquid fuels for automobiles. The enormous reserves of natural gas in the world are an important alternative of the depleting petroleum reserves. Involvement of huge expenditure has discouraged the development of such types of alternative fuels. Many research projects still focus on the development of alternative fossil fuels.
- **Use of Nanotechnology:** Nanotechnology is the latest development of science. It involves the use and creation of those devices that fall in the range of 1 to 100 nanometers (nm). One nm is equal to the one billionth of a metre. It is 50,000 times smaller than the diameter of a hair. Some devices have already been made and are being used like catalytic converters in automobiles that remove air pollutants. Several devices are fitted in the computer that read from the hard disk. It is also used in the sun screen lotions in cosmetics that transparently block sunshine. Some sports goods and clothes are also made with this technology. This technology is still in its infancy stage but it has definitely a promising future.
- **Efficiency of devices:** Different types of devise are used at different places like auto vehicles on roads, computers and air conditioners in offices and variety of home appliances at home. All these devices

need power to run. Devices made with traditional technology consumed a lot of energy but modern devices consume little energy and are safe to operate. Such devices are fitted with such equipment that automatically shut down when it is not in use or when it performs its job completely for example thermostat is fitted in geysers, washing machines, television, computers, electric iron, air conditioners etc. Modern technology is therefore more energy saving. Such technology therefore should be encouraged.

- **CFC free Products:** The use of CFC or chlorofluorocarbons was started in the beginning of twentieth century. It was used in a range of products like refrigerators, air conditioners, freezers, medical inhalers, insulating foams in packaging material, car seats, dry cleaning processes, cleaning electric circuit boards etc. Later its adverse effect of ozone depletion in stratosphere was noticed. Many international conventions were held to impose ban on the use of CFC. But the efforts were not very successful. Nowadays, many companies have started making goods without the use of CFC. Such products are labeled as 'CFC free.' Buying of these goods is an important step towards environment conservation and should be encouraged. In the developed countries, the production of CFCs ceased at the end of 1995. The developing countries will phase out its production by the year 2010. A substitute of CFC has been developed in the form of HCFC or Hydro-chlorofluorocarbons. It causes much less damage to ozone layer as compared to CFCs.
- **Using alternatives:** Use of alternatives is an important step towards environmental management. These alternatives replace the things that damage the environment. Most of the machinery consumes the fossil fuels and it is difficult to switch over abruptly to the alternatives but new technologies can be looked for, which use the renewable sources of energy like solar power, hydropower, wind energy, tidal energy, geothermal energy etc. Some cars have been made that run on battery and gas. Efforts should be made to improve these technologies so that all vehicles run on these energy sources. Solar energy can be made popular in cooking. Use of plastic is not encouraged because it is non-biodegradable. Scientists are working on making of biodegradable plastics. They are trying to mix the starch with plastic. After these plastic things are discarded the bacteria will consume starch and plastic molecules will break apart allowing the plastic to decompose. Leather goods manufacturing involves techniques that pollute the water, soil and air. A variety of substitute material of leather is being discovered. Such material

resembles leather and it is difficult to distinguish between them. These goods are made of polyvinyl chloride and non-woven fibres. This material costs much less than the leather and is becoming popular. Use of compressed Natural Gas (CNG) is a very important alternative of the diesel. In Delhi, the government has made it compulsory to use CNG for auto rickshaws and buses. Biogas Chullha is another substitute of firewood which is used in the villages. Burning of dead bodies also consumes a lot of wood, therefore, electric crematorium have been made as an alternative to the wood.

- **Recycling:** Many materials are recycled to conserve energy, reduce pollution, conserve land and save money. It is a type of reusing a thing but in a different form. It involves sorting and processing of waste products. It serves as a new material for new product. This method reclaims the original material and is used for new products. Important materials that are recycled include:
  - **Steel:** The scrap of steel is melted in the furnace with the new steel and can be used again. This method is known as Basic Oxygen Furnace (BOF). The other method is Electric Arc Furnace (EAF) which uses 100 per cent recycled steel. The scrap steel is placed in a furnace and melted by electricity. Limestone and other materials are added to remove the impurities. Around 64 per cent of the steel is recycled.
  - **Aluminium:** Many beverage containers are aluminium made which can be melted and recycled. They are crushed and baled before sending them to the reclamation plant. Here they are put into furnace and melted to form ingots or sheets. Around 100 billion aluminium beverage cans are used in USA and 55 per cent of them are recycled.
  - **Plastic:** Recycling of plastics is difficult than the metals because of seven different categories of plastics. All seven types cannot be mixed. In many countries these seven types of plastics are marked with identification marks. The process of recycling of plastic involves cleaning, shredding in flakes and then melting flakes into pellets.
  - **Paper:** The paper products that can be recycled are newsprint paper, office paper, wrapping paper, cardboard etc. The newsprint paper is the most common recycled paper. The waste paper is collected, mixed with hot water to make pulp. The pulp is filtered to remove small contaminants. The pulp is dipped in a vat or large container where ink is separated from the paper.

The ink can be dried and reused again. The cleaned pulp is mixed with new wood fibres to make paper.

- **Glass:** Scrap glass is called 'cullet' which melts at lower temperature than other raw materials thus saving fuel and money. Scraped glass in sorted by colour and made free from impurities. The cullet is melted in a furnace to make new glass.
- **Chemicals:** Many chemical wastes are hazardous. People are often warned to take their hazardous chemical waste to the site where trained workers can sort it and recycle and release the remaining to the leak proof containers or lab packs for safe disposal. Motor oils and paints are common materials that are recycled.

Some of the major factors which are required to be imparted as a part of environmental management are as follows:

- Use of 3R's i.e. recycle, reduce and reuse.
- Use of alternative sources of energy instead of conventional energy sources.
- Designing of treatment plants like waste water treatment plant or sewage treatment plant.
- Use of pollution control devices in industries.
- Changing the raw material or process in any industry.
- Using modernised machines to reduce pollution load in the environment.
- Minimise the use of non-biodegradable products like plastics and polythene.

By emphasising these factors in environmental management we can help in improving the conditions of the environment. For example, Delhi was among the most polluted cities of India. But the use of Compressed Natural Gas (CNG) which is pollution free, helped in reducing the pollution levels in Delhi. This was possible only by the use of innovative technology. Environmental problems can be solved to a great extent with the participation of the government authorities. The Government of India instituted a scheme in February, 1991 known as Eco-mark Scheme for labelling environment-friendly products. This scheme is administered by Bureau of Indian Standards (BIS).

The following primary environmental criteria for products are prescribed here:

- Cause less pollution than other comparable products in production, usage and disposal.
- Can be recycled while other comparable products cannot be recycled.

- Save non-renewable resources or minimise the use of non-renewable resources with comparable products.
- Reduce adverse environmental health consequences.
- Should not have high prices when compared with other products.

Eco-mark criteria of products covered under the scheme include the following categories notified by the Government of India:

- Soaps and detergents
- Paper
- Food items
- Lubricating oils
- Packaging materials
- Architectural paints and powder coatings
- Batteries
- Food additives
- Electronic goods
- Wood substitutes
- Cosmetics
- Aerosol propellants
- Plastic products
- Textiles
- Fire extinguishers
- Leather

The logo of eco-mark of India is an earthen pot which signifies use of renewable resource which causes no harm to environment during its production or consumption.

23.8.4 Social Aspects of Environmental Management

Social aspects of the environmental management are associated with the general awakening of the people towards environmental issues. In a way it is the direct result of the literacy level of the people. Some societies have tremendous awareness towards environment protection. Almost all governments try to protect the environment and several campaigns are also launched in this direction. People who are aware of the consequences immediately react to the government policies. Regular pollution check-up of the vehicles is one example. Similarly, throwing of garbage in the dustbin and keeping surroundings clean are the efforts of people which they do because of awareness. Immunisation of children, using CFC-free products, switching of fans and lights when not in use are social aspects of environment management.

Consumer education

In the modern world the consumer has been made to endure sub-standard products and services like adulterated foods, spurious and hazardous drugs, exorbitant prices, short weights and measure, unfulfilled manufacture guarantees, and several other ills. Consumer protection is provided with the efforts of government, non-governmental organisations and individuals to make the people aware about the goods they purchase and services they avail. Nowadays, special courts have been set up in India for the consumer protection. These courts are called Consumer Disputes Redressal Forum. These courts take minimum time to give decision so that the consumers get justice at the earliest.

Consumer Rights

- **Right to Safety:** This right protects the consumer from undue risk or physical harm. Such harm can be caused by adulterated food, defective vehicles and tyres, drugs, other defective home appliances etc. In case of any mishappening the consumer can approach the law for justice.
- **Right to be Informed:** All consumers enjoy the right to be informed about the product. It helps them to choose among the products or services that are available in the market. Although there are many advertisements but they do not provide sufficient information. In today's competitive market the consumer wants to compare the prices, quality, safety and sustainability of the product.
- **Right to be Heard:** This right protects the consumer when he feels cheated. When a consumer has bought a product and it is not functioning properly he has the right to seek a refund or replacement of product. There are many deceptive business practices that are illegal. The consumer in such cases has the right to sue the businessman.

Community Participation for Conservation

Involvement of people is must for the ecological restoration and conservation. Many societies and clubs like Citizen groups, National Audubon Society and the Sierra Club educate people on various environmental issues. They support environment-friendly legislation, and help in the implementation of environment protection laws. They also keep vigil and point out violation of laws. Japan has world's strictest standards for the control of water and air pollution. Every individual has the capability to maintain peace, harmony and equity in nature. Such an attitude will make the environment clean and healthy. Further degradation of environment can be checked immediately.

In India several environmental movements started in the form of Chipko Movement, Appiko Movement, Tehri Dam Conflict, Silent Valley Movement and Narmada Bachao Andolan. All these movements started as a direct result of people's awareness and their participation in the environment conservation programmes. It is suggested that the local people must be involved in the local governing bodies because they are the best judge of their surrounding environmental issues. They can also suggest the practical aspect of the various environmental policies laid down by governmental agencies.

We are also part of community and should make all out efforts to restore the ecological balance and practice various environmental conservation programmes. We should try to follow the techniques that do not bring any harm to environment. Such techniques are: use of solar cooker and minimum use of cooking gas; closing all taps when not in use; to switch off electric appliances when not in use; to make minimum use of auto vehicles; use of public transport vehicles; minimum use of air conditioners and heaters; avoiding wastage of food; strict self-imposing ban on deforestation; segregate garbage as biodegradable and non-biodegradable. Some people cannot distinguish between these types of garbage. We should guide them properly that things which mix in soil are biodegradable like fruit and vegetable peels, leaves, grass, wood, paper, clothes, wool etc. The non-biodegradable waste includes: plastic goods, polythene bags, synthetic clothes, metals etc. People should also be able to pick out things that are recyclable. Such things are paper, plastic goods, metals, glass etc. Keeping pollution emission of the auto vehicle under control is very important. Using fuel efficient vehicles is a significant measure. All electrical appliances should be fitted with thermostat so that it switches off automatically.

We should make efforts for environmental management by improving status of entire society. Following efforts should be made on behalf of the poor, with particular emphasis on the women:

- Education, especially improving literacy and education of girls and women.
- Improving health, especially bringing down infant mortality rate.
- Enhancing income through employmental opportunities.
- Improving resource management.

Numerous programmes, both private and government-funded have been in existence and knowledge has been gained. The result of success in these efforts is called social modernisation.

Education

Illiteracy rate among the poor in developing countries commonly ranges between 50-70 per cent. Providing basic literacy will empower people to gain information from written materials. An educated populace is, thus, an important component which contributes in enhancing wealth of a nation. Investing in the education represents a key element of the public policy options of a developing country, one that will give good results.

Improving Health

Like education, healthcare facilities required by most of the poor countries in the developing world are necessary. Healthcare in developing world must emphasise on hygiene, nutrition and sanitation. This will also involve prenatal and postnatal care of mother and children to reduce infant mortality rate.

Enhancing Income

The basic requirement of a economic system is the exchange of goods and services. People belonging to poor section of society have the potential to provide goods and services but often lack the monetary backing. Efforts are required to improve the economic status of these people so that even they can have equal access to resources. So that the gap between the rich and the poor can be reduced.

Improving Resource Management

The poor section of the population are depends on local resources for water, food or fuel wood. The population explosion is causing degradation these resources. However, a considerable part of this problem lies in poor utilisation of resources. A major factor in enhancing income is, providing the technical skills and information necessary to manage those basic resources more effectively. All these efforts if put together can help in proper environmental management.

23.9 Legal Provisions for Environmental Management

Every individual should be aware of the laws. However, most of the people are unaware of the laws and their legal rights. Often people choose to play the role of mute spectators to many serious problems that threaten their peaceful lives. This primarily happens because they are ignorant of their rights. Environmental degradation is a problem which everyone faces, such as vehicular exhaust, offensive smell from the open drains, loud noise or music, etc. These problems can be solved with the aid of specific laws that have been formulated for the very purpose. There are about two hundred laws dealing with environmental protection, enacted both before and after independence in India. However, pre-independence laws have not dealt with environment protection exclusively. For example, Indian Penal Code (IPC) in 1860 had a chapter XIV which dealt with offences affecting public health, safety and convenience, which covered aspects like water, air and noise pollution whereas post-independence laws mentioned above deal exclusively with environment protection.

23.9.1 Provisions in the Indian Constitution

The 42nd amendment in the Constitution was brought about in 1974 and two new Articles were inserted. Article 48 (A) and 51 (A) (g), both are related to the environmental protection.

Article 48 (A)

"The state shall endeavour to protect and improve the environment and to safeguard the forests and wildlife of the country."

Article 51 (A) (g)

"It shall be the duty of every citizen of India to protect and improve the natural environment including forests, lakes, rivers and wildlife and to have compassion for living creatures."

Seventh Schedule

Some subjects were also included in Seventh schedule of the Indian Constitution. These are stated below:

Union List

52 : Industries.

53 : Regulation and development of oil fields and mineral oil resources.

54 : Regulation of mines and mineral development.

56 : Regulation and development of inter-state rivers and river valleys.

57 : Fishing and fisheries beyond territorial waters.

State List

6 : Public health and sanitation.

14 : Agriculture, protection against pest and prevention of plant diseases.

18 : Land, colonisation, etc.

21 : Fisheries.

23 : Regulation of mines and mineral development.

24 : Industries.

Concurrent List

17 (A) : Forests.

17 (B) : Protection of wild animals and birds.

20 : Economic and social planning.

20(A) : Population control and family planning.

The Constitutional provisions are backed by a number of laws, acts, rules and notification.

23.9.2 Environmental Planning

In India, the environmental action formally started with the participation of Smt Indira Gandhi in United Nations Conference on Human Environment in 1972. A National Committee on Environmental Planning and Coordination (NCEPC) was established as the apex body of the Department of Science and Technology. The term 'Environment' figured for the first time in the Fourth Five Year Plan (1969-74), which recorded that harmonious development, is possible only on the basis of a comprehensive appraisal of environment issues.

The Tiwari Committee in its report in 1980 recommended the creation of a Department of Environment as a nodal agency to ensure environment protection, to carry out environment impact studies of the proposed developmental projects and to have administrative responsibility for pollution monitoring and control. Later this department was raised to the status of Ministry of Environment and Forest (MoEF) in 1985. After Fourth Five Year Plan, issues related to with environmental protection were included in all further Five Year Plans.

23.9.3 Environmental Legislations in India

Most of the post-independence environmental legislations were formulated after 1970s. Following is the list of some environmental legislations that have come into effect.

- General Acts
- Forest and Wildlife
- Water
- Air

General Acts

- Environment (Pprotection) Act, 1986
- Public Liability Insurance Act, 1991
- National Environment Tribunal Act, 1995

Forest and Wildlife

- Wildlife (Protection) Act, 1972
- Forest (Conservation) Act, 1980

Water

- Water (Protection and Control of Pollution) Act, 1974
- Water Cess Act, 1977

Air

- Air (Prevention and Control of Pollution) Act, 1981

23.9.4 Environment (Protection) Act, 1986

This Act came into force on 19th November 1986 and the main objective of this Act is to protect and improve the environment. To fulfill this objective the central government was provided with many powers.

Powers of the Central Government

- Planning and execution of programmes for preventing pollution.
- Laying down standards for environmental quality in various aspects.
- Laying down standards for discharge of pollutants.
- Examining processes, materials and substances which cause environmental pollution.
- Restricting areas where industrial operations and processes shall not be carried out.
- Establishing environmental laboratories.

23.9.5 Public Liability Insurance Act, 1991

This act laid down that insurance was necessary for the people who own, control or handle hazardous chemicals.

23.9.6 National Environmental Tribunal Act, 1995

This act laid down liabilities for damages arising from accidents while handling hazardous substances.

23.9.7 Wildlife (Protection) Act, 1972

This Act was enforced in 1972 and the main features of this Act are:

- Prohibiting the uprooting of specified plants from restricted areas;
- Prohibiting cultivation of selected plants without license;
- Considering specified plants as government property;
- Declaring any area to be under sanctuary;
- Restricting entry in any sanctuary and if necessary then only with prior permission of Chief Wildlife Warden;
- Prohibiting any destruction activity in a sanctuary;
- Declaring any area under national parks;

- Permitting the use of some enlisted species for the purpose of education, research and conservation.

23.9.8 Forest (Conservation) Act, 1980

This Act was later amended in 1988. Some salient features of this Act are:

- Restricting the de-reservation of any forest for non-forest purpose;
- Restricting use of any forest land for the purpose of reforestation by clearing naturally grown trees;
- Restricting cultivation of tea, coffee, rubber, etc. on forest land;
- Granting license for growing horticultural crops;
- Restricting mining in any forest land; and
- Appointing forest guards to prevent illegal activities in the forests.

23.9.9 Water (Prevention and Control of Pollution) Act, 1974

The main objective of this Act is to prevent and control water pollution and to maintain wholesomeness of water. There is a provision for the establishment of Pollution Control Boards, as per requirements.

Functions of the Boards

- Promoting cleanliness of streams and wells.
- Advising governments on matters of prevention and control of water pollution.
- Laying down or modifying water quality standards where required.
- Organising programmes to bring mass awareness.
- Evolving efficient methods of sewage and industrial effluent disposal.

Power of the Boards

- Restricting applications of the Act to certain areas.
- Prohibiting use of any stream or well for disposal of polluted matter.
- Restricting the new outlets and new discharges.
- Removing pollution matter from any water source during accidental situations.

Water Cess Act provided for levying and collection of cess on water consumed by selected industries.

23.9.10 Air (Prevention and Control of Pollution) Act, 1981

The main objective of this Act is to prevent and control air pollution. According to this Act, "Air pollutant means any solid, liquid or gaseous substance (including noise) present in the atmosphere in such concentration as may be or tend to be injurious to human beings or other living creatures or plants or property or environment." It has provision for the establishment of Central Pollution Control Board, State Pollution Control Boards and Pollution Control Committees for Union Territories.

Functions of the Boards

- Advising governments on issues related to improvement of air quality and prevention, control or abatement of pollution.
- Executing programmes for pollution abatement.
- Laying down standards for air quality.
- Providing technical assistance where necessary.
- Collecting information on pollution related matters.

Powers of the Boards

- Laying down standards on emissions from automobiles.
- Closing industrial units which cause air pollution.
- Lodging petition in court against defaulters.
- Punishing and fining those who do not comply with provisions of the Act.

23.9.11 Drawbacks of Different Acts

- Under Environment (Protection) Act, 1986 all the powers are vested with the central government which interferes with effective enforcement of laws in the states to protect the environment.
- Although there is a provision of making appeal by any person against the one who is defying law, under the Environment (Protection) Act, 1986 but the provision of 60 days notice is a big hindrance in this regard.
- Under Water (Prevention and Control of Pollution) Act, 1974 civil courts have power to grant permission to industrialists on various aspects, thus, restricting the enforcement area of the Act.
- Forest (Conservation) Act, 1980 ignores the role of tribals.
- There should be provision for providing loan to small industrial units for installing pollution control devices.

23.10 Environmental Clearances

Environmental clearance of polluting or degrading developmental activities is performed by the central and/or state governments, with the following objectives:

- Optimal utilisation of finite natural resources through use of better technologies and management practices;

- Incorporating suitable remedial measures at the projects formulation stage.

Till January 1994, acquiring environmental clearance was only an administrative requirement for mega projects. However, the new notification issued by the central ministry in January 1994 (as amended in May 1994) makes Environmental Impact Assessment (EIA) statutory for 29 different identified activities. From time to time and all developmental activities in these areas need to secure environmental clearance from the Central Government irrespective of whether they are listed under EIA notification or not. Some of the areas notified so far include:

- Doon Valley, Murud-Janjira, Dahanu Taluka, Aravali ranges in Gurgaon district of Haryana and Alwar district of Rajasthan;
- Identified coastal areas as per the Coastal Regulation Zone notification;
- Forests, Wildlife Sanctuaries, National Parks, Wetlands, Mangroves, Biosphere Reserves, Hill and Mountain areas, etc.

The 29 projects listed in Schedule (I) of the EIA notification can be broadly categorised under the following sectors for the sake of convenience:

- Industries
- Mining
- Thermal Power Plants
- River Valleys
- Ports, Harbours and Airports
- Communication
- Atomic Energy
- Transport (Rail, Road, Highway)
- Tourism (including hotels, beach resorts).

While all projects may have some environmental effects but all of them are not significant. The projects which could be subjected to detailed EIA include:

- Those which can significantly alter the landscape, land use pattern and lead to concentration of working and service population;
- Those involving manufacture, handling and use of hazardous materials;
- Those which are located near ecologically sensitive areas and places of religious importance; and
- Industries with constituent units of various types which could cumulatively cause significant environmental damage.

Thus, legal provisions can help in environmental management to a great extent, if followed carefully and strictly.

It has been observed that economic development of a nation is primarily responsible for deteriorating the environmental conditions. Environmental management can play a vital role in reducing the degradation of the environment. But the environmental management can only be best achieved through considering various important aspects like ethical, economic, technological and social. Governments also formulate many legal provisions which play a valuable role in management of environment. However, public awareness is essential for securing good results in this regard. Apart from all these efforts, some other approaches are also necessary for environmental management. The major approaches which are necessary for environmental management are:

- Economic policies;
- Environmental indicators;
- Setting of standards; and
- Information exchange and surveillance.

23.10.1 Economic Policies

Projects and programmes are structural elements of an economic system which generates several kinds of changes in the environment. For example, a thermal power plant emits pollutants like carbon monoxide, carbon dioxide, sulphur dioxide, particulate matter, etc. into the air, and cause air pollution. This affects the health of people, who breathe in the polluted air and damages the ecosystem also. On the other hand, the power plant provides electricity to people who are utilised in agricultural productivity or in industrial production. There are several examples of such effects associated with economic activities like production, consumption, distribution and trade. Hence, it is the task of environmental economists to identify and analyse all kinds of possible impacts associated with economic activities.

Economists treat environment as an asset. An 'asset' is defined as possession of value by an individual or group of individuals or nation as a whole. So, environment is an asset but its value may be eroded because of pollution. To avoid this erosion or pollution of environment, some economic policies are required to be developed by economists. These economic policies should be formulated in such a way that environmental harm is minimal.

Two broad sets of policies are required to affect the underlying causes of environmental damage.

Policies Built on Positive Links

These seek to harness the positive links between development and the environment by preventing policy failures, improving access to resources and technology and promoting equitable income growth. These policies include the following:

- Removing subsidies that encourage excessive use of fossil fuels, water and pesticides.
- Clarifying rights to manage and own land, forests and fisheries.
- Giving greater priority to provision of sanitation, clean water, education and extension of agriculture.
- Taking measures to empower, educate and involve farmers, local communities, native men and women so that they can make decisions in their long-term interests.

Policies Targeted at Specific Environmental Problems

Specific policies are required to induce or require resource users to take account of the effects that their actions have on the rest of the society. Policies designed to change behaviour are of two types.

- Those based on incentives, which penalise the polluters according to the amount of damage they do.
- Those based on quantitative restrictions.

However, policies must be drawn while considering

- The value of cost and benefits in developing countries, where resources are scare and basic needs must be met;
- The administrative traditions and enforcement capacity of a country;
- The participation of local people in drawing up and implementing policies;
- The cost of protecting and improving environment as compared to benefits from the economic growth.

23.10.2 Environmental Indicators

Human societies and their economic activities have the potential of causing great damage to the environment. Damage has a direct impact on the present and future human welfare. The effects of pollution and the misuse of resources are clearly visible in those parts of the world where environmental policy is often not well established i.e. in the developing world. Environmental indicators are the indicators which show an increase or decrease in the level of pollution. Some major environmental indicators, whose presences indicate the deterioration of environment, are given below as:

Greenhouse Gases

Increase in concentration of greenhouse gases like carbon dioxide, methane, etc. shows an increased temperature of the earth, i.e. global warming.

However, reduction in greenhouse gases implies a balance in the earth's atmosphere.

Eutrophication

The algal bloom or excessive growth of algae on surface water bodies implies presence of excessive amount of nitrates and phosphates in the water bodies. The excessive nutrients result in increased growth of algae and damage aquatic ecosystems. This implies pollution of water.

Acid Rain

Acid rain is the result of series of chemical reaction between oxides of sulphur and nitrogen and water, forming acids. Normal rain water has some amount of carbonic acid but acid rain has high amounts of acids. This indicates increased air pollution.

Escherichia Coli

Presence of Escherichia coli in drinking water supplies is an indicator of its contamination with sewage supplies.

Ozone Hole

Depletion of ozone layer implies an excessive use of chlorofluorocarbons by humans.

Soil Erosion

The removal of top fertile layer of soil is termed soil erosion and deforestation is a major factor responsible for it. Thus, more soil erosion indicates increased deforestation.

23.10.3 Setting of Standards

'Think globally Act locally' is a well-known slogan for addressing environmental issues and also expresses the objective of International Standards Organisation. These standards reflect global consensus on positive environmental practices in international context, which can be applied by organisations all over the world

International Standard Organisation (ISO) has two main benefits:

- ISO offers a wide range of standards for sampling and test methods to deal with specific environmental challenges. It has developed more than 350 international standards for the monitoring of aspects such as quality of air, water and soil as well as noise and radiation.
- ISO has developed standards which help organisations in chalking up a more easy approach to manage environmental issues. Strategic Advisory Group on Environment (SAGE) was set up in 1991.

SAGE brought together representatives of a large number of countries and international organisations to define new International Standards that could support better environmental management.

ISO 14000 SERIES

The pollution all over the world has several consequences on people over the globe. This forced ISO to develop environment management standards known as ISO 14000 series. ISO 14000 series is a set of standards relating to Environment Management System. The structure of standards is as follows:

- Environment Management System (EMS)
- Environmental Auditing (EA)
- Environmental Labelling (EL)
- Environmental Performance Evaluation (EPE)
- Life Cycle Analysis (LCA)
- Terms and definitions

The ISO 14000 has five basic principles:

- Focus on what needs to be done.
- Formulate a plan to fulfill its environmental policy.
- Develop the capabilities and support mechanisms necessary to achieve its environmental policy.
- Measure, monitor and evaluate its environmental performance.
- Review and improve its environmental management systems.

The first two standards of the series were published in 1996 and these are:

- ISO 14001 Environment Management System- Specification with guidance for use;
- ISO 14004 Environment Management System- General guidelines on principles, systems and supporting techniques.

Both ISO 9000 (Quality Management System) and ISO 14000 (Environment Management System) are gaining sufficient popularity in developing countries. Although initially ISO 9000 was successful, yet now ISO 14000 is also gaining success. This is because both these systems are appropriate, effective and reliable. Global Environmental Monitoring System (GEMS) is a worldwide collective effort to monitor global environment and make a periodic assessments of the health of its constituents. GEMS was first proposed in 1971 by Scientific Committee on Problems of Environment (SCOPE), latter it was formally created in 1975, as a small secretariat of UNEP.

23.10.4 Information Exchange and Surveillance

Environmental auditing is a management tool designed to provide information on environmental performance to the right people at the right time:

- To all levels of management and
- For a variety of purposes.

Environmental audit can be defined as a planned and extensive analysis to effect of an organisation on environment. It is a devise of surveillance. The scope of the audit will depend on the information that is required by management to monitor environmental effect of organisation.

A full environmental audit will cover:

- Compliance with environmental regulations;
- Implementation of environmental policies and procedures;
- Good environmental management practice; and
- Past activities.

The environment audit proposal however does propose that certain information should be made available to the public on the environmental performance of the developmental activity. This would be an environmental statement specific to each activity. Such a statement would:

- Describe the activities at site;
- Provide a detailed assessment of all significant environmental issues of relevance;
- Summarise the figures on pollutant emissions, waste generation, raw material requirement, energy and water consumption, etc.;
- Include the environmental policy programmes; and
- Include an evaluation of the environmental performance of the environmental management system.

Information gathered from environmental audit is valuable in corporate planning; crisis management and in making decisions. In India, the industries are now required to submit their audit reports to the concerned State Pollution Control Boards on or before 15 May every year.

23.11 Importance of Environmental Management

Environment and development are above all, and in a number of ways, global concerns. Environment and development are complementary and are in fact, two sides of the same coin. Environmental sound development concepts apply to all countries. Development is pursued in all countries and is aimed at increasing the well-being of their people. Development is a never ending process with continually changing targets reaching further but never really satisfied. Nations can be categorised as developed or developing, individuals within any particular state can also be classified by their relative or absolute affluence or poverty. Although a handful of the most affluent people in the world live in the developing nations, most affluent people, by definition, live in the developed nations. Similarly, most poor people live in developing nations. The aim of development is to increase the well-being of the people of the world, measured not only by an increased supply of goods and services, but by social and cultural indices as well. The rates and kinds of change in economic and social activities over time constitute the process of development.

Environment can be thought of as the stock of physical or social resources available at a given time for the satisfaction of human needs. This stock can and does change over time, and the rates and kinds of change are important dimensions of environmental concern. The resources available for the satisfaction of human want and need comprise the physical environment. These resources include not only forests, minerals and the like, but also, for example, adequate and reliable rainfall, moderate temperature, and other aspects of climate which make agricultural production possible. What is considered to be part of the resource stock is, of course, partly cultural and relative. Moreover, over time new uses or new technologies can increase or deplete the available stock of resources.

Environmental management is therefore, important because most physical resources are limited and some not at all. Human actions range along a continuum from enhancement of available resources to irreversible damage to them not repairable at any cost.

An example of total irreparability is soil eroded by wind and water action and accumulating at the bottom of the sea. An example of near irreparability is that when forests are cut down, seeds for regeneration are destroyed, and soil previously held by the root system are washed away. It may be impossible to replace them. Less irreparable, but still costly is forest destruction which results in seed loss but not extensive soil loss; the lands affected could be replanted, but it might take a century or more for them to become productive again.

It is, therefore, clear that strategies and actions need to be decided on an assessment of the risks involved. Those chosen should either involve minimum risk of major consequence or should have repercussions which are easily reversible should the need arise.

23.12 Neglect of Environmental Management

At present environmental management is too often neglected because governments and others whose activities can affect the environment lack the necessary information, political will or resources, or find it hard to respond to the long-term and trans-sectorial nature of environmental problems.

Sometimes even the existing administrative, professional, legal, financial and other institutions are poorly adapted to the needs of environmental management.

In general, there is a lack of environmental concern in international policies which are designed to meet development objectives, because of:

- Poor or inadequate information.
- Lack of political will, due, for example, to conflicting and/ or vested interests or general inertia (i.e., lack of a positive approach to overcoming problems).
- Lack of resources, in particular trained personnel.
- Failure to adopt long-term perspectives, i.e. over-concentration on short-term objectives.
- Failure to respond to the trans-sectorial nature of the environment.
- Poor institutional arrangements which usually produce fragmented action, i.e. the actions and processes of environmental management take place in an ad-hoc manner.

If the principles of environmental management are to be applied effectively, then two kinds of innovations would have to be considered, one is the consultations that must be engaged in, and the other is the environmental analyses which need to be carried out as an integral part of the planning behind environmental management and its adoption in any country.

These areas of innovation require considerable exploration and development, and some of this has already been initiated in many countries.

23.13 Need for Environmental Management

Uncontrolled damage to the environment resulting from the destructive developmental activities compelled the government and several international institutions to come out with comprehensive regulations and alternatives so that the environmental damage could be repaired. Many countries have already started their efforts to protect the environment. Several international conventions are held and treaties are signed to improve the environment. Since, 1992 around 160 countries have met regularly to discuss the various methods to develop different environmental management programmes.

Strong, flexible and effective environmental management is required to mitigate the negative impacts of reform. Environmental management needs to adapt to the changing social, economic and political reality. The need for environmental management also arises to build bridges between public and private sector entities. Even the businesses of today now views the environment as an opportunity to add value to investment, gain competitive advantage and achieve higher margins through eco-efficiency. There are many potential options in developing public-private partnerships in environmental management, such as increasing access to capital and technology for enterprises to raise the effectiveness of implementing environmental policies. All these considerations indicate the need to develop a strategic concept of environmental management. Environment must not be understood as a resource that can be exploited. On the other hand it must be viewed as a capital that has to be managed carefully so that it can yield returns for generations to come.

24

Sustainable Development

24.1 Introduction

The concept 'sustainable development' can be known by pondering over few questions. Let us consider our needs. We need clean air to breathe and a car for transportation. These two needs although may appear simple but are conflicting. This is precisely because fuel burning from car will invariably produce carbon which will affect clean air of the environment. With each passing day, the number of cars will increase and so will the extent of damage to the environment. So within our limited needs, we have conflicting requirements, which undoubtedly will multiply when we look at whole community, city, country or the world. A quick look at our present needs and that of future will make clear that needs conflict with each other. Which one would you choose and how would you make your decision. If we wish to meet our present needs, we will be at risk to sacrifice our future needs. This is where concept of 'sustainable development' has come which comes with sustainable use of resources.

The concept suggests the approaches for meeting the present needs as well as our future requirement. According to this concept, fulfilling of future needs depends on how well we balance social, economic, and environmental objectives needs today. The concept has gained momentum in view of adverse effect of climate change, ozone depletion, unprecedented flood, rain, scorching sun, etc. The world at large has started considering seriously on the measures to suggest ways and means to arrest the deterioration of ecological balance.

A number of definitions for the concept 'sustainable development' have been devised by the scientists, thinkers and others. The most accepted and the landmark definition was coined during Brundtland Commission in 1987. According to Brundtland Commission, "*Sustainable development is the development that meets the needs of the present without compromising the ability of future generations to meet their own needs.*"

The United Nations Conference on Environment and Development (UNCED), held in Rio de Janeiro in June 1992, is a milestone event, which effectively focused the world's attention on environmental and development problems faced equally by the global community. The Summit brought together governments from around the globe, representatives from international agencies and non-governmental organisations with the objective of preparing the world for attaining the long-term goals of sustainable development. It has therefore become imperative that countries come together to chart a sustainable course of development.

24.2 Concept of Sustainable Development

The most acceptable definition given by Brundtland Commission in 1987 contains two key concepts of sustainable development:

- The concept of ***needs,*** in particular the essential needs of the world's poor, to which overriding priority should be given; and
- The idea of ***limitations*** imposed by the state of technology and social organisation on the environment's ability to meet present and future needs.

All definitions of sustainable development require that we see the world as a system - ***a system that connects space*** and ***a system that connects time.*** When we think of the world as ***a system over space***, we grow to understand that air pollution from Europe may affect air quality in Asia. Similarly, insecticides and pesticides sprayed in one part of globe may affect marine resources of another part of the globe. When we think of the world as ***a system over time,*** we start to realise that the decisions our grandparents made about how to farm the land continue to affect agricultural practice today; and the economic policies we endorse today will have an impact on urban poverty when our children are adults. The concept of sustainable development is rooted in this kind of systems thinking. It helps us understand ourselves and our world. The problems we face are complex and serious and we can address them if we take serious consideration to the damages it can cause to environment even at far off places beyond our own country.

24.3 Definitions of Sustainable Development

The term sustainable development has been defined differently by different organisations and individuals on different occasions. Some of them have been quoted here.

"Sustainable development is development that meets the needs of the present without compromising the ability of future generations to meet their own needs. It contains within it two key concepts:

- The concept of **needs**, in particular the essential needs of the world's poor, to which overriding priority should be given; and
- The idea of **limitations** imposed by the state of technology and social organisation on the environment's ability to meet present and future needs."

– *International Institute for Sustainable Development (1987)*

"Sustainable development concerns a wide range of **interrelated issues** which may be approached through the following seven principles or dimensions. The first concerns the interdependent nature of the world. This gives rise to the need for a participative response through the exercise of **citizenship and stewardship**, which is the theme of the second concept. The third through to sixth concepts cover further key dimensions of sustainable development, leading to the seventh which, as a logical consequence of those that proceed, is concerned with the limits of knowledge and exercise of the precautionary principle."

– *Teachers in Development Education (TIDE) Annual report (2008)*

Sustainable development means a better quality of life now and for generations to come. It means not using up resources faster than the planet can replenish, or restock them and joining up economic, social and environmental goals. It also influences decision-making within organisations, and therefore can go towards forming principles and business values - for example, providing information to the public in an open and accessible way and involving people and communities who are affected by those decisions. Or in openly reporting how they run their business and the care they take about the local environment and the people that work for them. These principles can also apply to **government** policies – for example, in planning regulations for green buildings and technologies. It is also about being clear and **responsible** about the use of scientific, and other, evidence – for example, about levels of pollution or carbon emissions.- *UK Government website*

24.4 Components of Sustainable Development

According to Gilbert, Stevenson, Girardet, Stren (1996), the concept of sustainability relate to the maintenance and enhancement of environmental, social and economic resources, in order to meet the needs of current and future generations. The three components of sustainability are:

- ***Social sustainability***

Social sustainability is based on twin principles of justice and equality for all. All citizens should have access to minimum standard of security, and social benefits such as food, health, education, shelter and opportunity through distributive equity of weak resources. While the individual needs, such as health and well-being, nutrition, shelter, education and cultural expression should be met; social goals of cultural diversity, social justice and public participation should be achieved. This requires cohesion between society and its ability to work towards common goals be maintained.

- ***Economic sustainability***

Economic sustainability means growth in income along with the maintenance of basic stock of manmade capital, human capital and natural capital, internalising all costs including the environmental costs associated with production and consumption. This occurs when development, which moves towards social and environmental sustainability, is financially feasible.

- ***Environmental sustainability***

Ecological component is basically related to the environment part. It requires sustainable use of resources so that ecological stability can be maintained and natural capital remains intact. This means that the source and sink functions of the environment should not be degraded. Therefore, the extraction of renewable resources should not exceed the rate at which they are renewed, and the absorptive capacity to the environment to assimilate wastes should not be exceeded. Furthermore, the extraction of non-renewable resources should be minimised and should not exceed agreed minimum strategic levels.

These three components are dependent on one another in terms of sustainable development. The objective of sustainable development is to maximise the goals in three systems, and a balance among these three components. Thus, the main features of the concept of sustainable development can be briefly stated as follows:

- It emphasises the need for striking balance between the need of the present generation and future generation.
- It emphasises distributional equity.
- It requires preservation of human capital, physical capital and natural capital.
- It emphasises that the costs of environmental loss should be taken care of.
- It involves changes in the production methodology.
- It involves use of environment-friendly technology.
- In involves government to set higher environmental standards in its energy consumption policies.
- Most important of all, individuals must recognise that the products they buy and use do not harm the environment in any way.

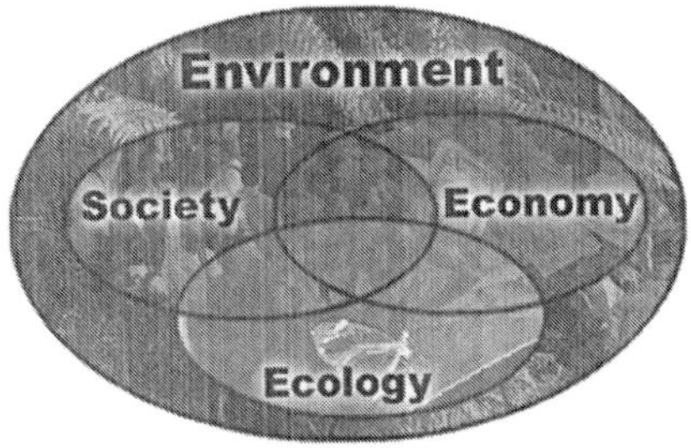

Figure 24.1: Interdependence of three components in sustainable development.

24.5 Objectives of Sustainable Development

In 2002, World Summit on Sustainable Development was held at Johannesburg from 21 August to 4 September 2002. The Summit was attended by 40,000 delegates from 190 countries. It specially took note of the fact that Agenda 21, a plan of action for sustainable development adopted by Rio Summit in 1992, was not implemented. The Conference identified five thrust areas such as Water and Sanitation, Energy, Health, Agricultural productivity, and Biodiversity and Ecosystem management.

This 2002 Summit expanded the definition given by 1995 World Summit on Social Development by identifying the three main objectives of sustainable development i.e. Eradicating poverty, Protecting natural resources, and Changing unsustainable production and consumption patterns. Let us discuss them in detail.

Eradicating Poverty

Sustainable development stands for meeting the needs of present generations without jeopardising the needs of future generations, a better quality of life for everyone, now and for generations to come. Poverty is one of the root causes of numerous problems related to environment. Poor people do not have sufficient money to meet their basic needs. They do not even have access to clean, fresh drinking water supplies and most of them are forced to drink the unsafe, contaminated and polluted water. This results in many waterborne diseases and can even cause death due to lack of proper medical facilities. Unhygienic conditions in slums due to lack of sanitation poses many problems to the poor. Hence, eradication of poverty should be one of the main objectives of sustainable development.

It is a well known fact that education solves a number of problems as it empowers the people through knowledge and making them aware about their surroundings. Effort should be made to educate the poor people through literacy programmes, so that they can realise the value of educating their children.

Education of one generation naturally leads to education of future generation. If a poor person gets educated, he would be able to earn sufficient for meeting his basic needs. It offers a vision of progress that integrates immediate and long-term needs, local and global needs, economic and environmental needs as inseparable and interdependent components of human progress.

Protecting natural resources

The air we breathe, the water we drink and the land we live and grow food on, all are natural resources. All organisms use resources but man is exploiting these natural resources at a fast pace in this race of growth and development. Economic growth is must for a nation but it should not be at the expense of depletion of natural resources.

Brundtland Commission noted that natural resources should be used to meet the 'needs' of the people but not their 'wants', which are increasing day by day. Needs can be defined as the basic requirement of people which are necessary for leading a quality life. Once needs are fulfilled, the wants arise, which are not essential for quality life but only for leisure. These wants are primarily responsible for the over exploitation of natural resources. Thus, it is necessary to protect natural resources, so that they can be made available to all. Managed use of natural resources is an effort in this direction.

Sustainable development is a development that attempts to bridge the gap between economic growth and environmental protection while taking into account other issues traditionally associated with development. Protection of natural resources is an issue closely associated with sustainable development. It also seeks to develop means of economic growth while supporting natural environment as well as abstaining the use of natural resources on short-term basis at the expense of long-term development.

Changing unsustainable production and consumption patterns

Sustainable development is often misinterpreted as focusing solely on environmental issues. In reality it is a broader concept as it encompasses three general policy areas: economic, environmental and social. Sustainable development will not occur solely by formulating policies, but steps must be taken by society at large. Sustainable development globally demands working and living in a way that enables people to lead healthy, fulfilling and economically secured lives without destroying the environment and endangering future welfare of people and planet.

Populations of developed nations largely rely on the unsustainable production and consumption patterns. Huge amounts of energy and natural resources are wasted annually during production or at consumption stages. The inefficient technologies are mainly responsible for this wastage of energy and other natural resources.

Shifting from this unsustainable production and consumption pattern to a sustainable one will prove beneficial for the environment as a whole. Use of eco-friendly products, reusing, recycling and efficient technologies is good alternatives in this regard. This will help in minimising generate stress on the environment and minimum waste, leading to sustainable development, which is of long-term benefit.

Thus, keeping these three objectives in mind, we carry forward sustainable development.

24.6 International Events on Sustainable Development

Major international events are mentioned below:

Stockholm Conference (1972)

The United Nations Conference on the Human Environment (also known as the Stockholm Conference) was an international conference convened by United Nations in Stockholm, Sweden during June 1972, at the initiative of the Government of Sweden. It was the UN's first major conference on international environmental issues, and marked a turning point in the development of international environmental politics. The Conference was opened and addressed by the Swedish Prime Minister Olof Palme and Secretary-General Kurt Waldheim to discuss the state of the global environment and was attended by the representatives of 113 countries, 19 inter-governmental agencies, and a large number of non-governmental organisations. It is widely recognised as the beginning of modern political and public awareness of global environmental problems. The meeting agreed upon a Declaration containing 26 principles concerning the environment and development, an Action Plan with 109 recommendations, and a Resolution. Some argue that this Conference had a real impact on the environmental policies of the European Community (that later became the European Union). In 1973, the EU created the Environmental and Consumer Protection Directorate, and composed the first Environmental Action Programme. Such increased interest and research collaboration paved the way for further understanding of global warming and eventually, led to the Kyoto Protocol.

Brundtland Commission (1987)

The World Commission on Environment and Development (WCED) is commonly known as Brundtland Commission (1983-87) was named after its Chairman Gro Harlem Brundtland, former Prime Minister of Norway. The mission of this Commission was to unite different countries to pursue sustainable development together by identifying sustainability problems worldwide, raising awareness, and suggesting the implementation of solutions. The Brundtland Commission released its Report in October 1987. The organisation, Center for Our Common Future, started with effect from

April 1988 to facilitate initiation of suitable steps for implementations of the Commission's recommendations by all stakeholders. The first volume of Commissions' report "Our Common Future," strongly influenced the Earth Summit in Rio de Janeiro, Brazil in 1992 and the third UN Conference on Environment and Development in Johannesburg, South Africa in 2002. The Commission is also credited with creating the most prevalent and modern definition of sustainability.

"Sustainable development is development that meets the needs of the present without compromising the ability of future generations to meet their own needs." It contains two key concepts: the concept of 'needs', in particular the essential needs of the world's poor, to which overriding priority should be given; and the idea of limitations imposed by the state of technology and social organisation on the environment's ability to meet present and future needs.

Earth Summit (1992)

The United Nations Conference on Environment and Development (UNCED), also known as the Earth Summit (also known as Rio Summit or Rio Conference) was a major United Nations conference held in Rio de Janeiro from 3 to 14 June 1992. Representatives of 172 governments and 2,400 non-governmental organisations participated in the conference. The important issues such as systematic scrutiny of patterns of production (particularly the production of toxic components, such as lead in gasoline, or poisonous waste including radioactive chemicals); alternative sources of energy (to replace the use of fossil fuels which are linked to global climate change); new reliance on public transportation systems (in order to reduce vehicle emissions, congestion in cities and the health problems caused by polluted air and smog); and the growing scarcity of water; etc. were addressed in the Summit.

An important achievement was an agreement on the Climate Change Convention which in turn led to the Kyoto Protocol. Another agreement was to "not carry out any activities on the lands of indigenous peoples that would cause environmental degradation or that would be culturally inappropriate." The Convention on Biological Diversity was opened for signature at the Earth Summit, and made a start towards redefinition of measures that did not inherently encourage destruction of natural eco regions and so-called uneconomic growth. The important documents (Rio Declaration on Environment and Development; and Agenda 21) and two legally binding agreements (Convention on Biological Diversity; and Framework Convention on Climate Change) were brought out in the Summit.

Agenda 21 (1992)

Agenda 21 refers to an agenda for the twenty first Century. It is a comprehensive blueprint of action to be taken globally, nationally, and locally by organisations of the UN, governments, and major groups in every area in which humans directly affect the environment. The full text of Agenda 21 was revealed at the United Nations Conference on Environment and Development (Earth Summit), held in Rio de Janeiro on June 13, 1992, where 178 governments voted to adopt the programme. The Commission on Sustainable Development acts as a high level forum on sustainable development and has acted as preparatory committee for summits and sessions on the implementation of Agenda 21. The United Nations Division for Sustainable Development acts as the secretariat to the Commission and works within the context of 'Agenda 21'.

There are 40 chapters in the Agenda 21, divided into ***four main sections as detailed below***:

Section I: Social and Economic Dimensions: Deals with combating poverty, especially for developing country, changing consumption patterns, promoting health, change population and sustainable settlement in decision making;

Section II: Conservation and Management of Resources for Development: Includes atmospheric protection, combating deforestation, protecting fragile environments, conservation of biological diversity (biodiversity), control of pollution and management of biotechnology and radioactive wastes;

Section III: Strengthening the Role of Major Groups: Includes the roles of children and youth, women, NGOs, local authorities, business and workers and strengthening the role of indigenous peoples, their community and farmers; and

Section IV: Means of Implementation: Implementation includes science, technology transfer, education, international institutions and financial mechanisms.

Besides, there is 'Local Agenda 21'. The implementation of Agenda 21 was intended to involve action at international, national, regional and local levels. Some national and state governments have legislated or advised that local authorities take steps to implement the plan locally, as recommended in Chapter 28 of the document. These programmes are often known as 'Local Agenda 21'.

Convention on Biological Diversity (1993)

The Convention on Biological Diversity (CBD), known informally as the Biodiversity Convention, is an international legally binding treaty. The Convention has three main goals:

- Conservation of biological diversity (or biodiversity);

- Sustainable use of its components; and
- Fair and equitable sharing of benefits arising from genetic resources.

In other words, the objective of the Convention was to develop national strategies for the conservation and sustainable use of biological diversity. It is often seen as the key document regarding sustainable development. The Convention was opened for signature at the Earth Summit in Rio de Janeiro on 5th June 1992 and brought to force on 29th December 1993.

The Convention recognised that the conservation of biological diversity is "a common concern of humankind" and is an integral part of the development process. The agreement covers all ecosystems, species, and genetic resources. It links traditional conservation efforts to the economic goal of using biological resources sustainably. It sets principles for the fair and equitable sharing of the benefits arising from the use of genetic resources, notably those destined for commercial use. It also covers the rapidly expanding field of biotechnology through its Cartagena Protocol on Biosafety, addressing technology, development and transfer, benefit-sharing and biosafety issues. Importantly, the Convention is legally binding; countries that join it ('Parties') are obliged to implement its provisions.

The Convention reminds decision-makers that natural resources are not infinite and sets out a philosophy of sustainable use. While past conservation efforts were aimed at protecting particular species and habitats, the Convention recognise that ecosystems, species and genes must be used for the benefit of humans. However, this should be done in a way and at a rate that does not lead to the long-term decline of biological diversity.

Rio+5 (1997)

In 1997, the General Assembly of the UN held a special session to appraise five years of progress on the implementation of Agenda 21 (Rio +5). The Assembly recognised progress as 'uneven' and identified key trends including increasing globalisation, widening inequalities in income and a continued deterioration of the global environment. A new General Assembly Resolution promised further action.

The Earth Charter (2000)

The Earth Charter is an international declaration of fundamental values and principles for building a just, sustainable, and peaceful global society in the twentyfirst century. Created by a global consultation process, and endorsed by organisations representing millions of people, the Charter "seeks to inspire in all people a sense of global interdependence and shared responsibility for the well-being of the human family, the greater community of life, and future generations." It calls upon humanity to help create a global partnership at a critical juncture in history.

The Earth Charter was approved by Earth Charter Commission at the UNESCO headquarters in Paris in March 2000. The official launch was on 29 June 2000 in a ceremony at The Peace Palace in The Hague, Netherlands in presence of Queen Beatrix of the Netherlands.

The Earth Charter's ethical vision proposes that environmental protection, human rights, equitable human development, and peace are interdependent and indivisible. The Charter attempts to provide a new framework for thinking about and addressing these issues. The Earth Charter Initiative organisation exists to promote the Charter.

The four pillars and sixteen principles of the Earth Charter are:

Respect and Care for the Community of Life

- Respect Earth and life in all its diversity.
- Care for the community of life with understanding, compassion and love.
- Build democratic societies that are just, participatory, sustainable and peaceful.
- Secure Earth's bounty and beauty for present and future generations.

Ecological Integrity

- Protect and restore the integrity of Earth's ecological systems, with special concern for biological diversity and the natural processes that sustain life.
- Prevent harm as the best method of environmental protection and, when knowledge is limited, apply a precautionary approach.
- Adopt patterns of production, consumption and reproduction that safeguard Earth's regenerative capacities, human rights and community well-being.
- Advance the study of ecological sustainability and promote the open exchange and wide application of the knowledge acquired.

Social and Economic Justice

- Eradicate poverty as an ethical, social and environmental imperative.
- Ensure that economic activities and institutions at all levels promote human development in an equitable and sustainable manner.
- Affirm gender equality and equity as prerequisites to sustainable development and ensure universal access to education, healthcare and economic opportunity.
- Uphold the right of all, without discrimination, to a natural and social environment supportive of human dignity, bodily health and spiritual well-being, with special attention to the rights of indigenous peoples and minorities.

Democracy, Nonviolence, and Peace

- Strengthen democratic institutions at all levels, and provide transparency and accountability in governance, inclusive participation in decision-making, and access to justice.
- Integrate into formal education and lifelong learning the knowledge, values and skills needed for a sustainable way of life.
- Treat all living beings with respect and consideration.
- Promote a culture of tolerance, nonviolence and peace.

The Charter has been formally endorsed by organisations representing millions of people, including the UNESCO, over 250 universities around the world, the World Conservation Union of IUCN, the Indian National Capital Territory of Delhi, the 2001 US Conference of Mayors, and dozens of youth organisations. Various groups from several religions support the Earth Charter.

The Johannesburg Summit (2002)

The Johannesburg Plan of Implementation, agreed at the World Summit on Sustainable Development (Earth Summit 2002) affirmed UN commitment to 'full implementation' of Agenda 21, alongside achievement of the Millennium Development Goals and other international agreements.

24.7 Sustainable Consumption

Man as the master of earth, bears the responsibility to respect the integrity of nature and stability of essential ecological processes. "Sustainable consumption implies consuming the resources in such a manner that satisfaction is maximised and wastage is minimised." It is basically an adoption of lifestyle in a just and sustainable manner.

Sustainable consumption is not a new concept as numerous traditional societies were aware of the rule of nature and they developed the ways to live in harmony with the nature. Today, increase in production has caused consumerism, ever increasing needs and greed. All these resulted into unsustainable use of resources. Thus, it lays emphasis on sustainable consumption.

Issues in Sustainable consumption

- Enriching the quality of life by using cheaper goods and services.
- Minimising the use of non-renewable energy resources.
- Using environment-friendly technologies.
- Minimising the waste through recycling and reusing.
- Reducing the gap between rich and poor that is taking equitable distribution of resources in various programmes and schemes.

No country can progress without considering the development of its people. But development in a sustainable way requires sustainable consumption of resources. Sustainable consumption threatens competitiveness and profitability and it goes against the economic mantra that encourages citizens to spend, spent and spent, sustainable consumption lies at the care of sustainable development. Sustainable consumption addresses the demand side looking at how the goods and services can be delivered in ways that reduce the burden on the carrying capacity of the earth. These goods and services are required to meet the basic needs of food, shelter and clothing; and improve quality of life through health, leisure and mobility.

Centre for sustainable production and consumption (C-SPAC)

Consumer's rights to basic needs cannot be denied which encompasses entitlements of healthcare, safe drinking water and sanitation as inalienable elements. Besides, a consumer is also entitled to safe goods, services and environment for it affects his/her life directly. Sensing the need for more focuses action in the area of consumer safety, centre for sustainable production and consumption (C-SPAC) was established in 1993.

The centre is closely involved in the promotion of sustainable patterns of consumption and production along with its involvement in other related areas such as production patterns, poverty, under and over consumption, etc.

The mission of C-SPAC is to achieve the consumer's right to be protected against unsafe goods, services and environment; to promote sustainable consumption and production; and provoke questioning and action. C-SPAC works simultaneously at the grassroots, national and international levels on various issues which directly or indirectly affect the consumers.

24.8 Benefits of Sustainable Consumption

Sustainable consumption can provide many benefits as noted below:

- Reducing degradation and deterioration of environment;
- Reducing the amount of waste generation;
- Reducing excessive stress on natural resources;
- Enhancing equitable distribution of resources between the rich and the poor;
- Reducing competitiveness between producers of the same products;
- Restoring natural resources for future generations;
- Enhancing health and hygiene for everyone;
- It raises the standard of living of existing generation;
- It checks that no harm is caused to the living standard of the future generations;
- It protects people against the environmental pollution;

- It also helps in conserving environment for the present and future generations.

24.9 Ways of Achieving Sustainable Consumption

Unsustainable consumption can be reduced and controlled by adopting following:

Checking the Population Growth

The rate of population growth corresponds with the increasing degradation of environment. As the population increases, more and more forests and farmlands are encroached for setting up of housing of complexes and industries. The growing population will eventually result in water and food shortage. Thus, it is important to educate people on the need to adopt family planning measures and the benefits of a small family.

Encouraging Sustainable Consumption

We need to encourage re-using of the products. Besides, recycling of products will not only held in reducing the waste but also avoid use of new raw material for manufacturing goods.

Popularise the use of eco-friendly goods to avoid environmental degradation Sustainable consumption through eco-friendly goods

An important step in the sustainability movement is the availability of goods and services which have been produced in a more environment-friendly manner than the goods or services of similar category.

Consumers became aware of the environmental-friendly goods or products through ecomark scheme. In India, Ecomark scheme was launched in 1991. The scheme was designed to cover 16 product categories, of which one of the categories; i.e. drugs was later dropped. Eco-labelling is done for a product which is made and disposed off in a way that significantly reduces the environment harm. A product with ecomark will be the right choice from the environment point of view. The Bureau of Indian Standards (BIS) is the authority which assigns and oversees the scheme of eco-labelling and use of its logo, i.e. earthen pot.

Two Committees were also set up to implement the scheme. These were:

- Steering committee identifies the products and promotes the scheme; and
- Technical committee debates and sets the product criteria.

24.10 Need for Sustainable Development

Economic development has caused excessive exploitation of natural resources. In the past few years, economic activities have brought along with them pollution and wasteful use of resources. Demand for the natural resources such as oil, wood and water is rapidly increasing. Excessive mining of minerals like iron, coal, gold, silver and extraction of crude oil will result in gradual depletion of their stocks. On the other hand toxic smoke and other injurious pollutants released from factories and vehicles cause pollution of environment.

People are then bound to spend a lot to clean up the mess because damaged environment minimises the quality of life of the present and the future generations. In such a situation, present generation has to ensure that the quality of life of the future generations is not jeopardised. For the future, people need ways to achieve social, economic and environmental objective in a balanced manner and consider the long-term implications of a decision.

Thus, it is necessary to improve the efficiency with which resources can be used and acquire international cooperation to overcome environmental problems. There are many reasons which clearly indicate the urgent need of sustainable development. Some of them are noted below.

Poverty

Although there has been a significant drop in poverty level since 1990, yet there is a large section of population living below the poverty line. This poverty can be reduced with the help of sustainable development.

Gap between Rich and Poor countries

The average income in rich countries is much more than the average income in poor countries. This is mainly due to lack of sufficient economic growth in poor countries.

Air Pollution

Urban areas in developing countries have alarmingly high level of air pollution. Heavy dependence on fossil fuels for energy production has led to growing concern over excessive release of greenhouse gases. The emission rates are bound to increase unless serious efforts are made for sustainable development.

Scarcity of fresh water

Consumption of fresh water is increasing rapidly but its availability in all parts of the world is unequal. Besides, over consumption and wastage also enhance the water scarcity problem. Better conservation and allocation of water is necessary and which can be done through sustainable development.

Soil Degradation

Nearly 20 lakh hectares of land has been degraded since 1950, which has resulted in sharp decline in productivity. This necessitates sustainable development.

Disappearing Biodiversity

Deforestation is proceeding at an alarming rate, leading to loss of huge amounts of biodiversity. Through a series of local extinctions, a large range of plants and animals have been reduced. One-third of the world biodiversity is threatened due to encroachment by humans for various purposes.

Declining Fisheries

The fisheries and their productivity are constantly declining. About 70 per cent of world's commercial fisheries are fully exploited or overexploited and are experiencing low yields.

Thus, there is an immediate need for sustainable development. It is development which can be sustained over a long period of time without causing any decline in the quality of life of future generations. Such a development process has been termed as sustainable development.

24.11 Challenges for Sustainable Development

Achieving sustainable development is not an easy task. It can however, be achieved by overcoming some challenges. Challenges mean the impediment in catering to the need of present generation without compromising with future generations' needs. These challenges include social, political and economic considerations, in relation to the present system.

- ***Social considerations***

People are highly influenced by status determined by their caste or class. Every caste or class has its own values or ethics, which make possible for people to live in a society. Some of the major problems which come in the path of sustainable development are noted below.

Population

A rapidly increasing population leads to increased demands of food products, clothes, houses, etc. But their supplies cannot be increased immediately due to lack of raw materials, skilled labour, etc. Subsequently, the costs of these essentials will increase, which will subsequently raise the cost of living for the masses.

Widening of economic gap

The wealthier class is mainly responsible for the uncontrolled expenditure, which further limits the capacity to save and invest. There is a common saying the 'money attracts money.' Through savings and investments, rich people are getting richer day by day. However, poor people die amidst poverty. Poverty encourages people to have large number of children because more children mean more hands to earn living. Thus, poverty increases poverty. It forms a vicious circle.

Education

Social attitude towards education is also a constraint in development. A large section of population in underdeveloped or developing countries is not seriously concerned over the education and more particularly to the girls. On the other hand, academic education is preferred over technical and professional education in some developing countries.

Essential facilities

Due to scarcity of resources it is not possible to provide educational, health, medical, transport and housing facilities to the entire population. Rapid increase in school going population and decreasing number of labour force put greater pressure on educational and other training facilities. Thus, retards quality of education.

- ***Political Consideration***

Political conditions of a country play a very important role in its growth and development. But on the other hand, it may even emerge as one of the greatest challenges in the path of sustainable development of a country. Some of the important political aspects which should be considered are the noted below:

Political Stability

The development of a nation relies heavily on political stability. The development and growth of UK, Germany, Japan and France has been due to their political stability and strong administration since the nineteenth century. All of them were involved in two world wars and were devastated. Still they continued to progress due to the strong political and administrative traditions.

On the other hand, Italy has not been able to grow up to their level due to political instability and appropriate administration. Peace, stability and legal protection encourage development. Technical progress can only take place under stable political conditions.

Government policies

A government must offer society helpful services that stimulate sustainable development. Policies made by the government can play an important role in giving impetus to interactions between environment and man. A good government can help in capital formation by adopting the policies and by providing timely overhead capital facilities.

Compatibility between nations

No nation can achieve the objectives of sustainable development alone. This can be achieved through compatibility between nations. The governments of nations are quite important in this respect. If there is some sort of incompatibility, then there will be no transfer of technologies, skilled manpower and other natural resources. For example, there are only a few nations in the world with rich oil reserves. Others have negligible oil reserve. So they have to import oil from the oil rich nations. This is possible only if there is a good compatibility between them.

- ***Economic Considerations***

All countries are not economically self-sufficient. There is high economic backwardness in some of the underdeveloped and the developing countries. Overexploitation of natural resources and energy has resulted in deterioration of quality of environment. The major economic constraints in sustainable development are as follows.

Low Labour efficiency

The low efficiency of labour is mainly due to poverty. Poverty is the root cause because it results in low nutritional standards, ill health, illiteracy and lack of training. Lack of money results in insufficiency of essential facilities. Apart from this there is occupational immobility of labour due to joint family system and caste system.

Low Capital

In underdeveloped countries, there is not only limited capital stock but the rate of capital formation is also very low. Deficiency of capital hinders the process of scrapping off the old techniques and installation of new and modern techniques. Besides, illiteracy and absence of skilled techniques in the backward economy also proves to be a hurdle. Thus, technological backwardness is not only the cause of economic backwardness but is also the result of it. In other words poverty is both a cause and consequence of low capital.

Support Base for Sustainable Development

Economic development may aggravate the problem of pollution. This may affect adversely the quality of life of present and future generations. In such a situation, present development may be at the cost of future development. This calls for sustainable development. Sustainable development maximises long-term net gains for the present and the future generations resulting from economic development.

Elements of Support Base

Sustainable development is a process of change, in which exploitation of resources, the orientation of technological development and institutional changes are in harmony with one another and enhance the current as well as future potential to meet human needs.

Sustainable development can be achieved in a better way by providing some essential elements for its support base. The major elements of support base for sustainable development are:

- Political and administrative will;
- Dynamic and flexible policies;
- Appropriate technologies;
- Comprehensive review and revision mechanisms;
- Humane approach.

Political and Administrative Will

All living species have an equal right on their environment and natural resources. Hence, protection of environment and conservation of natural resources are the responsibilities of all inhabitants of the earth. Each country has its own government for administrating the people. Thus, the governments and different administrative groups can play an important role in changing the opinion of the people of a country for the betterment of environmental quality and conditions.

Political stability and honest administration are the two key elements of sustaining development. It is a well known fact that greater political stability motivates the progress of a country, organised by an army of honest people at the administrative level. It is only the government or other related administrative authority, which can easily communicated between all the sectors of the society. This is why; these are considered as support base for sustainable development.

The political and administrative system can help in achieving sustainable development by working in following fields:

- Creating awareness of the deteriorating of the environment.
- Arranging for training of people who can further help in the protecting the environment.
- Promoting programmes related to conservation of natural resources.
- Assisting various governmental and non-governmental organisations working in different areas of the environment.
- Punishing the defaulters who do not comply with the rules made by the government.
- Prohibiting the excessive outflow of natural resources for strengthening of economy.
- Monitoring the activities of industries and other such sectors which may otherwise enhance environmental degradation.

- Strictly implementing laws, rules and regulations formulated for the protection of the environment.

Dynamic and Flexible Policies

Government and policy-makers should formulate dynamic and flexible policies to enhance sustainable development for the present as well as for the future generations. The government policies prove to be important support base for sustainable development. Policy statement pronounced by the Union Ministry of Environment and Forests (MoEF) in June 1992 outlined India's National Conservations Strategy on Environment and Development. It emphasised 'Sustainable Development' as the key element in Ministry's action plan. Based on this policy, an integrated strategy has been adopted by the government for protection and conservation of the environment. The strategy aimed at strengthening the existing programmes of pollution control; ensuring better disposal of solid wastes and hazardous substances; conserving forests and other biodiversity rich ecosystems.

Appropriate Technologies

All developmental activities are economic activities. Hence, development of a country is highly dependent on the economic growth. Since Industrial Revolution many countries of the world have developed due to their high economic growth. But the technologies used by the industries initially were known to cause many harmful effects on the environment. Traditionally used technologies are considered as the main factors causing degradation of environment. Thus, it is an urgent need for calling for sustainable development.

Industry is one of the sectors mainly responsible for draining of natural resources. All the industries require one or the other natural resources thus these resources get depleted. Some important adverse impacts of excessive use of natural resources are given below:

- Pollution of the environmental components like air, water and land.
- Depletion of non-renewable resources.
- Deterioration in quality of the environment.
- Erosion of top fertile layer of soil thus reducing agricultural productivity.
- Increase in frequency of disasters like landslides, floods, etc.
- Degradation of natural ecosystems of the earth.

Hence, all these adverse impacts call for an urgent need of shifting towards appropriate technologies, which cause no harm to the environment. Technologies should be so selected that they are eco-friendly and in perfect harmony with the environment. Use of alternative sources of energy in industrial as well as transportation sectors can be of great benefit. These alternative sources of energy include solar, wind, hydel, tidal, geothermal and biomass energy. The use of these sources of energy will help in reducing the increasing stress on the non-renewable sources of energy like coal, petroleum and natural gas.

The benefit of using appropriate and new technologies will be:

- Reduced stress on natural resources;
- Reduced environmental degradation;
- Reduced level of pollution in components of the environment;
- Enhanced use of recycled and reused substances;
- Reduced wastage of natural resources;
- Increased availability of resources for future generations;
- Healthy and hygienic environment.

Comprehensive Review and Revision Mechanisms

Environment is not static but keeps on changing with the passage of time. Hence, policies formulated for the betterment of environment are not suitable for all the periods of time. They should be revised periodically, so that they become appropriate according to the changing environment.

This is the prime duty of all the policy-framers to review the policies from time to time, so that policies can give better results. Some major points which should be kept in mind by the policy-makers and other dealing authorities are:

- Changing conditions of the environment;
- Depleting natural resources;
- Increasing public awareness of environmental issues;
- Enhancing the rate of sustained development;
- Solving environmental problems.

Policies should bc formulated in a manner that will give best results, i.e. increased economic growth and development under changing conditions of the environment. Periodic review of essential policies will help in checking whether the policies are yielding the results, for which they were once formulated. If some policies have shortcomings, they can be rectified through comprehensive review of the policies. This comprehensive review of policies will ensure:

- A better environment;
- Preservation of natural resources;
- Sustainable development.

Following are the important methods of carrying out a review:

- Questionnaire method;

- Interview method;
- Direct observation method;
- Environment Impact Assessment.

Humane Approach

In the words of Robbert Repetto, "Sustainable development is a developmental strategy that manages all natural resources and human resources as well as financial and physical assets for increasing long-term wealth and well beings."

Sustainability is a matter of sharing development opportunities by all and also raising people from the level of poverty and humane deprivation. According to late Professor Mahbub-Ul-Haq of Pakistan, "Sustainability does not mean sustaining the present levels of poverty and human deprivation. If the present is miserable and unacceptable to the majority of world people, it must be changed before it is sustained. In other worlds, what must be sustained are worthwhile life opportunities, not human deprivation."

The ability to meet the needs of people depends on three types of capital:

- Natural capital, i.e. natural resources;
- Physical capital, i.e. machine, tools, etc;
- Human Capital, i.e. education and technical advancement.

The Concept of Human Development Index was introduced by the United Nations Development Programme (UNDP), in its first human development report in 1990. The human development report has ranked nations according to the level of human development index.

The Human Development India (HDI) is based on three main indicators:

- Longevity, as measured by life expectancy at birth.
- Educational attainment, as measured by a combination of adult literacy and combined primary, secondary and tertiary enrolment ratios.
- Standard of living, as measured by purchasing power of people or their capacity to buy goods and services.

The development of human resources required adequate provisions of :

- Health services;
- Water supply;
- Housing;
- Nutrition;
- Family Welfare facilities.

All of these are essential determinants of the quality of life. The provision of one without the other is bound to affect the life adversely; hence the strategy of human resource development is to take an integrated view of these factors.

24.12 National Programme for Sustainable Development

National Food Security Mission (NFSM)

- To increase the production of rice by 10 million tonnes, wheat by 8 million tonnes and pulses by 2 million tonnes by the end of Eleventh Five Year Plan (2007-2012); and
- Measures include bridging the yield gap with respect to the identified crops through dissemination of improved technologies and farm management practices.

Rashtriya Krishi Vikaas Yojna (RKVY)

- Considers a holistic development of the agricultural and allied sectors; and
- Aims to achieve an annual growth rate of four per cent in the agricultural sector during the Eleventh Five Year Plan (2007-12).

Integrated Watershed Management Programme (IWMP)

- Main objectives are to restore the ecological balance by harnessing, conserving and developing degraded natural resources such as soil, vegetative cover and water; and
- Key outcomes include prevention of soil run-off, regeneration of natural vegetation, rain water harvesting and recharging of the ground water table.

National Watershed Development Project for Rainfed Area (NWDPRA)

- Promotes agriculture productivity and production in rainfed areas; and
- Programme is planned, implemented, monitored and maintained by watershed communities.

Command Area Development and Water Management Programme (CADWM)

- Objectives of improving the utilisation of created irrigation potential and optimising agriculture production and productivity. Area Development Authorities provide technical support.

National Project for Repair, Renovation and Restoration (RRR) of Water Bodies

- To restore and augment storage capacities of water bodies; and
- Recover and extend their lost irrigation potential.

Kisan Credit Card (KCC) Scheme

- Provides adequate and timely credit to farmers under single window, with flexible and simplified procedure.

National Agricultural Insurance Scheme (NAIS)

- Addresses the issue of production risk faced by the agricultural farmers.
- Funding is divided between the Central and State Government on a 50-50 sharing basis.

Macro Management of Agriculture (MMA)

- Works on ensuring that the central assistance on agriculture is spent on focused and specific interventions for the development of agriculture in the state.

Integrated Scheme of Oilseeds, Pulses, Oil Palm and Maize (ISOPOM)

- Works on providing flexibility to the states to diversify crop production; and
- Provides a focused approach to the programme keeping in mind the regional differentiation of each state.

Weather Based Crop Insurance Scheme (WBCIS)

- Mitigates the hardship of the insured farmers against the likelihood of financial loss; and
- Provides coverage against weather parameters like rainfall, temperature, frost, humidity, etc.

24.13 National Strategy for Sustainable Development

The problems of environment are closely linked to one another. So the solution to one problem may in turn solve another associated problem.

Role of various agencies in Sustainable Development

Environmental conditions are deteriorating with every passing day and it is clear that the development activities are mainly responsible for degrading environment. Today all the components of the environment, essential for human beings and other organisms are getting polluted, thus calling for an urgent need of sustainable development. It is the changing and affluent lifestyles and high standards of living, which is adversely affecting the environment. So there is an urgent need of such a developmental strategy, which can be sustained for long.

Although Earth Summit had discussed many of the main problems posed by the developmental activities, showing a global concern over deteriorating environment yet a lot of work is required to be done in this regard. Increasing population and exploitation of resources are the prime cause of concern with regard to sustainable development.

It is a general human tendency to blame others for one's own faults, thus, keeping oneself away from solving the problematic issues. Sustainable development can be achieved only, if individuals, communities, governmental and international agencies come together and discharge their responsibilities as noted below.

Role of an individual and community

Every individual on the earth has an equal right to live a quality life. However, looking at the conditions today, it does not appear possible for all to live a quality life. We should seriously consider whether we will be able to give our children a sustainable environment or an environment with polluted air to breathe and contaminated water for drinking. If we want to give a clean environment to our children, we must preserve the environment and use it sustainably, so that the present as well as the future generations can lead a healthy and quality life.

A majority of individuals are of the opinion that it is the duty of the government to preserve the environment. This is not correct. Individual and the community have to play a pro-active role in preserving the environment. This can be done by adopting following:

- Using alternative sources of energy like solar energy, wind energy, etc. to reduce stress on non-renewal resources.
- Avoiding wastage of natural resources like minerals through reuse, reduce the use or recycle of the products.
- Encouraging programmes related to the conservation of natural resources like afforestation, water conservation, etc.
- Adopting and employing environment-friendly technologies to improve the quality of environment.
- Segregating waste at initial stages or at the source to reduce the amount of energy utilised during their disposal or treatment.
- Avoiding use of vehicles for short distances and preferring public transport systems.
- Reducing the use of products which are non-biodegradable in nature.
- Following rules and regulations made by the government for prevention and control of pollution.

Role of Governmental and Non-governmental agencies

Governmental and Non-governmental agencies play an important role in promoting Sustainable development. In a vast country like India, government alone cannot be expected to achieve. The role of non-government organisations is also assuming equal importance. NGOs work at grass-roots level and are well placed to motivate people on issues of national and international importance.

The legal provisions enacted by the government for environment sustainability are:

- Wildlife (Protection) Act, 1972
- Forest (Conservation) Act, 1980
- Water (Prevention and Control of Pollution) Act, 1981; and
- Environment (Protection) Act, 1986

Government of India established a new Department of Environment in 1980 and exhausted its status to a Ministry of Environment and Forests in 1985 to reaffirm GOIs commitment towards Environment. Central Pollution Control Board, State Pollution Board and Pollution Control Committee have also been established to oversee the activities relating to environment conservation and protection.

Role of International Agencies

A large number of International Agencies are also involved in enhancing sustainable development. Some important agencies are:

- **United Nations Environment Programme (UNEP):** This is a UN agency responsible for cooperation of inter-governmental measures for environmental monitoring and protection. It was set up in 1972, with headquarters in Nairobi, Kenya. UNEP was established to study and formulate international guidelines for management of environment.
- **United Nations development programme (UNDP):** It was established in 1965 to combine the expanded programme of Technical Assistance and UN special fund. In 1971, the two organisations were successfully merged into UNDP. It mainly focuses on creating awareness of environmental policies UNEP and UNDP work in coordination with one another.
- **International Council of Scientific Union (ICSU):** This is a non-governmental organisation based in Paris that encourages the exchange of scientific information and initiates programmes requiring international scientific cooperation.
- **International Union for Conservation of Nature and Natural Resources (IUCN):** It is an autonomous body, founded in 1948, that initiates and promotes scientifically based conservation measures. It also cooperates with UN and other intergovernmental agencies and sister concerns of world wide fund for nature (WWF) for environmental conservation.

Bibliography

Ashby, W.R. (1958). *An Introduction to Cybernetics*, John Wiley and Sons, Inc., New York.

Ager, D.V. (1963). *Principles of Palaeecology*, McGraw-Hill, London.

Ager, D.V. (1976). *The Nature of Fossil Record*, Proceedings of the Geologists Association.

Allen, J.R. (1975). *Physical Geology*, George Allen and Unwin, London.

Arvill, R. (1967). *Man and Environment*, Crisis and the Strategy of Choice, Penguin, Hamonds-worth.

Ash, M. (1972). *Planners and Ecologists*, Town and Country Planning, Vol. 40.

Atkinson, B.W. (1981). *Precipitation in Man and Environmental Processes* edited by K.J. Gregony and D.E. Wailling, Butterworths.

Bahuguna, S. (1990). *Tehri the Dam of Discontent, Yojana*, Vol. 34(10), pp. 9-12.

Begon, W.D. and Mortimer, M. (1981). *Population Ecology*, Blackwell Oxford.

Bharucha, M. P. (1994). *Environment Compliance Litigation*, Chartered secretary. Bhatnagar, R.P. and Agrawal, V. (1995). *Educational Administration*, R. Lall Book Depot.

Billings, W.D. (1964). '*Plants and Ecosystem*', MacMillan and Co., London.

Bird, E.C.F. (1981). *Coastal Processes in Man and Environmental Processes* edited by K.J. Gegory and D.E. Wareling, Butterworths, pp. 82-101.

Botkin, D.B. and Keller, E.A. (1982). *Environmental Studies*, C.E. Merrill Company.

Botkin, D.B. and Keller, E.A. (1982). *Environmental Studies*, C.E. Merrill Publishing Company, A Bell and Howell Company, Columbus, p. 505.

Bridge, E. (1978). *World Soils*, 2nd edition, Cambridge University Press.

Brock, T.D. (1967). *The Ecosystem and Study of State*, Bioscience, Vol. 17, pp. 166-169.

Browen, H.J.M. (1966). *Trace Elements in Biochemistry*, New York, Academic Press.

Brundtland Report (1987). *Our Common Future*, Report of the World Commission on Environment and Development, Oxford University Press, p. 383.

Bryan, R.B. (1981). *Soil Erosion and Conservation in Man and Environmental Processes* edited by K.J. Georgoy and D.E. Walling, Butterworths.

Cain, S.A. (1971). *Foundations of Plant Geography*, Hafner Publishing Co., New York.

Cariquist, S. (1974). *Island Biology*, Columbia University Press, New York.

Clapham, W.B. (1973). '*Natural Ecosystem*', Macmillan, London.

Clark, G.L. (1954). '*Elements of Ecology*', John Wiley and Sons Inc., New York.

Cloud, P.E. (1969). '*Resources and Man*', W.H. Freeman and Company, San Francisco.

Cole, M. (1971). *Plants, Animals and Environments*, Geographical Magazine, Vol. 44, pp. 230-31.

Dassaman, R.D. (1976). *Environmental Conservation*, Wiley, New York.

Daubernmire, R.F. (1974). *Plants and Environment*, 3rd ed., John Wiley, New York.

Deshbandhu and Berberet, G. (1987). '*Environmental Education for Conservation and Development*' Indian Env. Society, New Delhi, p. 537.

Det Wyer, T.R. (1971). *Man's Impact on Environment*, McGraw-Hill, New York.

Dikshit, R.D. (1984). '*Geography and Teaching of the Environment*'. Poona University, pp. 68-83.

Elton, C.S. (1967). *Animal Ecology*, University of Washington Press, Washington.

Elton, C.S. (1989). *The Ecology of Invastion by Plants and Animal*, Methuen, London.

Embleton, C. (1989). *Natural Hazards and Global Change*, ITC Journal (1989), pp. 169-78.

Etherington, J.R. (1975). *Environment and Plant Ecology*, Wiley, New York.

Furley, P.A. and Newey, W.W. (1983). *Man and the Biosphere*, Butterworths, London.

Garg, R.K. and Prakash T. (1988). *Paryavan Shiksha*, Community Centre, p. 36.

Goel, M.K. (1995). *Apna Paryavaran,* Vinod Pustak Mandir, Agra, p. 314.

Goudle, A. (1984). *The Nature of the Environment*, Basil Blackwell Publisher Ltd., p. 331.

Govt. of India, (1986). *The Environment (Protection) Act 1986*, Ministry Environment & Forests, GOI, New Delhi, p. 14.

Gregory, K.J. and Wailing, D.E. (1981). *Man and Environment Process*, Butterworths, London.

Hewitt, K. and Hare, F.K. (1973). *Man and Environment*: Conceptual Frameworks, Commission on College Geography Resource Paper 20.

Holliman, J. (1974). *Consumer's Guide to the Protection of the Environment*, Ballanine, London.

Hutchinson, G.E. (1978). *An Introduction to Population Ecology*, Yale University Press, New Haven.

Jeffers, J.N.R. (1973). *System Modelling and Analysis in Resource Management*, Journal of Environmental Management, Vol. 1, pp.13-28.

Kendeigh, S.C. (1974). Ecology with special Reference to Animal and Man, Prentice-Hall, New Jersey.

Kerbs, C.J. (1985). *Ecology,* 3rd ed., Harper & Row, New York.

Khoshoo, T.N. (1984). *Environmental Concerns and Strategies*, Indian Environmental Society.

Komondy, E.J. (1969). *Concept of Ecology*, Prentice-Hall, New Jersey.

Kumar, V.K. (1982). *A Study in Environmental Pollution*, Tara Book Agency, Varanasi, p. 205.

Lee, N. and Wood, C. (1972). *Planning and Pollution*, The Planner, Vol. 58, pp.153-58.

Lohani, B.N. (1984). *Environmental Quality Control*, South Asian Publishers, New Delhi, p. 448.

Marsh, G.P. (1984). *Man and Nature (Physical Geography as modified by Human Action)*, Charles Scribner, New York.

Mishra, R. (1968). *Ecology Work Book*, Oxford & IBH, New Delhi.

Nelson, I. G. and Byrne, A. B. (1986). *Man as an Instrument of Landscape Change*, Alberta Geog. Rev., Vol. 58, pp. 226-38.

Nicholson, M. (1972). *The Environmental Revolution*, Penguin, Harmondsworth.

Odum, E.P. (1979). *Fundamental of Ecology,* Saunders, Philadelphia.

Odum, E.P. (1983). *Basic Ecology*, Holt Saunders Intel ed., Japan.

Odum, H.T. (1971). *Environment, Power and Society*, Wiley Interscience, New York.

Oestereich, J. (1994). *The Concept of Environmental Monitoring in the Indian Context, Productivity*, 35(2): pp. 85-191.

Pal, B.P. (1981). *National Policy on Environment,* Deptt. of Enviroment, Government of India, New Delhi, p.15.

Pal, S.K. and Malhotra, S. (1994). *Environment Trend and thoughts in Education,* Vol. XI, 1994, Published by Innovative Research Association, Allahabad.

Paric, C.C. (1980). *Ecology and Environment*, Longmans, London, p. 272.

Pattern, B.C. (Ed.) (1971). *Systems Analysis and Simulation in Ecology*, Academic Press, London.

Phillipson, I. (1986). *Ecological Energetics*, Arnold, London.

Pimm, S.L. (1982). *Food Webs*, Chapman & Hall, London.

Rao, K.L. (1975). *India's Water Wealth*, Orient Longman Limited, New Delhi, p. 235.

Rao, M. S. (1987). *Introduction to Social Forestry*, Oxford & IBH, p. 87.

Ricklefs, R. E. (1979). *Ecology*, 2nd ed. Chiron Press, New York.

Rouse, W.R. (1981). *Man-Induced Climates in Man and Environmental Process* (ed.) Walling Butterworth, pp. 38-54.

Sandbrook, R. (1992). *From Stockholm to Rio, in Earth Summit 92*, Regency Press Corp. London.

Sapru, R.K. (1987). *Environmental Management in India*, Ashish Publishing House, p. 288.

Saxena, A.B. (1986). *Environmental Education*, National Psychological Corporation, Agra, p. 191.

Sharma, C.B.S.R. Panneerselvam, N. and Arumikkili, K. (1985). *Environmental Genetic Toxicology in India.*

Sharma, P.D. (1990). *Ecology and Environment, Rastogi Publishers,* Meerut (U.P.).

Sharma, R.A. (1995). Distance Education -*Theory, Practice and Research,* Meerut, p. 392.

Sharma, R.A. (1996). *Fundamental of Educational Psychology*, Surya Publication, Meerut.

Sharma, S.P. (2003). *Teacher Education - Principles Theory and Practice* Delhi, p. 574.

Sharma, Y.K. (2002). *Fundamental Aspects of Educational Technology*, Delhi, p. 454.

Simmons, I.G. (1974). *The Ecology and Natural Resources*, Edward Arnold, London.

Singh, S. (1995). *Environmental Geography*, Prayag Pustak Bhawan, Allahabad, p. 517.

Singh, S. and Dubey, A. (1989). *Environmental Management,* Geography Department, Allahabad University.

Strahler, A. N. and Strahler, A. H. (1986). *Geography and Man's Environment*, John Wiley, New York.

University of Poona (1981). *Integrated Studies in Western Ghats*, University of Poon Press.

Valiathan, M.S. (1993). *Presidential Address*, 68 Annual Meeting, Association of Indian Universities, AIU, New Delhi.

Verma, P.S. and Agarwal, V.K. (1993). *Environmental Biology (Principles of Ecology),* S. Chand & Company, New Delhi, p. 592.

Vernadsky, W.I. (1884). *Studies in Geochemistry*, Leningrad.

Vyas, A.B. and Golley, F.B. (1975). *Ecological Principles*, International

Index